Excavations at Jawa 1972 - 1986

Stratigraphy, Pottery and Other Finds

To the memory of Dame Kathleen Kenyon

Excavations and Explorations in the Hashemite Kingdom
of Jordan

Excavations at Jawa 1972 - 1986

Stratigraphy, Pottery and Other Finds

Edited by

A.V.G. BETTS

S. W. Helms
and
A. Betts, R. Unger-Hamilton, N. Vaillant

EDINBURGH UNIVERSITY PRESS

© A. Betts 1991
S Helms 1991
R. Unger-Hamilton 1991
N. Vaillant 1991

Edinburgh University Press
22 George Square, Edinburgh

Printed in Great Britain by
The Alden Press Limited, Oxford

British Library Cataloguing
   in Publication Data
Excavations at Jawa 1972 - 1986:
Stratigraphy, Pottery and Other Finds
I. Betts, A.V.G.
935.695

ISBN 0 7486 0307 7

Contents

List of Illustrations   vii

Abbreviations   xii

Editor's Preface   1
A.V.G. Betts

Preface   3
S.W. Helms

1. Introduction   6
S.W. Helms
Jawa   6
Exploration history   6
Periods of occupation   10
Jawa in the 4th millennium BC   11

2. Stratigraphy   19
S.W. Helms
Background   19
Excavated areas   26
General   46

3. The Pottery   55
S.W. Helms
Introduction   55
Analysis of genres, types and variants   55
Size and volume analysis   65
Comparative study   69
Fabrics   105

4. Stamped, Incised and Painted Designs on Pottery   110
S.W. Helms
Stamp seal impressions   110
Incised and embossed patterns and
miscellaneous forms   128
Painted patterns   135

5. **The Chipped Stone Assemblage**   140
    A.V.G. Betts
    Tools   142
    Discussion   144

6. **The Microwear Analysis of Scrapers and
    'Sickle Blades'**   149
    R. Unger-Hamilton
    The experiments   149
    The gloss   150
    The microwear analysis   151
    Conclusion   153

7. **Other Finds**   154
    S.W. Helms
    Comparative study   155
    Summary   162
    Catalogue   163

8. **Rock Carvings and Inscriptions**   168
    S.W. Helms
    Rock art   168
    Inscriptions   178

Appendix A. The Jawa Area in Prehistory   181
    A.V.G. Betts
    Site inventory   181
    The Jawa area in prehistory   183

Appendix B. A Note on the Early Pottery   191
    N Vaillant

    Illustrations   194

    Bibliography   383

List of Illustrations

FIGURES

1. Landuse Map of southern Syria and Transjordan: if, irrigation farming; df, dry farming; fo, forestry; h, horticulture; g, grazing; lg, limited grazing; npu, no possible use (but for minerals)
2. The Near East: 200 mm isohyet (average year) and relevant sites
3. The Jawa Area: C, microcatchments (local runoff); A, animal pens (?); B, burial ground (?); Da, deflection dam; P, revetted pools; F, irrigated fields
4. Jawa and the Jordan Valley: relevant sites
5. The site of Jawa
6. Depth of archaeological deposition at Jawa
7. The Upper Settlement
8. The 'citadel': excavated areas and key to sections
9. Square C1: section 6 with piers and corbels
10. Square X1: section 5 with pier and corbels
11. Square C2: entrance to the 'citadel'
12. Square C2: key to loci
13. Square C2: building phases and features
14. Square C2: section 1
15. Square C2: section 2
16. Square C2: section 3
17. Square C2: section 4
18. Area C: stratigraphic matrix
19. Area F: plan of squares
20. Square F1: section 1
21. Square F1: section 2
22. Area F: squares F2, F3, F4
23. Square F2c/d: wall W5 and features on bedrock
24. Square F2c/d: plan of oven and other features
25. Squares F2a/c/d and F4d: plan of the latest structures
26. Square F2c: section 3
27. Square F2c: section 4, fortifications built on bedrock
28. Square F2c: section 6
29. Square F2d: section 7
30. Square F2d: section 8
31. Square F2d: section 9
32. Square F4a(c): section 1
33. Square F4a(c): section 2
34. Squares F1, F2a, F3a/c, F4d: stratigraphic matrix
35. Squares F2c/d: stratigraphic matrix
36. Square F4a(c): stratigraphic matrix
37. Gate G1 and sondage
38. Square TT1 (1973): rounded structure and finds *in situ*
39. Square UT1: sub-circular structure
40. Square UT1: features on bedrock
41. Square UT1: internal modifications
42. Square UT1a: the latest features
43. Square UT1: section 1
44. Square UT1: section 2

45. Square UT1: stratigraphic matrix
46. Squares UT2 and UT3: MBA structures
47. Square UT2: EB I A and MBA structures
48. Square UT2: stratigraphic matrix
49. Square UT2: section 2
50. Square UT4: sub-rectilinear structure
51. Square UT4: stratigraphic matrix
52. Area D: general plan of the dams and location of squares
53. Square D1a against the waterface of dam D2
54. Area D: section through dams D1 and D2
55. Squares D2a/c-f: plan of features
56. Square D2a: section
57. Square D1a/b: stratigraphic matrix
58. Squares D2a/c-f: stratigraphic matrix
59. Square LF2: general plan
60. Squares LF2a/d: latest features
61. Square LF2(1973): section 1
62. Square LF2(1973): section 2
63. SquareLF2(1973): section 3 and the outer lower fortifications
64. Square LF2a: section 4
65. Square LF2a: section 5
66. Square LF2a: section 6
67. Square LF2b: section 7
68. Square LF2b: section 8
69. Square LF2d: section 9
70. Square LF2d: section 10
71. Square LF4: general plan
72. Square LF4: section 1
73. Square LF4a/c: section 2
74. Square LF2: stratigraphic matrix
75. Square LF4: stratigraphic matrix
76. Square LF3: general plan and key to sections
77. Square LF3: stratigraphic matrix
78. Square LT1: stratigraphic matrix
79. The upper fortifications
80. The lower fortifications (South)
81. The stratigraphic matrix of Jawa
82. Pottery vessels from square TT1
83. Genre A: reconstruction of forms
84. Genre A: rim profiles (type A)
85. Genre A: rim profiles (types B/C/I)
86. Genre B: reconstruction of forms
87. Genre B: rim profiles (types A/C)
88. Genre C: reconstruction of forms
89. Genre C: reconstruction of forms (types A/B)
90. Genre C: rim profiles (types B/C/D/E/F)
91. Genre D: reconstruction of forms
92. Genre D: rim profiles (types A/B)
93. Genre E: reconstruction of forms (Types A/B/C/E)
94. Genre E: rim profiles (types A/B/C/D/E)
95. Genre G: rim profiles (types A/B/C/D/E/F/G)
96. Genre X: profiles of bases
97. Summary of Genres and Types: genre A (types A-G)

98. Summary of Genres and Types: genres A (types H-K), B (types A-C), C (types A-F), D (types A/B)
99. Summary of Genres and Types: genres E (types A-E), F (types A/B), G (types A-J)
100. Form and volume: parameters
101. Rim diameter: parameters
102. Volumetric analysis: genre A
103. Volumetric analysis: genre B
104. Volumetric analysis: genre C (types A-C)
105. Volumetric analysis: genre C (types D-F)
106. Comparison of rim dimensions: genres A-C
107. Frequency of occurrence: genres and types
108. Frequency of occurrence: (a) genres; (b) fabrics
109. Frequency of occurrence: genres, (a) test area; (b) excavation
110. Pottery catalogue: genre A (1 - 10)
111. Pottery catalogue: genre A (11 - 19)
112. Pottery catalogue: genre A (20 - 29)
113. Pottery catalogue: genre A (30 - 47)
114. Pottery catalogue: genre A (48 - 59)
115. Pottery catalogue: genre A (60 - 72)
116. Pottery catalogue: genre A (73 - 87)
117. Pottery catalogue: genre A (88 - 102)
118. Pottery catalogue: genre A (103 - 115)
119. Pottery catalogue: genre A (116 - 128)
120. Pottery catalogue: genre A (129 - 140)
121. Pottery catalogue: genre A (141 - 161)
122. Pottery catalogue: genre B (162 - 173)
123. Pottery catalogue: genre B (174 - 179)
124. Pottery catalogue: genre B (180 - 181)
125. Pottery catalogue: genre B (182 - 192)
126. Pottery catalogue: genre B (193 - 203)
127. Pottery catalogue: genre B (204 - 212)
128. Pottery catalogue: genre B (213 - 225)
129. Pottery catalogue: genre B (226 - 240)
130. Pottery catalogue: genre C (241 - 273)
131. Pottery catalogue: genre C (274 - 287)
132. Pottery catalogue: genre C (288 - 296)
133. Pottery catalogue: genre C (297 - 313)
134. Pottery catalogue: genre C (314 - 328)
135. Pottery catalogue: genre D (329 - 337)
136. Pottery catalogue: genre E (338 - 350)
137. Pottery catalogue: genre E (351 - 361)
138. Pottery catalogue: genre E (362 - 377)
139. Pottery catalogue: genre E (378 - 392)
140. Pottery catalogue: genre F (393 - 417)
141. Pottery catalogue: genre F/H (418 - 428)
142. Pottery catalogue: genre F (429 - 439)
143. Pottery catalogue: genre F/E/M/A (440 - 454)
144. Pottery catalogue: genre M/G (455 - 469)
145. Pottery catalogue: genre G (470 - 489)
146. Pottery catalogue: genre G (490 - 503)
147. Pottery catalogue: genre G (504 - 518)
148. Pottery catalogue: genre G (519 - 530)

149. Pottery catalogue: genre H/X (531 - 550)
150. Pottery catalogue: genre X (551 - 567)
151. Pottery catalogue: genre X (568 - 585)
152. Pottery catalogue: genre X (586 - 602)
153. Pottery catalogue: genre X (603 - 619)
154. Pottery catalogue: MBA (622 - 628)
155. Pottery catalogue: MBA (629 - 640)
156. Pottery catalogue: MBA (641 - 653)
157. Pottery catalogue: MBA (654 - 667)
158. Distribution of pottery parallels (repertoires and genres)
159. Seriation: 4th millennium BC pottery repertoires
160. Stamp seal impression: J162
161. Stamp seal impression: J163
162. Stamp seal impression: J174
163. Stamp seal impression: J176
164. Impressions: J449
165. Location of parallels for stamp seal impressions and seals
166. Stamp seal impressions: Tell Um Hammad (TUH4729 and 5346)
167. Survey of seal impressions
168. Blank impressions on handles: a, Jawa; b, Tell Um Hammad (Sharqiyah);
     c, Tell Mafluq; d, Katarat al-Samra'; e, Tell Handaquq; f, Jericho (O.T.);
     g, Katar Yuba; h, Dhiyaba; i, Ras Abu Lofeh; j, Fakhat; k, Jerash Survey;
     l, Azor; m, Megiddo; n, Tell al-Fara'ah (North); o, Beth Yerah; p, Affulah;
     q, Kinneret; r, Beth Shan; s, Ghrubba
169. Stamp seal impressions: numerical ranking?
170. Incised sherds
171. Impressed and decorated handles
172. Distribution of handle types and stamped impressions
173. Painted Designs
174. Chipped stone: scraper (a)
175. Chipped stone: scraper (a)
176. Chipped stone: scraper (a)
177. Chipped stone: scrapers (a)
178. Chipped stone: scrapers (b)
179. Chipped stone: 1-5. scrapers (b), 6-10. (c), 11. point (a)
180. Chipped stone: points (b)
181. Chipped stone: 1-8. points (b), 9-17. (c)
182. Chipped stone: knives (a)
183. Chipped stone: knives (b)
184. Reconstructed Sickle
185. Distribution of parallels for chipped stone
186. Wear Analysis
187. Ground stone vessels
188. Ground stone vessels
189. Ground stone vessels
190. Ground stone vessels
191. Ground stone vessels
192. Ground stone vessels
193. Ground stone pounders and grinders
194. Ground stone saddle querns and mace-heads
195. Ground stone mace-heads
196. Ground stone objects: pierced stones
197. Ground stone objects: pierced stones

198. Basalt pebbles
199. Basalt pebbles and pierced stones
200. Pierced stones
201. Drilled objects
202. Animal figurines
203. Animal figurines
204. Figurines
205. Rock carvings: cattle (A1)
206. Rock carvings: cattle (A2)
207. Rock carvings: cattle (A3)
208. Rock carvings: cattle (A4)
209. Rock carvings: cattle (A5)
210. Rock carvings: cattle (A6)
211. Rock carvings: horned beasts (A7)
212. Rock carvings: horned beasts (A8)
213. Rock carvings: cattle from a, al-Wusad; b, al-Wusad; c, al-Ghirqa
214. Rock carvings: cattle from near Qasr Burqu`
215. Rock carvings: Safaitic text (A9) and hunting scene
216. Rock carvings: hunting scene (A9a)
217. Rock carvings: ibex (A9b), deer ? (A9c), ostrich (A9d)
218. Rock carvings: ostrich (A10)
219. Rock carvings: various animals (A11 and A12)
220. Rock carvings: various horned animals (A13, A14, A15)
221. Rock carvings: camels (A16, A17)
222. Rock carvings: animal (A18)
223. Rock carvings: human figures (A19, A20)
224. Rock carvings: animals [A6: cf. Fig. 210], enigmatic figures and designs (A21)
225. Rock carvings: enimatic design (A22)
226. Rock carvings: enigmatic designs (A23)
227. Rock carvings: enimatic designs (24)
228. Rock carvings: man and camel (A25)
229. Rock carvings: wasms (A26), various designs (A27, A28, A29)
230. Rock carvings: cross and inscription (E1) and a cross
231. Lamp fragment from tumulus north of Jawa
232. The Jawa Survey Area: location of sites
233. The Jawa Survey Area
234. Desert "Kites" near Jawa (cf. Figs 232/3)
235. Chipped stone (misc. epipaleolithic sites)
236. Khallat `Anaza: plan of visible remains
237. Khallat `Anaza: plan of excavated structure
238. Khallat `Anaza: ground stone basin
239. Khallat `Anaza: chipped stone
240. Mugharet al-Jawa: plan of visible remains
241. Mugharet al-Jawa: chipped stone

TABLES

1. Schema of recording system
2. Schema of the pottery assemblage
3. Distribution of parallel repertoires
4. Fabric codes
5. Genre/Type - Fabrics
6. Fabrics - Genre/Type
7. Frequency of fabric clusters in Test Area UT4

8. Frequency of fabric clusters in Excavation Sample
9. Frequency of Genre/Type according to typology
10. Frequency of Fabric according to typology
11. Stamp seal impressions: numeration?
12. Chipped stone: provenance of samples
13. Microwear analysis: provenance of samples
14. Pottery fabric analysis: provenance of samples

PLATES

1. Polish and striations on experimental blade used to harvest domestic emmer (M 100x)
2. Polish and striations on tabular scraper from Jawa (M 200x)
3. Polish and striations on flake scraper from Jawa (M 100x)
4. Polish on experimental reed scraper (M 200x)
5. "Sickle blade" from Jawa (M 100x)
6. "Sickle blade" from Jawa (M 100x)
7. "Sickle blade" from Jawa (M 50x)

ABBREVIATIONS

The following abbreviations are used in the text. A list of abbreviated bibliographical references appears at the beginning of the bibliography.

bs   body sherd

catno(s) catalogue number(s)

CNRS   Centre Nationale de Recherche et Science (Paris)

dno(s) decimal number(s)

EB   Early Bronze

EB-MB Early Bronze - Middle Bronze (= EB IV)

EBA   Early Bronze Age

ED   Early Dynastic

ext   external

fb   fabric

hmj   holemouth jar

horiz   horizontal

IFAPO Institut Française Archéologique du Proche-Orient

int   internal

KS   Kataret es-Samra

MB   Middle Bronze

MBA   Middle Bronze Age

Neo   Neolithic

N.T.   New Testament

NRA   Natural Resources Authority, (Jordan)

O.T.   Old Testament

pno(s) page number(s)

PN   Pottery Neolithic

PN   Pre Pottery Neolithic

PU   Proto Urban

ref(s)   reference(s)
TH   Tell Handaquq North
TM   Tell Mafluq
TUH   Tell Um Hammad (esh-Sharqiya)
vert   vertical

Editor's Preface

A.V.G. BETTS

This volume is the first in a series of three concerning excavations at the sites of Jawa and Um Hammad in Jordan. Jawa was excavated over several seasons by Svend Helms in the 1970s. The first occupation at the site dates to the very beginning of the Early Bronze Age, and is remarkable for its massive fortifications and complex water systems. Jawa lies in the modern Kingdom of Jordan, and yet belongs more properly to the ambit of ancient Syria. At the time of excavation, the only known sites of this period were in Palestine, northern Syria, and Mesopotamia. Lying midway between these centres of ancient civilization, Jawa was something of an anomaly, its relationship within the archaeological sequence of the Near East considered unclear. To resolve this difficulty Helms started work at a second site, Tell Um Hammad in the Jordan Valley. Here, for the first time, distinctive vessel forms from the Jawa repertoire were found stratified together with recognisable Palestinian pottery. Even more importantly, these 'Jawa' forms occurred within a very close stratigraphic context, while developed forms in local wares appeared later in the sequence. Thus the two sites can be closely linked in time, and in the nature of the contact between them. Initial direct contact was followed by assimilation of imported traits into local traditions. Tell Um Hammad lies near the mouth of wadi Zerqa, one of the main routes from the plateau down into the Jordan Valley. Much of the 'Jawa' pottery seems only to occur in a restricted zone: along wadi Zerqa, in the uplands about Jerash, northern Transjordan and, perhaps, in southern Syria.

However, Jawa was not only important in the Early Bronze Age. A Middle Bronze Age outpost was built within the walls of the earlier occupation, taking advantage of the strategic location of the site. Similarly, Tell Um Hammad was also re-occupied at the end of the Early Bronze Age, when a widespread village grew up, over and beyond the earlier settlement.

The reports presented in these volumes are the result of the inspiration and the dedicated inquiry of Svend Helms, and the fruits of much hard work in the field by a number of individuals. This first volume concerns the pottery and stratigraphy of Jawa in both the Early Bronze Age and the Middle Bronze Age. The second volume will consist of reports on the stratigraphy and finds from the early stage of occupation at Tell Um Hammad, Early Bronze Age I-II (Betts [ed.] in press). The third volume will cover the later stage at Tell Um Hammad, Early Bronze Age IV and Iron Age.

My connection with excavations at both sites is a close one. I was a member of the field team excavating at Tell Um Hammad, and of field teams from the Department of Antiquities of Jordan and the British Museum, excavating the associated cemetery, Tiwal esh-Sharqi. While I did not participate in the original excavations at Jawa, I have spent a long time in the *harra*, a landscape which has a continual fascination for me, and I have attempted to provide a prehistorical background against which Jawa might be better understood. I consider it a privilege to be asked to edit this series of reports and I thank all those whose work made these publications possible.

Preface

S.W. HELMS

The excavations at Jawa were sponsored by the British School of Archaeology in Jerusalem (BSAJ). Fieldwork was conducted with the permission and cooperation of the Jordanian Department of Antiquities under the Directorships of Mr Yacoub Oweis and Dr Adnan Hadidi. Support, particularly from His Royal Highness Crown Prince Hassan bin Talal and the Jordanian Armed Forces, has already been acknowledged (Helms 1981), but I would like once again to reiterate my gratitude, since without such help the fieldwork could easily have become impossible.

Between 1972 and 1976 the work at Jawa was financially supported by the following organizations: the British Academy, the British School of Archaeology in Jerusalem, the British Museum, the Seven Pillars of Wisdom Trust, the Ashmolean Museum, the City of Birmingham Museum and Art Gallery, Manchester Museum, the Central Research Funds Committee (London University), the Palestine Exploration Fund, and several anonymous sources. Subsequent explorations and additional survey work (1983-86) were conducted as part of Alison Betts' Black Desert Survey (Betts, refs *passim*) under the auspices of the British Institute at Amman for Archaeology and History.

The British Institute at Amman has also sponsored and supported excavations and post-excavation studies in regard of Tell Um Hammad, and provided generous grants towards the production of the final publications of the findings from both sites. Staff of the excavation seasons are listed in Helms 1981: I would like to thank again all those who took part, particularly Lucy-Anne Hunt and Archie Walls. Survey staff between 1983-86 consisted of the writer, Alison Betts, Brian Hitchcock, Catherine Maclaughlin, Lucinda McClintock, Alison MacQuitty and Rebecca Montague. Arif Abu Ghannem and Ibrahim Hajj Hassan represented the Department of Antiquities.

My first explorations of Jawa and the eastern 'desert' of Jordan (the so-called Black Desert) began in 1966 on the advice of Professor Basil Hennessy (Director, BSAJ to 1969), who also funded a short survey season. Gerald Harding, who had visited Jawa early in the 1950s and identified it as an Early Bronze Age settlement (see also Winnett 1951, 1957), was the first to confirm my preliminary 'pottery reading'. In 1972 Crystal Bennett (Director BSAJ/BIAAH to 1983) supported a short survey of Jawa which was conducted by the writer, Lucy-Anne Hunt and Archie Walls, with the permission of the Department of Antiquities. Further evidence of an early date was found at that time. Since 1972/3 and up to 1976 it was the constant support and encouragement of the late Dame Kathleen Kenyon which made the excavation of Jawa a reality.

The vexatious problem of dating Jawa in a way that would be acceptable to Near Eastern archaeologists was not properly solved until 1982-84 when my excavations at Tell Um Hammad revealed pottery identical to that of Jawa. These decisive parallels occurred in 4th millennium BC contexts (EB I A), confirming the date proposed in 1975 (Helms 1975) and, of course, before that by Gerald Harding. I owe my decision to excavate at Tell Um Hammad to James Mellaart and Albert Leonard Jnr, who first showed me some of the relevant pottery forms from the site. During the excavations of Tell Um Hammad in the Jordan Valley I also benefitted from discussion with Walt Rast and Thomas Schaub, the excavators of Bab edh-Dhra`, who shared information about EB I pottery typology. Similarly, I was able to see an important pottery assemblage from the recent excavations at Tell Shuna North through the generosity of Carrie Gustavson Gaube. Still on pottery typologies and related studies, I am indebted to Genviève Dollfus (CNRS), the co-excavator of Tell Abu Hamid with Zeidan Kafafi (Yarmouk University), who arranged for the analysis of the early pottery from Tell Um Hammad. This work is being done at the Institut Française Archéologique du Proche-Orient (IFAPO) by Nathalie Vaillant who has also contributed a preliminary note on the early pottery of Jawa in this volume (Appendix B). Cooperation with IFAPO in Amman also included valuable discussions with its director Frank Braemer, who made it possible for the writer to see his survey pottery from the Hawran in Damascus (IFAPO), and to visit the important sites of Khirbet Umbachi and Leboué in 1988.

I am most grateful to Michael Macdonald who kindly read and corrected parts of Chapter 8, and to Jack Hanbury-Tenison for showing me his survey results from wadi al-`Arab and the Jerash Region. Thanks are also owing to Peter Dorrell and Stuart Laidlaw (Institute of Archaeology, University College, London University) who offered advice and assistance in the production of many of the illustrations which required lengthy and complicated photographic processing. I am also indebted to Denise Homès-Fredericq (Musée Royaux d'Art et d'Histoire, Bruxelles) for discussions on stamp seals, as well as support of the work at Tell Um Hammad, and to Jonathan Mabry (University of Arizona) for giving me pre-publication access to his findings at Tell Handaquq North. And, finally, I would like to thank those who have contributed to the final publication, particularly Alison Betts whose work on the prehistory of the Black Desert has established an important background against which to measure the significance of Jawa in the 4th and the early 2nd millennia BC.

1. Introduction

S.W. HELMS

"How often have I said to you that when you have eliminated the impossible, whatever remains, however impossible, must be the truth."
(Conan Doyle. *The Sign of Four*)

JAWA

Jawa lies in eastern Jordan at an elevation of 1000 metres above sea-level. Environmentally, the site straddles the wet-dry steppic interface, today receiving an annual average rainfall of between 150 and 200 millimetres (Source: NRA). This can be much higher in some years; it can be drastically lower in others. It is likely that the climate of the 4th millennium BC (the major period of occupation at Jawa) was similar to the modern one (Helms 1981). Local topography and drainage from the Jebel Druze uplands to the north has resulted in deeply cut wadi systems of which wadi Rajil is the major one in the area. Jawa was built on a rocky island between wadi Rajil and a smaller, subsidiary wadi in which water could easily be stored by the construction of earth and stone dams. It is estimated that about 2×10^6 cubic metres of water was discharged annually past Jawa during the wet season (about September to April), and that a much smaller percentage of this was captured and stored at the site (Helms 1981: *passim*). Soils in the area are suited to cereal cultivation using dry farming methods, and other crops with irrigation; spring and some summer grazing are possible (Moormann 1959).

EXPLORATION HISTORY

Jawa can be said to have been discovered by Poidebard (1934) who photographed the site from the air and took it to be a Roman installation, partly because of the remarkably regular walls, and partly because at that time *limes* studies were at the forefront of research interest in Syria. At about the same time Sir Aurel Stein (see now Gregory and Kennedy 1985: 250 ff.) visited the area and described the remains in some detail. Nelson Glueck (1951) surveyed in the general area a decade later, as an eastern extension of his survey of Transjordan. He missed the main occupation site - at noon

Jawa becomes almost invisible from the main track - but located `Ain Jawa, some kilometres to the south.

Jawa was first explored on the ground and also 'dated' with remarkable precision by Gerald Harding (cf. also Winnett 1951) when he and Winnett surveyed the area for pre-Islamic inscriptions (see Chapter 8). Harding described the massive fortifications and the main dam (Fig. 5:P4, Area D), and suggested that Jawa may have been built during the Early Bronze Age (Department of Antiquities: records in the Registry Section). His 'dating' is remarkable, not only because it was more or less accurate, but also because it was a daring suggestion in the 1950s when many of the major interpretative hypotheses about the 'history' or, rather, protohistory of the 4th and 3rd millennia BC in Palestine and Transjordan were being formulated.

Many of the major sites with substantial EBA remains had already been under excavation by that time (e.g. 'Ai/et-Tell [Marquet-Krause 1949]; Megiddo [Loud 1948]), or were just being opened up to reveal heavy fortifications in stone and mudbrick whose presence appeared to signal a fundamental social, economic, and political transformation in ancient Palestine. De Vaux had been excavating at Tell el-Far'ah, near Nablus, since the late 1940s (de Vaux and Steve 1947) and ultimately published his socio-economic reconstructions in the Cambridge Ancient History (1970a, 1971; cf. also 1970b on interpretation in archaeology). Kenyon began re-excavating at the tell of O.T. Jericho (1952b) and began also to publish her hypotheses regarding the change from village to 'urban' culture in Palestine (Kenyon 1960, 1965, 1979), introducing the term 'Proto Urban' to describe the period between the Chalcolithic and the 'urban' EBA. 'Proto Urban' was regarded as suitable parallel terminology to the proto-literate and proto-dynastic stages of southern Mesopotamia (Sumer) and Egypt, respectively. Hennessy published an hypothetical reconstruction on an international level based on a detailed examination of one trench at O.T. Jericho in 1967, in which he reiterated much of Kenyon's thinking, setting out apparently precise periodization based on pottery typology. Anati had already produced a summary of Palestinian history 'before the Hebrews' in 1963, where he presented an alternative terminology in which the term 'urban' predominates. James Mellaart (1966) attempted a more international summary, paralleling somewhat Hennessy's work at the time (see especially references to Tell Um Hammad; see also Mellaart in Leonard n.d.). Wright (1958, 1961, 1971) reformatted ideas based on his seminal pottery analysis (1937) which (the pottery analysis) can be regarded as the basis for all typology-based formulations since then. Paul Lapp started excavations at EBA Bab edh-Dhra', a site which had become well-known because of its extensive EBA cemetery. Lapp added further interpretative models (1966, 1968, 1970), again some of them on an even wider international level. About the same time Amiran began to excavate the large walled settlement of Arad on the northern edge of the Negev Desert, and from that source have come a series of ever-expanding hypotheses regarding the 'urbanization' of Palestine (e.g. Amiran 1968, 1970, 1978, 1986; see also Beit-Arieh 1984, and remarks below). Kantor (1965) and Dothan (1971) both hypothesized on the foreign relations of Palestine in the 4th and 3rd millennia BC, as did Perrot (1962). The data from Tell el-Fara'ah and other sites was the basis for yet another reconstruction by de Miroschedji (1971) which was severely criticized by Kenyon (1974).

Thus there already existed an ostensibly accepted interpretative framework (despite differences in many details) when the excavations at Jawa began in 1972 and when, shortly thereafter, I first suggested that the fortified settlement and its extensive water system could indeed be attributed to the EBA or late Chalcolithic period: not, however, to the 3rd millennium BC (i.e. contemporary with the 'urban' EBA to the west), but to the 4th millennium BC. However, this made Jawa earlier than almost all of the so-called urban settlements of Palestine, with the exception of Tell Sheykh al-`Areyny (Tel Gath: see Yeivin 1961; see now Weinstein 1984, and also Kempinski and Gilead 1988), perhaps Khirbet Iskander (Parr 1960), and PPNA Jericho which has often been called the 'earliest city in the world' because of its massive stone tower and walls (cf. also Mellaart 1975). The stratigraphic matrix of Tel Gath is, however, still uncertain; the position of Khirbet Iskander in the 4th millennium BC remains unresolved (but see now Richard 1987 and references); and the 'urban' status of PPNA Jericho is arguable and, in any case, too far removed in time from Jawa. But this did not alter the perception of social, economic and perhaps even political transformations (many of which are still current; e.g. Beit-Arieh 1984, and the 'city-state'), which were thought to have occurred in the southern Levant about 3000 BC. Jawa simply did not fit comfortably into such a scenario.

Perhaps the basic reason for contention - now regarded as a misconception by most scholars in cognate disciplines such as anthropology and sociology - was the praxis of assuming walls or fortifications to be synonymous with an urban status: Jawa could not predate the other EBA sites of Palestine and Transjordan in such a tight definition. That was the 'state of the art' of Near Eastern archaeological interpretation in the early 1970s, when not only the interpretative framework was (in retrospect, of course) far too limited, but when the model of 'civilized' Mesopotamia served as the most compelling source of inspiration (e.g. Kempinski 1983 - a decade later - and references there). Such canons of 'civilizations' (and therefore subsuming 'urbanization') were presented by Childe long before this (1950).

By the early 1970s rescue excavations in north-central Syria produced a perfect example of 'urbanization' and even 'colonization' in the impressive, formally fortified site of Habuba Kabira (Strommenger 1979, 1980) whose date in the 4th millennium BC was unequivocally demonstrated, and whose monumental architecture could easily be accommodated in the current interpretative framework since the foundation of the site could be linked directly with the Uruk sphere of southern Mesopotamia. A sophisticated, fortified settlement in north-central Syria could be accepted because it was not only dated by its pottery sequence, but also because it was culturally (therefore perhaps also economically) linked with 'civilized' lands in the south.

In due course, and as more excavated data were presented in preliminary form, there followed a number of developed hypotheses concerning EBA Palestine/Transjordan. These new hypotheses, however, were still based on old models. All were preoccupied with the notion of 'urbanization'; all of their proponents (once the relevant preliminary data from Jawa were to hand) either chose to leave out Jawa, or doubted the evidence altogether. These hypotheses have been summarized by Hanbury-Tenison in yet another reconstruction, without resolving the debate (1986; see now a review by Braun 1987). The main publications, apart from those already noted above, are as follows : Amiran (1970); Beit-Arieh, beginning work on Chalcolithic and EBA camps sites in the Sinai peninsula in the early 1970s, regards the walled EB II settlement of Arad as 'undoubtedly the capital of a city-state' (1984: 22), but also presents a compelling economic analysis (cf. also *idem* 1986); Callaway (1972, 1978, 1980) bases most of his interpretations on his own site of 'Ai (et-Tell) and the notion of predominant, if intermittent, Egyptian interference in Palestine; Esse (1984) presents some preliminary re-appraisals of the important EBA site of Beth Yerah (Khirbet Kerak), including a reasonable critique of some 'current' EBA terminology (i.e. 'EB I C' does not exist); Gophna (1984), has compiled a useful listing of survey results, although Jawa is somehow attributed to EB II; Lapp (1970); Levy (1986) seems to have accepted 4th millennium Jawa, more or less; Rast (1980) also stresses a close and complicated Egyptian connection with Bab edh-Dhra', but fails to mention Jawa; Richard (1987) doubts the evidence from Jawa; Ross (1980), like many others, ignores Jawa inexplicably; and Schaub (1982, 1987) presents an hypothesis which is largely pottery-based (e.g. the 'B Tradition'), and coins the phrase 'walled town culture'; while Kempinski (1986) thinks that the fortifications and water systems belong to the Middle Bronze Age occupation (see also Helms [1989a: *passim*] for other critiques of Jawa).

But, back in the 1950s, Harding had realized that Jawa was (and had to be) linked, in some way, to this phenomenon of EBA 'urbanization' (perhaps because he thought in terms of a date in the 3rd millennium BC). Kenyon herself was to agree with this in due course (in 1975), including the proposed 4th millennium BC date. But the question of how and why such a settlement came into being remained to be answered.

My first explorations at Jawa and in its vicinity took place in 1966 when a short survey was conducted at the suggestion of, and with personal support from, Professor J. B. Hennessy who was then the Director of the British School of Archaeology in Jerusalem. The site was 're-discovered', roughly planned, and a collection of surface material was made and eventually published in a short, somewhat misleading, note (Helms 1973). Work was resumed in 1972 when a sondage was made in the 'citadel' of the Middle Bronze Age at the summit of the site. This was done with the permission of the Jordanian Department of Antiquities under the nominal sponsorship of the British School of Archaeology in Jerusalem and the support of its Director, C. M. Bennett. Excavations proper began in 1973 and continued over three seasons until 1975 (Helms 1975, 1976b, 1977). A short survey season was conducted in 1976. Thereafter occasional explorations were undertaken as part of the Black Desert Survey (Betts 1986, and references *passim*; see also Appendix A below), ending in 1986 when the outbuildings of the 'citadel' complex were surveyed (see now Helms 1989a). A popular account of the project was published in 1981 (Helms) in which the major aspects of the site were documented.

PERIODS OF OCCUPATION

The major periods of occupation at Jawa may be summarized as follows.

Natufian: flint scatter in and around pool P1 in the ancient water systems north of Jawa (see Appendix A below);

Neolithic: a number of desert 'kites' (animal traps) in use near the site (see now Helms and Betts 1987), some of them over-built by structures which might have been animal pens (Fig. 3: A2)

Late Chalcolithic/EB I A: the fortifications, water systems and domestic installations on and about the site; this was the major occupation of Jawa;

EB IV/MBA: the construction and occupation of the 'citadel' at the summit of the site (Helms 1989a) in about 2000 BC or a little later;

Roman/Byzantine: various inscriptions on and about the site (Safaitic and Greek), sherd scatter outside the ancient site, cut stone fragments (including crosses), tombs, and a small tower near the site (see Chapter 8 below);

Islamic/Recent: Arabic inscriptions (also in Kufic script) on the site and nearby, and finally the reconstruction of part of the ancient water system (1983) by the NRA accompanied by destruction of the visible remains in some sectors of the site and the adjacent areas.

JAWA IN THE 4TH MILLENNIUM BC.

As we have said, Jawa lies in the semi-arid steppe of the Southern Levant and, at first glance, far away from what is normally considered to be the verdant, southwestern end of the so-called Fertile Crescent (Fig. 2).

The volcanic origin (Bender 1968) of the landscape in the region (*harra*) has left a good record of man's passing - from the Upper Paleolithic to the present day (Betts 1986, references *passim*). This record mostly concerns unsettled folk, from hunter/gatherers to nomadic pastoralists. But not all of this well-preserved evidence has exclusively referred to nomadic peoples; there were times of sedentization when different life patterns existed, probably the product of different social and economic systems. The difficult, but essential, question is whether such changes were internal: that is to say, whether they occurred within the steppe, or whether they came from beyond; whether they represent the occasional and temporary sedentization of nomadic peoples, or the implantation of populations from the verdant agricultural zones bordering on the steppe in the west and the north (see also Helms 1990).

Jawa was permanently settled only twice: once for a short time (but very extensively) during the 4th millennium BC, contemporary with what is called the late or later Chalcolithic and EB I (also 'Proto Urban' by Kenyon), and then again after 2000 BC (EB IV/[EB-MB] - MB II A). Both of these periods are still regarded as problematical and have attracted widely divergent interpretative treatment. Various interpretations concern perceived changes in the material archaeological record (artefacts, funerary practices, architecture, settlement strategies, etc.) which appear to suggest social, economic and political transformations. The later occupation - about 2000 BC - poses historical questions which are still under study (but see now Helms 1989a) and are not discussed further at this time but for presenting the technical data (Chapter 3). The earlier occupation raises questions regarding the proto-historical era, as we have noted above, which concern the basic mechanisms of social transformation in the southern Levant.

The location and complexity of the site generated the most difficult questions. The construction of Jawa was obviously an enormous undertaking, a great investment of human energy and ingenuity which found expression in the massive stone fortifications, extensive water harvesting systems, and densely packed domestic quarters. Over ten hectares were enclosed in two rings of walls with chambered gates and simple posterns, forming a central upper enclave surrounded on three sides by lower quarters which were likewise fortified (Fig. 5). Excavations revealed closely built-up domestic structures throughout the site. Dwellings were made of stone foundations and form-made mudbricks; floors were often sunk below the external surfaces. Oak from Jebel Druze was used as roof supports, joists, and rafters. Domestic installations consisted of hearths, clay-lined pits, stone-lined bins, storage cells, and induced draft ovens.

Jawa of the 4th millennium BC could, therefore, be described as a large, 'militarized', nucleated settlement, and this presents a stark contrast to what went on before in the eastern steppic areas of Transjordan and southern Syria and - but for the 'citadel' complex - after its abandonment. What is more, the establishment of Jawa can be securely dated before the general trend towards the nucleation and 'militarization' of settlements took hold in Palestine and Transjordan to the west (see also remarks above on hypotheses). It is for this reason that the very existence of the site demands answers to so many questions, the most problematical of which are, of course, why was Jawa established, and how did the population exist in the semi-arid region (see Helms 1981, in progress).

It is hypothesized that the population (or sectors within it) were experienced in hydraulic engineering and built what is today the oldest, most extensive and complete water harvesting system known anywhere in the world. Over eight kilometres of structural remains comprising stone gravity canals, diversions, earth and stone-lined dams and reservoirs can still be seen along wadi Rajil and at Jawa itself. It is possible to restore the original scheme completely, to measure its efficiency and to predict the available amount of water within an hypothetical hydrological model (Helms 1981), and thereby to realize that a delicate balance was maintained between consumption and annual recharge. It is also possible to suggest that a sector of the population knew how to control this limited water budget, that human and animal watering places were kept deliberately separate and that the population of Jawa, or a sector of it, may have had a notion of public hygiene. All of these postulated attributes are typical of what has been called an 'hydraulic civilization' (van Laere 1980 and references there). Such attributes are also part of the formative mechanisms, along with a complex economic system (and writing, organized religion, social stratification, etc.) which are the foundations of 'oriental despotism' according to some scholars (e.g. Wittvogel 1964).

The water system is simple in principle (Fig. 3). (The system as well as the settlement's architecture will appear in detail in Helms in progress.) The annual winter discharge of wadi Rajil was deflected into canals at three points (Da1 - Da3) and these canals led the water to the reservoirs (P1 - P10). However, this annual yield was probably never completely reliable. Local rainwater catchments based on surface runoff were incorporated and together these two sources - wadi Rajil and the micro-systems (C1 - C5) - provided Jawa with water. The balance of the subsistence economy has been documented in terms of macro-sampling. Faunal remains (Köhler 1981) include a significant proportion of cattle, and traces of what may have been animal pens (A1 - A4) can be seen scattered about near the site. Rock carvings of cattle appear in wadi Rajil (see Chapter 8). Botanical remains (Willcox 1981) suggest that irrigation was practised, along with dry farming. Fields linked with canals have been identified (F1 - F6), although their antiquity cannot be substantiated in any technical, archaeological way (see Chapter 2, Nature of the evidence). An extensive cairnfield nearby may be Jawa's burial grounds, (B1 - B2), but the graves cannot be securely related to the occupation of the site during the 4th millennium BC since no material remains have been found, despite extensive exploration.

Two deductions are as obvious as they are vexatious. Jawa had a large, for the most part permanently settled, 'hydraulic' population and, secondly, the time-span of construction and occupation of the site was apparently short. It is suggested (see also Chapter 2) that Jawa was perhaps occupied, built up and abandoned within as little as ten, and probably no more than fifty to one hundred years. In order to account for this, a broader perspective of the Southern Levant must be taken. Hypotheses have been constructed covering a broad spectrum of speculation upon social, economic and political mechanisms which include long-range migration, expansion outward from adjacent verdant zones (i.e. the Hawran and the Damascene) and nomadic confederation and temporary sedentization (e.g. Helms 1984b, 1987a, 1987b). All of these mechanisms have historical and ethnographic parallels in the region; none of them is mutually exclusive (cf. also Helms 1989a, 1990). These hypotheses are still being tested, for the most part using comparative pottery typology and the reconstruction of settlement patterns, with all the limitations of such processes.

As a result, a different view of the Southern Levant emerged: a view from the steppe outwards towards the verdant lands. Traditional scholarly focus was on the settled lands, particularly those of Palestine. Now an extensive sub-region - the Hawran, Jebel Druze and the basalt 'desert' or *harra* (i.e. the *badyiat al-sham*) - appeared as a viable part of ancient economy, both for limited agriculture (dry farming as well as pastoralism, even trade, including smuggling: cf. Lancaster 1981; Lancaster and Lancaster 1990 for local ethnographic parallels). Moreover, there are stretches of fertile land lying beyond Jebel Druze whose history before the MBA (early 2nd millennium BC) is almost unknown. Nearly all of the evidence in regard of our area for the MBA and later, comes only from fragmentary and problematical texts. The Hawran and the Damascene (al-Ghuta) are key components in all hypotheses concerning 4th millennium Jawa. Whatever social or economic reconstructions may be proposed, they must all take into account the well-watered plain about Damascus and the fertile Hawran to the south; and whatever value historical parallels might have, the rise of Aramean Damascus during the Iron Age (which may have been preceded by a period of gradual sedentization of nomadic pastoralists, or bedouin - i.e. ahlamu/Arameans), as well as the later predominance of Damascus as an administrative centre, are significant elements in the debate (Helms 1989a).

Unfortunately, no comparable materials have yet been published from the various recent surveys in and about the Damascene (Braemer 1984, 1988; but see now Maqdissi 1984). 'Datable' and potentially relevant evidence comes from farther to the west where a proto-historical material culture has long been defined (i.e. Chalcolithic - EBA, specifically EB I A). These data stem mainly from excavations at Tell Um Hammad in the Central Jordan Valley (Helms 1984a, 1986; Betts [ed.] in press) and a number of surveys in the upland regions of northwestern Transjordan (Hanbury-Tenison 1986). Other surveys (e.g. Gordon p.c.: wadi Zerqa) remain essentially unpublished to date, but will add considerably to the distribution maps in relation to Jawa's connections with the west. A number of excavations, once their findings are published formally, will also be relevant.

Recently excavated Tell Um Hammad (Helms 1984a, 1986, 1987a) is a large open settlement in the Jordan Valley close to the confluence of the Jordan and Zerqa rivers (Fig. 4). It lies near the crossing of two major routes: north-south along the Rift Valley from Beth Shan, the 'Esdraelon' Plain and the Mediterranean Sea to the Dead Sea, and east-west via wadi Zerqa, the Damiya ford and wadi el-Far'ah: that is to say, from the hills of Ajlun and the steppic borderlands south of

Jebel Druze (Gilead, Bashan, Hawran, and of course Jawa itself), to the core of the Palestinian highlands. Tell Um Hammad consists of several occupation stages, of which the second (TUH2) saw the use, and perhaps even the introduction, of pottery which is identical with some of the repertoires at Jawa (see Chapter 3). This stage is dated in the late Chalcolithic or EBA I A period (i.e. from the mid-4th millennium BC onwards); and as a confirmation of this significant connection with Jawa, identical stamp seal impressions have been found at both sites (see Chapter 4). Furthermore, it seems as if the relatively sudden appearance of a cultural link with the north-east (i.e. Jawa and the Hawran, also perhaps the Damascene) is limited to specific areas, to the exclusion of others (see Figs 158, 172). There are no known parallels in the northern Jordan Valley, but there are parallels near Jerash, along wadi Zerqa and at nearby sites in the Jordan Valley (i.e. Tell Handaquq North and Jericho). In the other direction (west, across the Jordan River) only slight stylistic and technological 'echoes' can be discerned in the pottery of contemporary sites (e.g. at Tell el-Far'ah). From this we might eventually be able to deduce a notion of territorialism as well as routes along which ideas, objects and perhaps also people and their animals moved, as they did in later period, up to the present (see now Helms in press and references there; see also Wirth 1971; Hütteroth and Abulfattah 1977).

Jawa (and perhaps the Damascene and its territories) is, therefore, probably linked with a specific part of Transjordan, and a western and southern steppic 'frontier' may now be more clearly defined. The three causative mechanisms of migration, expansion (implantation or colonization), and nomadic confederation accompanied by (temporary) sedentization must be explored further (see now Helms 1990).

At present the most appropriate model may be a combination of all three mechanisms. The presence of nomadic pastoralists (ever since the Neolithic; Betts 1986 and references *passim*; Helms 1990) and their interaction with agricultural lands whose core was always the Damascene and the Hawran, has to be acknowledged. This was not done in any effective way before when the various hypotheses regarding the 4th and 3rd millennia BC were constructed. Both an outward extension from the oasis of Damascus and its well-watered countryside (including the Hawran and Jebel Druze) and some temporary nomadic sedentization could thus have been in balance at some time, as it was later on, and still is today. However, lands far beyond the southern Syrian landscape may also have been relevant. A fourth mechanism can, therefore, be introduced and this concerns the far-reaching effects of Sumerian economic and political development.

Two kinds of evidence are of signal importance. On the one hand, the existence of huge nucleated, fortified but, like Jawa, relatively short-lived settlements such as Habuba Kabira on the upper Euphrates River (Strommenger 1979, 1980; see also Sürenhagen 1978 and Chapter 2 for pottery parallels) evinces 'international' events which must have affected adjacent lands, as well as socio-economic systems existing within them, even if only indirectly. On the other hand, it is now known that Uruk type pottery was in use far into the Syrian Steppe (i.e. at el-Kowm: (Cauvin and Stordeur 1985), perhaps in the hands of pastoralists. Until this discovery, the south-western 'border' of the international Uruk sphere was Hama (Fugmann 1958). It is this 'international' view which allows us to retain the notion of migration in the debate which may, in turn, not only contribute to the explanation of why Jawa was established, but also shed light on more general social, economic and demographic trends in the Southern Levant during the 4th millennium BC.

The relative chronological framework and its terminology are in a state of confusion. They always have been. Today there is a tendency to avoid proper names as much as possible and to use instead phrases like 'mid-4th millennium' for the Chalcolithic/EB I stage, 'early 4th millennium' for the later stages of the Chalcolithic, and so forth. The dates, however, are not to be taken as absolute. I have adopted this practice, but also use the most commonly recognized term for the early EBA since that 'period' can now be extended in time directly as a result of the excavations at Tell Um Hammad and related sites. Thus EB I A is roughly equivalent with Kenyon's 'Proto Urban A' (though probably longer than she once estimated), and EB I B the same as her 'Proto Urban B' which is also more or less the same as Schaub's 'B Tradition' (1982). (See Helms 1987a for this arrangement of terms with a relative chronology; the absolute dates, as I have noted, are uncertain. *Idem*: Table 1 also presents the preliminary findings from the excavations at Tell Um Hammad. See Helms in press for a fuller description.) Population estimates in the subregion of Um Hammad (the Zerqa 'triangle') were calculated on the basis of settlement size and, where possible, density. One result of this has been the notion of a population increase at the beginning of EB I A, with pottery parallels with some of Jawa's repertoires appearing a little later, though still within EB I A (see Chapter 3). Preliminary calculations indicate that the total population appears to remain constant thereafter, but that settlement strategies change. Locations in the open countryside (without fortifications) were favoured in EB I (A and B), as they had been in the Chalcolithic period; fortified, nucleated settlements on hills, or spurs of the nearby foothills, were increasingly preferred through EB II to EB III, leaving the countryside virtually empty of occupation (although the fields were probably still worked as before); and, finally, the time between EB III and EB IV saw a return to the original open settlements of the Chalcolithic and EB I periods. Pottery analysis and stratigraphy at Tell Um Hammad and some related sites further suggest the possibility of regional variations, including the continuation of some older traditions (i.e. Chalcolithic pottery repertoires), side by side with newer ones. Therefore, the end of the Chalcolithic may overlap with EB I A. EB I A and B may also be partly contemporary, representing regional variations which merge at some time at some sites. The same 'loosening up' of traditional terminology is suggested for the end of the EBA (i.e. III/IV) when the later stages can also be contemporary with whatever might be meant by MB II A (see now Gerstenblith 1983).

But, before any of these speculations can be taken further, the empirical evidence, such as it is, must be presented and discussed (and in that sense the popular publication of Jawa [Helms 1981] was premature). In this volume of the final publication of the excavations and various explorations at Jawa up to 1986, we want to present the basic archaeological data as well as to highlight the nature of the site and the peculiar character of the evidence which may be regarded as 'steppic archaeology' (see Chapter 2). This first volume presents the stratigraphic matrices and an overall site matrix as well as the record of material culture, in order to place the two establishments at Jawa in a chronological framework with regard to the north and west - southern Syria, western Transjordan and Palestine - and, therefore, also in a geo-economic and geo-political context in the ancient Near East. (A second volume will include a presentation and detailed analysis of the architecture and the various water and irrigation systems [Helms in progress].)

Despite currently available data which has definitely proved the date of the major occupation at the site in the 4th millennium BC, Jawa can still be regarded as an enigma or conundrum, as it has been up to now. In the past, the contention was that the massive fortifications as well as the extensive water systems could not have been built in the 4th millennium BC (e.g. Kempinski 1986; Hanbury-Tenison 1986; Richard 1987; Parr p.c.); rather, it has been argued, all of this actually happened in the MBA, about 2000 BC (see now also Helms 1989a). The interesting notion has been suggested (Parr p.c.) that the fortifications of Jawa were built in carefully excavated foundation trenches which cut through 4th millennium BC layers: in some cases (see particularly Figs 23 - 30 below) even beneath them so that clay floors with 4th millennium BC depositions upon them only appear to abutt them. I am reminded of an appropriate joke made by the late Père Francis Hours that the great PPNA tower of Jericho (i.e. part of 'the earliest city in the world') was actually a very large, bell-shaped pit of the Byzantine period.

2. Stratigraphy

S.W. HELMS

Nature of the evidence

We have already touched on some of the aspects which made Jawa an oddity in the archaeology of the Near East (Chapter 1), a peculiarity which gave rise to doubts. A brief examination of the nature of evidence pertaining to a steppic setting might, therefore, be a useful prologue to presenting the stratigraphy, the traditional backbone of controlled archaeology. Behind this discourse lie broader questions regarding the nature of archaeological evidence: whether one should merely record or also interpret data. Normally recovery of stratigraphic data has not been a problem; at Jawa, however, it might easily be, and in the greater region about the site, in the Syrian Steppe (*badiyat al-sham*), it certainly is. The question of interpretation is left for later publications once all of the empirical data have been presented. Nonetheless, various interpretative models must be noted since many of them were constructed in relation to environmentally different zones and, therefore, contributed to the perception of Jawa as a 'conundrum'.

The core of the problem lies in the environment of Jawa and the essentially silent history and prehistory of its ancient populations. We are dealing with a steppic zone with Jawa on its 'verdant' boundary, a zone where physical and socio-economic conditions contrast with those in the verdant zones of the Near East. We have also been faced with a serious imbalance in terms of what has been studied, where archaeological and, say, anthropological and historical work has been conducted. The steppe (wet and dry) is still under-studied. Moreover, virtually all historical reconstructions have necessarily been 'city' orientated, leading to the risk of misunderstanding the role of steppic populations in relation to sedentized ones. This environmental dichotomy affects the nature of evidence in two ways: physically, it limits technical archaeology in terms of stratigraphy and other standard empirical processes; intellectually, it affects the use of current interpretative models.

On the physical side, socio-economic realities imposed on steppic populations by the environment results in shallow occupational depositions and multiple and intermittent use of camp sites. Lack of vegetation has lead to heavy deflation and erosion of many sites leaving, in some cases, no more than a mixed artefact scatter.

Furthermore, mobile populations leave little behind and most of that is biodegradable. We also realize now that although steppic populations can be identified 'archaeologically' before the 4th millennium BC when they used characteristic flint tools and built shelters and corrals in stone, thereafter, it seems, both their tool kits and their shelters changed and are not readily recognizable. Shelters, for example, could now have been tents without stone footings; corrals are almost impossible to date: their chronology relies on juxtaposition with identifiable shelters; their use - specifically for domesticated animals - is similarly hard to prove. Therefore, although we can now 'populate' the Syrian Steppe before the 4th millennium BC (Betts 1986 *passim*; Betts *et al.* 1990, 1991), the nature of evidence makes this difficult in the strictly archaeological way during the time when Jawa was first established. We thus face a demographic 'vacuum' beyond the walls of Jawa. And although we can assume the presence of a mobile (nomadic pastoral) population (e.g. as in Helms 1981), we are only beginning to prove it 'archaeologically'. The only presently appropriate, or admissible, evidence consists of some flint tools which could be dated in the 4th millennium BC (Betts 1986; Betts *et al.* 1991), one EB II/III sherd which was found some 60 kilometres east of Azraq (Betts 1984), and a rock shelter occupation at al-Hibr (Betts in press). The single sherd is a case in point regarding 'steppic archaeology' and, in contrast to the same sherd being found in a verdant context, it says everything. One identifiable artefact is presently the only 'archaeological' evidence for a human presence in the dry steppe during the 3rd millennium BC; it is the first concrete evidence which might identify nomadic pastoralists who could be paralleled in contemporary texts (i.e. MAR.TU: Dossin 1956). This is an important aspect of 'steppic archaeology' which is naturally a difficult one to accept from the traditional point of view. Like the steppic population whose presence we have to surmise, we must maximize our limited resources and use everything to hand in order to begin to reconstruct the past. This is perhaps the most compelling justification for a multi- and inter-disciplinary approach.

There are three further aspects of 'steppic archaeology': the availability of comparative data (and their socio-economic contexts), chronology, and rock carvings.

The first - comparable data - has been a major problem with regard to Jawa: there simply were none until the excavations at Tell Um Hammad in the central Jordan Valley (Helms 1984a, 1986, 1987a), recent surveys in Transjordan (e.g. Hanbury Tenison 1986; see also Braun 1987), and surveys in southern Syria (Braemer 1984, 1988, p.c.). In other words (as we noted in Chapter 1) when the evidence from the excavations at Jawa first appeared in the 1970s, the major zones in which comparable data could be expected were unexplored. On the other hand, Palestine was almost over-explored and thus also perhaps over-interpreted.

Secondly, the chronological framework of the 4th millennium BC was (and still is) unreliable. 14C determinations are relative and the standard deviations already too large when we are dealing with periods of less than half a millennium. Pottery typologies have not been detailed enough and, in any case, are almost exclusively Palestinian: moreover, they are limited to the Chalcolithic period up to the middle of the 4th millennium BC (e.g. Commenge-Pellerin 1987), and to the 'Early Bronze Age' which is best documented in the 3rd millennium BC. Thus, even when we accept the limitations of ceramic typologies as a comparative, chronological tool, there is a gap in the usable data set of about 500 years.

Thirdly, rock carvings carry with them the same limitations as steppic depositional stratigraphy or, rather, its normal absence. By their nature, rock carvings cannot be dated 'archaeologically' unless they are accompanied by texts (and we do not really expect to find these in the *harra* during the 4th millennium BC), or when they are found in stratified contexts. Only a few carvings have been found in this 'acceptable' way (e.g. Betts 1988 for PPNB examples at Dhuweila). However, such undated works are still evidence and may yield meaningful results in conjunction with whatever else we can find.

We not only face (or faced) the admitted restrictions of the more traditional 'old' models which were summarized above (Chapter 1), but also specific questions regarding the nature of steppic populations in the past. Various hypotheses and definitions have been presented about the nature of nomadic pastoralists, their 'evolution' and, perhaps more relevant here, their relationship with the states about them, or even their own role in state formation (e.g. Fried 1967; Service 1962, 1975; Sanders and Webster 1978; Peebles and Kus 1977; see also Rowton 1974, 1976, among his other works). Two main points in the debate have received attention recently. One is the notion that nomadic society may be regarded as ideally egalitarian, while it is in fact stratified (as opposed to hierarchical society within the state) in the economic sense (see, among others, Lancaster 1981; Lancaster and Lancaster 1990; Bocco n.d.; Fabietti n.d.; Marx 1980, 1984). The second point concerns the notion of ethnicity and its appropriate application to the history (and prehistory: certainly proto-history) of the ancient Near East (e.g. Kamp and Yoffee 1980 and references).

The available evidence from Jawa cannot resolve these questions in anything but a speculative way (see, for example, Helms 1989a on MBA Jawa). However, we might plausibly assume (as in Helms 1981) that nomadic folk (i.e. multi-resource nomads: see Salzman 1978) were present in the *badiyat al-sham* during the 4th millennium BC. Furthermore, we may advance the hypothesis that such nomads, including pastoralists, were there ever since the Late Neolithic period (see now Helms 1990: 'Prolegomenon'; Betts *et al.* 1990).

It suffices to give two examples of the nature of steppic archaeological evidence and its problems. The first concerns the 'mysterious walls of the Desert', the so-called 'Desert Kites'. Some of the various arguments and counter-arguments regarding 'Kites' have now been documented with new evidence (Helms and Betts 1987). Yet many scholars still appear to be uncomfortable. The problem, briefly, is this. If we are dealing with animal traps (for which there are many ethnographic and structural parallels), we may assume the presence of hunters. We may also assume that animals would be butchered (processed) away from the traps and that we should not expect to find domestic occupation deposits within these traps. What we expect to find (and do) is projectiles in the main killing ground. And, if these projectiles can be shown to have been fired, and if they can be dated, then we might reasonably assume a period of use. Furthermore, if the dated projectiles are most commonly attributable to one specific era, we might then hypothesize that that era represents a floruit in the use, if not also the first construction, of some characteristic 'kite' systems whose design uniformity can also be recognized on the grounds of architectural characteristics. The artefactual evidence consists of PPNB arrowheads, many with impact fractures. The archaeological purists would have us 'dig' a 'kite' to prove this hypothesis, which by its nature precludes finding 'admissible' evidence.

A second example is the 4th millennium BC date of the walls and gates of Jawa. Despite published sections and descriptions of clearly, though relatively, 'dated' occupational depositions (Helms 1975, 1976b, 1977, 1981), serious doubts were raised (see Helms 1989a for some references; see also Chapter 1 above) as to the date of Jawa's most monumental feature: its massive and extensive fortifications. (The complex water systems were another, cognate problem.) Two standard criticisms were brought: (i) the walls were built in foundation trenches (i.e. the fortifications must belong to the MBA); and (ii) we should have excavated more extensively (see 'Excavation and exploration strategy' below). The first is unfortunate and basically stems from narrow, probably unsuitable, interpretative models which produced notions such as 'urbanism', 'city states', and other constructs grafted onto Palestinian proto-history from the Mesopotamian realm, with the later 4th millennium BC of the southern Levant being perceived as an evolutionary prelude (hence Kenyon's 'Proto Urban'), and notions such as the origins of the 'walled town culture' of the EBA (linked with the 'B tradition' of painted pottery: Schaub 1982). Jawa, therefore, should either not be fortified in the 4th millennium BC, or it ought to be 'dated' later than the first walled 'towns' of EBA Palestine: i.e. sometime after 3000 BC.

Excavation and exploration strategy

The main objective of the excavations was to provide a date-range for the fortifications and the water systems, most of which lay above ground and could be recorded by aerial photography and other rapid planning procedures. In order to do this, suitably preserved depositional configurations had to be identified in which material remains (apart from those suitable for radio carbon dating) could be found and 'linked' with the albeit limited artefactual repertoires and typologies in the adjacent verdant zone (i.e. Palestine). The major artefact categories here are pottery, and to a lesser extent, flint tools.

Given the great amount of visible structural evidence, both on the site and nearby (i.e. the 'kites': see Fig. 234 and Appendix A), exploration had to take into account not only the fortified perimeter of Jawa, but also its extramural features, of which the water systems were the most impressive and, of course, also the most significant. (An *a priori* requirement for prolonged life at Jawa was the capability to procure and store water.) Additionally, we had to consider other visible extramural features: notably, a rounded tower-like foundation on a spur to the south of the site, several tumuli to the north and east (one a formal 'architectural' complex: see Chapter 8 below), at least two fields of smaller tumuli which could have been the cemetery of ancient Jawa (Fig. 3: B1, B2), complex corral systems which might have been animal pens (Fig. 3: A1 - A3), field walls (Fig. 3: F1 - F6), as well as 'kites' and other sites in the vicinity (see Appendix A).

While the remains of the intramural settlement held some possibility of preserved, superimposed occupational depositions, the balance of extramural features lay, for the most part, exposed on bedrock. With the exception of elements within the water systems (see below: especially area D) and the remains which obviously belonged to the later historical periods (i.e. Roman/Late Antique), no stratigraphic evidence was found beyond the walls of Jawa. The 'dated' elements of the water systems, however, can be used in an argument for dating virtually all of the visible remains (i.e. dams, canals, and pools) in one period (the 4th millennium BC) by a form of inductive reasoning whose premise was that if some important parts (e.g. both dams in pool P4 and the revetment of pool P3: Figs 5, 6) were dated, the rest could be included on the grounds of similar design. This was particularly the case with the major water system (I): i.e. if pools P3 and P4 belonged to the 4th millennium BC establishment of the site then, logically, so must have done the feeder canals and their deflection dam in wadi Rajil (Fig. 3).

Figure 6 sets out the results of a soil-depth survey (which was also eventually augmented by the excavations). It was obvious that there were few areas within the walls of Jawa where any reasonable amount of occupational debris might be preserved against the fortifications. Only one area in the upper settlement (Fig. 5: area F) was suitable and turned out to be fruitful; area LF(2/4) in the lower settlement was the best candidate for excavations there. Therefore, more extensive excavations are not a pressing requirement, although they would perhaps extend the artefactual sample size as well as providing more domestic architectural information. Regarding the water systems, only the area of pools P3 and P4 offered a chance of deep stratigraphy. There, however, lay a potentially serious stratigraphic problem in that the fill behind revetments or dams need not strictly speaking provide a date of first constructions (but see area D below). The basic tactics of the excavations were, therefore, clearly determined by the visible and measurable remains at the site. The areas to be excavated were set out accordingly.

Table 1. Schema of recording system

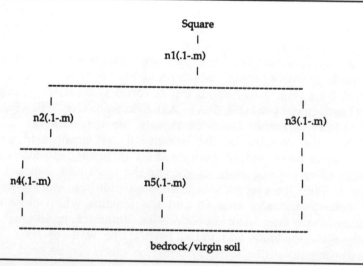

Recording system

Field notation was based on the 'page number' system developed by Kenyon in her excavations in the Near East. This system strove to distinguish between loci within a square ('page number' [pno] = locus) which were determined by horizontal stratigraphic disruptions (e.g. walls), and stratified depositions ('decimal numbers' [layers, etc.] = dnos). A certain amount of subjective judgement was unavoidable in such a decision-making process whose aim was to facilitate meaningful stratigraphic seriation. It did not always work. The schema is outlined in Table 1.

All material remains were numbered according to square (e.g. Area C, Square 2: C2) followed by the pno.dno, a subjective soil description (e.g. 507.14 'dust') and a categorization according to the material (e.g. 'pottery', 'flint', 'bone', etc.). But for some purposive sampling (mainly botanical material), no sieving was carried out. All material encountered was kept. Finds were processed partly in the field and partly in Amman, under various working conditions. Unfortunately, logistical difficulties in Amman forced us to reduce the collected material drastically. As a result, all undiagnostic sherds were 'dumped' after a rough fabric seriation and counting. However, all diagnostic sherds (rims, bases, and body sherds with distinctive features) were kept and form the basis of the typology as it is presented here. Similarly, the flint material had to be reduced. A preliminary sorting was done by R. Duckworth (1976; see also Helms 1981: Appendix B2) and the typology (less debitage) was finally processed by Betts (see Chapter 5). A selection of identifiable animal bones was studied by I. Köhler (1981). Some botanical samples were processed by Willcox (1981).

The recovery strategy was, therefore, a macro-sampling only which, under the circumstances, was deemed adequate since Jawa's location and nature required answers to basic questions in order to relate the site to the current (1970s) state of Near Eastern archaeology: i.e. the date of occupation, cultural links with the verdant zone, and a general idea of the (macro) subsistence economy.

Since so much of the ancient site was visible above ground (and so little remained below: see 'Nature of the evidence'), including the site's most remarkable feature, its water systems, the recording of structures became the most pressing need. To this end various time-saving devices were used, including a movable bipod for vertical photography (Fleming 1976), and an airfoil for remotely controlled low level air photography (ceiling about 250 metres). In 1975 a helicopter was made available through the generosity of HRH Crown Prince Hassan and the Jordanian Air Force. Use was also made of the 1:60,000 series of air photographs (Hunting Surveys: NRA Jordan) and satellite imagery (NASA: Skylab, Landsat, etc.).

The Upper Settlement

Test Area B.

Area B1 was a 1 x 2 metre cut against wall W2, a cut which revealed 25 centimetres of undistinguished soil depositions resting on bedrock, and against wall W2 which was also built directly on bedrock at this point. All material recovered (sherds) belonged to the 4th millennium BC assemblage (according to fabric designation only; see also Appendix B). B2 was a similar cut (2 x 3.5 metres) against wall W2, south of the point where the internal wall W2a (cf. gate G1a) abutts the fortifications. Soil depth was 30-40 centimetres at this point, but the deposition was undistinguished. Wall W2 rested on bedrock; all materials recovered belonged to the 4th millennium BC assemblage (sherds: by fabric designation only). B3 was a larger area (25 x 25 metres) and was set out across the projected trace of the upper fortifications on the eastern flank (projection of wall W9, beyond gate G3). Bedrock exposure is typical of the area. No traces of the upper fortifications were preserved. However, a few fragmentary sub-circular stone structures were visible. All material collected within and about these soundings belongs to the 4th millennium BC assemblages (sherds: diagnostic and fabric designations; see also drill bits and beads in Chapter 5 below). The concentration of beads and drill bits may suggest a craft specialization in this location of the site.

Area C: the 'citadel'

The 'citadel' in the upper settlement forms the core of the latest occupation at Jawa (see Helms 1989a) and consists of a tripartite complex (Fig. 8): (i) a rectangular unit divided into a series of square and rectangular, inter-connected cells (walls BH/K/L/M); (ii) a transverse unit divided into three corridors by a double row of stone piers (walls BE/F/I/G/H); and (iii) a transverse entrance wing made up of a 'kitchen' (walls BA/C/D/E/G), an entrance with vestibule (walls BA/B/C/D/F), an unexcavated section of rubble with some visible internal wall lines, and a rectangular cell (walls BJ/B/I). There is an offset in the external line BI-BL which may indicate a two-stage construction sequence. On the whole, however, investigation of the structure (where this has been possible) showed that the entire building complex was probably constructed at the same time and as one design and construction project. All of these stone walls were set directly on eroded and deflated remains of the 4th millennium BC occupation at the site. There is a series of extramural walls - rough stone corrals - which must post-date the first construction of the 'citadel' (Fig. 7:30). Their precise date of construction has not been established: it could be any time after the construction of the 'citadel', up to the recent (bedouin) past (see square LF3 for Late Antique activities at Jawa).

Four sectors of the building complex were partially excavated. Square C1 represents the clearance of one of the cells (walls BM/N/O/P) in the northern unit (Fig. 9). Two stone piers, still partly supporting the corbelled stone roof, were cleared down to their bases which were set on and into brown/grey mud plaster (200.3), itself set directly on deflated and eroded layers of the 4th millennium BC. Square X1, the first test cut to be made at Jawa (1972), was set against the southern wall of the transverse corridor (wall BF), in line with a stone pier and under a surviving part of the original roof (Fig. 10: Sec. 5). The test cut was stopped when eroded layers of the 4th millennium BC were encountered. Square C2 covers the southwestern corner of the 'citadel' (Figs 11-17) and consists of three major loci: the so-called kitchen, bounded by walls BE/G/A and a door between walls BC/D (loc. 502); the entrance vestibule (loc. 501); and the area immediately outside the main entrance to the 'citadel' bounded by walls BA and BB (Fig. 12. loc. 500/ 503/ 504/ 505/ 506/ 507).

Square C1 (loc. 200)

The lowest layers encountered consisted of ashy compacted soil with pottery of the 4th millennium BC occupation at Jawa (Fig. 9). These layers - exposed in several small sondages - were totally different in character from the clean, yellow clay floor (200.3) which covered all of the exposed area in the square and also continued up over the lower courses of the walls and door jambs of the cell. There were no recognizable signs of occupation on this floor surface: no ash, no burning, no traces of any (recognizable) organic remains. The floor surface was covered with a 20 - 30 centimetre deep layer of fine grey soil in which three sherds were found. Some of this grey earth (200.2) covered fallen stones, particularly in the western area of the cell. This, in turn, was covered by grey/brown/yellow loose soil, some of it wind-blown and generally homogeneous, up to the present-day surface (200.1). There were no organic, nor any artefactual remains in these layers.

Square X1 (loc. 1)

The lowest layers encountered in this sondage (1.4) consisted of hard-packed clay with some charcoal flecks and a number of sherds typical of the 4th millennium BC occupation at Jawa (Fig. 10). These layers appeared to run beneath the base of wall BF. A hard clay floor was set on these earlier depositions and was covered by a 3 centimetre deep layer of black ash. Both floor and ash (1.3) abutt the lowest course of wall BF which was plastered with the same material as the floor (cf. square C1 above). Grey ashy soil, more dense near the black ash layer, tipped down from wall BF. The wall plaster was broken off some 80 centimetres above the floor. Several fallen stones lay in the grey ash (1.2). The rest of the depositions, up to the modern surface, consisted of water-laid earth and fallen roofing slabs and smaller stones (1.1).

Square C2 (loci 500-507)

Locus 502 ('kitchen'). The lowest layers reached consisted of a solid, continuous floor over the entire sector (= floor 501.4: see below) which was covered by a series of deposits and features (Figs 11, 14). A circular clay oven (502.6) was set onto the floor and supported by loose stones (502.8) which included a number of querns and several large pieces of pottery (see Chapter 3: catalogue nos J656, etc.). These features, and the rest of the floor surface, were covered by grey/black ashy lenses, brown/grey soil, mudplaster lumps, and patches of powdery white plaster intermingled with fallen stones, some of them large enough to have come from the surrounding walls (502.5/4). This in turn was covered by brown soil, also containing large stones, but no artefactual material whatever (502.3/2/1), up to the modern surface. There were no signs of any of the typical flat basalt slabs which serve as roofing beams elsewhere in the citadel. The 'kitchen' may, therefore, have been open to the sky.

Locus 501 ('entrance vestibule'). The area of the entrance vestibule was joined up with locus 502 at the end of the excavation season of 1973 (Figs 11, 14, 16). The lowest layers rested on the clay floor which was discoloured through burning ('chestnut brown') and covered with patches of grey/black ash and patches of white powdery plaster. Several stone pounding basins were set onto the floor. A number of burnished sherds lay scattered in this debris (501.4). These floor depositions were in turn covered by brown earth with soft white patches (plaster?) (501.2 = 502.5/4) and some large stones. Brown earth and stones continued up to the modern-day surface (501.3/2/1 = 502.3/2/1).

Loci 500/503-7. Locus 507 is defined by the outline of walls AA/B/D. Bedrock and virgin soil (507.16: reddish/brown coarse deposits, completely sterile; beneath 506.8) were reached in the central parts of this sector (Figs 11 - 13, 15 - 17). An ash-filled stone circle (AF + 507.15) was set directly onto virgin soil, just south of the bedrock outcropping. This represents the earliest occupation in Area C. Grey ashy depositions covered the stone circle (507.14). At this point the first 'architecture' appears in this sector: stone walls AA/B/D were set into the grey ash and on bedrock farther north (see locus 506/504 below), leaving a narrow doorway between walls AA and AD. Wall AA appears to be contemporary with the stone circle, AF (see Fig. 17). A semi-circular stone-paved surface was set against wall AD (507.11) and consisted of basalt querns, some of them 'saddle' querns. A brown clay floor (507.9) flecked with white plaster fragments covered the rest of the chamber up to walls AA/B. Floor depositions included ash, brown clay, and other organic material (507.6/7/8/10). This was sealed by a clay floor which was paved with basalt querns and other flat stones (507.13/5) reaching up to walls AA/B/D and making a shallow step up into the chamber from the north. The stone surface was covered by ashy brown/grey depositions (507.4/12/3-1) which were sealed by a yellow clay floor (= 504.3/4).

Loci 506/504 are defined by the north section beneath the main doorway of the 'citadel', and bound in the south by walls AA and AC. The lowest layers consisted of virgin soil ('brick' coloured) and bedrock, the former mixed with flecks of white ash and dry, crumbled clay lumps (506.8), corresponding to the stone circle in locus 507 (feature AF) above. A platform made of querns was part of this phase (Fig. 16), covered by brown earth (500.10) against wall AA. This was overlaid by a 2 to 3 centimetre-thick layer of dark ash (506.7) which covered the whole of the sector and abutted walls AA/D. Walls AA/D (= walls AB) were constructed as part of this phase. A series of grey, crumbly clay and soil layers (506.6/5 = [upper] 500.10) covered the dark ash and were, in turn, sealed by a floor. A series of depositions lay on this floor: brown, lumpy soil with stones (506.4 = 500.9), yellow/brown earth (506.3 = 500.8), and brown ashy soil (506.2 = 506.1 = 500.7). 506.1 is sealed by 500.6 and 504.13/12. The doorway between the northern and southern chambers, in walls AA/D, was now blocked with a stone packing (AG) which is associated with occupational debris consisting of soft brown earth (504.11/8/7) which in turn is sealed by a hard gritty surface (a floor?) covered by occupational debris (504.6/5) and an internal wall. Another floor (504.4/3) seals the whole of the sector, and is covered by grey topsoil and stones (504.2/1) in the open areas, corresponding to hard-packed and silted layers which ran beneath the footings of the southern flank of the 'citadel' (wall BA).

Loci 500/503 comprise the original square (1973) measuring 2 x 4 metres (Fig. 12). The lowest layers consisted of virgin soil (500.10: brown earth with stones and the quern platform noted above = 506.8 and 507.16) which was overlaid by small stones and yellow/brown clayish soils (500.9/8) and ashy lenses (500.7). These layers abutt wall AA which was set directly on bedrock/virgin soil at this point. Layers 500.9-.7 correspond to 506.4/3/1 and were sealed by a thick deposition of decomposed mudbrick 'crumble' (500.6) which corresponds to 504.12/13 and is in turn sealed by a whitish layer (500.5: 'washline') which covered the entire square. 503.1/2 lay beneath this in the southern end of the square. 500.4 represents fill beneath the 'lower threshold' in the doorway to the 'citadel' and contained only 4th millennium BC materials. The whole of the square was sealed by a layer of roughly set stones (500.3) which abutted the thresholds and the southern flank of the 'citadel', perhaps to serve as a dry access ramp. This in turn was covered by grey, loose topsoil (500.2/1).

With reference to Figure 18, the following sequence can be established: Stage 1 (i) wall AF on virgin soil, followed almost immediately (i.e. the relationship between AF and wall AA noted above) by (ii), the construction and use of the chambers, with many sub-phases represented by the various stone pavements; the blocking AG (iii), is followed by abandonment; and finally Stage 2, the construction of the 'citadel' and perhaps also the stone pavement leading up to the entrance. Stage 1 belongs to the 4th millennium BC occupation at Jawa; Stage 2 to the Middle Bronze Age (c. 2000 BC onward).

Area F: upper fortifications and occupation within

Area F consists of the southwestern corner of the upper fortifications, running from the 'breach' between walls W2 and W4 (W3) and the rounded corner in wall W4/5 some 50 metres east along wall W5 (on special problems see 'Problems of Stratigraphy' below). Walls W4 and W5 are bonded in their exterior faces and form a continuous, unbroken line, as far as the jog and wall W6 (130 metres east). Sets of squares were laid against the inner faces of these walls in locations where sufficient depth of deposition (see Figs 7, 22) was indicated. Square F1, the first to be opened in the area (1973) and isolated from the rest of the area measured 7.80 x 2.50 metres and linked fragmentary structures (standing stones) with the fortifications. Squares F2 to 4 were set out in the corner of walls W3/4/5, originally on a 10 metre grid.

Square F1 (loc. 300)

Bedrock was reached in a 2 metre-wide cut beside the upper fortifications (W5), 1.25 metres and 0.6 metres beneath the lowest courses of the curtain. Bedrock slopes down southwards and eastwards (Figs 19 - 21). By analogy with other areas (e.g. F2) the outer base of the curtain was probably built directly on bedrock, while the inner one was set into earlier occupational debris (i.e. 300.5/4/3), consisting of brown earth and lenses of grey ash. No structures were found in the small excavated area. The upper parts of layers 300.2/3 (Figs 20, 21) appear to be the surface contemporary with the construction of the curtain. Some time thereafter wall W5 collapsed inwards (Figs 20, 21: 'collapse') and this event may be paralleled in area F2-4 at the southwest corner of the upper settlement (see below). The fallen stones are sealed by layers 300.1/2 (grey ashy lenses, brown earth and stones) which, in turn, are associated with the line of standing stones in the northern part of the trench. These are the only signs of any formal structure near the fortifications in this sector.

The sequence of events, therefore, consists of (i) a considerable period of occupation on bedrock while the immediate area was not fortified, (ii) the construction of the upper fortifications (W5), (iii) a partial, inward, collapse of the curtain wall, and (iv) further occupation, still in the 4th millennium BC (EB I A). After a long abandonment, the area to the north was reoccupied (v) during the MBA (see Fig. 7).

Squares F2a/c/d and F4d

Square F2d (loci 400, 401, 413, 414) was the first to be opened in the area (1973) and partly excavated down to the floor level in the rounded dwelling (Figs 22 - 31). Subsequent excavations in F2c (1974) were extended eastwards into square F2d (i.e. loci 413 and 414).

Virgin soil (brown 'crumbly' soil similar to vs. [virgin soil] in square C2) was reached in a restricted area at the base of curtain wall W5 (414.6 and probably also 414.5). Wall W5 was built directly on and partly in virgin soil in this sector, its lowest course 50 to 60 centimetres offset and wider than the upper parts. This footing was sealed and/or abutted by a yellow clay floor (414.2/3) sealing occupational debris (414.4: ashy lenses). Comparison may be made with square F2c (Fig. 27) where the same floor and offset in the curtain appear. Some time after the floor was in use (not long: there are very few signs of occupational debris) part of the curtain wall appears to have fallen down (414.1: ashy soil and rubble, including some large boulders) and this event parallels a similar stone fall in square F1. Occupational debris (400.4a: ash lenses etc., about 20 centimetres) sealed the stone fall and indicates a period of occupation prior to the construction of the sub-circular house (walls BA-G).

Wall BA was set directly on the stone fall (414.1), partly over occupational layers (400.4a), the foundations being made of a grey/yellow earth packing against the fortifications (W5: 400.4/3/2) and faced with stones set in rough courses. It appears that the new work included a partial excavation into earlier occupational levels: this is particularly clear in section 8 (Fig. 30), whereas sections of the original floor surface there (414.2/3) may have been reused. About 20 to 40 centimetres of occupation and several floor surfaces (413.8: black ash, decomposed mudbrick) and a shallow pit (401.5) lie between the original floor surface and the final floor of the dwelling (413.4). The house walls were plastered over with yellow clay, the same material as the floor surface. Hard white ashy lenses and grey soil indicate use of the floor surface in this area. However, very soon after this episode, the house was severely burned and allowed to collapse inward: charred wooden roof supports, roof beams, and other structural parts were found in tumbled mudbricks (some of them hard-fired and form-made) and decomposed brick and wall plaster (401.3). These depositions were sealed by loose brown soil, some of which was probably wind-deposited, some water-laid.

Square F2c was linked with square F2d by cutting through the intervening baulk (see Figs 23, 24: locus 413). Virgin soil and bedrock were reached over half the square. As in the other sectors here, the curtain wall (W5) was built directly on sterile ground and showed the same offset of the first course, abutted by various occupation layers (405.30), including a shallow ash-filled pit (405.21/22) and a yellow clay floor surface (= 414.2/3) which itself was overlaid by compacted brown earth and decomposed mudbrick debris (405.25). These layers were sealed by a stone pavement, partly made of 'saddle' querns, which forms the outer end of a flue for an induced draft oven (feature AA: 405.20/23/24/28/29 and 413.12/15). The oven was cut through earlier layers, including floor 414.2/3 (cf. Figs 24, 28) and was fired at least once, followed by an inward collapse of its clay superstructure (413.11/14 and 405.26/27) and the deposition of layers nearby (405.17/18/19 and 413.10/13) which, in turn, were sealed by the first of the next series of clay floors (405.15/16 and 8) of the rounded house (BA, etc.) up to floor 405.12 (= 413.4). Removal of the baulk between squares F2d and F2c revealed the rest of the shallow pit sealed by this last floor (413.5 = F2d:401.9). Layers 413.3/2/1 link the fill and collapse within the northern part of the rounded house: = 401.3/2/1 and F2c 405.10/9/8/7/6/5 as roof collapse and 405.4/3/2/1 as top soil. The last floor (405.12) sealed two pits (405.11/13/14 = 413.5 and 413.6) and a mudbrick-lined hearth (413.7). After the last plastering of the floor (405.12), a stone bench was set against the back wall of the house, which at this point was partly the original inner face of the curtain wall (W5). Some plaster lines ran beneath this 'bench' (BH), others up against it (Fig. 27).

Square F2a (Fig. 25) revealed the return of the house wall (BB), a second building to the north (CA), and bedrock almost immediately below the surface. Depositions were undistinguished.

Square F4d contained the rest of the rounded building (BA, etc.) and a small rounded bin (BD) which was reached through a narrow doorway from the main chamber of the house (Fig. 25). The bin, like the house, was bonded into the pre-existing inner face of the curtain wall (W5) and had a mud plaster floor. The exterior depositions (410.1/2) consisted of undistinguished soil and rubble on bedrock, only 10 to 20 centimetres below the present-day surface. The interior of the main chamber and the bin (411.1/2/3) consisted of ashy soil with decomposed mudbricks and roof tumble with heavy black ash lenses lying on the equivalent of floor 405.12.

Squares F3a and F3c

Squares F3a and F3c contained a few round wall fragments, some internal features (a pit in F3a covered by stones and querns), and fugitive plaster floors, all only 10 to 20 centimetres below the modern surface (Fig. 22). All material recovered from these squares belongs to the 4th millennium BC assemblages at the site, despite the close proximity of later structures (MBA 'citadel' outbuildings, units 7 - 9: Fig. 7; cf. also squares UT2 and UT3 below).

Squares F4a and F4c

These squares (Figs 22, 32, 33) presented many difficulties typical of the 'archaeology' of Jawa (see Chapter 1 above). The proximity of a repaired breach of the upper fortifications (W3 between wall W2 and W4) and the collapse of walls on either side of this event have obliterated most of the stratigraphy. Furthermore, bedrock steps down sharply to the south and west. And, finally, the original occupation build-up was probably never very deep. However, a sequence of building events can be reconstructed with some confidence.

As in the southern flank of the upper trace of fortifications, the curtain walls and the repaired breach were all built directly on bedrock on the exterior, but not on the interior. The earliest depositions (420.22: fine grey ash lenses and decomposed mud plaster or brick) lay directly on bedrock in square F4c and probably also in square F4a. Because of the abrupt drop in bedrock contours towards the south from square F4a to F4c, the latter had deeper occupational depositions which can be shown to 'fit' between bedrock and layer 420.22 and layer 420.15a in F4a: in other words, there is a 'phantom' phase in the northern square.

A series of yellow clay floors (420.21/19) sealed ashy, occupational depositions (420.20, etc.) in square F4c. A compact clay floor (420.17; 421.1) was the first feature which could be linked to a structure in this area: it abutted wall FB which was part of a rounded unit excavated through earlier depositions, down to bedrock. It was very similar in structure and in terms of its features (i.e. the step down through the doorway and a door socket on the left hand side). A foundation cut was visible in the section (Fig. 33: section 2, 'ft'). The circular unit collapsed inward (large stones and earth), and the floor was covered with a series of rubble and decomposed mudbrick layers

(420.15a and 405.15b), the former sealing the remains of the rounded unit (walls FA & FB). At this point topsoil was reached in F4c.

Layer 420.15a was traced into square F4a and lay beneath grey ashy depositions (420.13/15) in the east sector, the equivalent of layer 420.14 in the west where it ran beneath the repaired breach of the fortifications (wall W3) which must therefore post-date everything described so far. An oven was installed on these layers and was eventually abandoned and filled with ashy and decomposed mudbrick depositions (420.6/7/8/11/12; 422.1). A large amount of heavy stone work collapsed inwards at about this time, presumably from curtain walls W2/3/4 (420.2/5), and was surrounded by ashy and melted mudbrick layers (430.1/2). This last 'event' was sealed by tumbled stones and earth up to the modern surface (420.3/10/1). All materials recovered from the two squares belongs to the 4th millennium BC assemblages.

With reference to the matrices in Figures 34 to 36, various phases and sub-phases can be loosely linked with the adjacent area (F1/2/3).

(*i*) Ashy depositions on bedrock and a series of clay floors are roughly equivalent to the first occupation in squares F2 and F3, including the induced draft oven.

(*ii*) The construction of rounded units may correspond to the rounded house(s) in squares F2 and F3, followed by collapse.

(*iii*) This was followed by the construction of an oven and the repair of the breach (W3), and, in turn, by another wall collapse and then the end of 4th millennium BC occupation in the area.

(*iv*) The construction of the 'citadel' outbuildings in the north of the area during the early MBA.

Area G: main gate in upper fortifications (G1)

The gate is bonded into the adjacent curtain walls (W1/2). Everything was built directly on bedrock. There was very little in the way of soil deposition within the gate; the same held for both interior and exterior spaces with regard to the defence line. The gate was blocked by large fallen boulders from its upper courses and from the adjacent curtains. These were removed and a trench of 4.5 x 5 metres was set out about the southern, exterior pylon of the gate where the soil depositions were deepest. Most of the rest of the interior of the gate was exposed bedrock.

Excavations revealed a shallow curb or threshold (Fig. 37:AA) between the two exterior pylons and a narrow stone socle or footing against the southern flank of the gate chamber (Fig. 37:AB). It was impossible to say which came first: the curb/threshold and socle/footing, or the pylons and chamber of the gate itself. The total depth of soil deposition (grey/brown clayish earth) was only 20 centimetres and internally completely undistinguished. The few finds consisted entirely of 4th millennium BC pottery and flint.

Square TT1 (1973)

The test trench was opened upon the discovery of an apparently unique sherd concentration (see also Figs 38, 82). Clearance was limited to the interior of a partially eroded rounded or elliptical chamber (walls AB/AC), part of a larger complex which lay to the south. A small doorway in wall AB/AC was blocked with a large, flat stone (AD). A rock scarp (partly crumbled away) ran eastwards and curved around a natural cave in the basalt bedrock. A 'cup-mark', or artificially drilled depression, was cut into bedrock half-way between the test trench and the cave.

Square TT1 is the only example of a domestic floor surface on which an appreciable amount of material culture was preserved on a reddish clay (plaster) floor set directly on bedrock and virgin soil. All depositions (grey/brown soft earth) were unsealed. The area had been heavily eroded, probably as a result of collapse in the rock scarp. A shallow pit (AE) was set against wall AA and sealed by flat stones, including several 'saddle' querns. Because of the shallowness of the depositions it is impossible to assign a relative position within the site matrix, although everything in the square belongs to the 4th millennium BC 'horizon' at Jawa.

Area UT: interior of the upper settlement

All areas are unconnected with the upper fortifications. Squares UT1 and UT4 are concerned with structures of the 4th millennium BC; squares UT2 and UT3 with the western flank of the outbuildings associated with the 'citadel'. Square UT4 was cleared of stones (20 x 40 metres) and used as a test area; the interior of a rectangular structure was cleared down to occupation levels (floor) in two unconnected cuts.

Square UT1 (loci 700 -707)

Much of the excavated structure in squares UT1a to UT1d was visible above ground, and formed part of a series of rounded and semi-rectilinear dwellings in this area. The western flank of the structure was bonded into a series of stepped revetments (Fig. 39: AI, etc.) which make up the east flank of an open passage or 'street' leading from gate G1 into the upper settlement. There probably were two internal gates, (G1a) and perhaps a gate at the northern end of the passage (Fig. 79). The excavated portions in square UT1 revealed a sub-circular dwelling with one square corner (Fig. 39: square UT1b, AD/AA), a narrow doorway giving onto a lane in the south (Fig. 39: square UT1c, between walls AA and AB), and flanked by a spur wall (AH). The interior of the dwelling was subdivided into three sections:

(i) the main sub-circular room bounded by walls AA/AB/AF; (ii) a long, apsidal chamber (AC/AE); and (iii) a sub-rectangular chamber (walls AF/AA/AD) separated from the main room by a thin stone curb or wall (AF). All layers, but for those in square UT1a, were unsealed and consisted of 'topsoil' which lay on broken floor surfaces, some of which retained traces of mud plaster (e.g. Fig. 40: 700.4).

The earliest depositions (other than 'topsoil' in the shallower areas) consisted of compressed brown earth (705.12) and brown earth with ash and plaster fragments (705.11) with some orange discolouration (Figs 40, 43) on virgin soil or bedrock. Layer 705.11 may be regarded as a floor surface abutting wall AB. This appears to be set into sterile soils in the section, possibly in a shallow foundation cut. A low curb wall (AK) defined the northwestern limits of this floor surface. Two large, flat stones (AL) were set into the floor and may have served as a base for a central (wooden?) roof support (see also square F2C: BI, Fig. 25). Layers 707.10 (grey earth), 707.5 - .8 (fine ash), and 707.4 (ash) in square UT1b, and layers 700.3/.4 (floor surface and plaster) in square UT1d must belong to this phase in the area.

Two further phases might be identified. The first of these consists of internal modifications of the dwelling in terms of stone partitions (705.6:BA), wall BB and enclosure or bin BC with a fill (702.5). The second of these phases consists of two pits in square UT1a: a pit (CA) surrounded by small stones (unexcavated); and a pit (CB) with two larger stones set into opposing sides (Fig. 43: Sec. 1).

The dwelling in square UT1, therefore, represents one main phase of construction and occupation, followed by two phases of occupation accompanied by some internal structural modifications (Fig. 45). Furthermore, the first establishment of a dwelling here (and a narrow lane) was associated with the construction of an inner gate (Fig. 39: G1a) and the stepped stone revetment (Fig. 39: W1a).

With reference to Figure 45, and in comparison with other areas (e.g. area F), we may suggest that the construction activity about gate G1a may have taken place late in the 4th millennium BC sequence, since there is only one main building phase. This, however, is only surmise (see 'Problems of Stratigraphy' below).

Square UT2 (loci 720, 721, 722)

This square demonstrates the same close proximity in stratigraphic terms of the two major occupations at Jawa. Bedrock was not reached at any point. The earliest remains here (4th millennium BC 'horizon') are represented by yellow/green sandy layers with some pebbles and ash lenses (Figs 47: 722.10, 49). This is followed by a series of features, all of them associated with the stone wall (AD): AA is a hearth (722.8); AB a stone-covered bin or shallow pit (722.6) next to wall AD;

and AC another stone-covered bin or pit in the east section. A long series of occupational deposition abutted wall AD, comprising greenish clay layers and ashy lenses (722.3/4/5/9). These layers, as well as the stone wall (AD), were sealed by a thin clay 'floor' (722.2) which abutted a stone scree next to a second stone wall (BA). Soil depositions on this 'floor' contained only material of the 4th millennium BC and must, therefore, 'date' wall BA within the earlier 'horizon' at Jawa. The area to the west of wall AD (locus 720) was cleared down to a brown, ashy deposition (720.3/4) which was associated with the wall and also ran beneath the east wall of the later structure here (wall CA). Layers 720.1/2 are 'topsoil'.

The later building (unit 3 of the 'citadel'complex': see Figs 7, 46) was visible on the surface as a rectangular mass of tumbled stones, all of them characterized by a lighter patina than the rest of the (earlier) structures at the site. Upon clearance within the small 'square' (2 metres wide), two parallel, narrow stone walls were found (walls CA/B). The lowest levels reached in this locus were cut through the floor of the building (721.8/10) and belong to the 4th millennium BC 'horizon'. They serve to reiterate the lack of any intervening occupation at Jawa between the 4th millennium BC and c. 2000 BC: i.e. Stages 1 and 2, as they were established in area C above (Fig. 48). Layers 721.4-7/9 represent an uneven plaster floor, its 'makeup' and occupational debris, for the most part concentrated along the central axis of the building. This was overlaid by rubble and yellow/grey soils (721.1-3).

Square UT3 (locus 750, 752)

A three metre-long trench was cut across the line of unit 5 of the 'citadel complex', and abandoned when a fragile and sterile clay floor surface was reached: layers 750.1-3 overlaid the floor and contained only MBA material (Fig. 46). A large flat stone (base plate of a roof support?) lay on the floor. Layers 752.1/2 lay within the units eastern courtyard, but consisted of no more than undistinguished 'topsoil'.

Square UT4 (loci 1700, 1710)

Clearance of the area revealed a series of sub-circular structures, one of which appeared to have at least two squared corners (Figs 5, 50). This structure was sounded, and represents the most regular plan to be found within the 4th millennium BC 'horizon' at Jawa so far. Bedrock was not reached. The plan, however, may represent the original construction here (see below: 1700.5), while the various internal features belong to the later phases of use (by analogy with other squares at the site).

The northern sondage, within the squared end of the structure (walls AB/AC/AD), revealed two low stone 'benches': one (AK) against wall AB and the internal dividing wall, AG; the other against internal wall AH and walls AC/AD. A door socket was found near the opening in the internal dividing wall (AG). The 'floor' surface associated with these features consisted of ashy soil with reddish/brown earth. A small sondage in the corner made by walls AB and AC reached a plastered area and a number of small stone features, both abutting the original structure. An auger hole reached what may be bedrock or sterile soil some 25 centimetres below the plastered surface.

The southern sondage uncovered what may be the continuation of the western 'bench' (AK/AL) and a shorter 'bench' just inside a doorway between walls AA and AE. The floor surface was the same as in the northern sondage.

Two phases of use can, therefore, be identified with certainty (Fig. 51). By analogy with other squares (and the evidence from the auger hole), it is possible that the rectilinear structure was indeed the first 'event' here (i), followed by a number (ii, iii [?]) of re-occupations and minor internal modifications, up to the final abandonment in the area.

Square X2

The square represents a clearance in 1986 which revealed a sub-circular structure partly on bedrock and also over earlier structures. All recovered materials belong to the 4th millennium BC assemblages at Jawa. The stratigraphy - limited to a small sondage - nevertheless shows that at least two major phases of occupation and construction occurred here: the earliest (?), perhaps on bedrock, consisting of heavier walls; the latest of flimsy, sub-circular ones (see also TT1 and LF2, particularly the latter for a similar 'architectural' sequence).

The Lower Settlement

Area D: dams retaining Pool P4

The visible stone dam (D2: straight water face) is interrupted at the east end, some 25 metres short of the projected line of the lower fortifications (Fig. 52). However, elements of an earlier dam (D1: curved water face similar to the retaining structures in pool P3) were visible for about 7 metres beyond the end of the straight dam. Relatively recent flooding between this area and the projected line of the lower fortifications had removed most of the stone structures. More recently (1983/4) reconstruction of part of the ancient water system has now obscured this area and has also caused serious erosion of the lower fortifications which were set on a rock ridge. The following squares were set out: D1a, a 2 x 2 metre cut against the water face of the straight dam; D2 at about the centre of its preserved line, reaching bedrock; D1a, a 2 metre wide trench behind the facing stones of the water face, across the hump of the dam, abutting a stone revetment on the air face; D1c, a 1 metre wide cut across the projected line of dam D2, down to bedrock, in which no trace of any structure was found, nor any datable materials, just yellow silt.

D2 designates the area across the projected line of the lower fortifications in line with both dams. A modern wall (Fig. 55) roughly follows the line of the curving dam (D1), but could not have served any water retaining function since it was only set on ash and silt layers. It must represent recent (and useless) bedouin efforts to retain water in pool P4. However, earlier (i.e. 4th millennium BC) structures were found in squares D2a, c, and d.

DX is a small, shallow test cut made behind the water face of the 'failed' dam in wadi Rajil opposite pool P5. An ash and yellow clay matrix contained nothing but (a small amount of) 4th millennium BC material (Fig. 5).

Squares D1a/b/c and D3

The sondage against the waterface of dam D2 (D1a) reached bedrock 2.50 metres below the modern surface (Fig. 53). The dam's airface was built directly on bedrock and its lower courses sealed by well-compacted rocks, clay and silts (1000.4) containing pottery sherds (4th millennium BC types) and animal bone fragments. This layer was in turn sealed by yellow clay with some rock tumble (1000.3) on whose surface lay a number of sherds (MBA types: see Chapter 3), charcoal and a scattering of animal bone fragments. Layers 1000.2/1 consist of sterile reddish/yellow compacted silts, up to the present surface within the reservoir.

The infrastructure of the dam D2 and that of the earlier dam (D1) are divided as follows (Fig. 54). Dam D2 and layers 1014.12/11 (silt and clay over a stone apron [AC] belonging to dam D1) are followed by thick layers of compacted brown soil (silt) alternating with thin layers of grey/black ash (1014.11-1), up to the present surface of the structure. Layers 1013.1-5 (= 1014.1) covered the top of the earlier dam (D1) and abutted and ran beneath an upper revetment (BB). These layers sealed a series of depositions over and against dam D1: from the lowest levels reached (on a sloping surface from the airface of D2 - wall AB) 1015.9-11 up to 1011.1/1014.13/14/1016.1, they repeat the structural sequence noted against and over the waterface of D2. These strata of hard, compacted brown silt alternate with layers of ash, up to the present surface.

The dam D1, walls AA/AB, formed the water and airface of the dam respectively; AC was a sloping stone paved apron within the reservoir. A sondage was cut between AA and AB, revealing a series of horizontal layers: the lowest reached, 1016.7/8, consisted of the same brown compacted clay or silt as we already noted in regard of later fill in the infrastructure; 1016.6 is ashy; 1016.5 brown clay; 1016.4 ash; 1016.2/3 brown clay.

A trench was cut across the western sector of the dam (Fig. 52: D3). Here the remains of dam D1 are represented by a solid stone wall (2.50 metres wide) encased by the same fill as elsewhere within the later dam's infrastructure (layers 1058.1-6; 1059.1-8), limited by the stone waterface and a stone revetment on the airface.

Squares D2a/c/d/e

In square D2a, the lowest levels consisted of 'crumbly' brown soils (1028.3) which lay against wall AA and were sealed by various ash layers (1028.1/2), the upper of which covered the top of wall AA and were linked with deep ashy deposit to the west (1025.2/1026.1/2/6-8/1027.1). All of these layers were sealed by reddish/brown topsoil and a scatter of large stones (Figs 55, 56).

Wall AA was traced into square D2c and also related to a fragmentary curving wall (AB). All of these structures were sealed by pale grey ash (1033.1) which was covered by 'crumbly' brown soil (1032.4-6) and that, in turn, by deep ashy deposits (? = those in square D2a: 1031.2/1032.1-4/ and 1034.1-4, a westward extension towards the dam). Reddish brown topsoil overlay all of these layers, including a later addition on wall AA, wall BA.

The area between walls BA and a single stone wall (CA) in square D2d was cleared down to an ashy layer (1040.3) beneath topsoil (1040.1/2) which ran against both walls.

The presently visible wall (DA), marking the eastern edge of the pool (P4) was set on topsoil in square D2e. A sondage to the west of this modern wall was excavated down to a hard brown soil (1065.12) which was covered by ash lenses alternating with hard brown clays, up to topsoil: 1065.11/10/9 ash; 1065.8 hard brown; 1065.6/7 ash; 1065.4/5 dark brown; and 1065.1-3 topsoil.

The stratigraphy in squares D2a/c/d/e/f is unreliable, but does at least show several phases of activity. On the other hand, the squares in the dam area show two major phases of construction of which the latest also appears to have been in use, in some way, during the MBA. Both dams (D1 and D2) were built during the 4th millennium BC, the earliest of them (D1) following the design of the other dams at Jawa; the later (D2) departing from this design. The evidence from cut D1c suggests that the latest dam (D2) may never have been finished, or that it failed dramatically, since no structural remains were found in situ (Figs 57, 58).

Area LF: line of the lower fortifications

Squares LF1/2/4 lie on the southern flank of the fortifications (wall LW1/2/3/4/5/6), in the southern lower quarter of the settlement

(Figs 5, 80). They are connected by a continuous curtain wall which has been traced both on the ground and through the use of air photographs. Square LF1 represents the clearance of a double (or triple) chambered gateway set into a casemated wall (square: about 13 x 15 metres). The remains were only centimetres below the surface: there were no distinguishable strata within these depositions. However, the few material remains which were found all belonged to the 4th millennium BC assemblages of the site. Squares LF2/4 (20 x 40 metres) lie some 75 metres farther east and are divided into two parts. Square LF2 (Fig. 59) consists of three squares abutting the lower fortifications: squares LF2a and LF2b against wall LW4, LF2e against both walls LW3 and LW4 at a postern (LP1); square LF2d against an internal wall (LW5). Square LF4 (Fig. 71) was set out across a major gateway in the southern trace of the fortifications (LG2) in three loci: LF4a within the internal wall LW5, west of the gateway; LF4b on the other side of wall LW5 and against wall LW4, bound by the west flank of the gate in the east; and LF4c inside the gate between walls LW5 and LW6, including a sondage within the central passage of the gateway.

Square LF3 (Figs 5, 76) was set out across the eastern flank of the lower trace of fortifications, opposite the deflection area (Da2) in the second of the water systems at the site, within wadi Rajil. Two loci consist of LF3a which connects the modern (bedouin) stone corral and the visible remains of revetments/fortifications along the edge of the settlement; and LF3b a small cut beyond the internal line of trace up to the outer trace which is clearly visible in air photographs, but built directly on bedrock.

Square LF2

Square LF 2 was excavated in two stages: a sounding in 1973 and an extension of this in 1975. The earlier sondage (Figs 59 - 63: sections 1, 2, 3, loci 1000 and 1001) may be summarized as follows.

The earliest occupation levels reached consisted of ashy tip lines (1000.4 and the lower parts of 1000.3) sloping down towards the south and running beneath the then visible line of the lower fortifications (LW4). Ashy lenses and decomposed mudbrick debris (upper 1000.3) abutted wall LW4 and contained only 4th millennium BC material, proving the early date of the lower line of fortifications at that stage in the project. The layers running beneath the wall suggested at that time that the lower settlement, at least in this particular sector, appeared to have been open and undefended during the first settlement of the site. The upper strata of layer 1000.3 consisted of grey/brown ashy lenses and washed mud plaster and brick overlying a similar soil matrix which sloped northwards off wall LW4. These upper strata, therefore, indicate a levelling off in the area immediately within the lower fortifications. This was followed by a partial inward collapse of wall LW4 (i.e. the stones in layer 1000.2): comparison can be made with the inward collapse recorded in the upper fortifications in area F. Sometime after this an oval stone building (wall BA) was set (or cut) into layer 1000.2 and represents the latest occupation phase at this stage in the 4th millennium BC.

The extension of the sondage in 1975 supplemented the earlier work. The new evidence revealed that there was an earlier defensive line (wall LW5). The immediately relevant square in the extension is LF2a (Figs 59, 64 - 66: sections 4, 5, 6, loci 801, 802, 803, 804, 805). Bedrock was reached 1.30/1.20 metres beneath the outer fortification (wall LF4). Immediately on this were signs of occupation: i.e. a hearth (Fig. 64: section 4, 805.32) surrounded by small stones and filled with grey/black ash), and sealed by a deep layer of compacted hard yellow clayish soil (805.31 [lower]/33/34), in turn sealed by a hard clay 'floor' surface (805.29). The 'floor', or at least a deliberately consolidated external surface, abutted the inner fortification wall (LW5). Thereafter followed a series of occupation layers (ash lenses, etc.) separated by thick strata of organic material mixed with earth (i.e. 805.31 [upper]/28-1; 804.22/21 = 1000.3/4), all running underneath wall LW4 in the south. What appears to be either a foundation or a robber trench against wall LW5 (Fig. 65: section 5, left hand) may simply be a localized feature; it does not reappear in the opposite section (Fig. 66: section 6, right hand). Section 6 also shows that, although interrupted by an eroded trough, layers 805.3/4/1 and others once linked the two defensive walls, suggesting that they were in use, or at least above ground, together for a time. This ceased with the erosion of the trough noted above, and the removal of the top courses of wall LW5, and was followed by new depositions (ashy lenses, etc.) and then the inward collapse of wall LW4, as we have already noted in the earlier sondage of 1973. The final stage (as in 1973) consists of the construction of the oval stone unit (wall BA).

Squares LF2b/e along the inner face of wall LW4 (Figs 67, 68: sections 7, and 8, locus 820) showed a long series of occupational layers, mostly striated ashy depositions separated by layers of decomposed mud brick. These layers served to 'date' the postern in wall LW4 (LP1) within the life of the wall, with several reconstruction phases.

Square LF2d produced evidence of the earliest occupation in this sector of the lower settlement (Figs 69, 70: sections 9 and 10, locus 810) which consisted of grey/brown ashy surfaces with carbonized organic material and some artefacts, immediately on bedrock. These layers (810.24/25/26) also ran beneath the inner face of wall LW5. The southern sector (as revealed here) may, therefore, have been open and undefended at the very start of occupation at Jawa. Layers 810.22 and 810.23 were clay floors, separated by occupational debris, which abut a house wall (AA), which, in turn, is built virtually on bedrock. Its footings in relation to layers 810.24-26 are uncertain: they may be contemporary; they are probably a little later. In any event, only the upper floor (810.22) also joins the lowest course of the fortifications (LW5) (obscured in Section 9 by a shallow pit, but traced throughout the square, and along the south profile). The early sequence here, therefore, is as follows: (i) occupation on bedrock; (ii) construction of wall AA; and (iii) construction of wall LW5 and continued use of wall AA. Both walls continue in use for a relatively long time. There is another series of clay floors (810.18/13, etc.) separated by occupational debris, up to layers 810.4/3, which is followed by undistinguished topsoil.

Square LF4

Squares LF4a/b/c can be directly linked with LF2: both inner and outer fortifications (walls LW4/5) were traced through. The deepest stratigraphy comes from square LF4a (Figs 71-73: section 1 and 2, locus 1500). There wall LW5, the inner and earliest fortification in this sector of the lower settlement, was built directly on bedrock and a series of floors, separated by occupational material, run off the wall. The first floor is layer 1500.18; this was followed by ashy layers (1500.15) at which point a 'house' wall (BA) was built, making a narrow doorway between its southern end and the west flank of gateway LG2. Floors and occupational depositions continued up to layer 1500.10, where the inner face of wall LW5 was either purposely stepped southwards, or altered to leave a narrower wall in the south. This point might also correspond with the construction of the new southern defence line represented by wall LW4. At any rate, surfaces associated with wall BA must have abutted this outer portion of wall LW5 up to layer 1500.7, at which point the doorway was blocked with stones (CB) and a stone-lined and -paved hearth (CA) was constructed on top of the northern part of wall LF5, next to a surviving southern part, of which one course remained *in situ*. This was followed by disturbed, undistinguished topsoil. Square LF4b (locus 1501) was not taken to bedrock. A series of disturbed ashy lenses joined walls LW5 and 4.

The gateway (LG2) was partly cleared of stone to facilitate planning. Its passage floor level was not reached, but probably consisted of a series of crude stone steps, just like gate LG1 and the small postern in wall LW4 (LP1). The eastward continuation of the trace in wall LW6 must have served both stages of the lower defenses (i.e. walls LW4 and LW5).

With reference to the sections (Figs 61 - 70, 72, 73) and the stratigraphic matrices (Figs 74, 75), the sequence of occupation in squares LF2 and LF4 may be summarized as follows. Occupation on bedrock (i), including stone structures (i.e. Figs 69, 70: wall AA in square LF2d), preceded the construction of the lower trace of fortifications. This was followed by (ii) the first inner defensive wall (LW5), including the construction of the main gate (LG2). A considerable amount of occupational debris (iii) then accumulated outside the fortifications (Fig. 65: layers 805.33-805.1, 804.22/21). Then followed (iv) the construction of the outer fortification wall (LW3), a process which perhaps involved the partial demolition of wall LW5 (see Fig. 65: traces of a 'robber trench' against the southern, upper face of the wall). Occupational depositions accumulated up against the inner face of the new construction (v), and at some point (vi) there was a partial inward collapse of wall LW4, followed by (vii) more occupation and, finally (viii) the building of a series of simple, sub-circular huts and open-air domestic installations near, and even over, the defensive works (Figs 60 - 63, 65, 71, 72). This was the last phase of occupation in this area, but for whatever activities might have left a scatter of Roman/Late Antique sherds beyond the fortifications (for which see Chapter 8).

Square LF3a/b (loci 1400, 1401, 1402)

It is possible to recognize an internal line of the lower fortifications in this area which parallels somewhat the similar arrangement of two wall lines in squares LF2 and LF4. The outer line was not examined archaeologically since it has little soil deposition against it (see Fig. 6). The inner line consists of heavy stone foundations, set into grey ashy soils and onto some water-laid silts. Wall BA (Fig. 76) represents an inward jog of the line from walls BD and BC (BE), making a right angle with wall BB. BF, a large boulder, may have fallen from this wall line. The sondage (LF3b) against the outer face of walls BA and BB revealed nothing but soft grey/brown topsoil (1400.1) abutting the walls. Beneath the footings of the inner defence (?) line lay a series of depositions consisting of soft grey/brown soil and ash (1400.2/.3), including some silty depositions. These layers ran beneath walls BA and BB and lay on a stony surface (1400.4 - .7) which was very compacted and totally barren of any occupational debris. It should be regarded as virgin soil here.

The internal sondage (LF3a) demonstrated the 'date' of the corral walls here (CA) which were set onto grey, undistinguished 'topsoil' (1401.1/.2, 1402.1 - .5) which also abutted the upper parts of wall BA in the east. These upper layers contained material from the 4th millennium BC as well as some body sherds of the Late Antique period (perhaps of the 5th - 6th centuries AD).

The earliest occupation encountered in this square consisted of soft brown soil (1402.7) on virgin soil, against a wall fragment (AC) and perhaps also against walls AA and AB (Fig. 76). This configuration (A) runs beneath the line of the so-called inner fortifications (BA, etc.) and may be contemporary with the outer, unexcavated line of fortifications noted above. Soft grey/brown depositions abutted walls AA and AB (1402.6). Wall AD appeared beneath topsoil and may be related to wall AA: the area was not sounded further.

Two major phases of 4th millennium BC occupation are indicated. The earliest (walls AA, etc.) may be linked to the outer defence line, the outer lower fortifications, which may be preceded by an open settlement, as in squares LF2/4. This was followed by the construction of the inner line (walls BA, etc.). A corral was constructed a long time after this (Fig. 77: matrix).

Square LT1: interior occupation

Only one square (about 10 x 10 metres) was laid out within the southern lower quarter of the settlement, below and against a distinctive rock scarp where the opening to a small cave was visible. The area was cleared to bedrock and the accessible parts of the cave were excavated to bedrock.

Depositions in the exterior area were very shallow and virtually indistinguishable from the normal grey/yellow 'topsoil' at the site. Loci 900 and 901 divide into two sets of layers, the upper of which (900.1/2/4/6-9; 901.1/2/3/7/9) are 'topsoil'. The lower levels consist of ashy lenses and decomposed mudbrick (900.3/5; 901.4-6/8), all more or less directly on bedrock, and all of them associated with a fragmentary matrix of stone walls of sub-circular plan.

Loci 902/903 concern the excavation of layers within the cave. The earliest of these, on bedrock, (903.2/3/4) included organic material and artefacts of the 4th millennium BC. These depositions were followed by a series of flimsy floor levels separated by decomposed mudbrick, ashes, and a large amount of fallen whitish plaster (903.1 through 902.9-2). Layers 902.1/4 represent 'topsoil' within the cave and link up with topsoil layers on the outside (Fig. 78).

Other Sondages

A1: rubbish pit excavated to bedrock: silts only.
A2: a very recent burial within the recent tip from the mechanical excavations of the ancient pool (since 1986 cemented over); ash and yellow silt/clay matrix similar to the fill in the other dams at the site. All recovered material (the corpse apart) belonged to the 4th millennium BC assemblages.

A3: a cut across the canal upstream from dams D1/2: yellow silt; no 'cultural' material;

A4/A5: cuts across the canal and the interior of the stone 'box' below dams D1/2; some 4th millennium BC flint objects.

GENERAL

Problems of Stratigraphy (Figs 79, 80)

As we pointed out repeatedly, stratigraphy (if it exists at all) cannot answer all questions. It can, however, present dilemmas. This is particularly so with regard to massive stone constructions which were built directly on bedrock and which were often kept deliberately separate from occupational loci. The water systems of Jawa are an obvious example, while the fortifications could only be examined in the traditional archaeological way in a few limited areas (Fig. 6). Other extra-mural features are even further removed from stratified matrices (Fig. 3). Most of these problems and dilemmas can only be solved, or resolved, through careful structural analysis which will be included in a second volume of the excavation report (Helms in progress). However, a brief discussion must be given at this time: at least in relation to the (limited) stratigraphical data presented here.

The first problem is the length of occupation of the major settlement, from the first construction to abandonment, all of which occurred in the 4th millennium BC. It is clear at once that occupational depositions are uniformly shallow everywhere at the site, and this in itself might argue for a short period of occupation. Analyses of the material remains support this to some extent. For example, there are no indications of any stylistic development in the pottery assemblage, although it is made up of several disparate repertoires (see Chapter 3). The overall combination of repertoires (i.e. making up the assemblage) is homogeneous through all phases of the earliest occupation at Jawa. However, even a guess as to an absolute time-range based on non-development (or, conservatism) in pottery styles is impossible, as is testing for time-range in, say, Palestinian assemblages of EB I A. That period can now easily be dated between c. 3500 and 3000 BC (Helms in press). Falling back on stratigraphy alone then, we may examine three areas in which depositions are preserved to some depth.

The first is area C and square C2 where layers of the 4th millennium BC are sealed by the foundations of the MBA 'citadel'. The maximum depth is less than one metre (Fig. 16). The structural sequence indicates a continuous process from features on bedrock or virgin soil (AF), through the walls of the rounded structure (AA, etc.), to the blocking of a doorway (Fig. 13: AG), accompanied by a series of floors and internal modifications. The impression (and that is all it can be) is of relatively short and continuous occupation from first foundation to abandonment which is then followed by new work in the MBA over a millennium later.

Area F, the second area, provides a similar development, but also expands the sequence of building activity somewhat. Again the depth of occupation is shallow (maximum under 2 metres) and is virtually continuous from foundation (which includes the upper fortifications: see also below) to final abandonment. But we can now distinguish two main phases in the use of the space immediately inside the fortifications. The first sees this area being used as a sub-industrial zone, open for the most part (see Figs 25, 28), with the construction and use of induced-draft ovens. The area was clear of internal structures for a short time before this. Then followed the construction, continuous use, and modification of a sub-circular dwelling (walls BA, etc.) which implies a 'planning' development. These data might suggest a longer period of use than those in square C2. Nevertheless, everything took place within the upper fortifications which, as we can show (see below), were perhaps still under construction further along the trace to the east: that is to say, we are probably dealing with a construction process which included the expansion of the core settlement. This, in turn, might suggest a relatively short time from beginning to abandonment.

A slightly different picture emerges when we examine the lower fortifications in area LF (2/4). With reference to Figures 59, 69, and 65, two major building events are evident, both of them within the 4th millennium BC occupation of Jawa. An earlier, inner fortification (wall LW5) was preceded by occupation against a domestic structure (wall AA). Up to 50 centimetres of debris had accumulated on bedrock to the south of wall AA when wall LW5 was constructed (its outer face is on bedrock). Wall LW5 is associated with about one metre of occupation debris on the inside and outside followed by the construction of the second line of fortifications (wall LW4) about 3.5 metres farther south. This change of plan, or limited expansion of the lower sector, could suggest a longer time of occupation than was evident in the other two areas discussed here. How long is, of course, impossible to say. In addition to this, features in area LF (square 2) also indicate a final (minor) phase of construction which is different from the earlier ones. A rounded or oval dwelling (walls BA, etc.) was built partly on the outer fortifications, departing from the preceding pattern in both plan, type, and relation to the 'military' architecture of Jawa. However, the 'cultural' material associated with this last phase in the area was still precisely the same as before.

A tentative conclusion regarding the length of occupation in the 4th millennium BC is that we are probably dealing with a relatively short time: anywhere between 3 years at the lower end (see Helms 1981: Fig. 94) and perhaps 50 years at the upper. We are also dealing with two different phases which are none the less related and essentially contiguous: i.e. a formal, even a 'planned' phase, which saw the construction of the fortifications and dwellings within them, and a final phase typified by what might be termed a lapse in 'planning' control and a different, simpler form of domestic architecture. This sub-division in the 4th millennium BC occupation at Jawa can also be recognized in the main water system (see area D).

The second stratigraphic problem concerns the upper and lower fortifications and, once again, much of the potential solution will be achieved through architectural/structural analysis at a later time (Helms in progress). A summary suffices at this stage.

The basic question is: do all of the fortifications at Jawa belong to one period, specifically to the 4th millennium BC? This has been proven for most sections in the trace above, in the detailed stratigraphic analyses. However, as we have noted, many of Jawa's heavy stone walls now stand free of any occupational material. With reference to Figure 79 (and the relevant squares throughout) it is possible to present a preliminary architectural/structural appraisal which suggests a general building programme which must belong to the 4th millennium BC on the basis of the excavated areas (see also Helms 1989a).

The western upper fortifications were laid out in an almost perfectly straight line (Fig. 5, walls W1, W2, and W4), and turn the corner to wall W5 without a break, but for the repaired breach (wall W3). This breach has been 'dated' as a later repair, but one which occurred within the 4th millennium BC occupation period. The problem is gate G1 which interrupts the structural continuity (in the strict stratigraphical sense) and thus presents a dilemma. The argument, therefore, has to be an architectural one: i.e. if gate G1 is taken to be a homogeneous design (built as one project), it can be regarded to be 'bonded' into both walls W1 and W2, and since walls W2 and W3 are taken to be contemporary (i.e. the same line, the same building technique, continuous outer courses, and 'sealed' by the breach repair, W3), the entire line belongs to the first stage of occupation at Jawa. This is corroborated by the relationship between wall W2 and the internal revetment (wall WIa), both of which are abutted by, and incorporated with, sub-circular dwellings which (in turn) contain only 4th millennium BC materials (square UT1, for example). The northern end of wall W1 is 'bonded' into a shallow jog which forms the west return of the upper fortifications. This jog is also abutted by typical sub-circular structures (unexcavated). The west return lies directly on bedrock. Thus the major part of the upper western trace of the fortifications can be regarded as one building scheme, probably part of the very first occupation at the site. The eastern parts of the southern flank are uncertain in terms of their date of construction. For example, the southward jog at the east end of wall W5 (wall W6) is much narrower and also different in construction technique. Its east return (wall W7) is similar and comes to an end some 50 metres to the east. The projected line of the upper fortifications here can be regarded as either incomplete or destroyed, up to the southeast corner.

This leaves the eastern flank overlooking wadi Rajil. The best preserved portion is wall W9 which, however, is free-standing on bedrock. It may be related with the first building programme at Jawa on the basis of similar proportions and construction method. Thereafter only very low and fragmentary wall elements remain intact, including gateways (e.g. Helms 1981: Fig. 13: 3, 4); the plan of the former may be compared with other gates (e.g. gate LF1). Wall W12, however, can definitely be included in the first building programme. It is over-built by the characteristic sub-circular structures, all of which yielded exclusively 4th millennium BC material. Wall W12 is also over-built by an outbuilding of the MBA (Fig. 7: unit 27). Thus, but for the northwest return of wall W1, the major reconstructable trace of fortifications of the upper settlement at Jawa, including the chambered gateways, belongs to the original 4th millennium BC plan.

There is much less of a problem regarding the lower trace of fortifications; at least this is so in area LF (especially squares 2 and 4). Although 'stratigraphically' unconnected with the excavated areas, gate LG1 (LF1) can be considered as part of the early building programme (see also Helms 1989a). This is based on the type of plan (i.e. similar to G1, but for additional chambers), and the recovered material through surface clearance: all of which belongs to the 4th millennium BC. Walls LW4 and LW5 can be traced on the surface and (see details in squares LF2 and LF4) they are, therefore, also part of the earliest construction scheme. Thus the postern (LP1) and gate LG2 (Fig. 71) belong to the same period. Wall LW6, the east projection of the lower fortifications, must also belong to this scheme.

The balance of the lower fortifications can be similarly associated. The walls in and near area D (Figs 5, 52, 53, 56) are dated 'archaeologically', as is the inner line in square LF3, the eastern trace in wadi Rajil (Figs 5, 76). It is, therefore, a reasonable conclusion that virtually all of what can be seen (and reconstructed by projection and interpolation) of the lower trace of the fortifications, including of course the internal divisions (Fig. 5), should be included in the early planning stages of most ancient Jawa.

The water systems are the next potential problem. We have
already noted the difficulties regarding earthworks whose raw
materials may come from earlier occupation periods and whose
construction, and even use, cannot normally be 'dated' in the strict
archaeological way unless they are connected directly with
occupation depositions. Thus it is possible to regard these important
systems at Jawa as 'undatable' (see also 'Nature of the evidence'
above). This is the negative extreme of archaeological methodology
and interpretation. On the positive side, we might summarize the
available data, quite apart from the *a priori* requirement of some sort
of water system in order that a large population might have survived
at Jawa.

First of all, all material recovered from the various excavations in
area D belongs to the 4th millennium BC: that is to say, all material
from within the structural matrix of the two main dams in pool P4
(Fig. 5). By itself, the 'purist' counter-argument could be that nothing
later need be expected, since all of the raw material would come from
the 4th millennium BC settlement in any case. The total absence of
MBA material (i.e. sherds) is, therefore, not a conclusive point.
Although built and used about 2000 BC - the counter-argument would
continue - no pottery of the period was dropped anywhere in the
vicinity, either during construction or later. Given the amount of
pottery recovered in the excavations, however, and the proximity of
the occupation site, as well as the projected length of time the
construction programme of the water system may have entailed
(about 3 years?: see Helms 1981: Fig. 94), this is not a strong
argument. It is, moreover, an argument which is further weakened by
the stratigraphy against the water face of the second dam at Jawa's
pool P4 (Fig. 53: D2), where 4th millennium BC sherds were found in
rubble and silts against the lowest courses of the dam, which (layers)
were then sealed by sterile silts, followed by layers containing only
MBA pottery. The evidence is admittedly circumstantial, but together
with the rest of the information from the site, conducive to agreement
on a pre-MBA date for the construction of both dams: certainly for
the earlier, inner one (D1).

In terms of stratigraphical problems, this leaves the extramural
features such as the irrigation systems, 'animal pens', 'burial
grounds', and other features about Jawa. Apart from the logical
association of these with most ancient Jawa, no more can be said at
this stage. The logic is based on the nature of the two establishments
at the site: the earliest one was a large, nucleated, 'militarized'
settlement which required a complex and extensive water system as
well as other large-scale extramural features such as animal pens and
a cemetery. The fields can be included in this array of necessary

'service areas' (see Willcox 1981 on crops requiring irrigation). The MBA establishment, on the other hand, was much smaller and probably served a different function (Helms 1989a). Its requirements would have been more modest: but whoever built MBA Jawa would certainly have used what was already there (i.e. some, if not all, of the water systems), just as the modern bedouin today have rebuilt pool P3 in concrete.

The site 'matrix' (Fig. 81)

It is naturally impossible to correlate specific layers and domestic structures and features from one excavated area to the next. Although Kenyon never made direct reference to this limitation in publications (but see Kenyon 1952a), she always maintained that no correlation whatever was appropriate unless a physical and, therefore, stratigraphical connection were made. (Wheeler, from whom the notion might stem, once connected two distant trenches in this way: with doubtful results.) This absolute maxim represents the minimalist (or purist) position which is a serious physical and conceptual limitation. Admittedly, all attempts at linking up general phases and stages from one separate excavated area of a site to another are speculation to some extent. It is, nevertheless, part of an interpretative framework without which there can be no progress in the disciplines of prehistory and history. In other words, the maxim precludes the construction and testing of hypotheses; it tends to negate the process of studying more complex relationships such as inter-site relation in a landscape, among other things. To say this may appear to be a pleonasm in the 1990s; but a debate regarding pure recording of data versus interpretation is still occasionally argued in archaeology and some related disciplines. (Kenyon herself was not reluctant to speculate on the international level in Near Eastern history, despite her technical archaeological proprieties.)

The maxim, in its technical sense is, none the less, a useful cautionary precept with regard to Near Eastern 'tell' sites: that is to say, sites at which major structural features are buried and can normally only be exposed in limited areas, even if total clearance were financially possible. (The classic example is Megiddo.) Many such features would, in any case, be incomplete. Furthermore, extramural systems (e.g. hydraulic, agricultural, etc.) are almost invariably destroyed or seriously disrupted in the verdant zones. Jawa, however, is different. Most of the major ancient structures are still visible on the surface and almost completely preserved in their original plan, both within the main settlement and beyond (e.g. the water systems). Some cautious connections between excavated areas, therefore, may be attempted in order to reconstruct major episodes in the occupation, both during the 4th and early 2nd millennia BC, and perhaps also later.

Four main categories might be considered with reference to Figure 81: (i) the fortifications; (ii) the two 'dated' dams in pool P4; (iii) the main domestic occupation within the walls; and (iv) a somewhat fugitive last phase of occupation up to abandonment in the 4th millennium BC.

It may be hypothesized that almost all of the visible (and reconstructible) fortifications, both in the upper and the lower settlements, were constructed as one (planned?) scheme, beginning with the first occupation of Jawa. The evidence comes mainly from the analysis of area F where it appears that the upper trace was begun in the northwest area, construction proceeding southwards and around the corner made by walls W4 and W5 (Figs 5, 6). The proposed line of fortification was open for a time in square F1 (i.e. while the construction was in progress elsewhere) and, as we have argued above, further east still surface observations indicate that the trace was either never completed during the 4th millennium BC, or that it was partly destroyed. The existence of domestic structures on bedrock (e.g. in squares C2, UT1, etc.) may support the notion that both fortifications and internal settlement began at the same time.

A similar series of building events is evident in the lower trace, particularly in the southern sector (e.g. squares LF2/4). There we have clear evidence that substantial domestic structures existed well before (though by how much is not known) the construction of the first line of curtain wall, LW5 (see LF2, wall AA). Thus we can suggest that the lower trace, like the upper one, was begun in the western sector, perhaps next to pool P4 and its first dam (D1, see also below), and proceeded southwards and then eastwards. (Gate LG1 was set directly on bedrock: its position in the southern trace is roughly in line, though slightly farther east, with square F1 in the upper trace. We might argue that the construction of the lower trace, being smaller in proportions as well as on level ground, proceeded more quickly.) A second outer line of curtain (wall LW4) was added sometime after this.

Finally, still regarding the fortifications, we face a problem with regard to the visible signs of collapse (destruction?) in the upper and lower traces. There are four sets of data, the first three very similar in magnitude (i.e. they were minor events), the last a major disruption. The minor events are represented by inward collapse of stones from the upper fortifications in squares F1 and F2d, and from the lower ones in square LF2a. Those in the upper trace may have occurred on separate occasions, or have been contemporary (see also above: discussion on building progress): that in square F2d before the construction of dwelling B; that in square F1 close to the first construction of the curtain (wall W5). The event in square LF2a is probably later than either of those above: it occurs sometime after the construction and use of the outer curtain (wall LW4). The major event in square F4a/c could be related to this last collapse in the lower trace. A breach about 50 metres in length was made in the western sector of the upper curtain (walls W2/3) late in the building sequence there (i.e. after the construction of the main domestic units there), and then repaired (wall W3), still during the 4th millennium. This event was followed by some continued intramural occupation.

The first dam of pool P4 (D1) was set on bedrock (determined by an auger probe only) and probably bonded (but broken in antiquity) with the western lower fortifications. Therefore, it is assumed (and also most likely) that this dam was built close to the first occupation at Jawa, contemporary with the construction of the fortifications. As we have noted above, this dam may have burst at some time, but it cannot be established when in the sequence this might have occurred. It may have happened before the second straight dam (D2) was built, or later. The second dam (D2) may have been built near the end of the 4th millennium BC occupation of the site. It was never completed (see also above), although it, and perhaps also some remains of the earlier dam, were reconstructed in some way during the MBA, since silts built up during that period, and also later. It is pure speculation whether the second 'failed' dam is related to the breach and repair (wall W3) in the upper fortifications (but see Helms 1981 *passim*).

We argued above that the domestic sector of Jawa was constructed at about the same time as a beginning was made on the fortifications. This was a major domestic construction phase which expanded outwards towards and in some cases against the curtain walls (e.g. area F west). An extension on the lower, southern sector was needed at some point. In some areas (e.g. UT2 and area F) this phase is represented by two construction episodes: two 'dwellings' in the former; and a series of ovens followed by dwellings in the latter.

A final phase of occupation can be recognized in squares X2, UT1 and LF2/4 (and possibly also in TT1: see Fig. 38), as well as on the surface of the rest of the site (air photographs: on the basis of architectural style). This consists of small, rounded or oval, single-roomed (some are sub-divided) structures and isolated domestic features (hearths, lined pits, etc.), some of which are even built over the fortifications in the lower trace (e.g. LF2a, LF4). These structures may perhaps be associated with the still visible huts and other features beyond the lower fortifications and also across wadi Rajil (Helms 1981: Fig. 96, and *passim* for further speculations). The 'architecture' of this last domestic phase of occupation may be compared with other EB I A structures in the Jerash region (Hanbury-Tenison 1986: Fig. 18) and similar plans at Yiftah'el and `En Shadud (Braun 1984: 1985) in the 'Esdraelon' Valley, Dakerman on the Lebanese coast (Saidah 1979), Mumasakhim in southern Syria (cf. Hanbury-Tenison 1986: Fig. 18), and even Tell Um Hammad Stage 2 (Helms 1984a: Fig. 8) and énéolithique supérieur Byblos (Dunand 1973).

The general 'history' of occupation at Jawa can be summarized as follows.

Everything that is 'dated' in the 4th millennium BC can be regarded as one stage which consists of two phases: a major one, with many sub-phases, which saw the planning and construction of most of the visible fortifications, the domestic sector, and (most, probably all of) the water system; and a minor phase when the site was reused and overbuilt in some areas with smaller, architecturally different (or indifferent) dwellings and other features. Perhaps the straight dam (D2) belongs to this second phase of Stage 1. Jawa was completely abandoned (in so far as the evidence of material culture in concerned) in the 4th millennium BC, during the period called EB I A in Palestinian archaeology.

Stage 2 saw the reoccupation of the site, during the early part of the MBA. The pottery study suggests a date about 2000 BC, or a little later (see Chapter 3). The 'citadel' and probably all of its outbuildings were constructed at this time, and there is some evidence that at least parts of the water systems were in use at this time. The complex was abandoned, perhaps during MB II A, in terms of Palestinian archaeological periodization.

Stage 3 saw no direct occupation and/or construction on the main site at Jawa; however, sherd scatter, Safaitic and Greek texts (see Chapter 8), nearby tumuli, and other finds, indicate that the area was perhaps more actively used between about the 2nd century BC and the Roman/Late Antique era. This is not to say that there was no human population in the region (see also 'Nature of the evidence' above): we simply have no way (yet) of detecting such a presence in terms of material remains.

Stage 4 may be regarded as 'bedouin' (see also Helms 1989a) from the early Islamic period up to the present (i.e. by inference and the presence of Arabic texts).

Stage 5 is the 'renaissance' of Jawa. A faction of the Ahl al-Jebal reconstructed pool P4 in 1983. It was done in concrete and the system worked, more or less, but is rapidly failing because it did not copy accurately the schema of the original 4th millennium plan.

3. The Pottery

S. W. HELMS

INTRODUCTION

The two pottery assemblages at Jawa (EB I A and MBA) represent all of the diagnostic material to be recovered during the excavations and the various surveys between 1972 and 1986. The site is not rich in this respect. The assemblage of the MBA is very small (Figs 154 - 157) and not suitable for more than a listing and a brief discussion of 'dated' parallels in Syria/Palestine of the late 3rd and early 2nd millennia BC. The earlier assemblage, however, can be analysed further.

Preliminary typological analysis of the assemblage during the first seasons of excavations already showed that we were dealing with a short period of occupation; the assemblage was an essentially homogeneous one. However, it was also apparent that only some types could be recognized in the established pottery repertoires of the late Chalcolithic and/or EB I A period of Palestine. Many types, some of them representing significant percentages of occurrence, could not be identified in Palestinian/Transjordanian terms. Clearly, the early pottery of Jawa was made up of more than one repertoire and these repertoires had to be extracted from the data in the hope that they might lead to the identification of various cultural connections beyond Jawa. The first stage in the analysis is the establishment of genres, types, and variants. This selection was based on the following criteria: first order choices based on form and decoration; second order choices based on macro-fabric analysis (see also Appendix B) and size/volume analysis. Following the comparative study of these genres, it was possible to construct sets at repertoire level. The structure is summarized in Table 2 below.

ANALYSIS OF GENRES, TYPES AND VARIANTS

The very first occupation of the 4th millennium BC to be cleared at Jawa in 1974 revealed an almost complete set of pottery vessels (Fig. 82), and other objects (see Chapters 5 and 7), all on one floor within a small sub-circular stone structure (see Chapter 2: square TT1). All major genres are represented. This at once demonstrated the contemporaneity of vessels which, upon further analysis (see below) proved to belong to potentially different repertoires which, in turn, can be traced to different geographical sub-regions of Syria/Palestine.

Table 2. Schema of the pottery assemblage

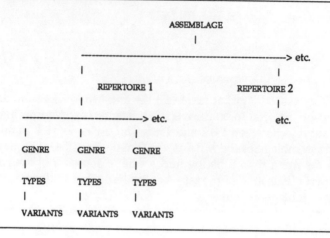

Typology and analysis are arranged according to closed and open forms, as follows: holemouth jars (hmj) (Fig. 97: genre A); jars of various kinds (Figs 97 - 99: genres B - F); bowls (Fig. 99: genre G); miscellaneous forms (M) and decoration (HB); painted wares (HA); and bases (X). Typological analysis deals with the following aspects: (i) the reconstruction of complete forms within the general genre sets (Figs 83, 86, 88, 89, 91 - 93); (ii) an analysis of attributes such as rim form (Figs 84, 85, 87, 90, 92, 94 - 96), lugs, handles, decoration (including surface treatment); and, where applicable and relevant, also construction method (see also Appendix B). Decoration is discussed in Chapter 4. These criteria are then used (iii) to establish types within genres (see also above) and variants within types. These analyses of the pottery assemblage are presented below under the various genre designations. In those cases where the sample is large enough (i.e. genre/types AA, BA-BC, CA-CF) a further analysis (iv) concerning size/volume ranking is attempted (Figs 100 - 106). Finally (v) the assemblage is presented in terms of frequency of occurrence of both genre/types and genres (Figs 107 - 109). Individual vessels or sherds are referred to by their catalogue numbers (see Figs 110 - 153). Catalogue captions precede the pottery illustrations.

Genre A: holemouth jars (Figs 110 - 121)

Reconstruction of complete forms

Only two restorable profiles were available (J1/2 and J3/4). These two examples represented two basic sub-forms (mouth radii are virtually constant: see 'Size and volumetric analysis'): a squat form (J1/2) and a taller form (J3/4), both with flat bases. This subdivision according to vessel proportions is typical of types A, B and perhaps also C within genre A (Fig. 83: AA, J1/2, J3/4; AB, J88/94; AC, J96/108/106). The other holemouth jars are more problematical in this regard, although bases must have been flat in all cases (this latter assumption is based on the distinctive fabric of bases which can be matched to rim fabrics and, of course, comparison with complete vessels in Palestinian assemblages). Type AF may belong to type AE. Types AE and AG may also be subdivided into round, squat, and elongated forms. J129 and also perhaps J130/131 (type AG) have straight shoulder profiles and may have had a lower centre of gravity; the rest of the holemouth jars have distinctive high shoulders. Neck and base radii tend to be equal.

Rim forms

Rims occur in two basic forms. By far the most common is a distinctive bulbous rim, for the most part made to produce a gradual thickening towards the lip (Fig. 84: 7), and occasionally a more abrupt swelling (Fig. 84: 12). The former occurs in thick as well as slightly thinner variants (Fig. 84: 13). A smaller set of variants consists of plain rim profiles (Fig. 84: 23) continuing the width of the body to the lip. Both major variants (bulbous and plain) are sometimes modified as follows: by bevelling the lip internally (Fig. 84: 9, 54) or by bevelling several internal rim facets (Fig. 84: 45); by rolling the rim to produce a scar line, or lines, beneath the lip (Fig. 84: 19, 23, 56), from either a pointed or a rounded lip; by grooving, or recessing the internal facet of the lip (Fig. 84: 51), or the underside of the rim, producing a 'bowed' form (Fig. 84: 61); and by recessing the upper side of the rim to produce a slightly up-turned lip (Fig. 84: 70). All of these rim forms occur in type AA.

Plain rim forms are also used in the next types (AB - AJ, Fig. 85: 96, 98), with similar modifications: rolled from a sharp lip (Fig. 85: 88); externally recessed (Fig. 85: 141). J94 (Fig. 85) is unique in the assemblage, with a slightly everted lip. Only a few types and variants depart marginally from these norms: notably J132 and perhaps also J159 (Fig. 97, type AG; Fig. 98, type AJ) by having pointed lips; J146 (Fig. 98, type AJ); J153 (Fig. 98, type AJ) with an internal pointed lip; and J152/154 (Fig. 98, type AJ) combining bevelling or grooving with a rolled rim.

Handles

The most common and characteristic handles consist of a set of four pushed-up and rounded lugs (e.g. J1/2), a form of devolved or 'vestigial' ledge handle (see genre B below for a clear development, or evolution) which are applied symmetrically, either just below the rim, sometimes rising above the stance-line (e.g. J1/2-10), or on the shoulder of the vessel (e.g. J24). Many of the recovered sherds were too small to have preserved lugs. However, with other attributes such as bands of punctate or slashed decoration in common (see below), most of them in genre/type AA probably had such handles. Types AB through AJ probably had no handles: that is to say, none appeared in the same symmetrical fashion, in sets of four. Only type AE (Fig. 100) was provided with small loop handles, occasionally in very small versions which may also be regarded as pierced vertical lugs (e.g. J177/128). Sherds were too fragmentary to determine whether such handles were applied singly, in pairs, or otherwise.

Construction method

All vessels were handmade. There are no traces of mat impressions on bases (see Appendix B).

Genre B: flared rim high-shouldered jars (Figs 122 - 129)

Reconstruction of complete forms

The 'generic' relationship of types is further developed below. All vessels in this genre have flat bases, the smaller versions with a distinctive concave profile towards the base (Fig. 86). All types have flaring necks and often grooved rims (see below), and high shoulders in relation to body curve. All types have two lugs or ledge handles on opposite sides, at, or very near, the widest point of the body. The largest range (BC) is often provided with additional 'vestigial' handles (up-turned, or pushed up, rounded lugs) near the neck/shoulder junction. Neck and base radii tend to be equal. In the largest range (BC) the body is identical (as are other attributes: cf. below) to those of genre/types AA (Fig. 86: 180, dotted profile).

Rim forms

Five basic rim forms occur in genre B, all of them on slightly everted, or near-vertical, necks: bevelled; plain rounded/pointed; grooved on the lip; rolled outwards; and slightly bulbous towards a rounded lip. Of these variants, plain forms occur only in type BC (Fig. 87: 186; cf. also Figs 124: 180, 125: 185, 189, 191, 126: 193, 195). The grooved form is most common in types BA and BC (Fig. 87: 163, 166, 181, 182, 183), either as a simple groove between the rounded sides of the lip (Fig. 87: 163, 181), or combined with an outward-rolled rim (Fig. 87: 166, 182). Rolled rims appear only in types BB and BC (Fig. 87: 178); they are sometimes formed into down-pointing lips (Fig. 87: 200), or less clearly defined, resulting in a slightly bulbous rim form (Fig. 87: 209). The fifth variant, bulbous towards a pointed/rounded rims, occurs only in type BC (Figs 87: 209, 127: 204-206, 211, 212), some of them resulting in a flaring or down-turned point (Fig. 127: 206).

Handles

Pushed up lug handles identical to those in genre/type AA occur on the largest range of vessels (Figs 124: 180, 129: 238-240) where they are applied on the shoulders. This location is the same, as we have already noted above, as that of the lugs on the holemouth jars (AA). Not enough remained of J180, the most complete example, to be certain of the number of such lugs. But by analogy with the holemouth jars and the smaller range in genre B itself (Fig. 122: 162-166), it is possible to suggest that sets of four were used. The same lug form also appears on the smallest range of vessels in genre B, preserved in two variants: a small lug precisely the same as those in genre/type AA (J162); and a larger version which clearly shows a development from up-turned, rounded ledge handles (e.g. J163: a set of four). Both of these vessels also demonstrate what might be called a 'migration' and concomitant development or modification of handles which depends on their position. The smaller, 'developed' handle is applied only on the shoulders (as in the larger vessels here, and also as in genre/type AA); the larger handles are placed on the waist or the widest point of the body.

Handles on the middle size range of genre B also show such an evolution which can be regarded to be directly related to the relative size of the vessel. The smallest vessels in this range are similar to the largest forms in type BA (e.g. compare J168 and J163). Slightly larger vessels have flatter and larger handles (J167), while even larger vessels still (J171, etc.) have what has long been regarded as the standard 'Palestinian' up-turned ledge handle (Wright 1937; cf. also Amiran 1969: Pl. 8 and *passim*). No complete forms of type BB were found at Jawa: however, the numerous direct parallels, as well as the relatively clear evolution of such vessels well into the Early Bronze Age of Palestine and Transjordan (if not also parts of Southern Syria), allows us to assume that type BB probably only had two sets of ledge handles, and that these were normally applied at the widest part of the body. The internal development or, more correctly, the formal preference at Jawa, as we have already pointed out, is clearly related to vessel size. Thus the largest variants in genre BB (Fig. 123: 174-177) have the largest ledge handles (see also size/volume analysis below). As handles get bigger, their slope becomes more horizontal.

Type BC, the largest range in the genre, was provided with the biggest handles, for obvious reasons: they were meant to be functional; they are certainly not decorative, as might have been the pushed up lugs. The form is no longer a ledge handle, it is now a thick, bulbous mass, solidly 'welded' into the wall of the body (Fig. 128). Variants within this handle form range from splayed handles, still reminiscent of ledge handles (Fig. 128: 223), through plain lumps

(Fig. 128: 221), to 'axe head' forms (Fig. 128: 215-217). It is assumed, by analogy with the middle size range in genre B, that these vessels were provided with only two handles.

Construction method

All variants were made by hand without the use of a wheel or a tournette. The smallest range was probably built up from a mass of clay without using coils, up to the neck/shoulder junction. J162 (Fig. 122) indicates that the rim was made separately and then joined to the body, leaving a thickened ridge, or scar, on the inside. Not enough was recovered of type BB to say anything about construction method. Type BC, however, was probably built using coils, at least up to the high shoulder. No signs of separate construction regarding the necks were found.

Genre C: everted rim jars with high shoulders (Figs 130 - 134)

Reconstruction of complete forms

Although at first glance these jars appear to be a heterogeneous group, analysis of other attributes (including fabric type: see also Appendix B) demonstrates their typological homogeneity. This is further supported by the volumetric analysis. There are two basic body forms: (i), globular with characteristic ring bases and everted rims (CA-CC); and (ii), elongated, high-shouldered forms with indented shoulders and rounded bases (CD-CF) (Figs 88, 89). This second body form may occur in two subdivisions: one more rounded or fuller (Fig. 88: 294); the other narrower (Fig. 88: 280), reflecting similar subdivisions in type A of genre A among the holemouth jars.

Rim forms

Similar to genre B and in contrast to genre A (see also size/volume analysis below), rim forms 'straddle' the types, but also reflect broadly a size/volume seriation. There are two main categories: one restricted to the smaller vessels (types CA-CC); the other to the larger vessels (types CE/CF). Type CD forms a 'transitional' group. There are also subdivisions within these categories. Types CA/CB have simple, everted, rounded/pointed rims which appear in a number of variants, as follows: simple, everted, rounded/pointed (Fig. 90: 250); internally recessed (Fig. 90: 251); and everted, internally bevelled (Fig. 90: 257), with a slight internal carination. Type CC has two variant rim forms: one is internally bevelled, well onto the neck, to a sharp transition at the lip, and a rounded, rolled form (Fig. 90: 259); the other, internally bevelled, sometimes slightly recessed, a bevelled lip and traces of rolling beneath that (Fig. 90: 260), resulting in an external groove below the rim. The 'transitional' type (CD) occurs as a simple, everted, rounded profile (Fig. 90: 274), occasionally showing traces of rolling on the exterior (Fig. 90: 275).

The larger size-ranges (types CE/CF) have two related rim forms. Both are everted, some more sharply than others, occurring (Fig. 90 Genre C: rim profiles [types B/C/D/E/F]) in two variants: rounded, sometimes also slightly bevelled (Fig. 90: 280, 282, 284, 291); and more pointed (Fig. 90: 294, 309, 306, 302). In both variants, external neck profiles sometimes show signs of scoring, or indentation (Fig. 90: 282, 309). Often the neck/shoulder junction is defined by a sharp internal carination (Fig. 90: 280, 294) which in some cases also resulted in a sharp transition from shoulder to neck (Fig. 90: 280, 302).

There were apparently no handles on any of these vessels. Very few complete profiles were recovered, but the fabrics are so distinctive (i.e. the only chaff-faced, burnished wares at Jawa) that this surmise is probably correct.

Construction method

Type CA is anomalous within the pottery assemblage at Jawa in terms of construction, fabric (see appendix B), and surface treatment. The necks, and probably also the bodies, were wheel-made (Fig. 130: 241, 245), the fabric was not chaff-tempered, like all the rest in this genre, and the exterior surfaces were given a light grey/green slip.

Types CB and CC were perhaps also wheel-made, at least from the shoulder upwards (Fig. 130: 250: note the reverse carination where the body may have been joined to the shoulder and neck, an analogous feature repeated in the indented shoulders in type CF, cf. also J259). In view of this (i.e. J250, etc.) and the sophisticated form of the base in contrast to other bases, it is possible to suggest that these vessels were made in two halves, the base formed upside-down, and then joined.

In contrast, the balance of the genre is completely handmade, with the possible exception of some of the rims which were either wheel-made, or (more likely) finished by slow turning or hand-finishing once they were joined to the body of the vessel. This latter possibility is perhaps indicated by the direction of pattern burnishing, both inside and outside the neck. J294/295 is the most complete example in this size range (Fig. 132). Its rounded base, perhaps made in a form of some kind, and the body up to at least the indentation at the shoulder, were certainly coil-constructed. These large vessels may have been made in three sections: the base, up to the shoulder (much like the holemouth jars of type AA: cf. also genre BC above, and its structural relation to genre/type AA); the shoulder, perhaps also coil-constructed in a form, but upside-down; and the neck. Traces of joins between these sections can be seen in J294/295 (Fig. 132), the lower being masked by the indented shoulder, the upper by the sharp internal (and sometimes external) carination. This was followed by applying a slip and burnishing the surfaces: mostly horizontally on the body; vertically or slightly radially on the shoulder; and again horizontally both inside and outside the neck (Figs 132: 294/295, 134: 320, 327, 328). Occasionally the external surface of the neck was also burnished vertically (Figs 24: 310, 134: 323).

Genre D: low everted rim jars with high, indented shoulders and rounded bases (Fig. 135)

Reconstruction of complete forms

Only nine identifiable examples of this genre were recovered, two of them complete profiles (J329/337). Necks are very low and almost flush with the shoulders of the vessels. Shoulders are indented, making a shallow trough about the base of the neck. Bases are rounded. As was the case above (genre/type AA and genre C), formal analysis may indicate a subdivision into rounded and more elongated forms (Fig. 91: DA, 329 and DB, 335), although the sherds in type DB are very small, but for J331 whose body profile definitely slopes down more acutely than that of either J329 or J337.

Rim forms and construction method

Rim forms are simple: everted and rounded (Fig. 92). Only J330 departs form the norm by being more pointed and internally bevelled (Fig. 135). The characteristic shoulder/neck profile is partly the result of construction method, the indentation masking the join between neck and shoulder. Construction probably included the use of coils up to the shoulder. The necks were perhaps made separately, although this is not clear in the small sample recovered. The base may have been made in a form. There are no handles.

Genre E: bag-shaped jars (Figs 136 - 139)

Reconstruction of complete forms

With the exception of J392, a unique type within genre E in any case, no complete profiles were found. Also, no bases could be attributed to this broad genre with any certainty, not even for J392 which could have had a pointed base as easily as a small disc base, or a rounded one. Nevertheless, form analysis (Fig. 93) suggests that most of the body forms tend towards high-shouldered profiles rather similar to those of the smaller type range in genre B (e.g. BA/BB). In most cases, projections of the shoulder slopes forced an abrupt profile change at the widest diameter. (For further details regarding types, see below.)

Rim forms

Genre E has the greatest variety of rim forms of all genres in Jawa's pottery assemblage. With two exceptions, type EA has two simple forms: rounded or slightly pointed (Fig. 94: 341); and rounded, internally recessed or 'bowed' (Fig. 94: 345). The exceptions are J338/339 (Fig. 136) which consist of a slightly 'bowed' neck and an everted, out-folded rounded/pointed lip. Rim forms in type EB are all bevelled on the lip and show signs of rolling, or folding, on the exterior surfaces. Some variants include a slightly internally 'bowed' neck (Fig. 137: 352/353).

The most varied set is type EC. The low lips, or rims, are everted in all cases. Their form is modified in the following ways: internally bevelled in two facets, to a rounded rim with an external fold (Fig. 64: 362); internally bevelled and recessed to a pointed/rounded rim which is deeply grooved at the neck/shoulder junction (Fig. 94: 366); internally grooved below the neck/shoulder junction and a pointed rim (Fig. 94: 373); a bulbous lip (Fig. 94: 377); and an internally recessed, near-vertical rounded rim (Fig. 94: 385).

Types EE (only one example) and ED have simple, rounded rims, those of type ED showing signs of outward rolling or folding (Fig. 94: 392, 390, respectively). There are apparently no handles on these vessels (but for J372 where they are identical to lugs in genre/types AA and BA/BC), a doubled loop handle (cf. also genre F below) on J351, and four vertical, pierced lugs on the shoulder of J392.

Genre F: narrow-necked jars (Figs 140 - 143)

Reconstruction of complete forms

Two complete forms (FB, J418 and FA, J419) and one semi-complete forms (rim to widest body diameter: FA, J393) were found. Type FB is represented by but one example (J418) and can probably be classed among the rest of the genre. The scanty sample might suggest a form subdivision similar to that of some of the other genres discussed here. J419 would then represent the more rounded, fuller form, and variants like J393/394/395 the taller, narrower forms. But for J418, all extant examples have a loop handle near the rim, in some cases a handle which extends or 'loops' above the rim stance line (e.g. J419). Bases are assumed to be flat throughout, although only two definite examples were recovered (i.e. J418/419). Many fragmentary body sherds (i.e. J396-417) are classed in this genre because of their embossed decoration (see below) of which analogous designs occur only in genre B (e.g. J234/237, etc.).

Rim forms and handles

All preserved rim forms of this genre are simple, and rounded/pointed. Many, if not most, variants have loop handles of some form near the neck. J419 has a high loop handle, J393 a smaller version, flush with the rim stance line. Loop handles vary from

simple to double (Fig. 142: 439 and 430). J419 was given a red slip.
J418 had no handles.

In addition to loop handles, many vessels also had small,
horizontal, 'vestigial' lugs, often on the shoulder or the widest point
of the body (Fig. 140: 393, 396-417). These features can be compared
with the general decoration of genre B and with the position of
'vestigial' or devolved lugs in the same genre.

M: miscellaneous jars (Fig. 143, 144)

These jar forms have rims which can be compared with some of the
variants discussed so far, with the possible exception of J468.
However, in that case comparison might be made with some variants
in genre C (i.e. Fig. 131: 282; see also the comparative study below for
external parallels).

Genre G: small bowls (Figs 144 - 148)

Reconstruction of complete forms

For the most part, the form of small bowls is obvious and even in
those cases where only a little of the body curve towards the base is
preserved, the general form can be reconstructed. Bowls J470-483
(genre/type GA) probably had both rounded and/or slightly
flattened (also omphaloid) bases by analogy with their better-
represented and -preserved parallels at Tell Um Hammad in the
Jordan Valley (see also Chapter 4). J484-489 can be reconstructed with
either small disc or flat (cut ?) bases, or gently rounded ones, again by
analogy with complete parallels elsewhere. The same is true of the
heavy flat forms (J511-522), all of which must have had flat or
flattened bases.

Rim forms

Most rim forms in genre G are simple, particularly those of types GC
and GD which are rounded (Fig. 95: 492/497). Type GA is recessed,
occurring in a number of variants ranging from everted, rounded
(Fig. 95: 470), through slightly recessed, with an external concave
profile (Fig. 95: 474), to sharply recessed and externally grooved (Fig.
95: 482). Rims in type GB are mostly simple and pointed or rounded,
but for J484 which is externally slightly recessed (Fig. 95: 488/484,
respectively). The horizontally bevelled and externally grooved rim
form in type GE is discussed further in Chapter 4 below. Type GF has
a rounded, externally rolled or folded rim (Fig. 95: 508).

The crude bowls and platters (type GG) have a number of variant
rim forms: rounded, slightly in-turned (Fig. 95: 511); pointed (Fig. 95:
518); and internally recessed, to a pointed/rounded lip (Fig. 95: 519).
J525 is anomalous with its external recessing and carination (Fig. 148;

see also external parallels in Chapter 4). The so-called lamps (type GH) have simple, rounded rims.

X: bases (Figs 149 - 153)

Form and construction method

Most of the base forms are very simple, but for two categories. One belongs to genre/types CA/CB/CC and consists of a ring base with a rounded profile and often an external groove at the junction of the base (ring) and the body (Fig. 96: 259). A distinctive feature of these bases is the bulb of the base which, in all examples, protrudes beneath the ring-base stance line. There is only one example of the second category, J550 (Fig. 149). It is a hollow pedestal with a flat foot, a straight interior profile and a sloping exterior forming a sharp pedestal/body junction, down to a splayed and slightly bevelled foot.

The rest of the base forms, some of which can be matched to rim forms through their common, distinctive fabrics, are summed up in Figure 96. Most are very simple, always flat (but without any signs of cutting or any mat impressions), either with a sharp transition from base to body, or a rounded one (Fig. 96: 609, 592). Some of these bases are slightly hollow (Fig. 96: 613, 592); some show a slight reverse curve in the profile from base to body (Fig. 96: 577). In some cases this reverse curve is developed into a near-pedestal (Fig. 96: 546). Other variants include rounded 'feet' and grooved transitions from 'foot' to body (Fig. 96: 581, 545, 564). Sometimes the 'foot' has been bevelled (Fig. 96: 574), or simply grooved, producing a sharp edge (Fig. 96: 571, 545). There are several examples of low, hollow pedestal bases with flared, rounded 'feet' (Fig. 96: 565, 567). Finally, some variants are rounded and, occasionally, also slightly hollow (Fig. 96: 592, 600, 601). Construction method sometimes includes a composite structure (Fig. 96: 566, 565, 567).

The seriation of genres, types and variants of the whole assemblage is summarized in Figures 97 to 99.

SIZE AND VOLUME ANALYSIS (FIGS 100 - 106)

The evidence to hand suggests that some genres might represent ranked series according to volume or capacity, and that others do not. A number of simple analyses may be conducted in order to demonstrate this. However, two serious limitations prevail. In the first place, we do not have enough complete vessel profiles; in the second, the sample sizes are too small to yield meaningful results in terms of more sophisticated statistical processes. In effect, only three genres (A, B, and C) lend themselves to any further studies at this time, and even these may not be significant.

The theoretical basis of analysis was established using tomb groups from Tiwal esh-Sharqi (the cemetery for EB IV Tell Um Hammad: Helms 1983; Tubb 1985, 1990) and Um Bighal (Helms 1989b; Helms and McCreery 1988) where a plot of certain points in the profile of complete vessels appeared to be distinctive and whose distribution according to size/volume might produce a significant regression which could serve as a simple tool (along with others) for constructing pottery repertoires. Figure 100 shows the similarity between two vessels, one from Tiwal esh-Sharqi (a), the other from Um Bighal, near Amman (b). The third vessel comes from the same tomb at Um Bighal (c), but is typical of the separate repertoire common in the Amman region. Three points were tested: r1, the widest radius at the lip of the rim; r2, the widest radius at the neck of the body; and r3, the widest point of the body. The first point was not useful; there was too much random variation in the hand-made rims. The other two, however, could be used to construct linear regressions and these measurements are used in the present analysis.

A second process was used here to test for volumetric ranking. This consisted of measuring the neck radii of closed forms which resulted in a normal distribution in the case of hole-mouth jars (see below), and a multi-modal one for jars. Once again, r2 (Fig. 101) was more suitable.

A broad division into two categories is possible with regard to capacity. The assemblage appears to consist of genres which are not significantly ranked (i.e. volume is essentially constant or, failing that, random), and genres which are produced in a ranked series in which certain attributes such as handle form, construction method and, occasionally, also rim form, among others, tend to cluster within definite volumetric parameters. As we have noted, only genres A, B, and C lend themselves to further analysis.

With reference to the introductory remarks above, two analyses have been attempted. The first consists of plotting radii of vessel opening - in this case r2 - the smallest opening, rather than radii of rim lips which tend to be more varied, and which are also not related to the intended capacity of the vessels. Basically we limit measurement to the most common 'container' form in the closed vessels. This is the holemouth form (i.e. genre A). Figure 106 summarizes these measurements for the three suitable genres, genre A being limited to genre/type AA.

Genre A (Fig. 102)

It is immediately obvious that the holemouth jars of genre/type AA were produced within much tighter measured parameters than genres B and C and, therefore, it may be reasonable to assume that a normal distribution would result, should we have a larger sample. (A similar analysis of the identical type at Tell Um Hammad yields such a curve.) Genre/type AA, therefore, can represent a relatively constant mensural approach to construction, with a possible volumetric division into two sets, if we recall (and agree with) the shape analysis above which suggested squat, as well as taller, forms. Other numerically less well represented vessels in the assemblage might be classed in this category, as being uniform or bipartite in capacity. This would include the other holemouth jars in genre A (the internal dimensions of type E are unreliable), genre D (both squat and taller forms), and genres E, F and G.

In contrast, genres B and C (Fig. 106) show much wider mensural parameters in their neck radii (r2) and this, as well as the relative position of other attributes, leads to the notion of volumetric ranking in the production process. This, in turn, may signify some awareness of formal measurement (see also 'Stamp seal impressions' in Chapter 4).

Genre B (Fig. 103)

Using the three complete, or near-complete, forms (i.e. J163/164/180), the regression lines (r1, r2, r3) may be plotted (Fig. 102: a). Vessels can then be plotted according to their rim forms, with the following results.

Combining bevelled and grooved rims, a broad distribution is achieved in which genre/type BA forms the lower range, and genre/type BC the upper in a broad range of volumes. It might be hypothesized that this division is characterized by forms with vestigial pushed-up lugs on the shoulders (Fig. 102: a, b). Vessels with plain rounded/pointed rims cluster more closely in the middle volumetric range (Fig. 102: c), as do outward rolled/down-pointed rims and bulbous rims (Fig. 103: a, b). The entire genre is plotted in Figure 102c, including the handle forms of both genres/types BB and BC.

Two tentative conclusions may be appropriate. First, it is relatively clear that a volumetric range was intended and produced at Jawa (or elsewhere). Second, we may be able to separate out three related types and variants (BA, BB, and the bevelled/grooved rim variants in BC) as a specialized series which was provided with stamp seal impression. The position of these impressions on the vessels, and possibly also their number and configuration, depended on capacity, as well as perhaps other things (see Chapter 4). Generally, the variants within overlapping capacity ranges might be regarded as the production of several workshops at Jawa, or wherever these pots were made.

Genre C (Figs 104, 105)

Similar results are achieved by plotting the regressions lines (r1, r2, r3: Fig. 104: a) by using the two complete, or near-complete, shapes at, or near, either end of the indicated size range. Plots according to variants (rim form, etc.) result in a cluster at the lower end of the size range in regard of genre/types CA/CB and CE. It may be significant (although the sample is far too small) that the correlation of clustering between types CA and CC, as against the tighter clustering of type CB, indicates copying of an 'imported' type (CA: different fabric, etc.) in two sub-types: in a smaller (CB); and a larger one (CC) (Fig. 104: b, c). Type CD (Fig. 105: a) overlaps with the bulk of type CC, while types CE/CF are broadly distributed from the upper end of CA/CC/CD onwards (Fig. 105: b, c). Of these two, type CF appears to cluster more tightly in the middle size range. The entire genre is plotted in Figure 105d.

As we have hypothesized with regard to genre B above, rim/attribute variants may indicate the existence of several workshops, some of which may have specialized in certain capacity ranges: or, that at the very least, a ranked series of 'standard' capacities was produced.

Relative distribution of genres and types

The frequency of occurrence of types and genres within the pottery assemblage at Jawa is plotted in Figures 107, 108, and 109. We must once more stress that the sample size is probably insufficient (i.e. total here 638). However, it would appear that type A is the most preferred variant in genre A and that holemouth jars in general were the most abundant vessels form. Similarly, type C is the most abundant form in genre B (i.e. large storage vessels) and ranked about equal in abundance (after genre A) with genres C. Types E and F are most abundant in genre C. Genre D (also large storage vessels) is rare. Other jar forms (genres E and F) are ranked next, and appear in about equal numbers, as do the bowls.

If we regard holemouth jars as cooking vessels (many are severely burned: i.e. used over, or in, a fire) which, moreover, are easily broken, then their apparent numerical superiority might roughly match the frequency of genre A. Assuming that genres E and F functioned as smaller storage vessels (for solids and liquids respectively: i.e. for immediate use in the household), their combined frequencies again roughly match the other two sets ('cooking' and 'macro' storage). This leaves genre G which may be regarded as serving dishes, ranked significantly lower in the assemblage. These combined distributions can be regarded as normal and typical of pre-industrial, vernacular domestic economies.

COMPARATIVE STUDY

The pottery of the 4th millennium BC

For a long time after the first publication of sherds from Jawa (Helms 1973) there have been difficulties in linking the site's 4th millennium pottery assemblage with currently documented material from either Palestine or Syria. One reason for this difficulty - one among several others which made Jawa's existence a conundrum - was that parallels from Syria, particularly southern Syria (the Ghuta/Damascene, Hawran, and Jebel Druze) were severely limited (e.g. the closest published assemblage comes from Hama [Fugmann 1958] and remains largely unpublished in any archaeologically useful way). The excavations at Tell Nebi Mend (Qadesh of the Late Bronze Age), resumed in 1975 and still in progress, are unpublished (but see Parr 1983; Mathias and Parr 1989). Transjordan was still virtually unexplored but for the ever-useful and inspiring surveys of Nelson Glueck (1951), surveys by Mellaart (1962; see now Leonard n.d., 1983), de Contenson (1960), and Mittmann (1970), the excavations at Tuleilat Ghassul (Mallon *et al.* 1934; Koeppel 1940; Hennessy, 1969) and the published pottery from the cemetery at Bab edh-Dhra' (Saller 1964/5; Lapp 1968; Rast and Schaub 1980, [eds] 1981; Schaub and Rast 1984; Schaub 1973, 1981, 1987). Isolated, unstratified depositions such as the cave at Arqub edh-Dhahr (Parr 1956) and the sondage at Khirbet Iskander (Parr 1960) added little on which to begin to construct typologies. Soundings at Tyre (Bikai 1978) were too limited in the periods concerned here to produce a meaningful sample. Byblos, the only extensively excavated site (apart from Ras Shamra) on the Levantine littoral, remained problematical until the publication of the 4th millennium strata (Dunand 1973; cf. now Saghieh 1983).

On the other hand, material from Cisjordan was always abundant, although somewhat skewed in favour of easily processed tomb groups. G. Ernest Wright's masterly compilation of the evidence and his periodization (1937) served as a basis which can be regarded as the most lastingly useful handbook, despite that author's subsequent re-appraisals (e.g. *idem* 1958, 1961, 1971). With the gradual - some would say revolutionary - introduction of more careful recovery methods (by Kenyon from the 1950s onwards), a new plateau of seriation and periodization appeared to have been reached. Wright's compilation and the work at Jericho served as the fundamental data-base for EBA pottery up to the present. This was followed by various excavations at key EBA sites (e.g. Tell el-Far'ah near Nablus: compare de Vaux and Steve [1947] and de Vaux [1952] onwards for a change in recovery etiquette at least) and developed, sometimes along apparently divergent lines, by adherents of one 'school of thought' or another. Hennessy (1967) followed Kenyon (but compare now Kenyon [1981] and Kenyon and Holland [1982, 1983] in which Hennessy's pre-publication data-base cannot be easily recognized). Lapp, and others, followed Wright with additions of their own. De Miroschedji (1971) presented a middle ground with somewhat unproven periodization (see Kenyon [1974] for a review). Mellaart (1966) provided some remarkably prophetic perspectives (e.g. Tell Um Hammad, among other sites in the Jordan Valley). Ruth Amiran summarized most of this material (1969) in what is still the best compendium to ancient Palestinian pottery up to the end of the Iron Age, although her Chalcolithic and EB I sections now need some revision and, certainly, expansion. However, since most of the assemblages and repertoires were constructed from tomb groups and on the basis of unpublished stratified (domestic) pottery, some of the more problematical groupings have remained enigmatic. This was particularly the case regarding the later 3rd millennium (EB IV/EB-MB/MB I, etc.) and the time (represented by pottery styles) between the 'terminal Chalcolithic' (e.g. Ghassul IV A/B, or 'Ghassul/Beersheba') and what was often called the 'full Early Bronze Age' characterized by the rise of so-called urbanism. Assemblages and repertoires from this 'horizon' (as well as the later one) were arranged and re-arranged within unproven hypothetical frameworks (e.g. Callaway [1964]; Kenyon [1979]). The material available for comparison with Jawa was - in retrospect - not truly representative of domestic preferences; nor was it representative of regionalism, which is now recognized as a normal phenomenon in pre-industrial vernacular environments: that is to say, in essentially rural landscapes. This corpus of pottery was also crammed into what now appears to be an illusory time-frame of between 100 and 200 years, beginning some time about 3200 BC (see Zeuner [1956] for a very early determination of 5210 +/- 110 b.p. [c. 4165 - 3870 BC]; Kenyon [1960: 8], for a radiocarbon determination for Tomb A94 and her Proto Urban period: c. 3400 - 3100 BC). Nevertheless, the presently published corpus of Chalcolithic and early EBA pottery serves as an essential source of parallels.

For many scholars Jawa's pottery assemblage therefore 'floated' sometime between about 3200 BC, or a little later, and 2000 BC, although Gerald Harding, the first to begin properly to understand ancient Jawa (Department of Antiquities in Amman [Records]; and p.c.), had already regarded the site as EBA in the early 1950s. Kenyon herself (p.c. at Jawa in 1974) confirmed this, accepting the then proposed stylistic relationships (Helms 1975) with her 'Proto Urban' period, and a little later (discussion, lecture by the author, 1975

[Palestine Exploration Fund, London]) publicly stating that the massive 4th millennium fortifications at Jawa rendered her terminology ('Proto Urban') less appropriate of what may have been going on in the southern Levant in the second half of the 4th millennium BC.

More recent work in the southern Levant (i.e. up to about 1982) produced very little apparently relevant material since, as before, only tomb groups or partial repertoires (based on the earlier typological seriations) emerged in print. Work in northern/central Syria - especially the Tabkha Dam Rescue Project - now added an important and monumental link with southern Mesopotamia (Uruk VII - IV: Sürenhagen 1978; Strommenger 1980) but, once again, little within these pottery repertoires could be linked directly and convincingly with the pottery assemblage of 4th millennium Jawa. The most southerly extent of Uruk-type pottery remained (and remains) Hama (Fugmann 1958) despite Hennessy's redrawing of a vessel from tombs K1 at Jericho (cf. Hennessy 1967; Kenyon 1965: Fig. 12: 6). A recent discovery of Uruk material near el-Kowm (Cauvin and Stordeur 1985) adds an important steppic perspective. What appears to be 'Palestinian' pottery of the 4th millennium BC has now been found at al-Hibr in eastern Jordan on the Saudi Arabian frontier (Betts, in press). This left the region of the Ghuta/Damascene and the Hawran/Jebel Druze where explorations, but for those at Khirbet Umbachi/Hebariyeh (Dubertret and Dunand 1954/5), have only begun in the last few years (Seeden 1986; Braemer 1984, 1988 and p.c.; al-Maqdissi 1984), and where some comparisons with 4th millennium material from Jawa have been mooted (Braemer p.c.); they have, however, turned out to be illusory, referring to slightly later assemblages in EB I B (Braemer and Vaillant p.c.). A recent publication of structures near Sidon (Saidah 1979), unfortunately without the pottery, adds a link in terms of architectural typology between Byblos and the Jordan Valley (i.e. via the Jezre'el valley, as far south as Um Hammad, and perhaps also into the Ajlun hills and Jawa). Unfortunately, recent surveys in the Jordan Valley (Ibrahim *et al.* 1976, Yassine *et al.* 1988) add little new information as published pottery illustrations are restricted to photographs of a few selected sherds. Similarly, a number of important surveys in the southern subregions of Transjordan have not yet provided any empirical evidence.

Connections between Jawa and the Palestinian assemblages of the 4th millennium BC (i.e. appellations such as late Chalcolithic, 'énéolithic superieur', 'Proto Urban', EB I, etc.) did, however, exist in print as early as 1951. Credit must again go to Nelson Glueck who published several sherds which find precise parallels at Jawa (1951:

Pls 100: 3, 103: 7, 162: 7). They come from Tell Um Hammad (Umm Hammad esh-Sharqiyah) near the confluence of the Jordan and Zerqa rivers and from Tell Mutawwaq on the Jordanian plateau at a bend in wadi Zerqa (Glueck: Meghanieh: see now Hanbury-Tenison n.d., 1986). These parallels were not recognized by the author until the later 1970s, following a viewing of Mellaart's pottery drawings from his survey and soundings at Tell Um Hammad (1962) and particularly after seeing the unpublished manuscript generously made available by Albert Leonard (n.d.) at the American Center for Oriental Research in Amman in 1980/1. This lead to the author's excavations at Um Hammad in 1982 and again in 1984 (Helms 1984a, 1986, 1987a, Betts [ed.] in progress) where a large proportion of Jawa's 4th millennium BC assemblage may now be recognized (see below). Um Hammad forms the most concrete basis for stylistic parallels with regard to the EB I A period of Palestine/Transjordan.

Very recent work, concomitant with that at Um Hammad and available in summary published form, in the Jordan Valley, the Ajlun hills, and the Jezre'el (Esdraelon) Valley, has underpinned this relationship. At the same time, these new data have provided regional variations which may be and will be used in socio-economic reconstructions (see now Helms 1984b, 1987a, 1987b, 1989c, in press, in progress; Betts [ed.] in progress). For the Jordan Valley new material regarding the 4th millennium BC has been found in excavations by Gustavson-Gaube (1985, 1986) and Dolfuss and Kafafi (1986; cf. also *Abu Hamid*) at Tell Abu Hamid, and Tell Shuneh North, respectively. Related material from the area of Jerash is represented in surveys by Hanbury-Tenison (1986, 1987, n.d.). Excavations in the Jezre'el valley (Braun 1984, 1985) now adds important parallels west of the Jordan river. Surveys in southern Transjordan were noted above: their presently published surmises, particularly regarding the EBA material, are still essentially undocumented, and in any event, will probably not be representative of the main stream of 'cultural' development in the southern Levant. Several surveys are under way up and down the Jordan valley, results from which will augment considerably the relations between sub-regions in the southern Levant.

Since the closest pottery connections with Jawa seem to be limited to the central Jordan Valley, wadi Zerqa and the north Jordanian plateau (Ajlun hills and north), Um Hammad and its neighbouring sites represent the most direct link with what is known about EB I in the southern Levant. The neighbouring sites are Tell Mafluq (Mellaart: see Leonard n.d.), Kataret es-Samra (Leonard 1983, 1989), perhaps Tell Abu Zighan (Helms in press) which is also known as Tell Handaquq South, and also Tell Handaquq North (Glueck 1951;

Ibrahim *et al.* 1976; Mabry p.c. and n.d.) where a stamp seal and an impression have now been found, which are very similar to those whose impressions appear on identical vessels at Jawa, Tell Um Hammad and Mafluq, and also at Kataret es-Samra (an actual seal from Tell Handaquq North in Mabry p.c., n.d.; Mafluq: Leonard n.d.; Kataret es-Samra: Leonard p.c.). In the first instance, parallels will be sought in the early stages at Um Hammad (stage 2) as they have been partly published (Helms 1984a, 1986, 1987a) and, thereafter, within the general EB I, or late Chalcolithic ('Proto Urban'), assemblages of Palestine and Transjordan. In some cases it is possible to identify proto-types for genres which suggests an indigenous, perhaps specifically Palestinian production or tradition; in the other direction, developed forms - when these can be cited - may indicate continuity. Parallels from the Syrian regions are still very limited, as we have noted above. They come, for the most part, from the soundings at Hama on the Orontes and from the Upper Euphrates region. With regard to Syria, some developed forms (i.e. dated in ED [Early Dynastic] II - III) are used to indicate the possibility of earlier forms in those places. The comparative study is arranged according to genres, each type being dealt with in sequence.

Genre A (types A - K: variants 1-161/452-454)

Holemouth jars (hmj) are the hallmark of Palestinian domestic assemblages and repertoires, and can be regarded as an almost continuous formal development from the Neolithic (Pottery Neolithic: PN) to the end of the EBA (ie. up to EB IV/EB-MB/MB I). Their form and rim shape are simple, as is their construction, and for these reasons holemouth jars have generally not been useful as diagnostic indicators in the construction of pottery-based relative chronologies. However, this state of affairs may be somewhat illusory since the bias which has affected typological arguments (see above) is particularly effective in regard of domestic vessels which have been either ignored altogether in tomb assemblages, or simply were not there in the first place. Amiran's necessarily preliminary outline of EB IV/EB-MB pottery is indicative of this. With the exception of tombs 1101-2 (Lower) at Megiddo (e.g. Amiran 1969: 78), not a single holemouth jar is illustrated. Yet these jars are very common in albeit recently excavated domestic depositions of the period (e.g. Dever 1974; Gitin 1975; Helms 1986), as well as in some tomb groups. Amiran's earlier EBA groups similarly lack serious reference to holemouth jars, because they were not considered to be diagnostic, although they are very common indeed in EB II - III assemblages (e.g. Amiran 1978: *passim*). On the other hand, Late Bronze Age and Iron Age cooking pots - the plausible functional equivalent to holemouth jars - abound, although their diagnostic value has also been challenged.

This poor opinion of holemouth jars may now be redressed. Careful seriation of pottery from stratified depositions now shows that these vessels (as also ledge handles whose chronological seriation has confounded various workers) can be diagnostic (e.g. Um Hammad: Helms 1986, 1987b).

Jawa's assemblage appears to have been in use for a short time (see Chapter 2), and yet a great variety of types within the genres can be recognized.

Type AA (variants 1-87). This type is the most abundant at the site and is precisely paralleled in stage 2 (EB I A) at Tell Um Hammad in the Jordan Valley (Helms 1987a: 54ff.). It is also found at Kataret es-Samra in EB I A contexts, immediately on Chalcolithic layers (= terminal [?] Ghassul) nearby (Leonard 1983: Fig. 8: 8), at Mutawwaq (Glueck 1951: Pl. 163: 9; Hanbury-Tenison n.d.), similarly among EB I material, and now also at Tell Handaquq North (Mabry n.d.).

The origin of this type, specifically in reference to the (four) rounded lugs near the rim, can be traced back to Palestinian Neolithic and Chalcolithic assemblages such as Abu Zureiq (Anati 1971: Fig. 35: 19), Arad V (Amiran 1978: Pl. 3: 11), and Ghrubba (Mellaart 1956: Fig. 4: 36). Related early types appear at Horvat Beter (Ben-Tor 1966: Fig. 3: 10), Byblos (Dunand 1973: Fig. 23: 261652), Tuleilat Ghassul (Koeppel 1940: Pls 77: 4), and Affula (Sukenik 1948: Pl. III: 15a).

But, although a case can be made for a Palestinian floruit of the general type (or the attribute = lugs), its precise correspondence to Jawa's type AA during the 4th millennium in Palestine is apparently very localized. This, however, may be simply a function of selective pottery sorting and/or publication.

As we have noted, Jawa's assemblage was in use for a short time: in any event, it shows no signs of local, internal formal, or stylistic development. At Um Hammad, on the other hand, where the stratigraphy indicates prolonged and continuous occupation in EB I A, the type (AA) does seems to 'develop' (cf. Helms 1986: Fig. 16: 6, 1987a: Fig.9: 1); it at least seems to have some devolved relatives. Farther afield in the Jordan Valley some slightly later (?) variants can be recognized in EB I B (?) levels at Jericho (Kenyon and Holland 1982: Figs 40: 22, 64: 3, 65: 10, 68: 19; Kenyon and Holland 1983: Fig. 133: 21; cf. also Kenyon 1952b: Fig. 5: 3), and perhaps even in related types (EB II) with short horizontal moulded ledges near the rim (Kenyon and Holland 1983: Fig. 131: 2). At O.T. Jericho the type evolves and merges with other holemouth jar forms which belong to EB I B (Kenyon and Holland 1982: Fig. 65: 10; cf. also Helms 1986: Fig. 16: 9, 11 = EB I B). Early cognate examples are known at Arad in

Stratum V (Amiran 1978: Pl. 3: 11). Other 'developed' or 'devolved' types come from Arad's Stratum IV and also Stratum II (Amiran 1978: Pls 3: 1 [cf. also J531 for similar painted decoration], 8: 15) in EB II contexts. Other parallels come from Tell el-Far'ah (de Vaux 1961: Fig. 3: 12). A hybrid form is said to come from the area of Bab edh-Dhra' (Saller 1964/5: Fig. 15: 3). One of the variants at O.T. Jericho finds formal parallels (without the lugs) in a well-defined genre at Um Hammad (Helms 1986: Fig.16: 9, 11) which is sealed in 'EB I B' layers there. This form seems to continue into EB II at Jericho (e.g. Kenyon and Holland 1983: *passim*).

The rounded lugs are a significant attribute which not only links Jawa and the west (see also stamp seal impressions below in Chapter 4), but which may also represent a discrete repertoire. This repertoire is represented at Jawa in the following genres and types: BA (Fig. 122: 162) and BC (Fig. 124: 180, shoulder), EA (Fig. 136: 342), and EB (Fig. 143: 449). Both of these genres (B and E) are directly comparable to examples in (discrete?) repertoires at Um Hammad (Helms 1986: Figs 12: 13, 3, 13: 6, 14: 4, 7; 1987a, Fig. 10: 12), as well as Mutawwaq, and less directly at Bab edh-Dhra' and Tell el-Far'ah North (cf. relevant Jawa types below).

Type AA, therefore, appears - at present - to be peculiar to Jawa, the Ajlun hills along and north of wadi Zerqa, and the central Jordan Valley. Its general attributes see a wider distribution, possibly via two mechanisms: (i) direct contact, and thus formal development, and/or (ii) parallel development from more indirectly related repertoires such as those in the partially published EB I A at Bab edh-Dhra' (cf. especially genre B below). The second possibility recalls the Palestinian or, rather, the southern Levantine floruit of related types from the Neolithic onward.

Type AB (variants 88-94). The type is related to AA in terms of form, fabric, and the punctate/slashed decoration, but does not appear to have any lugs. Of the three variants, only J94 is divergent in its characteristic rim shape.

Variants J88 to J93 and J95 find close parallels in stage 2 at Um Hammad (Helms 1987a: Fig. 5: 10) and in other early EBA assemblages of Palestine: for example, comparisons may be made with forms at O.T. Jericho (Kenyon and Holland 1983: Figs 58: 32 [EB], 60: 32, 33 [EBA], 78: 17 [PU/EB], 137: 4 [PU/EB], 157: 2 [EB]); Tell el-Far'ah North (de Vaux and Steve 1947: Fig. 5: 15 [?]; de Vaux 1961: Fig. 3: 11 [?]) although these vessels may be closer to type AA; the Jerash area (Hanbury-Tenison 1987: Fig. 8: 19, form only); and Meser II and III (Dothan 1959a: Figs 5: 3, 6: 13).

Variant J94 also has close parallels at Um Hammad 2 (Helms 1984a: Fig. 12: 6; 1987a: Fig. 5: 4), as well as in related forms at N.T.

Jericho (Pritchard 1958: Figs 56: 8, 57: 7 [?]), the Jerash area (Hanbury-Tenison 1987: Fig. 6: 51 [?]), Kataret es-Samra (Leonard n.d., 1983: Fig. 9: 22 [?]), Meser II (Dothan 1959a: Fig. 6: 6 [?]), Arqub el-Dhahr (Parr 1956: Fig. 14: 123 [?]), and perhaps also at Azor (Perrot 1961: Fig. 41: 2 [?]). Its form can be traced back to the Chalcolithic period. Comparison may also be made with vessels from Rasm Harbush site 'ii' (Epstein 1978a: Fig. 12: top row, middle), Tell Turmus (Dayan 1969: Fig. 4: 5), perhaps Beersheba (de Contenson 1956: Figs 2: 3, 4: 18 [?]), Neve Ur (Perrot *et al.* 1967: Fig. 16: 3 [?]), among others.

Type AC (variants 96-111/149/161). Thin-walled holemouth jars find their closest comparisons in Palestinian Chalcolithic assemblages (see below), but (apparently) only rare examples may be found in (early) EBA contexts: e.g. at O.T. Jericho (Garstang 1936: Pl. XXXV: 22; Kenyon and Holland 1983: Fig. 127: 16 [PU]); perhaps Megiddo XX (Loud 1948: Pl. I: 17); and Horvat Usa (Ben-Tor 1966: Fig. 3: 1).

The Chalcolithic parallels may be summarized as follows. Comparison may be made with vessels from Tell el-Far'ah North 'énéolithique moyen' (de Vaux and Steve 1947: Fig. 1: 5, painted), Tell Esdar IV (?) (Kochavi 1969: Fig. 18: 9 ?), Tell Fara South (Macdonald 1932: Pl. XXXIX: 17), Jericho (Garstang 1935: Pl. XLIIX: 2), Ghrubba (?) (Mellaart 1956: Fig. 4: 34, with ledge handle), Arad Stratum V (Amiran 1978: Pl. 6: 3), Beersheba (de Contenson 1956: Figs, 2: 12, 3: 1-3 etc.), and Horvat Beter I (Dothan 1959b: Fig. 8: 19).

Type AD (variants 112-115). These vessels are related to type AC, but otherwise fall into the 'undiagnostic' category.

Type AE (variants 96-111/149/161). Holemouth jars with narrow mouths and vertical loop- or pierced handles near the rim share some attributes with types AC/AD (fabric) and, like them, are most comfortably compared with Palestinian Chalcolithic examples. However, early EBA (or 'late Chalcolithic') and later EBA parallels may also be cited. Comparison may also be made with examples from Tell el-Far'ah North (de Vaux and Steve 1947: Figs 2: 22, handle on bowl, 3: 3, 4, handles on shoulder of jar = 'E B I', 5: 19-21), O.T. Jericho (EB II?) (Garstang 1932: Pl. VI: 12, note also decoration at rim = type AB). More examples of vertically and horizontally pierced lugs, very similar to Chalcolithic types, occur in the 'Proto Urban' tombs at Jericho (Kenyon 1960: Fig. 15: 7, tomb A94), and the tell (Kenyon and Holland 1983: Fig. 130: 20), Beth Shan XVIII (Fitzgerald 1935: Pl. 11: 16, 21-24 etc.), Tel Ras ha`ayin (Eitan 1969: Fig. 2: 27), and Affula (Sukenik 1936: Pl. VIII: 32, compare the EB II example from Jericho).

Chalcolithic parallels are very common, ranging from small pierced lugs (i.e. J117/128) to larger handles, usually at the waist of storage jars. Similar forms can be found at Azor (Perrot 1961: Figs 39:

7-9, 40: 6), Meser (Dothan 1957: Fig. 4: 11), Megiddo XX (Loud 1948: Pl. 2: 24), Jericho (Garstang 1935: Pl. XLI: 14,15), Tell Fara South (Macdonald 1932: Pl. XXI), Tell el-Far'ah North (de Vaux and Steve 1947: Fig. 1: 15-19), Pella (McNicoll *et al.* 1982: 89: 3, 4), Majami in the Jawlan/Golan area (Epstein 1978a: Fig. 5: 6, 12, bottom row), Tell Turmus in the same general area (Dayan 1969: Fig. 8: 4-6), Horvat Beter I - III (Dothan 1959b: Figs 10: 27 *passim*, 15: 9, 12-15, 17: *passim*), Beersheba (de Contenson 1956: *passim* and especially Figs 11: 1-10, compare Jericho tomb A94 here, 12: 19-26), Tuleilat Ghassul (Mallon *et al.* 1934: Fig. 47; North 1961: *passim*), and so forth.

Type AF (variant 447). A surface find, this anomalous type can however be classed among Jawa's EB I A assemblage on the basis of fabric type. Parallels for vertical loop handles at the rims of holemouth jars (or deep bowls) are common throughout Palestinian Chalcolithic and EBA assemblages (see also above). The applied decoration may be compared with Chalcolithic and EBA examples: e.g. for the earlier range the applied 'figurine' on a carinated holemouth jar from `Ein el-Jarba (Kaplan 1969: Fig. 7: 1a/b); for the later range, Arad Stratum II (Amiran 1978: Pl. 106: 4). In general, the special treatment of handles, or the exterior of otherwise purely domestic vessels (in clay as well as stone), is a common phenomenon in the ancient Near East from Anatolia to Egypt. Whether such peculiarities may be used to evoke a spiritual content is debatable (but see also Epstein, 1975, 1978b, 1982, 1985; see also Chapter 7).

Type AG (variants 129-136). These vessels are crudely made and their formal attributes, therefore, not very diagnostic. Variant J131 is related to type AF in terms of its shallow bosses below the rim. J129-131 may be distantly related to bag-shaped holemouth jars in stage 2 at Um Hammad (Helms 1987a: Fig. 9: 3) which, in turn, are distantly related to crude, sometimes slightly 'bow-rimmed', jars at Horvat Beter I-III (Dothan 1959b: Fig. 14: 9), Horvat Usa (Ben-Tor 1966: Fig. 5: 5), perhaps Arad Stratum V (Amiran 1978: Pl. 6: 1), and Beth Shan XVI (Fitzgerald 1935: Pl. I: 10). All of these forms 'straddle' the Chalcolithic and early EBA periods.

Type AH (variants 137-140). The characteristic in-folding of the rim can be compared with examples from Um Hammad's stage 2 (Helms 1987a: Fig. 5: 12, with punctate decoration, among others), and many other Palestinian examples from Chalcolithic, as well as late EBA, assemblages.

Type AI (variants 141-145). The externally recessed rim has a similar distribution in space and time as type AH.

Type AJ (variants 146-148/150-160). Like some of the previously described types, these vessels have few diagnostic attributes other than shape and fabric which allow them to be classed in this genres

(A) and generally within Jawa's EB I A assemblage. Variant J159 finds a parallel at Meser (Dothan 1957: Fig. 3: 7. Of the rest, only variants J152/153 may be taken further: but only to say that the elaboration of the rim (rolled/recessed) is a feature which becomes common first in late Chalcolithic and early EBA holemouth jars. But, some of these rims are indistinguishable from EB IV examples on the basis of shape alone. Even the fabrics tend to be similar. A good comparison is provided by genres in stage 2 at Um Hammad (Betts [ed.] in progress: TUH5195/38/2794 etc.) and N.T. Jericho (Pritchard 1958: Pl. 56: 1, 2). Comparison can also be made with the EB IV examples from Um Hammad's stages 6 to 7 (Helms 1986: Fig. 19: 4, 6, 7, 9, 11), demonstrating how typical the holemouth form is for not only the Early Bronze Age, but also the Chalcolithic period before that.

Type AK (variants 452-454). Spouted holemouth jars (or deep bowls), sometimes called 'trumpet-spouted', are common throughout the Chalcolithic period and continue 'in vogue' well into the late EBA. The Jawa examples are too fragmentary to make specific comparisons meaningful: however, as part of the assemblage, they recall Chalcolithic or early EB I (e.g. 'EB I B') examples, particularly on the basis of the painted rim.

Genre B (Types A - C, variants 162 - 240)

Apart from the general form of these vessels, one particular attribute - ledge handles, and to a lesser extent, sub-circular lugs - has long been. regarded as a Palestinian/southern Levantine peculiarity. The region of use may now be extended northwards, into the Hawran/Jebel Druze subregions, and perhaps as far as the Ghuta/Damascene because of the evidence from Jawa and the presence of at least one rounded (and impressed?) ledge handle in the earlier pottery assemblage at Khirbet Umbachi/Hebariyeh (Dubertret and Dunand 1954/5: Pl. VII: 2, 3rd sherd in 3rd row). The nearest relevant Syrian assemblage (Hama) apparently includes no such handles.

The generic relationship between the three types (A - C) has been demonstrated above. Of the three, only type A is idiosyncratic in shape: i.e. the high shoulders.

As is the case with genre A, genre B may be traced back, to some extent, to the Chalcolithic and even Late Neolithic periods of Palestine. Ledge handles were discussed above with regard to lugs on holemouth jars which are precisely duplicated on the shoulders of vessels in genre B (cf. J162/180 and J1 *passim*). Larger, rounded, and upturned ledge handles are known at Abu Zureiq (Anati 1971: Fig. 36: 15, 16), at Horvat Usa (Ben-Tor 1966: Figs 3: 12, 4: 1, 5, 5: 12, 13, one upside down [?]), and also in late Chalcolithic contexts at Jericho, and elsewhere. However, the ledge handles in Late Neolithic assemblages (i.e. 6th to 5th millennium BC) are reminiscent of what becomes a common type some one and a half thousand years later: but there is probably no generic, or evolutionary, connection between the two types. This is underlined by their almost complete absence from Chalcolithic assemblages (as these are published to date); and even the very common Chalcolithic lugs are usually quite different from the rounded ones of the later 4th millennium BC. The preference for ledge handles, once it was established in EB I A, continued throughout the whole of the EBA, up to about 2000 BC (EB IV). Rounded handles are the norm in the Middle and Late Bronze Ages, and their origins can be sought in Syria.

The characteristic decorative bands (see Fig. 129: 226-237) cannot, on their own, be used as indicators of periodization since rope moulded or thumb-impressed and applied bands have reappeared in pottery repertoires throughout the history of potting all over the Near East. On the other hand, they are not out of place in a 4th millennium BC setting.

In terms of shape, particularly the larger types (B-C) can be compared to Chalcolithic, and even earlier, storage jars, with the qualification that the form is simple and perhaps, therefore, not very diagnostic after all. Relevant comparisons may be made with vessels from Ghrubba (Mellaart 1956: Fig. 6: 122), Tuleilat Ghassul (Koeppel 1940: Pls 96: 1, 4, 79: 9), the large storage jars in the Huleh/Jawlan region (Dayan 1969: Fig.8; Epstein 1978a: Figs 6, 8, 11, 12), and Tell Abu Hamid (Dolfuss and Kafafi 1986: Pl. III; *Abu Hamid*: Fig. 74, *passim*), among many others. Of these only the painted vessel from Ghassul (Koeppel 1940: Pl. 96: 4) comes close to genre B in that it has (twinned) horizontal (pierced) lugs at the junction of shoulder and waist; the rest have either the typical Chalcolithic pierced lugs, or rounded vertical handles at the shoulder or the waist. Shapes, therefore, may be assumed to remain more or less similar (because, as we have noted, they were simple in any case), but handles changed. This is borne out at Tell Um Hammad where shapes and general decorative features of a whole set of genres within an almost discrete repertoire precisely parallel the so-called northern Chalcolithic vessels (i.e. such as those in the Huleh/Jawlan region), with only one difference: their handles are not pierced; they are horizontal ledge handles (Helms 1984a, 1986). This occurs in Um Hammad's stage 3 which is presently assigned to 'EB I B' (= 'Proto Urban' B). Again, it is evident that a change in preference must have occurred, here in essentially the same, continuing repertoire, between the (late) Chalcolithic (early 4th millennium) and the early EBA (later 4th millennium BC).

The closest parallels for ledge handles at Jawa come from the assemblage at Um Hammad's stage 2 (Helms 1987a: Fig. 6: 7; cf. also 1984a: Figs 10: 12, 11: 17, etc.). Other Palestinian ledge handles of the middle to later 4th millennium BC which may be compared with those at Jawa come from Horvat Usa (see also above) (Ben-Tor 1966: Fig. 5: 12, 13 - compare J173), Beth Shan XVI (Fitzgerald 1935: Pl. II: 1 - 3), Bab edh-Dhra' Tomb A76 (Lapp 1968: Fig. 9: 19), Affula where they occur together with 'Esdraelon' wares (Sukenik 1936: Pl. II; 1948, Pl. VII), and O.T. Jericho ('Proto Urban' tombs: Kenyon 1960: Fig. 18: 18; 1965: Figs 7: 7 ['EB I B'], 8: 23, 9: 5; tell: Kenyon and Holland 1983: Figs 12: 3, 14 [handle?], 13: 16, *passim*). Amiran's summary of the developments of ledgehandles (1969: *passim*), although generally in harmony with the recent results from Um Hammad and other sites, is misleading in detail at both ends of her sequence (i.e. EB I and EB IV).

In terms of shape, very close parallels occur in Um Hammad's stage 2 (Helms 1984a: Fig. 11: 17; 1987: Fig. 6). To this can now be added the conclusive evidence of stamp seal impressions (see Chapter 4) which makes the relationship in terms of this genres (as well as genre A) virtually direct. Other, almost identical, examples come from the Ajlun hills subregion and along wadi Zerqa, as well as from Um Hammad's neighbours, Tell Mafluq and Kataret es-Samra (i.e. Glueck 1951: Pl. 163: 1-3; Hanbury-Tenison 1987: Figs 5: 27, 46, 6: 35, 60, 61, 8: 14, 9: 1, 7, 8, 13, 39, 41-3, n.d.: Fig. 6: 8). More distantly related - but nevertheless related - examples are found at Bab edh-Dhra' in EB I A contexts. The nearest comparisons have ledge handles at the waist and vestigial lugs and punctate bands of decoration in the same positions on the vessel as, for example, J180 (Lapp 1968: Figs 9: 19, 11: 20). These vessels can be compared with the parallels from Um Hammad which were cited above (see also Helms 1986, 1987a on Bab edh-Dhra'). In addition to this, certain hybrid forms appear in the same repertoires (Lapp 1968: Fig. 11: 13) in which horizontal ledge handles are combined - not always comfortably - with vertical rounded loop handles. Similar hybrids are found in other early EBA assemblages (i.e. Jericho: Kenyon 1960: Fig. 14: 8 1965: Fig. 8: 25; Lachish/Tell el-Duweir, Tufnell 1958: Pl.60: 226, *passim*; see Helms and McCreery 1988, and Helms 1989b on EB IV survivals of this style; and Tell el Far'ah North: de Vaux and Steve 1947: Fig. 3: 11; 1949: Fig. 6: 31). The problem of hybrid forms - in relation to EB IV pottery production - has been discussed by Dever (1970).

We may conclude the following from this brief survey of parallels and related (or affected) forms. Ledge handles were re-introduced, or re-invented or preferred (after the Late Neolithic), in Palestine (Cisjordan) in EB I A, but local styles persisted: that is to say, rounded handles particularly in the north of the land. Ledge handles then evolved continuously, though perhaps not as uniformly as has been hoped (e.g. Amiran 1969: 35-40), up to the end of EB IV, and then apparently ceased to be made. In the process, the competition between (?) indigenous rounded handles and ledge handles expressed itself occasionally in the production of 'hybrids', if the somewhat subjective argument may be sustained. Apart from evincing the notion of continuity from EB I A to the end of EB IV (see also Prag 1974, 1986; Richard 1980), comparison with the pottery production of the Chalcolithic again suggests that something 'new' was introduced with the start of what we call 'EB I A'. It may be noteworthy that typical 'Palestinian' EB IV folded ledge handles re-appear in the later assemblage at Khirbet Umbachi (Dubertret and Dunand 1954/5: Pl. VII: 1).

The precise parallels with Jawa's genre B have the same localization as those for genre A/type A: i.e. perhaps Khirbet Umbachi/Hebariyeh, [the Hawran], the Ajlun Hills, wadi Zerqa, and the central Jordan Valley; but apparently not as far north within the Jordan Valley as Tell Shuneh North (cf. the typology in Gustavsen-Gaube 1985, 1986). The northern extent of precise parallels may be in the region of Tell Handaquq North where a stamp seal similar to those which made the impression on Jawa's and Um Hammad's vessels is reported (Mabry p.c., n.d.).

Related genres, such as those from Bab edh-Dhra', may suggest a diffusion and concomitant local interpretation of the genre in Transjordan and a little later the rest of the region, i.e. Cisjordan as far as Arad in the south.

And finally, it may be appropriate to guess that the ledge handles and the specific jar form of genre B had its origins and first floruit in the [Damascene] - Hawran, Jebel Druze, and the Ajlun hills regions and that its use and/or production spread from there to the central Jordan Valley about the middle of the 4th millennium, specifically along wadi Zerqa, and southwards as far as the southern Ghor.

The bulk of genre A and almost all of genre B can, therefore, be regarded as south Syrian/northern Transjordanian. Only type A of genre B may contain more foreign elements in its form. The high shouldered profile is more typical in north and central Syrian repertoires such as the Uruk related assemblage at Habuba Kabira (Sürenhagen 1978: cf. forms 63, 65, 69.1, *passim*). Generic relationships can be noted between such forms and types at Nineveh V and even later forms as far afield as Anatolia (i.e. Arslan Tepe: Palmieri 1981: Fig. 9: 2, 5). Such a notion is not conclusive by itself, or even appropriate; together with other genres at Jawa, however, it becomes very relevant (see genre C below).

Genre C (types A - F, variants 241 - 328)

Genre C ranks second only to genre A in terms of frequency in the Jawa assemblage and, along with others (see below), cannot be directly paralleled in EBA or late Chalcolithic assemblages in Palestine or in western and southern Transjordan. There are, however, some apparently related attributes in certain types of vessels in these regions, and these will be discussed first in terms of form and surface treatment.

Form. The genre divides itself into two basic groups of types: CA - CC with characteristic ring bases and CD - CF with (probably) rounded bases. The reason for this division is simply one of vessel size.

Ring bases. There are no direct parallels among jar forms, but for one distantly related vessel at Bab edh-Dhra' (Lapp 1968 Fig. 8: 9) which is really a large amphoriskos. It has a hollow base whose central parts ('bulb' or 'boss') protrude slightly below the base stance line. The balance of comparative attributes appear on juglets and shallow bowls. Ring-based forms, some of them with the characteristic protruding bulbs, are known in the Jericho Proto-Urban tombs (Kenyon 1960: Figs 13: 29, 14, 5, 6; 1965: Figs 10: 3 very close, and also 4: 23, 8: 11). Similar attributes appear on similar forms in tomb A 76 at Bab edh-Dhra (Lapp 1968: Figs 1 - 4, especially 1, 12). Two other relevant examples come from Horvat Beter (Dothan 1956b: Figs 7: 18, 19, 12: 3, 4). Most of the repertoires from which these parallels are taken include vessels with omphalos bases, and these are common in many early EBA assemblages. At Tell el-Far'ah North, omphalos bases, ring bases, and flat bases with internally protruding bosses appear on amphoriskoi and bowls (e.g. de Vaux and Steve 1949: Fig. 6), some forms recalling possible Chalcolithic prototypes (e.g. compare examples from Azor in Perrot 1961: Fig. 37: 6).

Only omphalos bases and, rarely, hollow stump bases (? ring bases) may be compared to Chalcolithic and, occasionally, Late Neolithic examples: and that is not to say that these earlier examples should be regarded as prototypes. Comparison, for example, can be made with burnished vessels from Abu Zureiq (Anati 1971: Fig. 18: 1, 2), Teluliot Batashi (Kaplan 1958: Fig. 10: 12), Beersheba (de Contenson 1956: Figs 4: 11, 11: 4), and Azor (Perrot 1961: Fig. 42: 15), among others.

Since we may compare only one formal attribute between Jawa and the Palestinian assemblages and not similar vessel forms, it seems likely that we are dealing with two quite separate repertoires. It is also important to note that, so far as is known, none of the Palestinian examples is wheel-made, whereas those at Jawa are (see also Appendix B).

Sharply everted rims and indented shoulders. Of these two attributes, the first is far too general to be of much use (but cf. for example Tell el-Far'ah in de Vaux and Steve 1949: Fig.1: 27). Many vessels with sharply everted rounded or pointed rims suddenly become very common in early EBA assemblages and make up the prototypes for EB II-III (and even early IV) jars and, together with EB I juglets, the prototypes for EB II and EB III piriform and other juglets. Compare, for example, such vessels at Um Hammad in both stages 2 and 3 (i.e. 'EB I A - EB I B').

Indented shoulders of the Jawa kind are almost completely unknown in published EBA assemblages. There are a few examples which, however, occur in quite different genres (e.g. Kenyon and Holland 1983: Figs 114: 25 [PU], 137: 27 [EB]). Indented shoulders also occur in EBA contexts but probably have nothing to do with Jawa's genre C (e.g. Kenyon and Holland 1983: Figs 17: 2, 87: 14, 914: 3, 94: 5, etc.). The indentation is partly, perhaps dominantly, a function of construction technique which itself is adapted to the size of the vessel. It can also be a function of stylistic preference (see genre D below), although the result is different. If this rough proportion of construction technique and style is valid, the absence or at least rarity of the 'expediency' in Palestinian assemblages may be significant.

The few examples which come anywhere near the Jawa types (e.g. J294/327/328) are from Lachish/Tell el-Duweir (Tufnell 1958: Pl. 57: 74) in a doubtful context, and from Tell el-Far'ah where the indentation is reversed, one on a jar, the other on a jug (de Vaux and Steve 1949: Fig. 1: 26; de Vaux 1952: Fig. 11: 20). Other possibly comparable vessels appear in tomb A94 at Jericho, very close in vessel form and other attributes to Chalcolithic types (Kenyon 1960: Fig. 15: 7), and at Beth Shan XVII (Fitzgerald 1935: Pl. I: 18). A structurally related 'expediency' is represented by a large class of juglets and small jars (even amphoriskoi) current in EB I B which are made in two halves, the join deliberately left as a ridge (e.g. Asawir in Amiran 1969: Pl. 9: 22; cf. also Tell Um Hammad in Helms 1984a, 1986, 1987a). This characteristic reappears periodically throughout the EBA: comparison, for example, can be made with vessels from Abydos (EB II) (cf. Amiran 1969: Photo 58, with a groove, Pl. 17: 5 very similar to one of the examples at Tell el-Far'ah) and a later one (EB III) from Beth Shan (Amiran 1969: Pl. 19: 13, 'Khirbet Kerak' ware). Throughout EB I, and before that during the Chalcolithic period, and up to the end of the EBA, various decorative bands were applied to the neck/shoulder junctions of medium to large jars. In many cases - particularly in EB IV - this was a purely structural expediency, resulting effectively in an indentation at or near the shoulder; but this is quite different from the practice at Jawa. No parallels, even distant ones, have been reported from the various surveys in the Ajlun hills subregion, nor do any exist at Um Hammad, Kataret es-Samra, Tell Mafluq, or any of the other Jordan Valley sites where EB I A assemblages have been found. One possible parallel, however, is reported from the vicinity of Shahba in the Hawran (Braemer p.c.).

Therefore, it is reasonable to assume that this peculiarity of Jawa's genre C has no prototypes in Palestine during the Chalcolithic period, was not in use during EB I A, and cannot be found in later repertoires which continued to develop up to the end of EB IV.

Surface treatment. Types CB through CF show traces of pattern burnishing; in the case of types CD through CF this consisted of burnishing a red slip. Types CB/CC may have had a slip made of slur from the same material as the fabric of the vessels. The majority of the genre, therefore, is typified by (pattern) burnished red slip.

The practice of burnishing slips giving red through black colouring (depending on the degree of kiln oxidation or reduction) is known in Palestine from the Late Neolithic onward, although this may have little to do with any of the later traditions, even if these were partly developed indigenously. None the less, some of the Chalcolithic examples may be relevant and, at any rate, serve to highlight changes in preference and technique at the beginning of the EBA. The best known examples of this surface decorative 'style' come from wadi Rabah (Kaplan 1958: Fig. 5: 10, 15-18) and Abu Zureiq (Anati 1971: Figs 18 and 35). Recent excavations at Tell Shuneh North (Gustavson-Gaube 1985: *passim*, 1986) report dark burnished sherds which are proposed to be 'dark faced burnished' wares of northern Syria. Where precisely this material might fit is uncertain at present. In any event, it probably has nothing to do with Jawa.

It can now be demonstrated, without too many reservations, that the practice of burnishing of all kinds of vessels increased rapidly - almost exponentially - about the middle of the 4th millennium BC: i.e. particularly in EB I A. Three distinctive repertoires may be defined (in a preliminary way) of which the first two have long been current in the literature of the EBA, where they have been subjected to much hypothetical seriation and sub-periodization (e.g. Wright 1958; Kenyon 1979: *passim*).

The first concerns the so-called 'Esdraelon' ware whose periodization is now more firmly established at sites like Tell Shuneh North (see especially Leonard n.d.; Gustavson-Gaube 1985, 1986) and Tell Um Hammad (Helms 1984a, 1986, and especially 1987a: 76, 10). None of this ware was found at Jawa; none is reported east of the Jordan Valley; and there is a demonstrable distance/frequency regression on a north-south axis in Palestine, more or less as it was outlined by Hennessy (1967).

Secondly, brightly burnished and/or polished vessels made of well-fired clay form a new repertoire whose distribution might suggest a region of concentration not only within Cisjordan, but also along the Levantine coast northwards as far as the Cilician plain and southwards as far as the Nile Delta (see Hennessy 1967; Helms 1987a). The repertoire consists of high loop-handled juglets, fine shallow bowls, spouted jars, some amphoriskoi, and bag-shaped vessels; this repertoire is well-represented in stage 2 at Um Hammad (Helms 1987a) where it occurs alongside genres which have now been directly related with Jawa. Very little of this red burnished ware occurs at Jawa (but see genre F below), perhaps underlining the directional regression noted above.

A third genre of vessels which was highly burnished and eventually pattern burnished consists of platters which first appear in late EB I B or early EB II (e.g. Amiran 1969: Pls 9: 7, 11: 3, 4, Pl. 13, *passim*). These vessel forms are foreign to Palestine, but may be seen to develop in north Syria and Anatolia. Their only possible prototype in Palestinian assemblages is represented by 'pedestal-based' bowls which share some attributes with the northern examples. None was found at Jawa (but compare the rough platters in genre/type GG below).

The last two groups (a repertoire and a genre added to it a little later) developed into the typical EB II and EB III forms whose use lasted down to the end of EB IV. The practice of burnishing slips diminished and died out early in EB IV. The so-called Khirbet Kerak ware is irrelevant to the argument here. The practice of burnishing, therefore, increased dramatically at the beginning of EB I A, concomitant with the manufacture (or introduction) of new forms: but little of this may be relevant to Jawa in generic terms.

We may, therefore, conclude that both form and surface treatment of Jawa's genre C has little or nothing to do with Palestine or Cisjordan, and may not ever be found in western and southern Transjordan. It, the genre, is thus either a very local invention at the site (almost completely unlikely), or it was current a little farther to the northwest (i.e. in the Hawran and the Ghuta/Damascene). On the other hand, it could stem from traditions localized even farther afield. The Hawran/Damascene, though under survey (i.e. Braemer 1984, 1988; al-Maqdissi 1984), has yielded up only one sherd for comparison, as we have noted above. Braemer (p.c.) has 'recognized' genre C as belonging to the 'Early Bronze Age' of those regions. It remains then to look farther afield without, however, implying any direct demographic connection at this stage of the argument.

The sondages at Hama (K) offer up little but for some small vessels with omphalos bases (Fugmann 1958: Figs 30: 5E 567 No 9, 37: 4B 958, 54: 4B 961, and a disc base in Fig. 54: 4B 962), although cognate shapes do occur as early as Hama L (*idem* 1958: Fig. 13: 7C 122 No 57). Possibly related, though later, forms appear in EBA contexts at Tell Nebi Mend (Mathias and Parr 1989: Figs 7: 5, 10: 45). Comparable shapes can also be found in the Amuq F assemblages (Braidwood and Braidwood 1960: Figs 175: 3, 4, 178: 5, 6, 8, all 'cooking pots' in chaff-tempered ware). Relatively close parallels can be found in the area of the Euphrates river in Uruk-related assemblages, notably at Habuba Kabira. A jar or bottle (Sürenhagen 1978: Tab. 16: 98), similar to the example noted at Tell el-Duweir above (Tufnell 1958: Pl.57: 64) may be compared generally with the indented shoulder of J294, as may the rounded base. A large jar with a moulded decorative band on the shoulder (similar to Palestinian examples, but not like the Jawa indentations) has a very characteristic ring base with protruding bulb (Sürenhagen 1978: Tab. 6: 63) which is the closest parallel for the Jawa base that can be cited at present (but see above regarding Palestinian examples). This type of base is common at Habuba Kabira (compare, among others, Sürenhagen 1978: Tab. 1: 12, 15, 16 bowls, Tab. 2: 12   Chalcolithic examples with internal bosses: i.e. Tell el-Far'ah above - 10: 72, 11: 74, 12: 12, all jars [= genre E type E below], 18: 125, and cf. 34: 15 'Ringfuss' ['ringbase']). The same type of base - quite foreign to Palestinian assemblages throughout the third millennium - continues to be used in northern Syria and in Mesopotamia, suggesting (obviously) a generic relationship with the earlier material represented here by the Habuba Kabira assemblage, among others. A few examples suffice to show this, and among them are types which also closely parallel Jawa genre C's indented shoulders: comparison may be made with vessels from the upper Euphrates (Kampschulte and Orthman 1984: Tafn 15:, 1a: 3); Tell Asmar in ED III (Delougaz 1952: Pl. 176: C.4666.370) with the indented shoulder; Tell Billa in ED I and ED II (Speiser 1933: Pl. LV: 2) also with the indented shoulder; and Tepe Gawra VII (Speiser 1935: Pl. LXV: 68).

Genre C is, therefore, related more to Syrian than to Palestinian pottery repertoires. What this might mean in economic and demographic terms cannot be established at this stage: too much is missing between the Euphrates, north/central Syria, and Jawa. The Uruk connection is likewise nebulous, though very provocative, even if the relationship is indirect. No bevelled rim bowls have been found at Jawa unless one re-draws J508-510; and none has been found in Palestine (but see Hennessy 1967) despite roughly similar examples from Jericho and Tell el-Far'ah, among others. The closest 'Uruk' connection regarding Jawa remains Hama (Fugmann 1958: Figs 37: 5B 840, 46: 4A 882, 49: 7A 617, 54: 4B 785, 4B 786) and el-Kowm (Cauvin and Stordeur 1985) which may be regarded as a 'bedouin' camp (cf. also Helms 1989a, 1990: Prolegomenon; Betts in press).

Genre D (Types A and B, variants 329 - 337)

This genre is related to genre C in terms of its characteristic high and indented shoulders and round bases; and, like genre C, its parallels lie beyond Palestine.

A search for parallels in Palestinian assemblages yields little (but cf. Kenyon and Holland 1983: Fig. 13: 24 [?]), and comparisons there are forced in contrast to material from 4th and 3rd millennium vessels from Syria. The more normal shape for Palestinian everted rim storage jars may be traced in an unbroken development, from EB I through to the end of EB IV (cf. Amiran 1969: *passim*). A few idiosyncratic Palestinian examples may be cited: e.g. Tell el-Far'ah North (de Vaux and Steve 1949: Fig. 6: 2, 'EB I', 7: 7 'EB II' with seal impressions), but the development further into the EBA at Tell Far'ah follows a different pattern (de Vaux 1955: Figs 13, 14 for périodes 1 to 5); one vessel from the mixed assemblage at Arqub edh-Dhahr (Parr 1956: Fig. 17: 211); a stone vessel from Azor whose rim and shoulder forms are somewhat similar to Jawa's genre D (Ben-Tor 1973: 49, bottom centre); Meser (Dothan 1957: Fig.3: 12); Jericho (Kenyon and Holland 1983: Figs 122: 25, 137: 27); and perhaps also Horvat Beter (Dothan 1959b: Fig.9: 18). A few sharply indented shoulders on wide-mouthed jars can be cited as possible, but distant, parallels in Palestinian Chalcolithic and even Late Neolithic assemblages, but it is unlikely that any of these have anything to do with Jawa: Teluliot Batashi (Kaplan 1958: Fig. 10: 10); Beersheba (de Contenson 1956: Fig. 4: 18); and Horvat Usa (Ben-Tor 1966: Fig. 5: 2).

The scarcity of even vague parallels in earlier, later, and contemporary pottery assemblages in Palestine (and at least central and southern Transjordan as well) would, therefore, indicate that genre D was either invented at Jawa (unlikely: there are too few), or might have been in general use somewhere else.

On the other hand, convincing Syrian and even Mesopotamian parallels abound. Comparison is possible with vessels from Hama K (Fugmann 1958: Figs 30: 6B 979, 37: 5E 565, 4B 622 No. 34, 46: 4D 212 No. 26,4A 892, 54, 6B 790, 4A 894). The same vessel form, though with a more developed rim, is found in late EBA contexts at Tell Nebi Mend (Mathias and Parr 1989: Fig.11: 60-63). Very close parallels can also be found at Habuba Kabira (Sürenhagen 1978: Tab. 12: 78, 79, among many related, high-shouldered types). Developed forms (compare here the later EBA Palestinian jars) come from Tell Chuera

in ED I to ED III (Kühne 1976: Abb. 231), and Tell Asmar in ED III
(Delougaz 1952: Pl. 194: D.555.5106).

Comparative study indicates that, like genre C, genre D's source
must lie beyond Palestine, presumably in Syria: possibly in
north/central Syria. Genres C and D, therefore, may be part of a
separate and recognizable pottery repertoire, parallel with, and in
contrast to, the repertoire represented by genres A and B, both of
which genres have close Palestinian/Transjordanian cognates and in
some cases also proto-types.

Genre E (Types A - E, variants 338 - 392/449)

Genre E is problematical since parallels for many variants can be
recognized in both Syrian and Palestinian assemblages of the 4th
millennium BC, though not so easily in developed forms of the EBA
(see also Appendix B and the variety of pastes).

Type EA (variants 338 - 350). The simple shape can be seen in Late
Neolithic assemblages (e.g. at Jericho, cf. Kenyon and Holland 1983:
Figs 4: 11, 8, etc.), and throughout the Chalcolithic period. Closely
analogous forms may be cited from Abu Zureiq (Anati 1971: Fig. 19:
11), Beersheba (de Contenson 1956: Figs 3: 1 - 17, 6: 1 - 6), Neve Ur
(Perrot *et al*. 1967: Fig. 16: 2, 3), Arad Stratum V (Amiran 1978: Pl. 5: 7,
8), Horvat Beter (Dothan 1959b: Fig.9: 21, 26), Tell Turmus (Dayan
1969: Fig. 5: 2, 6), Rasm Harbush site 'ii' (Epstein 1978a: Fig. 12, top
right), Ghrubba (Mellaart 1956: Figs 4: 27 - 29, 39, 5: 99, 101 - 106, 6:
107, etc.), and the 'énéolithique' of Tell el-Far'ah North (de Vaux and
Steve 1947: Fig. 1: 1-3).

Very close parallels exist in late Chalcolithic or early EBA contexts
in Palestine: i.e. roughly mid-fourth millennium BC. Remarkably close
comparisons may be made with vessels from Affula (Sukenik 1936:
Pl. I: 21 = J346; 1948: Pls IV: 7 = J345/345, V: 3 = J338, 9 = J342), Beth-
Shan (Fitzgerald 1935: Pl. I: 18), Meser (Dothan 1957: Fig. 3: 12; 1959a:
Figs 5: 6, 7: 8 = J338/339), and Tell el-Duweir (Tufnell 1958: Pls 6: 4 =
J344, 27 = rim J338/339, 57: 48, 59 - 60 = J338/339). Other parallels
exist in Tell Um Hammad's stage 2 (Helms 1984a: Figs 10: 4, 5, 12: 3,
4; 1986: Figs 12: 8, 14: 2, 3, 7, etc.), Megiddo XX (Loud 1948: Pl.1: 1),
and in Late Chalcolithic/Neolithic material from the tell at Jericho
(Garstang 1935: Pls XLII: 12, 20, XLIII: 8, 9; 1936: Pl. XXX: 3, etc.). Most
of Kenyon's tell material (but for the Late Neolithic) seems more
distant (compare Kenyon and Holland 1983: Figs 11: 14, 15, 44: 15, 46:
17, 113: 3 [PNA/PU: = J343, J350], 22 [with handle = J342?], 23
[PNB/PU] etc.: all apparently early in the 'Proto Urban' sequence, if
not actually in what Crowfoot calls 'Derived Ghassulian' [1983:
716ff.]). However, Kenyon's 'Proto Urban' tombs at Jericho do contain
some close parallels (see Kenyon 1960: tomb A94, Figs 13: 29, rim on
juglet = J338/339, 14: 8 etc., 1965: Fig. 8: 18 = J343). Comparison can

also be made with material from Tell Fara South (Macdonald 1932: Pls XXXIX ff.), Tel Esdar (Kochavi 1969: Fig. 17: 28, 30), Arad Stratum IV upwards (Amiran 1978: Pls 9: 1, 12: 10, etc.), N.T. Jericho (Pritchard 1958: Pl. 57: 4, 7-9), the mixed material at Arqub edh-Dhahr (Parr 1956: Fig. 14: 123-126), and Tell el-Far'ah North (de Vaux 1951: Fig. 4: 5, 6 for related [?] bag-shaped vessels).

Syrian parallels can be found in several variants at Hama K (Fugmann 1958: Figs 30: 5E 566 plus paint, similar to genres at Tell Um Hammad [Helms 1987a: Fig. 9]), although how valid these comparisons may be is debatable. Similarly, quite close parallels may be seen at Habuba Kabira (see Sürenhagen 1978: Tabn 24: 8 - 13, 25: 40 [?] = J343, etc.).

Type EA is thus at home in Palestine as well as in Syria during the 4th millennium BC; it does not seem to have any developed forms in the later EBA, possibly because it is a very simple, primitive form which was either no longer made, or has not yet been recorded in excavations.

Type EB (variants 351 - 361/449). The genre is represented in a small grouping in Tell Um Hammad's stage 2 (Helms 1987a: Fig. 7: 6, 8; see also 1984: Fig. 12: 2). A similar shape might be seen in a jar from Arad V (Amiran 1978: Pl. 4: 3). These (Um Hammad stage 2 apart) later Chalcolithic, late Chalcolithic or early EBA assemblages of Palestine have little to add, as they are presently published. Distant parallels can be noted, but these may not be meaningful: comparison can be made with vessels from the Jerash survey (Hanbury-Tenison 1987: Fig. 6: 7 [?]; N.T. Jericho (Pritchard 1958: Pl. 87: 10 [?]); Ghrubba (Mellaart 1956: Fig. 4: 44 [?]); Jericho (Garstang 1932: Pl. VIII: 15 [?]; Kenyon and Holland 1983: Fig. 96: 8 [EB: J361?]); Megiddo XIX (Loud 1948: Pl. 3: 1); Tell el-Duweir (Tufnell 1958: Pl. 56: 26); and Affula (Sukenik 1948: Pl. V: 6?, 12, 19 [?]). None is a very satisfactory parallel, and the conclusion at this stage must be that the genre, though present at least in the central Jordan Valley, did not become a common type. In this regard it is somewhat similar to genre/type AA which appears quite suddenly in the central Jordan Valley (e.g. Tell Um Hammad stage 2) and then disappears, via a few later derivations, by later EB I or early EB II.

On the Syrian side, nothing comparable to type EB can be seen in Hama K. But, Habuba Kabira and its Uruk type assemblage has numerous parallels, some of them quite closely related, not only with Jawa's type EB, but also the balance of the genre (see below). Comparisons may be made with rim forms throughout (e.g. Sürenhagen 1978, Tab. 4: 55) and rim/neck forms (*idem* 1978: Tabn 7: 66, 67, 9: 69.1, 27: 115 = J352/353, etc.).

For the time being, therefore, type EB must be regarded as Syrian, and a type which may have reached the central Jordan Valley (and of course also Jawa on the eastern steppic boundaries) sometime about the middle of the 4th millennium BC, but did not (apparently) enjoy a long floruit there.

Type EC (variants 362 - 388). There are no comparable shapes in the Late Neolithic pottery assemblages of Palestine that could serve as prototypes for this genre. At the other end of the time scale, there is also nothing in EB II - EB IV which can be regarded as derived forms. Some distantly related forms occur in EB I contexts (see below). However, very close parallels exist in the Chalcolithic period (i.e. up to the middle of the 4th millennium BC). This 'connection' with a part of Jawa's pottery assemblage may be illusory; on the other hand, it might indicate a common source because these types are the closest to 'Uruk-style' vessels which have also been recognized in pre-dynastic contexts of Egypt (e.g. Kantor 1965).

Parallels from Palestinian Chalcolithic assemblages include Tel Esdar (?) (Kochavi 1969: Fig. 17: 25), the Beersheba region (de Contenson 1956: Figs 1: 1, 7, 8, 2: 1, 2, and especially 11: 1-10; Commenge-Pellerin 1987: Figs 34, 47: 5, 6, 8), Tuleilat Ghassul (Hennessy 1969: *passim*), Neve Ur (Perrot *et al.* 1967: Fig. 15: 13), Horvat Beter (Dothan 1959b: Figs 9: 27, 28, 15: 15 - 17, very close to Jawa's variants J366/367), and in some tombs at Tell el-Far'ah North (e.g. de Vaux 1957: Fig. 1: 2, 3).

Comparable vessels of early EBA date (or late Chalcolithic) come from Affula (Sukenik 1948: Pl. IV: 19 - 24, 36, 37), Meser (Dothan 1959a: Figs 5: 5, 6: 6, 7: 16), Megiddo XIX (Loud 1948: Pl. 3: 2), and some of the Jericho tombs, rather like those at Tell el-Far'ah (e.g. Kenyon 1965: Fig. 9: 9 [?]). Very questionable parallels might be cited with regard to the tell at Jericho (e.g. Kenyon and Holland 1983: Figs 11: 13, 14, 22 - 24, 46: 23, etc.), and this is also the case at Tell Um Hammad where only vaguely derived forms have been found (Helms 1987a: Fig. 7: 4), as well as places like Arad (Stratum IV onward, Amiran 1978: Pl. 12: 12). Therefore, it could be argued that the type - should it have anything to do with Jawa - saw a floruit in the early to middle 4th millennium BC only: that is to say, if there should be anything in the notion of a cultural connection with the Uruk sphere, this happened before the so-called 'full' EBA, and even before most of what we now may call an 'extended EB I'.

Rather similar to type EB above, type EC is not recognizably represented in the assemblages of Hama K (but cf. Fugmann 1958: Figs 37: 4B604 [?], 47: 7A653 [?], 7A62-4B872 [?]). However, Habuba Kabira's Uruk-related assemblage has many close parallels for the Jawa type (Sürenhagen 1978: Tab. 7: 64, 24: 19, 25, 26 etc.).

Type ED and EE (variants 389 - 392). Type ED probably represents a variant of type EC and can be shown to have a similar distribution: e.g. Beersheba Chalcolithic (Commenge-Pellerin 1987: Fig. 50: 1 - 6). Type EE (= variant J392) - only one vessel at Jawa - is similarly related, including its pierced lugs on the shoulder of the vessel. There are some possible Palestinian parallels in EBA assemblages (e.g. Kenyon and Holland 1983: Figs 13: 8 - 10 [PU/EB], 80: 5 [PU/EB], 136: 5 [EB: J389]). Its closest parallels, however, come from Habuba Kabira (Sürenhagen 1978: Tab. 18, cf. especially 124).

GENRE F (Types A and B, variants 393 - 421/429 - 446/448)

Jugs and juglets represent a form which becomes very popular in the southern Levant in the EBA, reaching the status of export quality (or at least as the container for export commodities) in EB II, much like Cypriot and Mycenean vessels in the later Bronze Ages (i.e. 'Syrian bottles': see Amiran 1969: *passim*). The origin of the form has been long debated and still cannot be localized with any certainty. The Palestinian or southern Levantine floruit in the 3rd millennium BC can now be traced back to the first appearance of juglets in about the middle of the 4th millennium BC (Helms 1987a), when the most typical forms, the so-called high loop-handled juglets, occur together with other pottery whose formal origins lie in Chalcolithic traditions. Various attempts have been made to connect up similar repertoires throughout the Near and Middle East of the 4th millennium BC; none of these is conclusive. Hennessy's connection of Cilicia (e.g. late Chalcolithic Tarsus) and Egypt (1967) is perhaps the most plausible of these exercises (see now Helms 1987a), while de Miroschedji's hypothetical reconstruction (1971: cf. Fig. 27) possibly goes too far in linking up Uruk material as far east as Elam. A variety of hypotheses has been presented regarding the role of Anatolia, and even the trans-Caucasian/Caspian regions, as source areas for pottery, people, and other things (e.g. Lapp 1968, 1966; Ritter Kaplan 1981), often with very extraordinary conclusions. Yet none of these links is impossible; they are, however, not proved.

Genre F at Jawa appears to be germane to this argument but cannot, by itself, resolve anything. Study of parallels tends to favour a connection with southern Levantine assemblages. Little is known about other regions such as the Damascene, as we have noted throughout this discussion.

The genre has be subdivided (A/B) but this may be unnecessarily complex. Type B is represented by but one complete vessel (J418) which is not out of place among the other parallels.

In terms of shape alone, variants J393 and J419 can be related to high loop-handled juglets which first appear at Tell Um Hammad in stage 2, together with 'Esdraelon' wares and, as we noted above, vessels whose origins lie in the Chalcolithic period of the southern Levant, specifically Palestine/Central Transjordan (Helms 1986: Fig. 14: 8, 9, 13-16; 1987a). The form does not seem to be in use during the Chalcolithic period; only a few forms may be cited which are anywhere close in shape. Comparison can be made with examples from Gezer ('cream ware'; Amiran 1969: Photo 16) and also one from Tel Esdar (Kochavi 1969: Fig. 17: 21 [?]).

The shape is common in EB II contexts throughout Palestine (e.g. Beth-Shan, Fitzgerald 1935: Pl. V: 12, 13; de Vaux and Steve 1948: Fig. 8: 2, 11), but appears first in EB I ('énéolothique') assemblages, for example, at Tell el-Far'ah North (de Vaux and Steve 1949: Fig.1: 11-14, 25, 6: 31 - 37 for close parallels in an 'EB I B' group, 8: 17, etc.; de Vaux 1952: Fig. 11: 19; 1955, Fig. 1: 20 = J419). The general type also exists at Bab edh-Dhra', as a regional variant in terms of decoration and form (e.g. Lapp 1968: Figs 8: 10, 9: 15, 18, etc.). It is related to the high loop-handled juglet class, like forms at Tell el-Far'ah North. Painted high loop-handled juglets, close to types in stage 2 at Um Hammad, are well-represented in the mixed assemblage at Arqub edh-Dhahr (Parr 1956: Fig. 15: 149, 145, *passim*). Related forms come from coastal Palestine (e.g. Azor, Ben-Tor 1973: 49). Similar rim and handle forms are known at tell Fara South (Macdonald 1932: Pl. XXX: H, 3rd and 4th from left) very close to variant J393. Tomb A94 at Jericho is one of the best collection of these variants (Kenyon 1960: Figs 12: 5 - 34, 13: 1 - 33, all of then high loop-handled juglets, 14: 1 - 6 = J419, together with fine shallow bowls, just like at Tell Um Hammad and = late Chalcolithic Tarsus , cf. now Helms 1987a: Fig. 19). Variant J419 finds parallels in the same assemblages (compare Kenyon 1960: Figs 21: 4, 22: 10, in 'Proto Urban' B contexts; 1965: Fig. 4: 12, *passim* = Bab edh-Dhra' tomb A 76, cf. Lapp 1968). Material from the tell at Jericho is rarer, but for the most part designated 'PU/EB' (i.e. basically EB; cf. Kenyon and Holland 1983: Figs 62: 3, 64: 10, 80: 4, 92: 19, 116: 9, a 'tripled' loop handle, 118: 3, a 'doubled' handle, 133: 20, 138: 3, 159: 5). One parallel might be cited from Arad's Stratum IV (Amiran 1978: Pl. 9: 10); the rest of the material at Arad includes many of the typical developed jar and jug(let) forms, well into EB II. Similarly, the form is already present in phase I (= 'EB I B') at 'Ai (Callaway 1972: Fig. 15) and thereafter in developed forms up to EB III. Amiran has published a typical burnished high loop-handled juglet from the same site (1969: Photo 50). Most other EB I assemblages show the same trends, and Amiran's summary of the evidence (1969: Photos 29-31) has added valuable parallels from Lebanon which go some way towards affirming a Levantine coastal floruit for the general vessel form, rather than inland southern Syria or Transjordan. Here only Jawa and perhaps Khirbet Umbachi (Dubertret and Dunand 1954/5: Pl. VII: 2) -

but not found at the latter site during a visit in 1988 (Braemer p.c.) - have so far produced potentially related material.

In terms of specific details of handle form and decoration, Jawa's genre F is less diagnostic. However, some very close comparisons are possible and show the same distribution as the variants related to the characteristic high loop-handled juglets. Comparison can be made with examples from Affula (Sukenik 1948: Pl. VIII: 10 - 20) for stabbed, slashed, and scored decoration on handles, the Jericho tombs (Kenyon 1960: Fig. 12: 5, 22, 27, 28, etc.) for handles with decoration close to variants J421/441, applied decoration (Kenyon 1965: Fig. 4: 12) which is very similar to some of the vessels in tomb A 76 at Bab edh-Dhra' (Lapp 1968: Fig. 8: 4, 12), and Tell el-Duweir (Tufnell 1958: Pl. 57: 41, applied decoration). Jawa variants J440/441 are similar to an example from Horvat Beter (Ben-Tor 1966: Fig. 5: 9, cf. also Fig. 5: 3, related to high loop-handled juglets). The applied decoration could be derived from impressed or incised bands which are common throughout the Chalcolithic period (e.g. Tell Turmus/Golan, Dayan 1969: Fig. 4; Epstein 1978a: *passim*), perhaps used to express vestigial handles or lugs. But do such so-called vestigial forms necessarily have to be devolved from 'true' or complete ones? Applied decorative features similar to Jawa's genre F (variants J393-417) are also known at Ghrubba (Mellaart 1956: Fig. 4: 24, 25, probably 'EB I', and on bowls), in the Jerash and wadi Zerqa subregion (Hanbury-Tenison 1987: Fig. 9: 17, 29, 39), at Tell el-Far'ah (de Vaux and Steve 1949, Fig. 8: 32) on pedestal-based bowls which find close parallels at Bab edh-Dhra' (see now Helms 1987a: Fig. 17: 15 - 16), and on bowls (de Vaux 1951: Fig. 11: 11), as well as many plain oval applied or moulded 'vestigial' lugs throughout the assemblage (e.g. de Vaux 1951: Fig. 11: 23, 25, 26, etc.). In general, they may even be related to the raised lumps on 'Esdraelon' wares.

The closest formal parallels for type B (= J418) might be recognized at Tell el-Far'ah in various EB I jars (e.g. de Vaux and Steve 1949: Figs 1: 25, 6: 32).

M (= miscellaneous jar forms [rims only]: variants 450, 451, 456, 458-460, 463-469). The grouping may be subdivided into two jar variants according to the suggested body shape: (i) small 'bag-shaped' jars (J455, 456, 458-460) with near-vertical necks and red painted stripes, and (ii) everted rim jars (J463-469). Variants J457, 458 and 461 are discussed below under bowls (see genre G).

Both jar forms and their variants can be recognized in Palestinian Chalcolithic repertoires, generally categorized as 'jarres à col' (see now Commenge-Pellerin 1987): this applies particularly to the general form of J455 which occurs at Ghrubba (Mellaart 1956: Fig. 6: 108) and in stage 2 at Tell Um Hammad (Betts [ed] in press:

TUH1568). Good examples can also be found in the Chalcolithic
typologies of Palestine (see Commenge-Pellerin 1987: *passim*). Similar
forms occur in the 'Uruk' assemblage at Habuba Kabira (Sürenhagen
1978: Tab. 24: 9, 9, etc.). J458, with its horizontally pierced lug handle
(originally two?) near the rim, can be compared with lugs near the
rim of vessels at Tell Turmus (Dayan 1969: Fig. 8: 20), at Lachish
(Tufnell 1958: Pl. 56.4), Ghrubba (Mellaart 1956: Figs 4: 27, 28, 5: 117,
118), and at Jericho (Garstang 1936: Pl. XXXVII: 11). This type then
may be regarded as a Chalcolithic form in Palestinian terms, within
the qualifications noted above. The similarities may, of course, be
meaningless.

Everted rolled or rounded/pointed jar rims (J460, 463, 467) may
be compared with Chalcolithic examples (e.g. Commenge-Pellerin
1987: Figs 31: 1-6, 32: 2, 6, 50: 9, 14, 51: 2; Levy and Menahem 1987:
Fig. 12.13: 6, 9, etc.; Dayan 1969: Fig. 5: 9) in the Beersheba region and
the Huleh Basin, respectively. Comparable vessels are known at
Habuba Kabira (Sürenhagen 1978: Tab. 6: 63, etc.) although, as we
have already pointed out, such comparisons may be illusory in this
case. EB I A examples come from stage 2 at Tell Um Hammad (Betts
[ed] in progress: TUH1541, 1380). The balance of jar rims in this
grouping is undiagnostic, but for J468, 469 and 450.

J468 finds close parallels in the Beersheba region during the
Chalcolithic period (Commenge-Pellerin 1987: Figs 30: 6[?], 50: 3, 4) as
well as in stage 2 at Tell Um Hammad (Betts [ed.]in press:
TUH1010[?], 219, and 2957). 'Uruk' style examples include vessels
from Habuba Kabira (Sürenhagen 1978: Tab. 11: 74) and al-Kowm
(Cauvin and Stordeur 1985: Fig. 4: 3). Comparison may also be made
with vessels from Hama L (Fugmann 1958: Fig. 13: 3A 360). The rim
form reappears in EB IV in Palestine.

J469, an incomplete rim, can be compared with (Northern)
Chalcolithic vessels at Tell Turmus (Dayan 1969: Fig. 6: 20, 21),
although the slashed decoration at the neck/shoulder junction is a
common form of decoration throughout the Chalcolithic period and
particularly the Early Bronze Age. Finally, J450 (a surface find) recalls
typical EB I B decoration on jars of all sizes, with vertical 'trumpet'
spouts and ledge handles: a good example comes from stage 3 (EB I
B) at Um Hammad (Helms 1986: Fig. 13: 7). Another related vessels
comes from the region of Bab edh-Dhra' (e.g. Helms 1987a: Fig. 14: 11,
[after Saller 1964/5] and discussion there).

But for the one 'later' example (J450), the comparisons given here
fall into the Chalcolithic period and EB I A of Palestine with some
cognate examples within the greater 'Uruk' sphere of Syria,
conforming to the pattern set by the bulk of the Jawa pottery.

Genre G (Types A - K, variants 457, 458, 461, 470-530):

Like the holemouth jars, bowls (genre G) are not normally diagnostic; many of the recovered examples at Jawa are simple in shape and often only preserved as small fragments. Grouping according to types is also difficult for the reasons noted above and because the sample sizes are so small. Thus 'type' K represents but three disparate forms (J457, 461, and 462).

'Type' K (variants 457, 461, 462). J457 has a slightly everted, pointed rim which may relate it to type GA and any number of parallels in both Chalcolithic and EBA repertoires of Palestine and Transjordan. J461, particularly its painted rim, is reminiscent of small Chalcolithic vessels (e.g. types in Commenge-Pellerin 1987: Fig. 26: 8, 11). J462 may not even be a shallow bowl (as it is drawn here), but a flared, everted rim jar. If it is a bowl, its shape might be related to the much cruder shallow bowls of type GG.

Type GA (variants 470-483). It is possible to find apparently related bowl forms in Palestinian Chalcolithic assemblages. For example, several types from the Beersheba region have the same general rim form (e.g. Commenge-Pellerin 1987: Figs 18: 8, 19, *passim* on 'bassins', and 22: 1; Levy and Menahem 1987: Fig. 12.3: 9). Other examples also exist in the Huleh Basin (Dayan 1969: Fig. 5: 8). A similar form is known in the North Syrian 'Uruk' sphere (cf. Sürenhagen 1978: Tabn 1: 12, 21: 54, 66). However, the closest or most direct parallels come from EB I (A) contexts in Palestine and Transjordan (see Helms 1987a: 59 for discussion). Some examples include a broad genre in Tell Um Hammad's stage 2 (Helms 1986: Fig. 10: 4-7, 8; 1987a: Fig. 17: 15). Others come from Jericho - especially the 'Proto Urban' Tombs - Lachish and Bab edh-Dhra' (cf. Helms 1987a: Fig. 14: 4, 5, 7-9; cf. also Kenyon and Holland 1982: Fig. 36: 11-16, 1983: Figs 13: 23 [PU], 14: 5 [PU/EB], 44: 3 [PNA-PU], 50: 1 [PU/EB], 132: 18 [PU: = J482]). Recessed rims of similar form are known in contemporary and later contexts (Amuq F/G) in Northern Syria (Braidwood and Braidwood 1960: Fig. 172: 30-32, with a false 'trumpet spout' 34; compare J450).

The evidence from Tell Um Hammad and the area of the Jordan/Zerqa confluence indicates that the type appears there in a slightly different form just before the 'introduction' of some of the genres typical of Jawa's assemblage. These earlier forms can be shown to develop into shapes which are directly comparable with Jawa's type GA. Similarly, these types can be shown to develop further in the Jordan Valley, well into EB I B and even EB II.

Type GB (variants 484-489). These thin-walled bowls (but for J484) find their closest formal parallels in EB I A fine, red polished, shallow bowls which are common throughout stage 2 at Tell Um Hammad (Helms 1986: Fig., 10: 8, 12; 1987a, Fig. 7: 17; also compare examples from O.T. Jericho in Kenyon and Holland 1983: Figs 11: 6, 56: 30 [= J484], 84: 11 [J486], 130: 7, mostly 'PU'). I have argued that this type may represent a coastal Levantine form which can be traced as far north as Cilicia (Helms 1987a: Fig. 19, and discussion). The examples from Jawa, however, are plain, not as finely made, and never burnished or polished in the same manner. There may, therefore, be no relationship at all between them and the western types. J484, on the other hand, might can be regarded as a distant relative of smaller 'bols coniques' of the Palestinian Chalcolithic repertoires (e.g. Commenge-Pellerin 1987: Fig. 18, *passim*). Comparable forms exist in Hama L (Fugmann 1958: Fig. 13: 7B 410). Similar fine, shallow bowls are known in the assemblage at Habuba Kabira (Sürenhagen 1978: Tab. 2: 25).

Types GC (variants 490-496) and GD (variants 497-503). Both types can be considered together: their forms are simple and very similar, type GD being slightly heavier in fabric and deeper in body. Parallels from Palestinian Chalcolithic contexts come from the Beersheba area (Commenge-Pellerin 1987: Figs 17: 17, 19, 45: 2, 3, 5, etc.; de Contenson 1956: Fig. 6, etc.; Perrot *et al.* 1967: Fig. 15: 1, etc.), and also from Azor farther north (e.g. Perrot 1961: Fig. 37: 32) as well as the Jawlan/Huleh area (Dayan 1969: Fig. 4: 6, with impressed band decoration). Similar forms occur at Habuba Kabira and in Hama K9 and K8 (Sürenhagen 1978: Tab. 2: 27; Fugmann 1958: Fig. 30: 5B 829 No.7, etc.).

The same simple, not very diagnostic, shape also occurs in Palestinian and Transjordanian contexts in EB I: for example, at Um Hammad (Helms 1984a: Fig. 10: 1 where the form is related to local, early versions of type GA [see above]); at Ai and O.T. Jericho (see Amiran 1969: Pls 11: 2, 12: 4); N.T. Jericho together with 'Esdraelon' wares (Pritchard 1958: Pl. 57: 18; Kenyon and Holland 1983: Figs 12: 1, 16: 10, 126: 5, 130: 18 [J496] for type C, and 17: 27, 128: 9 for type D); and at Tell el-Far'ah in both 'énéolithique moyen' and 'supérieur' (de Vaux and Steve 1947: Fig. 1: 27-29; de Vaux 1952: Fig. 10: 10, etc.). Similar forms also occur at O.T. Jericho, but mostly in EB I B contexts (Kenyon and Holland 1982: Fig. 34: 26, 27).

Type GE (variants 504-507). Hardly worthy of the grouping 'type', GE further divides into two: J504/505 and J506/507. Both have bevelled rims; the former is externally grooved and more closed in form.

The rim form (especially J404/405) is somewhat reminiscent of rims common in Palestinian Chalcolithic repertoires: for example, in the Beersheba region (e.g. Commenge-Pellerin 1987: Fig. 20: 1, 6, 'bassin'; de Contenson 1956: Fig. 8: 12, large 'bols coniques'). But none of these parallels is convincing and we might, therefore, conclude that the form has no meaningful parallels in Palestinian Chalcolithic repertoires.

A similar situation pertains with regard to the EB I repertoires of Palestine and Transjordan (e.g. Kenyon and Holland 1983: Fig. 53: 2 [EB]?). Leonard (1983: 41) relates the Jawa type to a form of large, crude pithos or krater (EB I B: cf. Helms 1986: *passim*) at Kataret es-Samra near Tell Um Hammad. I find this hard to accept. Both form and scale of the vessels are very different; also, the 'date' is a little late. There appear, therefore, to be no parallels in EB I (A or B), but for some vaguely similar rim forms which probably stem from the Chalcolithic 'bassins' noted above (e.g. de Vaux and Steve 1948: Fig. 5: 5, 1949: Fig. 8: 7). A possibly related form (to the Jawa type) does, however, come into fashion during EB II (cf. de Vaux and Steve 1947: Fig. 7: 17) and is typologically related to the common 'hammer-rimmed' bowls or platters whose origins probably lie in north/central Syria and even Anatolia where such vessels occur during the 4th millennium (e.g. at Hama: Fugmann 1958: Fig. 37: 4B 958).

A few distant parallels can be cited from the repertoire at Habuba Kabira (Sürenhagen 1978: Tab. 22: 86), again closer to the Chalcolithic 'bassins', noted above, than small bowls. Reasonable parallels for J504/505 can perhaps be recognized in the Amuq F assemblages in northern Syria (Braidwood and Braidwood 1960: Fig. 174: 13, 14).

Type GF (variants 508-510). Rather like the previous 'type', GE finds no convincing parallels in either Chalcolithic or EB I repertoires of Palestine and Transjordan. Vaguely similar rim forms do occur in a class of conical bowls (or 'bassins') in the Beersheba area (Commenge-Pellerin 1987: Fig. 45: 15; Levy and Menahem 1987: Fig. 12.5: 3), often with thumb-impressed decoration along the rim. There is nothing of the kind at Tell Um Hammad during EB I. Therefore, we might conclude that type GE probably has nothing to do with the lands south and southwest of Jawa; but comparison might be made with forms at O.T. Jericho which include Hennessy's redrawn 'bevelled rim bowl' (see above; e.g Kenyon and Holland 1983, Figs 129: 7 [= J508], 130: 14 [= J509]).

However, several much closer comparisons can be made with vessels from Habuba Kabira (e.g. Sürenhagen 1978: Tabn 2: 24, 21: 44, 45, 52). A similar form comes from the Amuq F assemblage (Braidwood and Braidwood 1960: Fig. 174: 12). It may be possible that type GF is related to north/central Syrian repertoires.

Type GG (variants J511-525). These crudely made bowls and/or platters are, at first glance, undiagnostic. However, cognate forms do exist in some 4th millennium repertoires. The type can be sub-divided into shallow and deep forms and then, in turn, into round-based and flat-based platters, and rounded and (but one example: J525) slightly everted-rimmed bowls.

There are no obvious parallels in either the Chalcolithic or the EB I repertoires of Palestine/Transjordan, unless such poorly made vessels have simply not been published. Possible distant 'relatives' might be seen in the 'cuvettes' of the Beersheba area (Commenge-Pellerin 1987: Fig. 52: 2). Some distant cognate forms occur at Ghrubba (Mellaart 1956: Figs 4: 2-4, 18, 5: 62) and J525 might find a parallel in a vessel from Horvat Beter (Dothan 1959b: Fig. 13: 17). During EB I, the type (GG) may be distantly related to platters such as the one from Megiddo XVIII (e.g. Amiran 1969: Pl. 13: 1 = J520/521) which continue in use into EB II (e.g. Amiran 1969, Pl. 15: 6, 8). There may be some distant parallels at O.T. Jericho, mostly in 'Proto Urban' contexts (Kenyon and Holland 1983: Figs 48: 10 [= J525], 130: 12, 131: 16 [J525?], 137: 15). No parallels were found at Tell Um Hammad and we can probably suggest that type GG has nothing much to do with either Cis- or Transjordan, always with the understanding that the crudeness of execution and manufacture may render comparisons immaterial. But, there are some relatively close parallels among the shapes from Habuba Kabira (Sürenhagen 1978: Tbn 1: 15-18, 20: 28-34 = J525; Tbn 3: 38, 39, 43, etc., 22: C 2-7, 23, 10 = platters from Jawa). Platters, and one possible parallel for J525, exist at Hama in stage K (Fugmann 1958: Fig. 30: 7A 655 No 27a, 37: 7B 408 No 16). Tentatively, then, type GG may have a north/central Syrian origin.

Type GH (variants 526-528). On the basis of similar fabric, the purposive isolated depression in the rim of J527, and traces of burning on the rims, this type probably served as a lamp. Lamps have not been recognized in Chalcolithic repertoires as a purpose-made form, although broken vessels and small bowls with traces of burning along the rim have been found. Widely spaced depressions in the rims of some vessels were probably not used to hold wicks (e.g. Perrot 1961: Fig. 38: 18, etc. for 'coupes à pied fenestré'). Nor can a unique bowl from Abu Zureiq have been a lamp (Anati 1971: Fig. 18: a black burnished bowl with four symmetrical, up-turned, and pinched protrusions along the rim).

EB I repertoires do not appear to contain a purpose-made lamp form. However, small shallow bowls such as those from Tell Um Hammad's stage 2 (see genre GB above) commonly have traces of burning along their rims which has been identified as stemming from a vegetable oil (Moffat p.c.). Some possible parallels might exists in 'Proto Urban - EB I' contexts at O.T. Jericho (e.g. Kenyon and Holland 1983: Figs 17: 20, 18: 11 ['spout' = J527], 51: 7).

Types GI and GJ are undiagnostic, but for the obvious carination in J529, a design or manufacturing feature which does not become known in Palestine/Transjordan until EB II during the 3rd millennium BC. J529 comes from a context (see Chapter 2: Fig. 66) which may not be securely stratified. However, unless the form be regarded as a Middle Bronze Age type (its fabric militates against this: it is in keeping with other EB I fabrics at Jawa), it must belong to the early occupation at the site, i.e. in the 4th millennium BC.

Carinated forms earlier than those of the Palestinian EB II repertoires occur commonly in north/central Syria: examples may be compared at Hama (Fugmann 1958: Fig. 37: 4B 613, etc.) and at Habuba Kabira (Sürenhagen 1978: Tabn 3: 33-35, 20: 15, 19, 21: 64-66, 22: 72). Painted and other decorated forms are discussed below (Chapter 4, 'Painted Patterns').

Bases X (variants 551-619)

But for J550 (see also Chapter 4), which has a good parallel at Habuba Kabira, the balance of bases can be compared to Chalcolithic and EB I (and later) types throughout Palestine and Transjordan. They are simple and not very diagnostic. One clear connection with Chalcolithic/EB I types is represented in variants J560, 564-567, with their thumb-impressed pedestal bases. Another form (round-based) is more common in north/central Syria than in the southern areas during the 4th millennium BC. Ring bases with downward protruding central bosses have been discussed above under genres CA, CB, and CC. Their origin most likely lies in North/Central Syria, as we have said, despite a few Palestinian parallels in EB I (B) which, of course in their turn, could be derived from northern proto-types (see Helms 1987a).

The pottery of the Middle Bronze Age

Pottery from the later occupation at Jawa has been partly published in a study of Jawa's role in the economic history and historical geography of the early 2nd millennium BC (Helms 1989a). The pottery section of that work is included here in order to present all of the ceramic data from the site together.

All non-stratified sherds (i.e. UT ++++) come from the surface in either the 'citadel' or the immediate vicinity of the various outbuildings. Sherds designated with square numbers (i.e. C2 ++++) are surface finds in those loci, or derived from cleaning operations.

Very little pottery was recovered from the excavations and soundings into these later building complexes of Jawa. Intensive survey of standing remains and their immediate vicinity similarly yielded a meagre sample. It is doubtful whether further clearance would change the nature of the sample meaningfully. Any date range is, therefore, internally limited (by the size of the sample), and, in any case, necessarily imprecise when based on distant stylistic parallels whose reliability is not uniformly secure.

Cooking Vessels (Fig. 154)

The most common form appears to be a crude cooking vessel with rounded or slightly bevelled inturned sides, a flat base, and two horizontal, rounded and incised ledge handles near the rim. The form, though more elaborate, is typical of Palestinian repertoires in use during MB II A. Precise formal and decorative parallels can be found both in central Palestine and in northwestern Syria, in contexts which are dated in the EB IV/EB-MB period (late 3rd millennium). One Palestinian parallel - specifically a ledge handle on a bowl, not a cooking pot - occurs at Tell Iktanu 2 (Prag 1971: Fig. 25.1; 1974, Fig. 7: 5). Prag has also referred to a similar form in the Damascus Museum (1971). The Syrian parallels come from the Idlib area (Egami 1983: Fig. 4: 14, level VII = 'Early Bronze Age with Middle Bronze Age...'), contemporary with Syrian 'caliciform' pottery (e.g. Dever 1980: Fig. 5) which can be related to assemblages ranging from the Amuq valley (Braidwood and Braidwood 1960), to Qatna (du Mesnil du Buisson 1935), as well as to some tomb groups in northern Palestine: e.g. Ma'ayan Barukh (Amiran 1961: Fig. 6: cf. especially 7, 4); Qedesh (Tadmor 1978: Fig. 8); and Megiddo (e.g. Amiran 1969: Pl. 24: 1-6; also Dever 1980: Fig. 5). The general vessel form is also related to examples with wavy, thumb-impressed, folded and plain ledge handles, common in central Palestine in the later EB IV/EB-MB range (e.g. Glueck 1951: Pls 129: 1, 10, 130: 4-13, 131: 23, 24, 132: 15, 142: 13,5, 151: 10; Helms 1986: Fig. 17: 11, 12, 14). There is also a generic relationship with MB II A and later cooking pots, as we have already noted (e.g. Tel Burga, Kochavi et al.: 1979, Fig. 11: 7).

Bowls (Fig. 155)

Deep bowls with almond-shaped or collared rims and an external groove find parallels in EBIV contexts at Tell Hadidi (Dornemann 1979: Figs 12: 7-9, 23-27, 16: 5?, 18: 7, 8, 10) and in Hama J7 (Fugmann 1958: Fig. 62: 3K 227, 3H 189). Related forms appear in MB II A assemblages in Palestine: e.g. Megiddo XV and XIV (Loud 1948: Pl. 14: 7; cf. also Amiran 1969: Pl. 25: 4, 5, 8) and the Golan (Jawlan) dolmen (Epstein 1985b: Fig. 5: 2). The plain bowl (J631) may be compared with MB II examples (e.g. Golan dolmen, Epstein 1985b: Fig. 6: 7).

The krater rim (J632) is known from MB II contexts in both Syria and Palestine: convincing examples come from Tell Hadidi (Dornemann 1979: Figs 21: 32-37, 22: 17), Ebla III (Matthiae 1980: Figs 34, 35, etc.), and MB II A Tels Burga and Zeror (Kochavi et al. 1979:

Figs 10: 16, 17: 18). A related form exists at Hama in stage H5 (Fugmann 1958: Fig. 109: 3K 162).

Rolled-rim bowls (J633/634) could be related to 'caliciform' (EB IV) 'tea pots' (e.g. Dever 1980: Fig. 5: cf. top two rows), as well as MB II(A and B) krater rims (e.g. Amiran 1969: Pl. 29).

Carinated bowls (J635-638) with recessed rims are common in MB II (A) assemblages in both Syria and Palestine. Comparison may be made with shapes from Tell Hadidi (Dornemann 1979: Fig. 20: 46, 47; but note recessed rims in EB IV contexts there, Figs 16: 247, 19: 7), Megiddo XIV (e.g. Amiran 1969: Pl. 24: 1, 2), Tell Beit Mirsim G-F (Albright 1933: Pl. 4: 1, *passim*), Aphek/Antipatris, Tells Poleg, Burga and Zeror (Kochavi *et al.* 1979: Figs 4: 3, 14, 17, 27, 7: 4, 13, 14, 8: 3, 16, 10: 3, 11: 5, 17: 9, 18: 19; for Aphek cf. also Beck 1985: 196ff.), and the Golan dolmen (Epstein 1985a: Fig. 5: 3).

Rounded or globular bowls, one with reserved slip decoration in horizontal bands, (J639/640) stand half-way between EB IV ('caliciform') and MB II A forms: e.g. bowls (related to goblets) from Megiddo, Hama J5, Qatna, etc. (e.g. Dever 1980: Fig. 5: cf. bottom row), and Aphek/Antipatris and Tel Poleg (Kochavi *et al.* 1979: Figs 4: 29, 30, 8: 3). The characteristic ridge at the neck/shoulder junction may link one of the body sherds to this group (e.g. J657), but see also jars below.

Jars (Figs 156 and 157: body sherds)

All jars can be closely related to Syro-Palestinian forms current in MB II A. There are three types: triangular rims (J641-645); rilled rims (J646-649); and rolled or rounded rims (J650-653). The combed decorative bands, including wavy line patterns in horizontal registers (J655/656/658-661), belong to this general grouping (e.g. Holland 1980, *passim*). The body sherd (J657), with its ridge, can be linked to bowls (above), or to jars (e.g. = body sherd J655 here).

The first group of jars finds close parallels at Tell Hadidi (Dornemann 1979: Fig. 22: 7, 8, 10, etc.), Mardikh/Ebla (Matthiae 1980), Tell Beit Mirsim [D] E (Albright 1933: Pl. 7: 10), Megiddo stratum XIV (Loud 1948: Pl. 13: 2), Jericho (Kenyon and Holland 1983: Fig 164: 3, 166: 13, 192: 3), Aphek/Antipatris (Kochavi *et al.* 1979: Figs 4: 9, 11, 14), Hazor (Yadin *et al.* 1958: Pl. 113: 1, 3, 4), and the Golan dolmen (Epstein 1985b: Fig. 4: 20, 21 for decoration). Rilled rim jars of the second group (J646-649) may be compared with examples which come mostly from Palestinian MB II A assemblages such as Megiddo XIIIB/XIV (Loud 1948: Pls 12: 17, 18, 19, 27, 16: 10), Aphek/Antipatris, Tells Poleg and Burga (Kochavi *et al.* 1979: Figs 4: 10, 8: 19, 20, 11: 16?), and Jericho (Kenyon and Holland 1982: Fig. 127, *passim*, 1983: Figs 168: 16-18, 171: 8). Related forms might be seen at Mardikh/Ebla III[B] (Matthiae 1980). The third group (J650-653) has a similar distribution in terms of parallels (Epstein 1985b: Fig. 4: 21). Parallels may also be found at Tell es-Salihiyeh, in the Damascene (Osten 1956: Fig. 95). Comparison can also be made with examples in a summary of Syrian pottery by Dornemann (1984).

Body Sherds and Bases (Fig. 49: J654/662-667)

The loop handle (J654), though not very diagnostic, can be fitted into MB II [A] repertoires of Palestine (e.g. Ras el-`Ain/Aphek-Antipatris, see Ory 1938: 118: 88; see also Amiran 1969: Pl. 28: 2-5, from Megiddo XII-XIIA). The same holds for carinations (J662), and flat and ring-bases (J663/665/666). Button-based burnished [piriform] juglets (J664/667) have been considered to be limited to MB II B assemblages in Palestine (e.g. Amiran 1969: 112), but this may be illusory (compare now Tel Zeror 'MB II A pottery', Kochavi *et al.* 1979: Fig. 18: 23).

Relative Chronology

On the albeit limited basis of comparative ceramic study it is, nevertheless, possible to posit a date range for the construction and use of the later building complexes at Jawa. The majority of parallels suggest MB II A in Palestinian terms, and MBA in Syrian ones, with the possible exception of Mardikh/Ebla (i.e. some parallels in Mardikh IIIB). Moreover, several examples indicate a date early in the Syrian typological/chronological terminology (MBA), and this is underlined by the presence of forms - including a common genre (J622-628) - which can be placed late in both Syrian and Palestinian EBA assemblages of the later 3rd millennium BC and assemblages of the early 2nd millennium BC.

The stratigraphic evidence shows that the complexes were neither occupied for a long time, nor that they underwent obvious reconstruction. Therefore, we might suggest that the small sample of pottery is an isochronal assemblage representative of several repertoires which could be regarded as a 'transitional' stage between EB IV and the beginning of MB II A, at least in terms of 'Palestinian' and perhaps also South Syrian assemblages (i.e. the Hawran and the Damascene/Ghuta). This is the traditional and still current conception (see now Gerstenblith 1983 on terminology). The use of the term 'transitional' is, however, misleading and somewhat barren. It merely describes what is happening to pottery assemblages and no more. Usage such as heterogeneity or even eclecticism (in the art historical sense) might be more appropriate: i.e. with the notion here that Jawa's later pottery is a mixture of types taken from two or more contemporary repertoires. If this can be corroborated elsewhere, we may further suggest that the more recognizably Palestinian EB IV sherds published from Khirbet Umbachi (Dubertret and Dunand 1954/55; Braemer p.c.: some precisely paralleled in EB IV pottery of the Jordan Valley) could also be contemporary, though, of course, not represented at Jawa. And, if this is so, we may be dealing with a plurality of repertoire preference (an imposed, rather than aesthetic eclecticism) as well as a variety of settled, semi-settled, and nomadic folk in the *badiyat al-sham* and its more verdant fringes at about the turn of the 3rd millennium. The absolute time range in the widest terms of current typological constructs may be supposed to be a century on either side of 2000 BC.

The 4th millennium BC repertoires in time and space

A detailed analysis is not possible since, as we have said, the state of exploration and publication is in its infancy regarding all of the Near East during the 4th millennium BC so far as reliable pottery typologies are concerned. But a tabular arrangement (Table 3) showing the general localization of genres and types does provide some further insights. The important limitation to remember is the almost completely undocumented record in the south of Syria, in the Jawlan/Hawran Hawran, Jebel Druze, and the Damascene (but for personal communications). Table 3 is arranged according to zones (cf. also Fig. 158a): Palestine/Transjordan, the coastal Levant, southern Syria, and north-central Syria.

Four categories of genre/type distribution are evident. The first consists of genres which appear to be either exclusively Palestinian or Syrian. Some of these genres probably stem from local Chalcolithic traditions (i.e. genres A, B, and perhaps F are Palestinian or coastal Levantine; genres C, D Syrian). The second category consists of genres whose types occur exclusively either in Palestine or Syria (i.e. genres E, G); the third, genres whose types appear in both Palestine and Syria (also genres E, G); and the fourth, genres which are known or have been seen in southern Syria (i.e. genres B, C; Braemer p.c.). These localizations are plotted on the map in Figure 158b and suggest that we are dealing with two discrete repertoires, one Palestinian the other Syrian: i.e. repertoire 1 = genres A, B and F; repertoire 2 = genres C and C. Both are in use at Jawa which proves contact between the site and those two separate zones, a contact which may have been indirect but one which does not exist in the same way in either of the two greater zones. Secondly, the genres whose *types* can be exclusively traced to either one or the other zone, should be perhaps be sub-divided into separate genres and added to the two main repertoires (i.e. genres G: types D to G and I to repertoire 2 [Syria]). Those genres which share types might be regarded as of Syrian origin, reaching Palestine via an intermediate zone (e.g. southern Syria; i.e. genres E and G, types A, B, C). Genre F and genre G type B can have been introduced via the coastal Levant. Jawa's heterogeneous pottery assemblage, therefore, is typical of an interim zone in terms of diffusion and contact.

Table 3. Distribution of parallel repertoires

GENRE	TYPE	PALESTINE/ TRANSJORDAN	COASTAL LEVANT	SOUTH SYRIA	N/C SYRIA
A	A	•			
	B	•			
	C	•			
	D	•			
	E	•			
	F	•			
	G	•			
	H	•			
	I	•			
	J	•			
	K	•			
B	A	•			
	B	•	•		
	C	•			
C	A		•		
	B			•	
	C			•	
	D			•	
	E		•		
	F		•		
D	A			•	
	B			•	
E	A	•			•
	B	•			•
	C	•			•
	D			•	
	E			•	
F	A	•	•		
	B	•	•		
M		•			•
G	A	•			•
	B	•		•	
	C			•	
	D			•	
	E			•	
	F			•	
	G			•	
	H	•			
	I				
	J			•	
	K	•			
J550					•

Comparable material from northern upland Transjordan is still too sparse to make any concrete judgements in terms of local distribution patterns. However, it does appear as if there was a concentration of some parallels in the north/central part of Transjordan, along wadi Zerqa and in the central Jordan Valley (i.e Tell Um Hammad and its neighbours, including Tell Handaquq North). This distribution does not presently appear west of the Jordan River, nor in the northern Jordan Valley. Whether a distinct route of diffusion might be reconstructed is debatable, though not impossible.

The time-range of the comparable material lies in the 4th millennium BC. This can be made more precise in Palestinian terms because of the stratigraphy of Tell Um Hammad where the parallels for Jawa appear in only EB I A contexts (stage 2), definitely before the so-called EB I B pottery types. Of these (EB I B), a very characteristic type is the 'grain-washed' wares most typical of northern Transjordan, though also distributed as far as Megiddo in the Yezre'el Valley. These types have also been seen at Laboué and at Khirbet Umbachi (Braemer p.c.). No Jawa parallels were evident at these two sites. In terms of diffusion patterns through time, this could suggest that the Jawa assemblage represents a period of as yet limited contact between Palestine and Cisjordan.

FABRICS

With the exception of the small sample analyzed in Appendix B, the fabric codes (fb) of the assemblage have been based on subjective classification which is set out in Table 4. Table 5 summarizes the correlation between genre/types and fabric codes and gives a breakdown in terms of frequency of occurrence (see also Figs 107 and 108a). The correlation between fabric codes and genre/types is tabulated in Table 6, as is the frequency of occurrence of the former (see also Fig. 108b). The material collected from test area UT4 was recorded in terms of fabric clusters, as follows: a = fb 9; b = fbs 3 + 5 + 8; c =fb 10; d = fb 12; and e = fbs 1 + 2 (see Table 7 for frequency of occurrence in the test area and Fig. 109a). The relative frequency of occurrence according to this clustering in the excavated sample is tabulated in Table 8 (see also Fig. 109b) in which an additional cluster (f) comprises fbs 4 + 7 + 6 + 7 + 11 + fabrics of 'genres' X (bases). Results from the test area, where only five diagnostic shapes (genre B) were found, show a numerical inversion in comparison with genre frequency within the excavated assemblage. Notably, fabric code cluster b (representative of the largest genre [A]) is less frequent in the surface collection (compare Fig. 109a, b). Similarly, fine fabrics (cluster e) are less frequent in the surface collection. The rest follow the same order. Reasons for such results may be limited to the fact that body sherds of holemouth jars (genre A) are very friable and do not survive as well as others since most of these vessels were severely charred through use. Similarly, necessarily smaller body sherds of fine fabrics tend not to survive at the surface (or are easily overlooked), while diagnostic shapes encountered in excavation tend to be more numerous: that is to say, a small, fine pot will break into more recognisable, formally diagnostic fragments than a cruder, larger vessel. When the geographical distribution of genre/types (see 'Comparative Study' above) is expressed in numerical terms, 59.8 per cent can be related to the south, 26.5 per cent to the north (Table 9; see also Figs 158-9), leaving 13.7 per cent (= 'genres' M and X) unprovenanced. When this is expressed in terms of fabrics, the following distribution results: south, 65 per cent; north, 18 per cent; and unaccountable (fb 12 and fabrics of bases [X] 17 per cent (Table 10).

Table 4. Fabric codes

fb	name	colour	temper	comments
01	FINE	grey	?	grey-green slip ext., wheel turned
02	FINE CREAM	yellow/pink	?	some examples painted
03	CREAM	yellow/pink	?	some examples vitrified
04	IMITATION FINE	grey/brown	chaff	darkened cores, ext. pattern burnished (red/brown)
05	RED	light red/yellow	?	red slipped ext., some examples painted
06	MOTTLED	grey/black	calcite	over-fired
07	THIN HMJ	grey/black	calcite	
08	HMJ	grey/yellow	shell/flint	pink/cream, slip ext., many examples charred in use.
09	RED CHAFF	red/brown	chaff	blackened cores, ext. pattern burnished (red), coil built
10	CRUDE	grey/black	chaff	most examples over-fired
11	GREY-RED	light grey/red	?	
12	MISC.	various	various	anomalies, unclassified

Table 5. GEN/TYP fabrics

GEN/TYP	fb	n	%	tot./GEN	%
AA	8	101	15.9		
AB	8	8	1.3		
AC	7	19	3.0		
AD	7	5	0.8		
AE	10	19	3.0		
AF	3	1	0.2		
AG	10	8	1.3	185	29
AH	12	4	0.6		
AI	12	5	0.8		
AJ	12	10	1.6		
AK	12	3	0.5		
A?	2	1	0.2		
A?	8	1	0.2		
BA	2	5	0.8		
BB	3	13	2.1	79	12
BC	3	61	9.6		
CA	1	8	1.3		
CB	4	9	1.4		
CC	4	16	2.5	88	14
CD	9	6	0.9		
CE	9	14	2.2		
CF	9	35	5.5		
DA	11	3	0.5		
DB	11	6	0.9	9	1
EA	3	13	2.1		
EB	2		1.9		
EC	2	27	4.63	56	9
ED	2	3	0.5		
EE	2	1	0.2		
FA	3/5	48	7.6		
FB	10	1	0.2	49	8
M	12	8	1.3		
M	5	3	0.5	14	2
M	3/5	3	0.5		
GA	3/5	14	2.2		
GB	4	6	0.9		
GC	7	7	1.1		
GD	6	7	1.1		
GE	4	4	0.6	61	10
GF	12	3	0.5		
GG	10	15	2.4		
GH	3/5	3	0.5		
GI	12	1	0.2		
GJ	12	1	0.2		
HA	3/5	11	1.7		
HB	12	7	1.1	18	3
X	3/5	6	0.9		
X	12	1	0.2	76	12
X	?	69	10.9		
		TOTAL		635	

Table 6. Fabrics and GEN/TYP

fb	1	2	3	4	5	6	7	8	9	10	11	12
		A?	AF				AC	AA		AE		AH
							AD	AB		AG		AI
												AJ
												AK
		BA	BB									
			BC									
	CA			CB					CD			
				CC					CE			
									CF			
											DA	
											DB	
		EB	EA									
		EC										
		ED										
		EE										
			FA		FA							
		GA	GB		GA	GD	GC			FB		
			GE							GG		GF
			HA		HA							GI
			M		M							HB
												M

fb	1	2	3	4	5	6	7	8	9	10	11	12
n	8	49	|	35	|	7	31	110	55	43	9	40
				\176/								
%	1	8	|	6	|	1	5	17	9	7	1	6
				\28/								

x = 11%   n = 635

Table 7. Frequency of fabric clusters in test area (UT4)

fbc	n	%
(a)	376	37
(b)	304	30
(c)	183	18
(d)	147	14
(e)	16	1
	1026	

Table 8. Frequency of fabric clusters in excavated sample

fbc	fb(s)	GENRES & TYPES									N	%
(a)	9			CD CE CF							55	9
(b)	3/5/8	AA AB AF	BB BC			EA	FA	GA	HA	M	286	45
(c)	10	AE AG					FB	GG			43	7
(d)	12	AH AI AJ AK						GF	HB	M	40	6
(e)	1/2	A?	BA	CA	EB EC ED EE						57	9
(f)	4/6/7/11+X										154	24

n = 635

Table 9. Frequency of GEN/TYP according to typology

zone	GENRES AND VARIANTS					n	%
SOUTH	AA-K	BA-C	EA-C	FA-B	GA-C	380	59.8
NORTH	CA-F	DA-B	EC-E	GD-I	HA-B	168	26.5
		M	X			87	13.7

n = 635

Table 10. Frequency of fabrics according to typology

zone	fbs	%
SOUTH	2/3/5/7/8/10	65
NORTH	1/4/6/9/11	18
	12 + X	17

n = 635

4. Stamped, Incised, and Painted Designs on Pottery

S.W. HELMS

Jawa's pottery repertoire is small and Jawa lies at some distance from the more verdant regions of the southern Levant, southern Syria, and Transjordan. Any idiosyncracies within the repertoire are, therefore, of utmost importance, particularly when they may reflect specialization and long-distance stylistic or technical correspondence in other repertoires. Ostensibly decorative elements, some with potentially real economic functions, can be useful in tracing connections within the Late Chalcolithic and EBI landscape (see Helms 1987a, 1987b).

The decorative designs under discussion here fall into three categories: (i) stamped impressions on the handles and body of vessels, all made before firing; (ii) incised or embossed patterns added before as well as after firing; and (iii) painted designs, usually on a cream-coloured slip over yellow/reddish fabrics. Of these the first category is the most useful for long-range links since precise parallels have now been found on near-identical vessels at Tell Um Hammad and related sites in the central Jordan Valley.

STAMP SEAL IMPRESSIONS

Moorey has recently stressed the importance of stamp seals in the Ancient Near East, and the fact that they have too long been overshadowed by their more complicated and picturesque 'cousins', the roll seals (Moorey [ed.] 1984, 1988). This bias is particularly relevant to Jawa and its related sites in the southern Levant where the sudden appearance of stamp seals is roughly contemporary with the development of complex economic and social systems in Mesopotamia (Sumer) and north/central Syria; and where shortly afterwards (in the 3rd millennium BC) the southern Levant also saw the development of more complex socio-economic systems in contrast to the Chalcolithic period. The most monumental expression of the new order were nucleated and militarised settlements which, however, have been wrongly called 'cities' and even 'city states' (see Amiran 1986; Beit-Arieh 1986), precisely because of the Syro-Mesopotamian Vorbild. Others have tried to re-state principles of 'urbanism' in Palestinian terms, following Gordon Childe's hypotheses (e.g. Kempinski 1978, 1983 and references there; Childe 1950). At first glance, the stamp seals and their specialized use might seem to support these notions. This, however, is not the case: the answers, when we will have them, will be both simpler and more complex.

Catalogue

J162 (C2/503.2: Fig. 160). Vessel maximum width = 10.0 centimetres. There are three preserved sets, each consisting of two identical impressions which were applied to the vessel before firing. It is possible, indeed likely, that all impressions were made with the same carved object (see now Mabry n.d.: Fig. 14: 5). The pattern consists of a long vertical line from which sprout a series of shorter, oblique ones (average 0.15 centimetres wide), all within an oval register measuring 1.9 x 0.8 centimetres. The shorter lines or ridges sometimes cross the vertical line, sometimes not (cf. J163). The lines or ridges measure a maximum 0.1 centimetres high. Two sets of impressions were stamped on the up-turned lugs, and one half-way between and in line with the lugs. If the original vessels had four lugs (cf. J163), a maximum of eight sets of impressions could be reconstructed. All impressions are more or less vertical and in line with the vertical axis of the vessel.

J163 (F2/405.8: Fig. 161). Maximum vessel width = 6.5 centimetres. Two sets of doubled, identical impressions are preserved on the shoulder of the vessel, half way between the two preserved lugs. The pattern of the impressions consists of a vertical line bisected by shorter horizontal ones (average 0.12 centimetres wide, 0.16 centimetres high) within an oblong register, rounded at each end, measuring 2.26 x 0.63 centimetres. It is possible to reconstruct two further handles (compare also the hole-mouth jars in the repertoire: see Chapter 3, genre AA) and, therefore, a possible maximum of four sets of impressions. All impressions are vertical and in line with the vertical axis of the host vessel.

J174 (UT4/TA ++++: Fig. 162). Maximum estimated vessel width = 17/20 centimetres. The single impression was made on the upper side of a rounded, slightly up-turned ledge handle, offset to the left and at an oblique angle to the centre line of the handle. The ware of the host vessel is crude and hence the impression is unclear. It is, however, possible to see that the original design must have consisted of two vertical lines, crossed by shorter horizontal ones (about 0.1 centimetres wide, 0.07 centimetres high), within a rounded, oblong register (about 0.93 centimetres wide, up to 2.42 centimetres long: i.e. to the edge of the handle), resulting in more or less equally scaled squares. By analogy with related vessels, only two ledge handles would have been attached: thus a maximum of two impressions is possible.

J176 (F4c/720.18a: Fig. 163). Maximum estimated vessel width = 20/24 centimetres. A set of two, probably vertical impressions was made on the upper side of a rounded, slightly up-turned ledge handle at an oblique angle with and on the centre line of the handle. Both impressions are incomplete at the outer edges but may be reconstructed as consisting of a series of short horizontal lines crossing an off-centre vertical one (about 0.14 centimetres wide, 0.07 centimetres high). This pattern is set into an irregular oval register (? maximum 2.32 centimetres long, 1.08 centimetres wide). A maximum of two sets of impressions is possible (cf. J174 above).

J449 (+++++: *Fig. 164*). Maximum estimated vessel width = 10 centimetres. J449 does not have a stamp seal impression, but simply a pair of shallow holes stabbed into the pushed-up, rounded lug handle on the shoulder of the vessel. But by analogy with the shape and design of both J162 and J163, it is included here (see also impressed ledge handles below).

It has been shown (Chapter 3) that all of the seal impressions were made on related host vessels, all of them within one genre (B: but see also discussion of parallels from Um Hammad and the relationship with genre/type AA). These vessels are not burnished, and many have drilled mendholes which may indicate that they were meant to contain only dry goods, at least in their mended state. It is possible to see a broad pattern in terms of secondary features such as the size, number and position of handles, for example, in relation to overall size or capacity. This, however, cannot be taken too far since the sample is too small. Stamps appear to be related to handles or their vicinity and this reflects or, rather, presages much later practice in Syria and Palestine when such impressions were mostly made in the same places.

In so far as typological analysis may be relevant, the patterns can be divided into two basic groups: (i) single vertical line crossed by horizontal or near horizontal/oblique, shorter ones, all within an oval register resulting in rectangular components; and (ii) double vertical lines crossed by horizontal shorter lines within an oval register, resulting in a checkerboard pattern of roughly equally scaled squares. The first group can be subdivided in terms of horizontal cross-lines, oblique cross-lines, and long, closely-spaced horizontal lines (Fig. 167).

It is impossible to say what material or materials may have been used for the seals themselves, although copper, wood, stone, bone, or even clay would do (i.e. Mabry n.d.: chalk). The method of carving the seal, however, can be reconstructed in some cases. Those seals which left impressions in which the vertical line or lines are crossed by shorter horizontal ones were simply carved or sawn in some manner; the vertical lines which seem to sprout shorter, oblique ones may represent a more sophisticated carving technique. At any rate, many earlier parallels exists where both seals and their impressions are preserved (see below).

Comparative study

The closest, most direct and, in some cases, precise parallels (including related host vessel genres and types) for the stamp seal impressions at Jawa come from Stage 2 (EB I A) at Tell Um Hammad and its neighbours Tell Mafluq and Kataret es-Samra in the central Jordan Valley (Helms 1984a, 1987a, 1987b). An actual seal and a stylistically related impression on a sherd, both very similar in design to impressions from Tell Um Hammad, have been found at Tell Handaquq (North) (Mabry p.c., n.d.). A corpus of related impressions from northern Transjordan, but not apparently across the Jordan River in Palestine, can now be assembled; but before going further, it may be useful, in terms of background, to trace the basic designs of the impressions throughout the ancient Near East: if for nothing else than to show that they are not unique to the 4th millennium, nor to Transjordan and southern Syria; and, hopefully also to glean some inkling as to their possible function.

Earlier stamp seal designs

A cursory survey of stamp seals and their impressions demonstrates that the practice more or less began with the development of agriculture in the Neolithic period, from about the 8th/7th millennia onward. Almost all designs - a small set - were 'invented', probably at about the same time throughout the Near East. The design repertoire is simple, consisting most commonly of net patterns, crosses, radiating lines, clusters of dots, 'tree' or 'wheat sheaf' patterns (Fig. 167: OTJ3, Ar6, KM1), concentric circles, spirals, and so forth. Homès-Fredericq (1963) has summarized the most common of these. What the individual designs might represent is not established at any point (but see Schmandt-Besserat on tokens 1977, 1978; also a critique by Brandes 1980). However, a minimalist interpretation might consider the requirements of developing agricultural, horticultural, pastoral economies, which must have used various forms of exchange systems, with the concomitant need for rudimentary recording in the management of grown, stored, and exchanged resources. Stamp seals of the Neolithic period (and onward) may denote one, or a combination of, the following: (i) simply ownership, either individual or communal; (ii) identity of manufacturer of the stamped object (later, the equivalent of the most common name for anything stamped, scratched or carved into pottery vessels: 'potter's marks'); (iii) identity of the contents of the stamped/sealed container; (iv) measurement through repeated stamps, relative position of stamps, etc.: a very questionable interpretation (but see Schmandt-Besserat and critiques noted above); and (v) generally, a system of economic control (Helms 1987b).

Examples of stamped objects are relatively rare: but comparison may be made with one from Tell es-Sawwan, of the Samarran/Ubaid period (Fig. 167: TS1; Abu al-Soof 1968: Pl. XVBI: 2) comprising two impressions into a fragment of juss (plaster). The design consists of two vertical rows of rectangular spaces, or a vertical line (1.3 centimetres) crossed by shorter, horizontal ones (0.9 centimetres), all within an oval register (or cartouche), rather similar (but obviously unrelated) to the Jawa/Tell Um Hammad set. Two actual stamp seals with pierced vertical lugs (Abu al-Soof 1968: Pl. XIV: 3) represent the most common type of the Neolithic period. The designs consist of a net pattern and radiating, criss-crossing lines, both useful in recognizing the method of preparing the seal (here simply carving or sawing into the soft material of the seal). The former design recalls those at Jawa and Tell Um Hammad. Very similar impressions, as well as seals, are known in the Mesopotamian realm: e.g. Tepe Gawra XIII (Ubaid II) with three vertical lines crossed by shorter ones (Fig. 167: TG1; Tobler 1950: Pl. CLVIII: 5), Chagar Bazar (Halaf) with net pattern (Mallowan 1936: Fig. 7: No. 5), and Arpachiya (Halaf) with net pattern (Mallowan and Cruikshank 1935: Fig. 50: 15).

A northern Syro-Mediterranean example comes from Mersin (XVI?) where a copper seal with pierced lug is attributed to the 'Copper Age' (Garstang 1953: Fig. 70). The impression is a set of two, on the neck of a jar, on either side of a strap handle (*idem* 1953: Fig. 54: 11); the design - a cross within circle - as well as the relative position of the impression(s) is paralleled at Jericho (Garstang 1935: Pl. XLII: 16, in Jericho VIII which is roughly contemporary with Mersin XVI), where the same impression also appears on the recessed lip of a hole-mouth jar (1935: Pl. XLII: 8). There the design is stamped on the inside of the jar neck and consists of a cross with four dots. Several stamps and impressions with net patterns occur in Amuq A and later (Fig. 167: A1, A2; Braidwood and Braidwood 1960: Fig. 37, *passim*). Byblos of the 'néolithique ancienne' provides a similar stamp whose design is close to some of the Jawa/Tell Um Hammad patterns (Fig. 167: BYB 1, 2; Dunand 1973: Fig. 52): a vertical line crossed by a number of smaller horizontal ones within an oval outline made by the shape of the stamp itself.

Apart from the example from O.T. Jericho, which was noted above, a carved plaque of unknown date from the same site (Fig. 167: OTJ2; Kenyon and Holland 1982: 560: 10) consists of a net pattern of eight by thirteen lines of squares (seven by twelve dividing lines; see also Jericho, below), and perhaps also an impression on the foot of a 'pedestalled' vessels from Jericho VIII (Garstang 1936: Pl. XXXII: 33A).

Two further examples come from Chalcolithic contexts in Palestine. A stamped clay sealing has been reported by Gilead (public lecture: Institute of Archaeology, London University); Lee (1973: 292 - 3) reports a pierced carved plaque from Tuleilat Ghassul whose pattern consists of a vertical line crossed by shorter horizontal ones. A stamp seal impression consisting of criss-cross patterns has been found in 'early Chalcolithic' contexts at Tel Tsaf, near Beth-Shan (Gophna and Sadeh 1988-9). (For other symbols see 'Incised and embossed patterns and other forms' below.)

The central Jordan Valley

The following seal impressions, and one actual seal, were found in and about the alluvial fan and marl depositions near the confluence of the Zerqa and Jordan Rivers, and adjacent areas. All locations lie in Transjordan (but for one example from O.T. Jericho). Of these the assemblage from Tell Um Hammad is most important since it represents a stratified set; the rest are surface finds. Through Um Hammad and the related sites, it is now possible to link other seal repertoires, notably a sub-set of roll seals which allow a general synchronism with sites to the west of the Jordan River.

Tell Um Hammad (TUH)

TUH1205 *(Fig. 167: TUH5; Prov. 4029)*. Maximum vessel width is not known. There is one impression along the centre line of an up-turned, rounded ledge handle. The pattern is a vertical line (3.33 centimetres) and 'sprouting', slightly oblique shorter lines (0.72 centimetres), in oval register; line depth is about 0.07 centimetres.

TUH[M1] *(Fig. 167: TUH4; cf. Leonard n.d.: Pl. XXII: 16.138)*. Stamped along the centre line of an up-turned, rounded ledge handle almost identical in form with TUH1205 above, the design is also very similar, consisting of a vertical line (3.27 centimetres) and 'sprouting' small, slightly oblique ones (0.71 centimetres) in an oblong, oval register; line depth is about 0.08 centimetres.

TUH[M3] *(Fig. 167: TUH1; cf. Leonard n.d.: Pl. XXII: 11.144)*. A set of three parallel and identical impressions was made on the centre line of an up-turned ledge handle. The pattern consists of a vertical line (2.24 centimetres) crossed by shorter, horizontal ones (0.69 centimetres) in an oblong, oval register; line depth is about 0.1 centimetres.

TUH[M2] *(Fig. 167: TUH6; cf. Leonard n.d.: Pl. XXVII: 4.145)*. A set of three parallel and identical impressions was made across the centre line of an up-turned, rounded ledge handle. The pattern is a set of three vertical lines (1.93 centimetres) crossed by shorter horizontal ones (0.89 centimetres) making a network of equally scaled squares within an oval register; line depth is about 0.07 centimetres.

TUH[Reg. No. 8] (Fig. 167: TUH3; Prov. +++++). Body sherd. The design consists of a vertical line (preserved 1.6 centimetres) crossed by shorter horizontal ones (0.51 centimetres) in an oblong oval register; line depth is 0.07 centimetres.

TUH[G1] (Fig. 167: TUH2; cf. Glueck 1951, Pl. 103.7). Body sherd. A set of 5 parallel and identical impressions was made on the body of a vessel. The design consists of a vertical line, crossed by short, horizontal lines in an oblong oval register.

TUH4729 (Figs 166, 167: TUH7; Prov. 50005). Holemouth jar (= genre/type AA). A set of two impressions was preserved: one on a rounded, upturned lug handle, the other just above the handle, near the rim. The design consists of a net pattern within a circle of about 0.99 centimetres diameter; line depth is about 0.08 centimetres.

TUH3381 (Fig. 167: TUH9 Prov. 50006). Body sherd. Not strictly a seal impression, it may, however, be related to the corpus under discussion. A series of single impressions (7-8) in two parallel rows was made with a elongated star-shaped object or with two separate impressions made with a sharp point, before firing the vessel. 2.2 x 1.0 centimetres.

TUH5346 (Figs 166; 167: TUH8 Prov. 40017). Hole-mouth jar. It is difficult to say whether this is a stamp seal or roll seal impression; the latter may be more likely, if only by analogy with similar designs elsewhere (see below). The seal was applied in a set of two (one very blurred) on a rounded, upturned lug near the rim of a large painted hole-mouth jar. Only one of the jar's four handles was 'sealed'. The design consists of an obliquely set net pattern within a register measuring 1.75 centimetres wide. The impression survives to a length of 6.05 centimetres; line depth is about 0.07 centimetres. The hole-mouth jar is typologically complex. On the one hand, its four pushed-up lugs near the rim links it to Jawa's genre/type AA; on the other hand, its body form, construction technique, and its surface treatment are totally alien to anything at Jawa. However, the vessel belongs to stage 2 at Um Hammad (= the 4th millennium BC occupation at Jawa).

Tell Mafluq (M)

M1 (Fig. 167: M1; cf. Leonard n.d.: Pl. XXXII: 3.89). A set of four identical impressions was made in a curve about the centre-line of an up-turned, rounded ledge handle. The design consists of a net pattern in a circle of about 1.1 centimetres diameter; line depth is 0.09 centimetres.

Kataret es-Samra (KS)

For further discussion of the site in EB I see Leonard (1983). Two seal impressions are known to me now, both of them through cooperation with Albert Leonard, who kindly provided photographs.

KS1 (Fig. 167) consists of a series of parallel, identical impressions in two bands, about 7.5 centimetres apart, on a body sherd. The design consists of a vertical line (2.5 centimetres) crossed by shorter, horizontal ones (0.5 centimetres). The centre-lines of the individual impressions are about 0.5 centimetres apart, leaving a 0.2 centimetre-wide ridge between them.

KS2 (Fig. 167) is a single impression on the centre line of an up-turned, rounded ledge handle, near the body of the vessel. The impression is not clear, but probably consists of a vertical line crossed by at least three shorter, horizontal ones within an oval register. (No scale.)

Tell Handaquq North (HN)

For the first time an actual seal, carved in chalk, has been found. Its pattern is very close to some of the seal impressions from Um Hammad (Fig. 167: HN1; Mabry n.d.: Fig. 15: 5), and consists of five columns and six lines of square and rectangular bosses in an oval surround (= 'cartouche'). The main relief lies on a flattened oval surface, one long side of which is also carved with a series of bosses. The main design measures about 4.5 x 2.9 centimetres. A related seal impression on a sherd (Fig. 167: HN2) comes from the same site (*idem*). It consists of four (?) columns of small square impression, preserved in seven (?) lines in a rectangular field measuring about 3.0 x 2.6 centimetres, as it is preserved. In addition to this, two incised or impressed (pre-firing ?) ledge handles are reported (Fig. 167: HN3): one consisting of a single slash in line with the axis of the handle crossed by shorter slashes; the other of a double slash, also crossed by shorter slashes.

O.T. Jericho (OTJ)

We have noted the undated 'stamp' above. A stamp seal impression on a body sherd comes from a 'Proto Urban - EB I' context (Fig. 167: OTJ1; Kenyon and Holland 1983: Fig. 78: 16). It is broken off and so it is impossible to say whether it was rounded or oval (1.94 centimetres maximum remaining). However, it can be compared with the general class of Jawa/TUH stamp seal impressions, specifically with TUH[M2], as well as the seal from Tell Handaquq North (Fig. 167).

Wadi Zerqa Survey (Gordon p.c.)

Several impressed, up-turned and rounded ledge handles (similar to the types at Jawa and Tell Um Hammad) have been reported. The impressions are said to be related to those at Jawa and Tell Um Hammad.

All of these examples - with the possible exception of TUH3381 and TUH5346 - are closely related to the impressions at Jawa; they may be considered to be virtually identical.

Related examples

A single stamp seal which may be more distantly related to the repertoire at Jawa has been reported in the survey of Wadi al-`Arab (Fig. 167: AS1; Hanbury-Tenison, p.c.: No. 040-010). The incomplete impression is on a body sherd. There are signs of an oval register or 'cartouche' about a net pattern which might be generally compared with J174 or, better, TUH[M2]. A second, similar impression comes from the Jerash Survey (Fig. 167: JS1; Hanbury-Tenison 1987: Fig. 5: 48) and can be compared with examples from Um Hammad. All other comparable impressions were probably made by roll seals and are included here because of their similarity with TUH5346.

Glueck published two 'impressions' from his East Jordan Survey. One is probably a roll seal and comes from Tell Qurs - site 89 - near the Yarmouk River (Fig. 167: TQ1; Glueck 1951: Pl. 84: 10). It has also been published by Ben-Tor in his EBA typology (1978: Pl. 1: 6: 1B-2) and can be directly compared with TUH5346 (Fig. 166). A stabbed or slashed series of parallel impressions on a body sherd from the same site (Fig. 167: TQ2; Glueck 1951: Pl. 84: 7) may be compared with TUH3381 (Fig. 167: TUH9). Other relevant items are discussed below (incised pattern, etc). There is one further parallel which is also noted in Ben-Tor's typology (Fig. 167: TP1; 1978: Pl. 1: 1B-1). It comes from Tel Parur (= Khirbet Fureit) near the Carmel Ridge and has the same diagonally arranged squares within a register. In this latter detail it may be compared with the example from the wadi al-`Arab and Jerash surveys above, and may perhaps not be a roll seal impression after all.

If at least some of these impressions were made by roll seals (i.e. particularly TUH5346, the example from Um Hammad) we may be able to relate the entire extended corpus to other sites in Palestine, notably `En Shadud and Megiddo (Braun 1985).

Relation with other corpora of the 4th millennium BC

There are many collections which include Near Eastern stamp seals. Most of the designs, however, cannot be linked directly with the repertoire from Jawa: at least not during the 4th millennium BC. On the other hand, very little has as yet been published from the more recent excavations in Mesopotamia and Syria where occupation of the 4th millennium is known to have been found. Nevertheless, even a brief survey of what is to hand is enough to place the Jawa seal impressions into a general Near Eastern milieu of the 4th millennium BC, from southern Mesopotamia to Cilicia.

Byblos (Byb)

The best parallel from Byblos comes from the 'énéolithique ancienne' (see above). Among seal impressions or actual seals dated in 'énéolithique récent', only one is close to the Jawa repertoire. Seal 21352 (Dunand 1973: Fig. 201) consists of a vertical line, crossed by a series of horizontal ones within an oval register or cartouche. Two other seal designs (*idem* 1973: Fig. 200: 30912 and 21959) fall into the revised general design category noted above (after Homès-Fredericq 1963), consisting of circular registers enclosing concentric circles of dots and concentric circles, respectively. One incomplete design (Dunand 1973: Fig. 200: 2004) is linear, and may be reconstructed as a tree-like pattern within a lozenge or diamond-shaped register (Fig. 167). This last design may be related to a series of stamp impressions from Habuba Kabira (Fig. 167; see also below).

Tarsus (T)

The only relevant and stratified example appears to belong to EB II (Goldman 1956, Fig. 396: 5) and consists of concentric circles. Four other, unstratified, seals are much closer to the Jawa repertoire. The best parallel among these consists of a vertical line, crossed by shorter ones within an irregular oval register (Fig. 167: T1; *idem* 1956: Fig 394: 44). A related seal (Fig. 167: T2; *idem* 1956: Fig. 394: 42) is circular and consists of three adjacent sets of horizontal lines; another (Fig. 167: T3; *idem* 1956: Fig. 394.39) is made up of two sets of adjacent dotted lines at right angles and on either side of a horizontal dotted line within a register with rounded ends; another (*idem* 1956: Fig. 394.43) consists of a vertical line surrounded by dots and radiating shorter lines within a sub-circular register.

Kazarli Hüyük

Seals on storage jars which occur together with high loop-handled juglets and may, therefore, be tentatively dated in the 4th millennium, come from this site between Mersin and Tarsus (Garstang 1937: Pl. VIII: 26). The seal impressions consist of concentric semicircles and are applied in a double row on the shoulder of the vessel.

Hama (H)

One comparable seal was found in Hama L (Fig. 167; Fugmann 1958, Fig. 13: 7A 786), presumably from a 4th millennium BC context. Of all the seals published from 'horizon' K, only one - if it is a seal - is distantly related to the Jawa repertoire: it is a calcite plaque from Hama K1b (Fig. 167: H1; *idem* 1958: Fig. 54: 6B 941). The seal is cut into an irregularly rounded surface and consists of a vertical line crossed by several shorter ones. The balance of stamp seals is rounded and the designs or patterns more or less within the revised repertoire noted above: i.e. dots, crosses, combinations of the two, radiating lines, and even blanks (see also below).

North Syria (S)

A number of undated stamp seals has been published (Buchanan 1984 [Moorey ed.]). Some are close parallels for the Jawa repertoire. All of these stamp seals come from Syria. One, bought in Aleppo, consists of criss-crossing lines in an oval register (Fig. 167: S2; *idem* 1984: no. 3) which can be compared with TUH5346 (Fig. 166); another, bought on the north coast of Syria, is round with a net pattern (Fig. 167: S1; *idem* 1984: no. 7).

Habuba Kabira (HK)

Two examples suffice. The first, already noted above in relation to Byblos, is not really used in the normal sense of stamp seal, but rather to create a decorative pattern on the surface of a vessel (Fig. 167: HK2). On the other hand, such treatment appears to be relatively unique and the vessel may, therefore, have had a special significance. The impression (Museum 1982: Abb. 32) consists of an elongated cross and additional lines within a diamond-shaped register and is applied all over the body of the vessel. The second example is an actual seal (Fig. 167: HK1; Strommenger 1977: Fig. 13): the design, made up of a net pattern, is of the type which goes back to the Neolithic period. The individual lines making up the design, however, are much thinner than those of the Jawa examples.

Jemdet Nasr

Various seals and impressions relatively close to the Jawa/Um Hammad repertoire have been found: e.g. net patterns in sub-circular registers dated in the Uruk era (see Homès Fredericq 1970, *passim*).

Uruk (U)

A set of two impressions (Fig. 167: U2; Heinrich 1936, Pl. 16-c, p. 34) may be compared with the repertoires at Jawa and Tell Um Hammad. A second seal impression (Fig. 167: U1) is similar to J174 and other related examples.

Palestine/Transjordan

There are very few comparable examples from 4th millennium BC contexts from within Palestine/Transjordan, other than those already mentioned above. In a sense, this is remarkable, if only in view of their apparent abundance in the central Jordan Valley, at Jericho a little farther south, at Jawa, and in the Irbid/Ajlun/Jerash area. It may be that stamp impressions have simply not been noticed by surveyors and excavators, although this is unlikely. On the other hand, the much (and unjustly) maligned surveys of Nelson Glueck show up the scarcity of impressions, since he illustrated the few that he did encounter.

Only three sets of additional data may be noted at this time. The first comes from the 'dolmens', at least some of which have now been dated in the range of EB I (Yassine 1985) to EB IV-MBA (Epstein 1985b). Stekelis (1935) published the contents of one dolmen which included an EB I jar with a series of stamped or impressed dots making up three parallel lines on the shoulder of the vessel (Fig. 167: D1; *idem* 1935: Fig. 19: 189, and 167, a 'high loop-handled' juglet). This device can be compared with TUH3381.

The second set comes from Lahun (Homès-Fredericq p.c.). Seal impressions were made on a 'high loop-handled' juglet and a body sherd: they consist of concentric circles, either alone, or accompanied by a series of impressed dots.

Several impressed vessels from early Bab edh-Dhra' form the third set. The impressions consist of stabbed patterns forming individual sets of opposed semicircles (Fig. 167: BD1; Schaub 1981: Fig. 5: 2, 3) set about the handles of the vessels. By their position, at least, they are analogous with the Jawa repertoire. Their meaning, however, is far from clear. Their 'design' can be compared to purely decorative motifs used, for example, on spindle whorls as far afield as proto-Elamite Susa, with parallel at Uruk-Warka and so forth (Le Brun 1978: Fig. 35). On the other hand, they can also be compared with proto-Sumerian fractions of minor units (Friberg 1984: 83). The answer may lie somewhere between these two extremes.

Seals of the EB II and EB III

It may be instructive to survey the evidence for stamp seals and their typology immediately after 'EB I', at least in the southern Levant, southern Syria, and Transjordan, and to see whether parallels may be found which could suggest the continuation of the practice, as well as the particular Jawa/Um Hammad style. There are some related examples beyond this zone, but these are probably not significant: i.e. Tarsus (Goldman 1956: Fig. 393: 18); and Amuq G (Braidwood and Braidwood 1960: Fig. 253: 1).

The short answer is that the style and perhaps even the practice, to a large extent, disappear by EB II, the practice perhaps now served almost exclusively, though still relatively rarely, by roll seals (see also Helms 1987a, 1987b). Close examination of the large amount of pottery published from the excavations at Jericho, for example, indicates this quite clearly; indeed it shows that whatever we might make of 'PU' (= 'Proto Urban' A, B, etc.), no examples of stamp seal impressions of the Jawa/Um Hammad type have been found. It has been argued elsewhere (Helms 1987a) that the 'PU' ('Proto Urban') of Kenyon's Jericho publications is later than stage 2 at Um Hammad (later than the EB I A occupation at N.T. Jericho: see Pritchard 1958) and, therefore, later than Jawa. It can be argued that the practice and the style went out of fashion in the area of the central Jordan Valley during, or shortly after, EB I A (if we may use the term in this way), and was never in fashion a few kilometres farther south. The same holds for Tell el-Far'ah near Nablus where no comparable material has so far been published, although some of the earliest EBA occupation (or at least some of the tomb groups) must be contemporary with stage 2 at Um Hammad, and certainly contemporary with stage 3 ('EB I B').

Similarly, the exhaustive publication of pottery from 'Ai (Marquet-Krause 1949; Callaway 1972, 1980) has revealed nothing of the kind: that is to say, there are no comparable stamp seals or impressions in the assemblages from the earliest occupation at the site which can be dated (relatively) after stage 2 at Tell Um Hammad and roughly contemporary with stage 3 ('EB I B').

Farther south still, at Arad, another well-documented pottery assemblage reveals no close parallels to the Jawa/Um Hammad repertoire. The earliest relevant level (Stratum IV) belongs to EB I and shows only distant relation to the general pottery repertoire of early Um Hammad. There are no comparable seal impressions. The balance belongs to EB II, again without any developed parallels but for one example (Fig. 167: Ar; Beck 1984: Fig. 36). On the other hand, there is a number of designs cut into pottery vessels which may be relevant in a more general way. These examples are discussed below.

Blank impressions

Although stamp seal impressions appear to be rare in EB I contexts (but, to date, for Jawa, sites in the central Jordan Valley, and the hilly areas to the east), this really only applies to impressions with specific designs. There is an appreciable corpus of blank impressions (Fig. 168) on pottery vessels, which are applied before firing. Most of these impressions are on handles. These 'blanks' can be distinguished as a separate practice from the so-called potter's marks which are not made by impression but, rather, by cutting or slashing the wet clay; they are also separate from thumb-impressed marks (e.g. J167/216 etc.), and perhaps also from punctate or incised bands about handles (e.g. J171/172).

Having thus separated out 'potter's marks' (whatever they might mean), and incorporating here the whole of the Jawa/Um Hammad repertoire of stamp seal impressions, we may conclude that impressions on pottery (in some cases all the way back to the Neolithic) are normally associated with the handles: either near them, or directly on them. Two sets of locations are common: (i) near or around handles; and (ii) on the handles.

The first group is represented by examples from Tell Um Hammad (Fig. 167: TUH[Reg.No.8], TUH[G1]), and Kataret es-Samra (Fig. 167: KS1). In both cases multiples of impressions are set out in rows. The second group is analysed below.

Assuming, for the sake of argument, that there may be something in the grouping of identical seals impressions (e.g. perhaps some crude form of numeration), the Jawa/Tell Um Hammad repertoire can be set out accordingly (Fig. 169). At one end of the 'series' would lie empty or blank handles (i.e. J170/172/173/175/177), followed by a single impression (i.e. J174, TUH1205/M1, KS2; also two examples from Tell Handaquq North [Mabry p.c.]), then two impressions (i.e. J176), three (i.e. TUHM3/M2), four (Tell Mafluq), and so on. There are not enough complete vessels available at present to take this hypothesis further. However, a survey of blank impressions (not obviously decorative thumb-impressions) might at least show the extent of the practice (whatever it may have meant, if anything) throughout the late Chalcolithic/EB I landscape of the southern Levant. It may also be possible to delineate a geographical distribution.

Stamped and incised motifs on handles (EB I)

Jawa, Tell Um Hammad, Tell Mafluq, Kataret es-Samra', Tell Handaquq North, and perhaps also Jericho (see above: if the 'seal' was used to stamp a handle) form a discrete set in terms of stamped motifs on handles. These motifs can be reduced to a simple patterns consisting of criss-crossing lines, in two basic formats (or 'cartouches'): (a) elongated or oval (e.g. J163); and (b) round (e.g. TM1). The former consists of one or more - up to seven in the available corpus - long lines, crossed by a number of smaller ones (Fig. 169a, b). Parallels beyond Palestine/Transjordan have been noted above (i.e. at Habuba Kabira, Mersin, Tarsus, Byblos, etc.), although, as we pointed out there, the motif has a long history of use in those regions, going back to the Neolithic period. Table 11 summarizes the analysis of these motifs from Jawa and the Central Jordan Valley.

Examples of incised, slashed and/or punctate motifs on or near handles occur in the following variations. At Jawa, vessel J221 (?) has a series of irregular short slashes beneath a lump handle, and J449 has two punctate depressions on an up-turned lug handle. Tell Um Hammad TUH3107 is a plain handle, but has punctate bands along the sharp edge, and in a crescent on the body just above the handle. TUH3381 has two parallels lines of punctate depressions on the body of the vessel. Two of the examples from Tell Handaquq North consist of a single long slash and a double long slash, both in line with the axis of the handle, and both crossed by smaller slashes. Several examples on ledge handles are known at Jericho: a series of three short, parallel slashes in line with the axis of the handle; and a line of punctate depressions at right angles to the handle (Kenyon and Holland 1982: Fig. 76: 10, and 8, respectively, 1983: Fig. 117: 11, three impression in line, at right angles to the handle). Two ledge handles from Tell el-Far'ah fit into this category, both with punctate designs: one has two parallel rows of six and four depressions; the other two parallels rows of six depressions. In both cases the rows are at right angles to the axis of the handle (de Vaux and Steve 1947: Fig. 1: 32, 'énéolithique Moyen', and 7: 26, 'Ancien Bronze II', respectively). A loop-handled jar or jug from the Bab edh-Dhra' area (Saller 1964/65: Fig. 23: 12) has two small bosses, side by side on the shoulder opposite the handle. The bosses have four and five punctate depressions each and are subscribed with double slashes on the body of the vessel. Three relevant examples come from Beth-Shan, all of them on ledge handles: two separate converging slashes; two touching converging slashes; and two crossed slashes (Fitzgerald 1935: Pls II: 1 [Level XVI], VI: 10 [Level XIV], VI: 11 [Level XIV], respectively). Apart from a series of punctate and slashed loop handles (Sukenik 1948: Pl. VIII: 10 - 20; see also below), there are two comparable examples from Affulah, both on ledge handles: one has two or more (the handle is incomplete) parallel slashes in line with the axis of the handle (*idem* 1948: Pl. VII: 22); the other a long slash at right angles to the axis of the handle, with three shorter slashes crossing. Two examples come from Megiddo XIX, both on ledge handles: a 'U'-shaped incision; and two slashes on either side of a blank oval impression (Loud 1948: Pl. 98: 13, 14, respectively; see also below). Esse (1984: Fig. 5D) reports a ledge handle with two parallel rows of slashes from Beth Yerah in EB I. A ledge handle with crossed slashes comes from Kinneret (Fritz 1986: Abb. 9). Several closely related handles from the Jerash Survey have short slashes (punctate) in a line of seven at right angles to the axis of the handle, near the body, and two lines of four in line with the axis; a series of 'V'- and 'Z'-shaped slashes; and a set of three short slashes in line with the axis of the handle (Hanbury-Tenison 1987: Figs 6: 60, 61, and 8: 50, respectively). Finally, a number of examples from Glueck's survey of the Jordan Valley might be cited. All motifs appear on ledge handles, normally on the upper surface. The following variations occur: three parallel lozenge-shaped slashes or impressions in line with the axis of the handle, the middle line slightly offset, from Tell Kufr Juba (Glueck 1951: Pl. 87: 1); a group of blank, oval impressions in three rows at right angles to the axis of the handle, arranged in sets of three, four and again three from Tell edh-Dhiyabeh (*idem* 1951: Pl. 57: 3); three parallel, lozenge-shaped impressions or slashes in line with the axis of the handle from Ras Abu Lofeh, similar to the example from Tell Kafr Yuba above, and, from the same site, two handles with two impressions or slashes of similarly arranged motifs (*idem* 1951: Pl. 30: 5, 6, respectively). The same arrangement appears on a handle from Tell Qurs (*idem* 1951: Pl. 84: 8). A single oval, blank impression in line with the axis of the handle comes from Tell el-Fakhat (*idem* 1951: Pl. 4: 9). All of these sites also have plain, unadorned ledge handles.

Table 11. Stamp seal impressions: numeration

no. of vert. lines	(a) elongated/oval								(b) round
	1	2	3	4	5	6	7	[n]	
JAWA	J162	J174							|
	J163								|
	J176								|
TUH	1205	M2							4729
	M1								
	M3								
	Reg.8								
TM									TM1
KS	KS1								
	KS2								
HN			[X]	X					
JERICHO				X--->?				X	
				?	?		?		

Impressed, incised, punctate handles (EB I)

An attempt may now be made to assemble all of these variant motifs, specifically on ledge handles, including the stamp seal impressions, and to see whether there may not be some quasi-numerate or mensural arrangement. This analysis includes handles without any 'decoration' of this type, which - the handles - form by far the largest percentage in Palestinian/Transjordanian pottery assemblages of EB I. Following on the summary set out in table 11, beginning with the examples from the core corpus of the 'Jawa types', and then the sampling of others outlined above, the arrangement in Figure 168 may be presented according to the number of seal or other impressions (see also Fig. 167 which includes some parallels).

Summary

On the one hand, the presently available data are so sparse, while obviously important areas in the southern Levant (i.e. southern Syria) are still virtually unexplored, that hypotheses regarding the origins and diffusion of stamp sealing and related practices are inappropriate, as are speculations about the meaning (if any) of the phenomenon in the 4th millennium BC. On the other hand, some technical observations can be made at this time, which will at least form a foundation for further investigations, and perhaps also provide some directions of interpretation.

It is first of all evident that a close relationship exists between Jawa and the central Jordan Valley, and perhaps also the wadi Zerqa area in terms of a specific style of stamp seal. Secondly, related stamps (e.g. TUH5346) from the same archaeological contexts (EB I A) can be shown to have a local distribution in the Jordan Valley, the northern Transjordan uplands, and also towards the Mediterranean coast (e.g. Tell Parur). A third related category consists of a cognate practice (as we have argued above) of placing symbols on or near the handles of storage vessels before firing. The distribution of this set appears to be the widest of the three categories in the southern Levant; it also appears to continue into the EB I B period, and stop by about EB II. Finally, a fourth cognate practice, that of using roll seals in much the same manner, seems to be restricted to areas west of the Jordan Valley, at least during EB I A (and B). The available samples are not abundant, but their distribution may be significant. By EB II, the available evidence suggests that stamp seals or meaningfully (?) impressed or scored handles and vessels are replaced, almost universally, by roll seals. The over-all data set also indicates that plain, unadorned vessels far outnumber the 'specialized' ones.

A tentative conclusion may be suggested in which we also include the information gleaned from general typological relationships (see Chapter 3). This conclusion is that we may recognize an introduction of a new practice in EB I A about the middle of the 4th millennium BC (but for some isolated Chalcolithic examples) which can be interpreted as a form of economic control, reflecting a trend towards a new, or at least transformed, economic system or systems in the southern Levant. Furthermore, there may be a meaningful distribution in both space and time, which could have demographic import. It seems as if the distribution of the use of stamp and roll seals parallels that of certain pottery repertoires, specifically at Tell Um Hammad. Um Hammad is important because it has the best currently available pottery typology for EB I A (and B). Both practices (roll and stamp sealings) and ceramics are new and appear abruptly about the middle of the 4th millennium BC. One set (roll seals plus red burnished wares) appears along the Mediterranean coast - as far north as Cilicia and perhaps as far south as the Nile Delta - into the Jezre'el and Jordan Valleys south of Beth-Shan and the Palestinian uplands; the other set (stamps and related vessels, among others) flourishes in the south Syrian and northern Transjordanian uplands, and the central Jordan Valley. This is the spatial component of our conclusion here.

The temporal component concerns the wider apparent distribution, and thus perhaps diffusion, of the general practice of marking certain vessels during both EB I A and B. This general practice could be seen as derived from the more formal use of stamp seals in EB I A. As we have noted above, the limited sign repertoire (see Homès-Fredericq 1963) which can be recognized in EB I B as well, becomes a purely decorative element in the pottery of EB II (e.g. Arad, Amiran 1978: *passim*), or whatever is implied by 'potter's marks', by which time roll seals seem to have replaced stamp seals throughout the landscape. By EB II, or a little earlier, a second cognate system is introduced or used in southern Palestine, at Arad and Tell Sheykh al-`Areyny, where Egyptian serekhs (Narmer, etc.) of the early dynastic period are placed on pottery vessels, signifying some form of 'international' commercial contact (see now Weinstein 1984).

The meaning of the stamp seals and the significance of the general practice are more problematical: particularly the meaning of the reduced signs (Fig. 169a, b). I have speculated elsewhere (Helms 1987c) on whether there might be a connection between our two signs and the proto-Sumerian system which soon after our period (EB I A: or the 2nd half of the 4th millennium BC) developed into a writing system (Nissen 1985). This would seem to be unlikely. However, the practice, that is to say the significance of stamping some vessels, perhaps in a purposive and even mensural way, could easily be related. It could have been adopted and adapted as a system of controlling some resources, when such systems became necessary. This further suggests that there may have been a trend towards more complex economic systems as early as the middle of the 4th millennium BC (and not just in EB II when 'cities' are said to appear). Analysis of the ceramic typology at least allows us to suggest the possibility of cultural (if not commercial or political) contact with the Uruk sphere of north/central Syria (see Chapter 3). But the mensural aspects of our data set are still very questionable. All we might safely say here is that there may have been an economic component, and that this was expressed in a restricted way (i.e. only a few stamped vessels), perhaps indicating a developing hierarchical social structure, one of whose manifestations, a little later, was the establishment of nucleated, militarized settlements in Palestine and Transjordan in EB II.

These arguments can, to some extent, be supported by the evidence of sealings or stamped impressions on pottery vessels in later periods, in the same general regions. We know that stamp seals were already superceded by roll seals in the Uruk sphere in the 4th millennium BC. The same shift can be observed in the southern Levant a half century or so later in EB II, as we have noted above. The stamping or marking of pottery vessels, however, appears to have continued as a 'Syrian' or 'Levantine' peculiarity. The collapse, or rather the shift away from nucleated settlements (and also their causative economic and social systems) at the end of the 3rd millennium BC (EB IV) would naturally have been accompanied by an abandonment of economic controlling devices (e.g. roll seals); however, a case can be made for the continued use of marking the handles and bodies of specific pottery vessels in a 'familiar' way (Helms 1987d, 1989b; see also Potts 1981). Similar examples, including stamp seals, were in use in the same manner throughout the Middle and Late Bronze Ages (e.g. Albright 1938: Pl. 33: 5, 6). The best interpretative models, however, come from the Iron Age of Palestine and from the Persian and Hellenistic periods. Stamps of royal content - i.e. an hierarchical social structure - signifying economic control as well as special property are represented by the LMLK ('of king' x stamps: see Na`aman 1986). An appropriate example from the Hellenistic period shows the use of stamps on handles for specific contents as well as connoting economic control through an organized bureaucracy. Two impressed monograms illustrate this: the letter K for *krion* ('barley': cf. s̆e = 'barley' and 'granary', Labat 1948: no. 367; Brandes 1980; ATU 235, etc. in the Mesopotamian examples of one of our signs), and an anagram, perhaps *grammateos* ('secretary' or 'official') (Ariel *et al.* 1985). By the Late Antique period, many signs are used in a purely decorative way (e.g. Hayes 1972: Figs 38, 39, 42, 72).

INCISED AND EMBOSSED PATTERNS AND MISCELLANEOUS FORMS

Various minor decorative categories and some miscellaneous forms may be of some value in terms of relative chronology. These include graffiti (post-firing), incisions (pre-firing), various lumps and bumps added to the bodies of vessels, vestigial handles (other than those discussed in Chapter 3 above), knobs, marks near handles (not apparently mensural in any way), and decorative bands.

Graffiti: post-firing application

Graffiti applied to potsherds or the body of pottery vessels after firing are known throughout the EB I period in Palestine and Transjordan. Their meaning, if any, is obscure, and this is certainly the case with the scratched chevrons on the small holemouth jar J161 which are reminiscent of patterns applied to vessels of the Neolithic and Chalcolithic periods (e.g. Amiran 1969: Pls 1, 2: 5). The design on J161 is probably purely decorative. The other three examples from Jawa, however, form a group whose occurrence, either singly or in combination, is remarkably common. J620 and probably also J621 may be regarded as 'net' or 'fence' patterns, while J427 represents a tree-like design.

The closest Palestinian parallels for these graffiti come from 'Proto Urban' Jericho: similar 'net' or 'fence' patterns are cut into the base of fine, inturned rim bowls, themselves paralleled in stages 2 and 3 at Tell Um Hammad (Kenyon 1960: Fig. 10: 11; for Um Hammad, see Helms 1986, 1987a). A similar design appears on another vessel from Jericho (Kenyon and Holland 1983: Fig. 23). The combination of this pattern and the 'tree' motif comes from one of the earliest 'Proto-Urban' tombs at Jericho, A94 (Kenyon 1960: Fig. 12: 21). Other symbols common at Jericho include stylized animals (*idem* 1960: Fig. 13: 12).

'Trees' also appear on their own at Jericho (Kenyon 1960: Fig. 13: 23, 1983: Fig. 124: 14; Garstang 1935: Pl. XLI: 25). This symbol - most usually called 'tree' or 'wheatsheaf' - has been used in various ways to imply religious practices and even specific beliefs (notably Amiran 1972a, 1972b, 1981; Elliott 1977; see also below). Such speculation is certainly inappropriate when only one graffito is to hand. However, a brief survey of similar symbols serves to place J427 into a broad cultural context of the late Chalcolithic to Early Bronze Age period in Palestine and Transjordan.

The symbol can be traced back to the Neolithic period where it appears as a repeated element in registers made of chevron or herringbone (or 'wheatsheaf') bands (e.g. Byblos: see Jidejian 1968: Pl. 6: top) and also in association with dots or small circles, sometimes considered to represent grain. This use of the symbol cut into pottery vessels before firing is repeated at Byblos in the 'énéolithique récent'. Various combinations of chevron/herringbone/'wheatsheaf' bands and single or multiple 'tree' symbols made up of a vertical line and sprouting smaller 'branches' are common (e.g. Dunand 1937: Pls CLXXII: 6482, XCXCIV: 5968, CXCVIII: 5961, 5662, etc.; see also Dunand 1973: *passim*). An example from a PNB (Late Neolithic) context is known at O.T. Jericho (Kenyon and Holland 1983: Fig. 124: 14). Certainly in the Neolithic context it is not too difficult to accept the suggested meaning of the symbol(s) in their decorative function at least: that they are an early example of artistic expression which copies from the real world and thereby links the abstracted picture with the intended contents of the vessel. By the 4th millennium BC such speculation is more contentious, even when it is limited to the origins of pictographs in Mesopotamia.

The 'tree'/'wheatsheaf' symbols from Tuleilat Ghassul, Nahal Mishmar, and Gezer III have been summarized and discussed at length by Elliott who settles on the 'sacred tree' identification (Elliott 1977: *passim*, and Fig. 5: 2). Some of these Chalcolithic examples can be compared with J427 here.

Parallels abound in the EBA. We have already noted examples from 'Proto Urban'/EB I Jericho. To these can be added others from Megiddo (Loud 1948: Pls 5: 15, Megiddo XVII, 6: 5, Megiddo XVI) and, farther afield, even seals which show the same symbol (e.g. Ras Shamra, Schaeffer 1962: 96, Fig. 74, 'cachét en terre cuite') whose meanings - because of their contexts - might be rather closer to the one suggest for the Neolithic examples above, than exclusively religious. Related symbols comes from EB II contexts at Arad (Amiran 1978: Pl. 38: 2, 8) where they are cut into the false spouts of jars. They appear together with other 'symbols' (i.e. 'dot with radiating branches', *idem* 1978: Pl. 38: 1) which recall the revised set first outlines by Homès-Fredericq (1963, and remarks above). The branched symbol, cut into one of the copper alloy axe heads from Kfar Monash (Hestrin and Tadmor 1963: Fig. 2: 1), may be more securely in the realm of early writing. Turned upside down it could be regarded as part of an archaic hieroglyphic text. In this sense our symbol could mean 'bearded ear or emmer' (cf. Gardiner 1969: 34). In this regard we might also cite the roll seal of the so-called 'Tekhi' (Amiran 1970: 83ff.; Ben-Tor 1978; see also Rowe 1936: 30, Pl. XXVI: No. 1) where a revised 'emmer' sign appears with a plough as well as the symbol perhaps for 'village with cross roads' (cf. Gardiner 1969: 49), which itself is reminiscent of some of the Jawa/Um Hammad stamp seal impressions. This symbol could also stand for proto-Sumerian 'pasturage' (Falkenstein 1936; see also Helms 1987c). However, this would going too far, at least in terms of the single example from Jawa.

Representations of trees in a realistic, rather than abstract, form (palms) are known from the Bab edh-Dhra' region of Transjordan (Saller 1964/5: Figs 21: 14 and 22: 12. They are embossed, perhaps stamped before firing, onto a conical bowl. The technique of impression is somewhat similar to a more enigmatic one from Beth Yerah (Sussman 1980: Figs 2, 3). A jar, also discovered somewhere near Bab edh-Dhra' and said to be of Egyptian origin (Saller 1964/5: Fig. 18: 5, 5a [Naqada II]), is decorated with a variety of symbols, including stylized human beings with raised arms, chevron/'tree'/'wheatsheaf' symbols, clusters of circles and applied anthropomorphic handles in 'prayer-like' attitudes. The abstract symbols are relevant here and, minimally, recall the Neolithic examples noted at Byblos above. Amiran has made much more of this.

Arad was noted in regard of pre-firing incised 'symbols' of an international flavour. The discovery of a crudely carved stone with human stick figures in various enigmatic attitudes and 'tree'/'wheatsheaf' symbols instead of heads, has caused Amiran to pursue a specific religious identification which is irrelevant here (but see Amiran 1972a, 1972b, 1981, and also remarks above). She did, however link the scenes on the vessel from Bab edh-Dhra' noted above: partly in regard of the 'wheat' symbols.

The minimal interpretation regarding J427 would take into account the common association of container and cereals and suggest that the graffito stood for what was in the pot: most likely barley, emmer or bread wheat (cf. Willcox 1981). On the other hand J457 may just have been a random doodle.

Incisions (pre-firing)

Apart from incised decorative bands (see below), there is only one example of this practice, J395. It is, however, a surface find, although typologically within the range of the 4th millennium BC pottery assemblage. The design consists of three parallel vertical lines superscribed by a horizontal one. At least one further vertical line could be reconstructed since the horizontal one appears to continue to the right. Parallels may be sought in the very well-known 'potter's marks', mostly on hole-mouth jars, common in pottery repertoires throughout Palestine and Transjordan from about EB II onward (e.g. Tel Arad, Amiran 1978: *passim*). For specific parallels comparison can be made with a similar design of three vertical line bound by two horizontal ones from Bab edh-Dhra' (see *BiArR* 6.5: 27ff.), and others from the same site or area (Saller 1964/5: Fig. 21: 145, with punctate bands as well; Schaub 1981, *passim*). A close parallel comes from O.T. Jericho. It is incomplete: three long lines crossed by four shorter (?) ones remain (Kenyon and Holland 1983: Fig. 128: 23 [PU]).

Lumps and bumps

Various protruberances on pottery vessels may be regarded as either vestigial handles or lugs, or as decorative elements of unknown significance (but see Epstein 1975, 1978b, 1982) which may be loosely related to raised knobs on stone vessels (note here J686 and J687) and similar elements typical of 'Esdraelon' wares in northern Palestine, as well as a variety of similar decorations on EB I (B) jars (e.g. Amiran 1969: Photo 35, Pl. 10: 9).

Vestigial handles

These may be divided into two groups: (i) J238 - 240, with projections probably related to the rounded, up-folded lugs typical of holemouth jars (J1 - 24) and jars (e.g. J162/3/180); and (ii) (J393, J396-417) decorated horizontal applications which are related to lugs or ledge handles as well as impressed/incised bands of decoration (see below). Only one example occurs on a recognizable vessel (J393, genre/type FA), on the shoulder of the jar, below and in line with the loop handle. The rest may best be classed in the same genre (F) on the basis of similar fabric. The shape and size of these lugs varies from lozenge-shaped (e.g. J399) to elongated strip (e.g. J416); decoration consists of impressed, stabbed and incised circles, lozenges and lines. Parallels are common, particularly in EB I assemblages of Palestine and Transjordan: among many others, comparison may be made with examples from Tell el-Far'ah (de Vaux and Steve 1949: Fig. 13: 16; de Vaux 1951: Fig. 11, on a bowl); O.T. Jericho (Kenyon 1965: Fig. 4: 12, 23, on high loop-handled juglets in 'EB I B' context; see also related vestigial handles on holemouth jars); Bab edh-Dhra' (Saller 1964/5: Fig. 20: 2, on a bowl; Lapp 1968: Fig. 8: 4, a high loop-handled juglet [see the example from Jericho here]); Jebel Mutawwaq (Hanbury-Tenison n.d.: 29, 30 on body sherds, 38 on a 'lump handle', etc. [see J213 - 225 here]); Ghrubba (Neolithic or EB I [?], Mellaart 1956: Fig. 4: 24, 25, on deep bowls); and Horvat Usa and Tel Esdor (Ben-Tor 1966: Fig. 3: 10; Kochavi 1969: Fig. 18: 6 respectively; see the holemouth jars from Jericho above).

Distribution of parallels (in EB I contexts) appears to be limited to northern and central Transjordan, the central Palestinian uplands (i.e. Tell el-Far'ah), the southern Jordan Valley (i.e. O.T. Jericho), and southern Transjordan (i.e. Bab edh-Dhra'). Somewhat similar, though rare, examples come from southern Palestine (e.g. Arad, Amiran 1978: Pl. 79: 14). The majority of vestigial handles at Arad stem from a different genre altogether (*idem* 1978: *passim*), from 'Syrian Bottles', typical of EB II (but see Chapter 3, and Jawa's genre F).

'Knobs'

This category may be divided into three groups: (i) 'knobs' on handles (J447); (ii) 'knobs' near the rim of bowls (J136); and (iii) 'knobs' on the shoulder of jars. One example of each was found at Jawa.

J447 (Fig. 143) is unique (and a surface find) and combines a 'knob' with two snake-like bands of clay on either side, at the top of a small loop handle. General parallels, particularly for the snake-like element, may be found in Chalcolithic as well as EB I contexts (e.g. Khalil p.c., in the southern Araba Valley; Garstang 1936: Pl. XXXIV: 16, in an 'EB I B' context [?]; Kenyon 1960: Fig. 12: 7, Tomb A 94; 1965, Fig. 4: 20,

Tomb K2). Rows of knobs or short bands of impressed decoration on similar handles occur in EB I contexts (e.g. Saller 1964/5: Fig. 23: 5) where they are related to vestigial lug handles (see above).

J136 (Fig. 120), a hole-mouth jar, has one circular knob remaining near the rim. It may simply be a cruder version of the more normal up-turned lug handles, as we have noted in Chapter 3 above. On the other hand, its shape may be distantly related to similar features around the rims of bowls. Comparison may be made with a holemouth jar from Tell el-Far'ah (de Vaux and Steve 1947: Fig. 2: 10), and a bowl from the same site (de Vaux 1952: Fig. 12: 10).

J450 (Fig. 143) is a jar without rim or base. There are two small knobs side by side on the shoulder, just below the neck junction. Traces of pattern burnish survive beneath the knobs, making three vertical lines. Parallels for such paired protruberances can be found throughout EB I repertoires of Palestine, particularly in 'EB I B'. The following are close parallels: Tell el-Far'ah (N) (de Vaux and Steve 1949: Fig. 3: 16); Tell Um Hammad stage 3 (Helms 1986: Fig. 13: 7); Bab edh-Dhra' (Lapp 1968: Fig. 8: 4, [?] on a juglet in a raised, impressed band; Schaub p.c., on a small jar with two ledge handles; O.T. Jericho (Garstang 1932: Pl. VIII: 6, an EB II/III stump-based jug, and 9, a painted jar of [?] 'EB I B'; Kenyon 1960: Fig. 14: 10, on a large jar, 1965, Fig. 4, a single knob on a juglet); Azor (Ben-Tor 1973: 49, 1975, Pls 14: 4-8, 20: 3, Fig. 8: 9, 10, 12); Tell ed-Duweir (Tufnell 1958: Pl. 57: 59, a large jar); and Arqub el-Dahr (Parr 1956: Fig. 16: 205, a painted jar). The most common shape appears to be the small, rounded jar with two ledge handles at the waist and often a vertical false or pierced trumpet spout. This shape is completely new in the Palestinian pottery repertoire of the second half of the 4th millennium BC and may perhaps be traced westwards and northwards along the Mediterranean coast, in terms of origins (e.g. Braidwood and Braidwood 1960: Fig. 171: 34, in phase F).

A specific parallel comes from the unprovenanced collection from the Bab edh-Dhra' region published by Saller (*idem* 1964/5: Figs 13: 3, 14: 2) where more general parallels may also be found (1964/5: Figs 14: 3, with three knobs in a row, 23: 12, with stabbed patterns: four dots on the knob, two slashes beneath each one, 28: 14, a single knob on a juglet, and 32: 12, 13, double knobs on bowls). The specific example concerns two knobs, each decorated with stabbed dots, bracketing an incised (pre-firing) pattern (see also J395 above) made up of six vertical lines bounded by two horizontal ones (Fig. 167). The shape of the host vessel is similar to genre/type EA at Jawa (see Chapter 3) and may be compared with examples noted above which also have paired knobs on the shoulder (i.e. Jericho and Tell ed-

Duweir). The four vestigial, upturned rounded lug handles also parallel such features in vessels from Jawa.

The symbol created by the two knobs and the pattern between can be interpreted in a variety of ways, including the notion of an anthropomorphic intent (see Epstein on 'noses', etc., 1975, 1978b, 1982).

Marks on/near handles

Various decorative elements appear on ledge and loop handles. The former are either 'thumb' impressed or slashed, the latter 'thumb' impressed or stabbed.

'Thumb' impressed or slashed ledge handles (J167, 216, 221, 224: cf. also Chapter 3 on more formally treated handles) may be compared with the following: Tell Um Hammad (Betts [ed.] in press); Jebel Mutawwaq (Hanbury-Tenison n.d.: 43); the Jerash Survey (Hanbury-Tenison 1987: Fig. 6: 60, 61); and perhaps Tell el-Far'ah (de Vaux and Steve 1947: Fig. 1: 32 [?] 'Enéolithique Moyen'). Many related designs exist in EB I repertoires. The peculiar handle shape ('lump handle') appears to be limited to the central Jordan Valley, wadi Zerqa, and the Irbid/Ajlun/Jerash region and, of course, Jawa. Similar forms may also exist in the Hawran or southern Syria.

On the other hand, rounded and slightly upturned ledge handles (see Chapter 3: types J169 - 177 in genre/type BB) have a slightly wider distribution, as does the characteristic punctate decoration on J171 which runs along the sharp edge of the handle and up onto the body of the vessel, making an arch above the handle. Such special decorative treatment of handles can be traced back to the Chalcolithic period when handles are often highlighted by painted patterns (e.g. de Contenson 1956: Fig. 1: 5, 6). This scheme of impressed or incised decoration is paralleled directly at Tell Um Hammad in stage 2 (Helms 1987a: Fig. 6: 6) as well as many other sites in Palestine/Transjordan within EB I and specifically EB I A. Parallels come from wadi Zerqa (Gordon p.c.), Tell el-Far'ah (de Vaux and Steve 1947: Fig. 3: 6, a developed form in EB I/II [?], but nothing earlier), Bab edh-Dhra where related shapes occur on small jars (Schaub p.c.: 0224.62.11), and Jericho (Kenyon 1965: Fig. 8: 25, a punctate crescent above a ledge handle and a loop handle on a 'hybrid' vessel, from the tell: Kenyon and Holland 1983: Fig. 9: 31 [?]). The direct parallels, as before, seem to be limited to the central Jordan Valley about Tell Um Hammad, along wadi Zerqa, the Irbid/Ajlun/Jerash and Hawran/Jebel Druze regions.

'Thumb' impressed or incised loop handles (J421) are very common in EB I assemblages throughout Palestine (see also Chapter 3 on raised bands on loop-handles as a related trait). Comparison, among others, may be made with vessels from Tell el-Fara'h (de Vaux and Steve 1947: Fig. 5: 23), Bab edh-Dhra' (Saller 1964/5: Fig. 31: 13, an EB II/III jug; Schaub p.c.: e.g. 0401.10.12, 0416.62.22, 0408.62.22, etc., all loop-handled juglets), Jericho (Kenyon 1960: Figs 12: 22, 28, 13, from Tomb A 94, 1965: Fig. 4: 12), Affulah (Sukenik 1936: Pl. II: 28, 1948, Pl. VIII: 10 - 20), and Beth-Shan (Fitzgerald 1935: Pl. II: 19).

'Stabbed' or 'slashed' loop handles (J440/441) in EB I assemblages occur at the following sites: Jericho (Garstang 1935: Pl. XLIV: 13, 17 [?], slashed and stabbed, but from Chalcolithic context; Kenyon 1960: Figs 12: 5, 27, 13: 17, 30, 14: 3, all from Tomb A 94, 1965; Figs 4: 12, 8: 25, etc.); Horvat Usa (Ben-Tor 1966: Fig.5: 9); and Affula (see above).

Decorative bands

Continuous decorative bands occur in three variations at Jawa: (i) incised or slashed designs; (ii) punctate or impressed patterns; and (iii) impressed raised bands. The first two are most common on hole-mouth jars of genre/type AA, the third on jars of genre/type BC. Precise parallels for the hole-mouth jars have been given above (Chapter 3) and are limited at the moment to the Jerash region, wadi Zerqa, and the 'Zerqa Triangle' about Tell Um Hammad in the Jordan Valley. The balance can be compared to Chalcolithic, as well as EB I, practices throughout Palestine, Transjordan, and probably also southern Syria. The northern Chalcolithic of the Golan/Jawlan region may be related in some way, but not directly, in spite of superficial similarities. The patterns are, after all, determined by very common tools and, therefore, not by themselves very diagnostic (but see Helms 1986, 1987a for the most specialized form of this decoration in 'EB I B' at Tell Um Hammad in relation with the earlier northern Chalcolithic of the Golan/Jawlan region).

PAINTED PATTERNS

Painted decoration on pottery is rare at Jawa, representing a tiny percentage of the total sherd-count (Fig. 173). In most cases a red/brown pigment was used; the surfaces of the decorated vessels were usually prepared for painting by applying a cream slip. Most fabrics were light coloured, either yellow or light red.

Few recognizable vessel shapes were found in this category. There are three examples of loop handles (J444/446/448), six jar rims (J455/456/458/462/465/466), two bowls (J453/461), the former a spouted vessel, and six bases (J544[=533]/545-547[=542]-550). The rest are body sherds.

The painted patterns can be arranged in groups (see below), none of which can readily be recognized in the tradition Palestinian painted repertoires (notably 'EB I B'/'Proto Urban B', 'group-line painted wares', or 'B Tradition' [Shaub 1982]) of the later 4th

millennium BC. A reference to EB I B with regard to J535 in a
preliminary report was incorrect (Helms 1975). Some of the patterns
are so random (J547/542) or simple (J548) that the search for
comparisons is probably fruitless. The only presently available
parallels to the west and south of Jawa concern seal impressions,
which may be regarded as 'foreign' (see Ben-Tor 1978).

Chevron bands with net patterns (J534/535/531)

J534 (Fig. 173) is the clearest example. J531 and J535 (Fig. 173) may be
a separate group: it is possible to see a resemblance between J531 and
the net patterns separated by solid lines on a twinned juglet from
Jerusalem (Ophel) which clearly belongs to EB I B or the so-called B
Tradition (e.g. Amiran 1969: Pl. 11: 12); a related vessel, a typical EB I
spouted jar from Ghor es-Safi with ledge handles has large net-
patterned painted surface separated by vertical lines (e.g. Amiran
1969: Photo 44). At any rate, J534 finds no parallels in EB I pottery
repertoires of Palestine, but for some distant and extraordinary
examples such as some of the painted vessels allegedly from the Bab
edh-Dhra' region (compare Saller 1964/5: Fig. 13: 1 with a series of
linked diamond-shaped net patterns in vertical registers [EB I/II ?]),
and perhaps some of the undated vessels from Arqub el-Dahr (Parr
1956: Fig. 16: 191, 194). Net patterns in registers appear on a few
vessels of the Chalcolithic period, although in no case can a close
comparison be made: e.g. a painted Jar from Tuleilat Ghassul (e.g.
Amiran 1969: Pl. 2: 16); and a 'cream ware' jar from Gezer (e.g.
Amiran 1969: Photo 16, Pl. 5: 9).

   The nearest parallel in any Palestinian context is not a painted
vessel, but an impressed one. An impressed body sherd from Tel Dan
(Fig. 173: 3, 4; Ben-Tor 1978: Pl. 1: 9 [1C-4]) carries a design very close
to J534. The so-called seal impression from Tel Dan is attributed to EB
III (even IV) by Ben-Tor (1978: 89).

   Farther afield, any number of similar patterns may be cited,
mostly from much earlier assemblages (e.g. Garstang 1953: Fig. 54: 8,
12, 16, 22 from Level XXIII at Mersin). None of these, however, is
directly relevant to Jawa. Net patterns in rows of triangles are a
common form of decoration at Habuba Kabira which is roughly
contemporary with the establishment and occupation of Jawa
(Sürenhagen 1978: Tab. 37 [?], 38).

Chevron bands

Only one example of chevron bands was found (J540) and even it is
not absolutely certain in this category; it could, for example, be a
larger, better painted version of chevron and net designs. If the
pattern was a continuous one (Fig. 173: 1) we might cite certain roll
seal impressions as parallels (e.g. from `En Shadud, Braun 1985).

However, be the pattern continuous or discrete, the best parallels to hand come from Late Chalcolithic Tarsus (Fig. 173: 2b). Comparison can be made with continuous chevron patterns (Goldman 1956: Figs. 227: a, f, h3, i. q, 226: a) and also discrete sets of chevrons (*idem* 1956: Fig. 227: b, e, o, among others). These comparisons may well be significant: not on their own, but in conjunction with the evidence from Tell Um Hammad where the strata, which are unquestionably contemporary and directly linked with Jawa, also contain pottery vessels which find close parallels at Tarsus (see Helms 1987a and arguments; Goldman 1956: Figs 231, 232, 233, 343, high loop-handled juglets and fine shallow bowls from Late Chalcolithic graves).

Chevron bands in a vertical register (J532/536/538?/539)

The clearest example is J532 (Fig. 173: 6). The chevrons are applied in a similar way to J540 above, with the characteristic beading at the point. This feature, however, is not necessarily diagnostic of any one style; rather, it is the natural result of turning the wrist or twisting the brush at this point when applying the paint. There are some distant parallels among EBA pottery of Palestine: e.g. a jar base from Jericho (Garstang 1935: Pl. XXXVI: 10) whose decoration is similar to J549, and the 'Egyptian' vessel from near Bab edh-Dhra' (Saller 1964/5: Fig. 18: 5a). None the less, the closest Palestinian parallels within the EBA 'horizon' do not come from painted pottery, but from seal impressions (e.g. Ben-Tor 1978: Pl. 1: 1 [IA-1] and details of other impressions summarized in Fig. 12: 2a - 4) from Megiddo, Tell Ta'anek, and Tel Dan, dated between EB I and EB III (IV) (Ben-Tor 1978: 89). The Late Chalcolithic examples from Tarsus (cited above) may also be compared (especially Goldman 1956: Fig. 227: o). Earlier examples from Palestine come from the Chalcolithic period. The best comparison here is a late painted bowl with doubled ledge handles from Tuleilat Ghassul (Fig. 173: 7; North 1961: Fig. 15. 8469/8470).

Chevron bands in a horizontal register (J545)

Reconstruction of the design cannot be taken very far. The pattern of chevrons and oblique lines repeats about the base, within the horizontal register (Fig. 173: 8); some of the oblique lines appear to continue beyond the upper register line, onto the body of the vessel. No Palestinian parallel for such a design is known to me (but cf. Gophna and Sadeh 1988-9; Leonard 1989).

Vertical parallel lines with horizontal register(s)

There are broad net patterns of regular or irregular components (J533[=544]/537/448). J448 (Fig. 143) is a (high) loop handle (see also J444 below). Its ladder pattern can be paralleled in EB I assemblages in Transjordan and Palestine. Examples are known from stage 2 at

Tell Um Hammad (Betts [ed.] in progress), Jericho Tomb A 94, in a related (?) incised form (Kenyon 1960: Figs 12: 28, 14: 3, etc.), perhaps Affula (Sukenik 1948: Pl. VIII: 21; comparison can also be made with the related (?) incised versions, 11, 15, etc.), and Arqub el-Dhahr (Parr 1956: Fig. 167).

The designs on J533 [=J544] and J537 (Fig. 149), one of them a base, may be reconstructed as broad net patterns over most of the body of the vessel, in which the vertical lines are spaced more closely than the horizontal ones. At Tell Um Hammad, and elsewhere in Palestine, such patterns are more common in EB II assemblages (Betts [ed.] in progress). Distantly related EB I examples tend either to consist of vertical lines only (e.g. an example from Ai, Amiran 1969: Pl. 11: 24; see also examples in Tomb K2 at O.T. Jericho, Kenyon 1965: Fig. 8: 21, 26, and an example from Tell ed-Duweir, Tufnell 1958: Pl. 57: 59), or in much tighter net patterns in which the lines are oblique to the vertical axis of the vessel (see the example from Ghor es-Safi noted above [Amiran 1969: Photo 44]). The oblique net patterns continue to be painted on vessels well into EB II (e.g. at Beth Yerah, e.g. Amiran 1969: Photo 53) and may be regarded as originating, at least partly, in the Chalcolithic period (e.g. Amiran 1969: Pl. 2: 18, from Tuleilat Ghassul). The only vertical net patterns in later EBA assemblages concern incised or combed decoration (e.g. Amiran 1969: Pls 16: 1 and 18: 13, both from Beth Yerah, EB II and III, respectively). An example from Jericho (Garstang 1932: Pl. VIII: 9) has a series of vertical ladder patterns based on a double horizontal line some distance above the base. The jar has ledge handles and two knobs (see also above). Parallels for this pattern must, therefore, lie beyond the boundaries of Palestine/Transjordan, at least in terms of what is known about pottery assemblages.

Vertical/oblique/horizontal bands and filled circles/dots

J444 (Fig. 143) is a partial chevron pattern painted onto a doubled (high) loop handle. The closest parallel for this form of decoration comes from stage 2 at Um Hammad where it appears on high loop-handled juglets (Betts [ed.] in press; Helms 1987a, Fig. 10: 4). Related (?) incised versions in the same formal genre come from O.T. Jericho, predominantly from Tomb A 94 (Kenyon 1960: Figs 12: 5, 13: 17, 30). J446 may be compare with examples from Tell Um Hammad stage 2 (Betts [ed.] in press; Helms 1986: Fig. 14: 9; 1987d, Fig. 10: 4).

J453 and J461 (Figs 143, 144), a painted band about the rim of a bowl, can be found in both Chalcolithic and EBA assemblages. Most of the painted jar rims (J455/456/458/462/466) are too small to be diagnostic. The decoration of J465 may be compared with EB I examples from stage 2 at Tell Um Hammad (Betts [ed.] in press; Helms 1987a, Fig. 10: 4), Tell el-Far'ah (de Vaux and Steve 1947: Fig.

28), O.T. Jericho (Kenyon 1965: Fig. 4: 24, 29, from Tomb K2), the region of Bab edh-Dhra' (Saller 1964/5: Fig. 13: 1), Megiddo XX (Loud 1948: Pl. 94: 15), and Arqub el-Dhahr (Parr 1956: Fig. 15: 146, 169-171, 173, 174, 179, 180).

Free-style patterns (J543/547/542/549)

These patterns are obviously not diagnostic. However, the painted base (Fig. 149: J546) with its heavy vertical lines and round splashes of paint can be compared with examples from, albeit Neolithic, Mersin (Garstang 1953: Fig. 54: 19, 20) and also perhaps to the interior design of a bowl (exterior = continuous chevrons: see above) from Late Chalcolithic Tarsus (Goldman 1956: Fig. 226: a'). The closest comparison for the random patterns on J547 (= J542) comes from the Chalcolithic repertoire of Palestine (de Contenson 1956: Fig. 11: 21). (See Chapter 3 for parallels regarding the pedestal base J550 [Fig. 149].)

5. The Chipped Stone Assemblage

A. V. G. BETTS

The material described below comes from stratified and surface contexts on the main site of Jawa. All stratified material belongs to the earliest occupation at the site (4th millennium BC), and the material from surface collections appears to be closely related. There is no clear evidence for a chipped stone industry of the 3rd/2nd millennium BC, although it is likely that some *ad hoc* use of broken chert may have been made in the later periods. All chipped stone was collected by hand during excavation. The material has been supplemented by a series of purposive surface collections. Unfortunately logistic factors prevented a full study of the excavated material and the assemblage is discussed here without reference to quantitative data. (For an initial, and now superceded, description of the Jawa chipped stone see Duckworth 1976 and Helms 1981: *Appendix B2*)

The Jawa assemblage relates to assemblages from late Chalcolithic and EBA sites in Syria and Palestine (see Fig. 185 for sites mentioned). The industry is associated with 'urban'/village sites in the fertile areas and bears no close relationships to earlier industries in the *harra*. The assemblage is characterised by elongated cortical scrapers and broad blades which are produced using the Canaanean method of blade production (cf. Hours 1979: 59). These blades are used as knives, or broken into segments and hafted as composite sickles. Raw material for the Jawa assemblage comes from two sources. Most of the fine olive coloured flint used for the scrapers and the Canaanean blades is imported from an unknown source but is similar to flint associated with this industry in Palestine and may well have been obtained through the same trade networks (Rosen 1983c). Some use is also made of the coarser local cherts, mostly for sickle blades, and chert pebbles were collected from the wadi bed to chip into drill bits. Cores are rare at Jawa. No cores of the fine olive coloured flint were recovered, suggesting that the material was traded in either as blanks or as finished pieces. This seems to have been the practice on other sites within the 'Canaanean' trade network (Rosen 1983c), and adds weight to the notion that Jawa was part of the same exchange system. Small chips of olive flint among the debris show that some secondary working of this material was carried out on site.

A detailed study of late Chalcolithic/EBA chipped stone industries of Palestine has been made by Rosen (1983a). Although his typology is referred to below, it has been adapted slightly to accommodate the specific characteristics of the Jawa assemblage. Tools have been divided into three broad groups: scrapers, points, and knives. The second group is a loosely defined category including a variety of piercing tools, some of them possibly multi-purpose. The third category comprises all blade tools, including sickle elements.

Table 12. Chipped stone: provenance of samples

Fig.	No.	Provenance	Description
174		F3 408.1	scraper
175		LT1 901 ++	scraper
176		D2c 1032.2	scraper
177		UT1 707.3	scraper
178	1	F3 408.1	scraper (b)
	2	LF4 +++++	scraper (b)
	3	++++++++++	scraper (b)
	4	D1b 1014.13	scraper (b)
	5	F4c +++++	scraper (b)
	6	LF4 1500.2	scraper (b)
	7	LF4 1500.2	scraper (b)
	8	++++++++++	scraper (b)
	9	LT1 901.4	scraper (b)
179	1	LF2 903.5	scraper (b)
	2	LF4 1500.4	scraper (b)
	3	LF4 1501.1	scraper (b)
	4	D2a 1026.1	scraper (b)
	5	LF3 1402.3	scraper (b)
	6	++++++++++	scraper (c)
	7	++++++++++	scraper (c)
	8	++++++++++	scraper (c)
	9	++++++++++	scraper (c)
	10	++++++++++	scraper (c)
	11	D1b 1014.10	point (b)
180	1	+++++++++	point (a)
	2	++++++++++	point (a)
	3	++++++++++	point (a)
	4	F2 +++++	point (a)
	5	LT1 901.3	point (a)
	6	F3 409.2	point (a)

Fig.	No.	Provenance	Description
181	1	LF2 890.6	point (c)
	2	+++++++++++	point (c)
	3	UT2 722.4	point (c)
	4	D2a 1040.2	point (c)
	5	LF4 1509.3	point (c)
	6	+++++++++++	point (c)
	7	LF2 804.1	point (c)
	8	+++++++++++	point (c)
181	9	LF4 1500.20	point (c)
	10	+++++++++++	point (c)
	11	LT1 900.6	point (c)
	12	+++++++++++	point (c)
	13	+++++++++++	point (c)
	14	D2e 1065.1	point (c)
	15	LF2 805.20	point (c)
	16	LF2 804.1	point (c)
	17	D2a 1026.4	point (c)
182	1	F4c 420.3	knife (a)
	2	UT1 702.3	knife (a)
	3	D2a 1040.2	knife (a)
	4	C2 500.9	knife (a)
183	1	F4c 420.1	knife (b)
	2	LF2 820.6	knife (b)
	3	UT2 722.9	knife (b)
	4	LF2 830.5	knife (b)
	5	LF2 810.10	knife (b)
	6	+++++++++++	knife (b)
	7	LF2 800 +	knife (b)
	8	LF2 802.2	knife (b)
	9	LF4 1501.3	knife (b)
	10	LF2 805.17	knife (b)
	11	LF2 801.6	knife (b)
	12	LT2 800 +	knife (b)
	13	+++++++++++	knife (b)

TOOLS

Scrapers

a). Large subcircular or ovoid cortical flakes of fine olive coloured flint with facetted striking platforms (Figs 174 - 177). They have semi-abrupt or semi-invasive retouch around most of the working edge and are usually heavily smoothed and polished with a high silica gloss around all or part of the edge (see also Chapter 6). They form a low proportion of the cortical tool class. Measured examples range from 12.0 to 17.5 centimetres in length and 9.0 to 13.0 centimetres in width. These would fall into Rosen's category of round tabular scrapers, although their size clearly distinguishes them from the other scrapers in his 'Tabular' class. As he points out (1983a: 104), although these tools are commonly referred to as tabular scrapers, they are struck mostly from the level surfaces of large flat nodules and not from true veined or tabular flint. Since the source of the raw material used for the Jawa tools is not known, it is impossible to say whether this applied to the Jawa assemblage (Rosen 1983c; but see now Helms 1987a: Fig. 22).

b). Cortical flakes of fine olive coloured flint ranging in shape from rectangular to oval with semi-abrupt or semi-invasive retouch around almost all of the edge (Fig. 178: 1-5). Striking platforms are usually faceted. Several have flakes removed from the proximal end of the dorsal surface, clearly done after the original flake was struck, since on most pieces the secondary blow has produced slight flaking on the ventral surface as well. Several pieces have scratch marks on the cortex, probably signs of use, and some have silica gloss around part of the edge (see Chapter 6). Sizes vary from 4.0 to 9.0 centimetres in length and 2.5 to 8.5 centimetres in width. They form the largest group of the tabular class. In Rosen's typology these tools would correspond to his elongated and oval tabular scrapers (Rosen 1983a: 105).

c). Hollow scrapers made on cortical flakes with abrupt scalar retouch forming a shallow concavity usually about 1.5 centimetres across (Fig. 179: 6-10). They are only a very rare component of the Jawa assemblage. Rosen recognizes notches as an integral form within his typology and the hollow scrapers from Jawa are probably similar to forms which he describes as 'more elaborate concavities with internal retouch'. McConaughy also mentions notch/ spokeshaves at Bab edh-Dhra' (1979: 316) which he suggests were wood or bone working tools.

Points

a). Elongated pieces, roughly rectangular in cross-section with curved or slightly pointed ends, gently curved or sinuous in plan with sides shaped by abrupt scalar retouch (Fig. 180). Some have irregular invasive retouch on the ventral surface. Their use is unclear. Some may have been used as chisels or for other specialized tasks.

b). Borers. These are rare and mostly atypical. Two pieces are made on cortical flakes (Fig. 179: 11) and two have the point formed by alternate retouch. Rosen notes the '*ad hoc*' nature of borers in the Canaanean industry, a description which might also be usefully applied to the Jawa assemblage.

c). Drill bits made from small roughly flaked pebbles and chips worked to a short crude point with a triangular cross-section (Fig. 181). Many are heavily worn at the tip. They range in length from 2.0 to 3.5 centimetres and are common at the site. For this class Rosen only describes drill bits on blades. He has no equivalent to the typical pebble drill bits of the Jawa assemblage. The pebbles used for these tools are often heavily water-worn and were probably collected locally from the wadi beds.

Knives

a). Large blades or elongated blade segments made by the Canaanean method from fine olive coloured flint, with facetted striking platforms and a trapezoidal cross-section (Fig. 182). Some are snapped, others truncated, and most have sickle gloss along one edge (see Chapter 6). They correspond broadly to the reaping knife mentioned by Rosen in his discussion on sickles (1983a: 110; see also 1983b) although they do not always have traces of sickle gloss and were probably used more as general purpose cutting tools than as specific harvesting implements. There are no 'knives' on large blades with triangular cross-sections although blades of this type are sometimes produced from a Canaanean core.

b). Sickle elements on short blade segments with silica gloss along one or both edges (Fig. 183; see Chapter 6). Most are snapped, although one or two are retouched at the ends. They have both triangular and trapezoidal cross-sections and are mostly of olive coloured flint, although some local raw material is also used. Some pieces are backed and curved, probably to form the terminal segment in a composite sickle. Lengths range from 2.5 to 6.0 centimetres. The gloss tends to run parallel to the side of the blade, suggesting that the elements were hafted parallel to the handle of the sickle. Rosen (1982) notes that bilateral lustre is a feature of 'Early Bronze Age' assemblages and does not occur in the preceding 'Chalcolithic'.

DISCUSSION

A number of tool types listed by Rosen in his Canaanean and late Chalcolithic/EBA industries are not found in the Jawa assemblage. These include arrowheads which are rare in the Chalcolithic and EBA of Palestine and virtually absent on sites in northern and central Palestine. Rosen (1983a: 128) suggests that the general scarcity of arrowheads in the Chalcolithic period might imply a decline in the use of bows and arrows in hunting, and cites McConaughy (1979: 172) who considers that it is indicative of peaceful condition and a decline in warfare. Such interpretations must be qualified to some extent. The trend towards walled settlements in the EBA suggests a need for defensive weaponry of some kind, and yet there is no apparent increase in the number of arrowheads on EBA sites. If walled towns can be equated with a degree of social unrest then possibly stone-tipped arrows were replaced by other weapons of some kind, perhaps small copper points which have not survived, or even unretouched flint chips instead of the traditional carefully worked points (cf. Helms 1976a: 206ff.). At Jawa, where faunal evidence shows that hunting was practiced at least to a limited degree (Köhler 1981: 249), and where the heavy fortifications suggest that warfare was likewise a reality of life, one might assume that there were some weapons in use which have so far eluded recognition in the archaeological record (see also Chapter 7 for mace heads).

There is a certain degree of dissention in the literature on the subject of the flint industries of Syria/Palestine from the later Chalcolithic onwards. Crowfoot-Payne writes of 'the Canaanean industry' (1983: 722). She describes it as very simple, characterised by sickle blades made on Canaanean blades and tabular scrapers of various forms, including the fan scraper. Hours, on the other hand, saw the term 'Canaanean' as applicable only to the specific knapping techniques used to produce the large parallel-sided blanks commonly recognized as 'Canaanean blades' (Hours 1979: 61). One important aspect of this knapping technique is the preparation of the striking platform. "Le profil est plutôt rectiligne et les bordes parallèles, grâce à une préparation spéciale du talon. Ce dernier est presque aussi large que le corps de la lame, et toujours facetté, soit plan, soit convexe." (Hours 1979: 61).

Crowfoot-Payne (1983) states that the Canaanean blade was brought into Palestine at the beginning of the 'Proto-Urban' (EB I [A]) period and is widely known in Syria and Iraq. This view is also supported by Rosen (1983b: 23). Hennessy (1967: 44) has gone a step further and suggests that the 'Canaanean industry' spread out into Syria/Palestine from Mesopotamia. Both Hennessy and Crowfoot-Payne have recognised the similarity between the large blades found in Mesopotamia and the Canaanean blade of Palestine. Cores for producing these blades are also very similar (compare Tobler 1950: Pl. XCIVb and Anati 1963: 321). However, these similarities may not be quite as close as they appear, and there is some evidence that caution is needed in drawing close parallels between the Mesopotamian knapping techniques and those of contemporary Palestine. Many of the Mesopotamian blades are produced using a technique which creates a blade of similar form to that of a Canaanean blade, but with a small plain punctiform butt, and not the facetted, often quite broad platform of the true 'Canaanean blade'.

True Canaanean blades certainly occur in western Syria as far north as the Amuq plain (e.g. Braidwood and Braidwood 1960: 248, Fig. 8 - 10; Crowfoot-Payne 1960), and even well into Anatolia (Caneva 1973: 187, 189, Fig. 2: 6), but it is perhaps less certain that this precise technique for blade production is used consistently further to the east, and thus the suggestion that the Canaanean tradition is derived from Mesopotamian sources must be treated with caution. Although the tradition may have its origins outside Syria/Palestine, it is not necessary to look so far afield. Tabular scrapers with or without facetted butts occur in Palestinian assemblages from the late Neolithic onwards and it is not inconceivable that the technique of Canaanean blade production developed within its main area of distribution rather than outside it.

Whatever its origins, there is little doubt that the Jawa assemblage belongs to this tradition of flint assemblages found in late Chalcolithic/'Proto-Urban'/EB I levels on sites in Palestine and western Syria, and specifically to the industry described by Crowfoot-Payne as 'Canaanean'. There is general agreement that the appearance of elements of this industry - Canaanean blades and large well-made cortical scrapers - signifies trade contacts of some kind (e.g. Rosen 1983b, 1983c). The sources of raw material are uncertain although Rosen reports tabular scraper quarry sites in Sinai and the Negev (1983c: 80) but there is a marked visual similarity between tools of these types from different sites in Palestine, the predominant raw material being a fine-grained greyish/brownish/olive coloured chert, occasionally with faint banding. No such tools are known from camp sites within the basalt *hamad* although some similar pieces have been found on local coarse-grained grey cherts (Betts 1986: 295). Recent excavations at the al-Hibr rock shelter site (Betts in press) have provided evidence of a local (steppic) flint industry which, on the basis of typological comparison of pottery and lithics, can be dated within the 4th millennium BC, broadly contemporary with the Ghassul/Beersheba tradition. The flint assemblage uses local raw materials to produce a toolkit which has distant parallels in the Palestinian Chalcolithic, but has no shared features with the finds from Jawa beyond occasional use of platform faceting in flake production. The Jawa flint assemblage thus clearly exhibits strong links with 'urban' and village sites to the north and west but probably has little or no connection with indigenous steppic traditions.

Identification of tool use is a perennial problem and it is widely conceded that the use of generic terms such as 'scrapers', 'burins', and 'knives' may be quite erroneous, although convenient for the construction of general typologies. Most chipped stone tools were probably multi-functional to some degree as they were first shaped, and often saw secondary and again different use after they became worn or damaged. Despite these difficulties it is still possible to infer some ways in which particular tools may have been used. The cortical flake tools must have been used for tasks involving either scraping or cutting. Unger-Hamilton (see Chapter 6) suggests that the large flake tools (a) were used unhafted, and on the basis of the edge polish, postulates that they were used to cut reeds or to strip leaves from stems. Unlike the smaller elongated cortical flake tools (b), the larger scrapers show little sign of scratching or wear on the cortical surface.

Most of the smaller flake tools (b) do not have polished edges but some have marked striation on the cortical surface which gives an indication of the portion of the edge of the tool which received most wear, and the direction of the cutting or scraping motion. This varies from piece to piece. Some have a flake scar at the proximal end of the dorsal surface. These flakes represent secondary working and may have been removed to facilitate hafting. The prepared platform technique used to create the cortical blanks tends to produce a thick bulb of percussion which would make hafting of the proximal end difficult without secondary thinning. The hollow scrapers (c) may have been used in the manner of spokeshaves. Their concave profile would make them unsuitable for use as cutting tools.

The functions (or functions) of the elongated points (a) is (are) difficult to determine. Some may have been used as chisels, either hafted or unhafted. Others may have been used as hand-held borers. Macrowear traces seem to vary considerably and it seems likely that, although the tools appear superficially similar in form, they may have served a number of different purposes. The few borers recovered at the site (b) were most probably hand-held and used for such tasks as piercing skins. One class of tool can be readily identified, and that is the drill bits (c). These were found in large numbers together with debris which showed clearly that they were being used to pierce holes in stone beads. Material found in association with the drill bits included chunks of roughly chipped carnelian, bead blanks, partially drilled beads and some finished ring beads (Fig. 199; see also Chapter 7). The bits were probably hafted, possibly for use with a bow drill. The holes are quite regular and cut from both sides of the blank. Wear on some of the drill bits is extensive. The greatest concentration of drill bits and associated raw materials and finished beads come from test area B3 (Fig. 5). Although such tools have not been reported from other contemporary sites, there is a possible parallel in collections from sites on Jebel Druze (Beaulieu 1944: Pl. XXXI, top two rows).

Use of tools in the 'knives' class is easier to determine. The long blades (a) must have been used for cutting, either in the hand or in a haft. Extensive polish on some edges suggests that they were used as sickle blades. The smaller sickle elements (b) were probably hafted in composite harvesting tools (Fig. 184).

As discussed above, the Jawa assemblage has been classified using general typological grouping for convenience in comparison with other sites. As with all assemblages there are some pieces which cannot be fitted into the typology. These consist of miscellaneous retouched blanks and debitage. Many of the waste pieces may also have been put to temporary use as well but this cannot be determined without more detailed microwear analysis.

6. The Microwear Analysis of Scrapers and 'Sickle Blades'

R. UNGER-HAMILTON

Five tools with macroscopic gloss (one tabular scraper [Fig. 186: 1], one flake scraper [Fig. 186: 2] and three 'sickle blades' [Fig. 186: 3 - 5]) were subjected to microwear analysis based on the method pioneered by Keeley (1980).

Table 13. Microwear analysis: provenance of samples

Fig.	No.	Provenance	Comments
186	1	D2c 1032.3	scraper (cf. also Fig. 176)
	2	LF3 1402.3	scraper (cf. also Fig. 179: 5)
	3	F4a 420.21	blade
	4	LF2 830.4	blade
	5	++++++++++	blade

THE EXPERIMENTS

Over 300 blades were knapped with hammerstones and antler hammers. Unfortunately, flint types of the Jawa assemblage were not available. Instead, a variety of flint and chert from Britain, Israel, Syria, Egypt, and Lebanon was used, mostly fine and medium grained and similar to the Jawa material. The blades were used unhafted, or hafted in a straight wooden sickle (see Camps-Farber and Courtin 1982: Fig. 5 for a replica of a sickle found in the Fayyum in Egypt), or in a curved antler sickle (Fig. 184; see also Cauvin 1983: Fig. 5: 8 for a replica of a sickle excavated at Haçilar). Most had unretouched cutting edges; some had finely to coarsely denticulated cutting edges.

Experiments were carried out in Syria, Israel, Turkey and Britain, but not in Jordan; however, these experiments (Unger-Hamilton 1983) have demonstrated that the same plant species harvested in different localities normally generate similar wear-traces. (For exceptions connected with soils, see below.) It is possible that lack of knowledge of the local environment (but see Willcox 1981) may have meant that some relevant species were omitted in the experimental programme.

The following cereal species (in some instances green, ripe, and dried) were harvested: wild barley (*Hordeum spontaneum*); wild emmer (*Triticum dicoccoides*); wild einkorn (*Triticum boeoticum*); domestic barley (*Hordeum disticum*); domestic emmer wheat (*Triticum dicoccum*); domestic einkorn (*Triticum monococcum*); domestic spelt (*Triticum spelta*); *Triticum aestivum*; *Triticum durum*, and the following non-cereal species: tussocked steppe grass (*Stipa spp.*); *Aegilops speltoides*; *Juncus spp.*; reed (*Phramites communis*); bullrush (*Schoenoplectus lacustris*); *Sparganium ramosum*; *Cyperus longus*; *Scipus maritimus*; cane (*Saccarum sp.*); field poppy (*Papaver rhoeas*); oriental poppy (*Papaver orientale*); several species of weeds, as well as several species of wild and cultivated legumes, including *Vicia spp.*; *Cicer spp.*; *Lens spp.*; and *Lathyrus spp.*

13 blades were used to saw or whittle fresh and dried oak, ash, sycamore, and beech wood. 14 scrapers, including flake- and tabular scrapers, were used hafted or unhafted to scrape the same species of wood as above, as well as cane and reed. One scraper was used to strip leaves from reeds.

A full account of the experiments is given elsewhere (Unger-Hamilton 1984: 226-281; n.d.). Various interesting facts emerged: for instance, certain species such as legumes, could not be harvested by cutting with blades, while other species such as *Stipa* were much more easily pulled from their basal nodes than cut. This suggested that these species would not have been cut with sickles in the past.

Both the experimental and the archaeological tools were cleaned in water and detergent. They were investigated under the Olympus Vanox microscope and photographed using Ilford FP4 film at magnifications of 50x to 200x.

THE GLOSS

In the past, macroscopic gloss has been regarded as evidence for the cutting of straw (Spurrell 1982), wood (Vayson de Pradennes 1919), or any siliceous material (Curwen 1937), and has been termed 'sickle gloss, sickle polish, sickle sheen, corn gloss ...' (Diamond 1979: 159). My own experiments (Unger-Hamilton 1983) have demonstrated that moisture affected the speed of gloss formation considerably and that non-siliceous materials such as copper could cause gloss on flint (Unger-Hamilton 1984: 73-5). These findings indicate that terms such as 'sickle gloss' are misnomers. However, in practice I found that the only activity which produced a strong gloss evenly distributed over the cutting edges of flint blades was the harvesting of most of the plant species mentioned above, and to a lesser extent the working of wood (see below and also Curwen 1930). Levi-Sala's experiments (1986) have shown that rolling flint in wet sediment could generate diffuse gloss with an appearance that is identical to gloss derived from some plants; however, in this case all the edges of the tools were affected.

Experiments have also demonstrated that gloss and microscopic polish formed on fine-grained flint at the same stage; this was not the case with coarse-grained flint: on such flint gloss was often not visible long after microscopic polish had formed. It is, therefore, advisable to observe the graininess of the raw material before counting blades without gloss (with other indications of use such as edge damage) as 'sickle blades' (e.g. Otte 1976). Coarse-grained blades without gloss may well exhibit plant polish when studied under the microscope.

THE MICROWEAR ANALYSIS

Microscopic traces on tools from archaeological contexts were compared to the traces on all of the experimental tools mentioned above. Only the results which appeared to relate to the tools from Jawa are discussed here (for the overall results see Unger-Hamilton 1984: 226-81). The most important experimental finding was that there were some differences in plant polishes, apparently due to stem thickness, hardness, and moisture content. Cereal polish had a characteristic distribution with a polish concentration at the edge, diffusing gently inwards (Pl. 1). Experiments also demonstrated that no microscopic striations were visible on the experimental flint blades when water plants were harvested; a few striations were visible when plants were harvested from a grassy cover; and many striations were visible on the experimental blades when plants were harvested from tilled soil (Unger-Hamilton 1985). It is, therefore, likely that this striation criterion, which was first mentioned by Korobkova (1981), might be indicative of plant cultivation.

The Scrapers

The tabular scraper (Fig. 186: 1) was made of medium-grained flint and was 188 millimetres long, 92 millimetres wide, and 11 millimetres thick. It had a large notch (which appeared to be accidental, as it lacked a bulb of percussion) at its distal unretouched end, and a fine dorsal retouch on both lateral edges. The gloss (4 millimetres wide) was confined to the ventral aspects of the distal corners and adjoining lateral edges. No edge damage was visible on the ventral aspect.

The flake-scraper (Fig. 186: 2) was made of fine-grained flint and was 39 millimetres long, 37 millimetres wide, and 8 millimetres thick. It had somewhat irregular dorsal retouch on the lateral and distal edge and a notch on one lateral edge. The very strong gloss (9 millimetres wide) was confined to the ventral aspect and followed the curve of the distal edge. Some edge flaking was visible on the ventral aspect.

Confinement of the gloss to the ventral aspects and the alignment of micro-striations perpendicularly and obliquely to the distal edges, suggested that the tools had been used with a scraping motion.

The micro-polishes on both tools were similar (Pls 2, 3) given that the tools' raw material was of different grain size. The polishes were buoyant looking - a feature suggesting that the worked material had been fresh (see Unger-Hamilton 1983) - and they had the distribution of experimental polishes on tools used to scrape reed (Pl. 4). Two problems remained with the identification of the scrapers as reed scrapers: (i) the pronounced edge damage on the ventral aspect of the flake-scraper which was not found on experimental reed scrapers (this retouch may have been post-depositional, as it was unlustred); and (ii) micro-striations in the polish on both the scrapers which were not seen on my experimental reed scrapers. Striations had occurred when an experimental scraper had been used to strip leaves, and this may have been the case with the Jawa scrapers; alternatively, grit may have been present during use, or else another unidentified plant may have been scraped. It seems unlikely that this had been wood, as the often domed and striated polish from scraping fresh wood was confined to a narrow band on the very edge of the experimental scrapers (see Unger-Hamilton 1984: Pl. 5d), while the macroscopic gloss was much weaker than that on the scrapers from Jawa.

The 'Sickle-Blades'

The three 'sickle-blades' (Fig. 186: 3 - 5) from Jawa which were studied microscopically were between 60 and 27 millimetres long, 18 and 22 millimetres wide, and 5 and 6 millimetres thick. Two of the blades (Fig. 186: 3, 4) had bands of gloss and around 5 millimetres-wide micro-polish (Pls 5, 6); the distribution, flatness, and striations of these were consistent with the harvest of ripe cereals from tilled soils (see Unger-Hamilton 1983, 1984: 71-2, 226-81, 1985). This suggested that the blades had been used to harvest cultivated cereals. One of the blades (Fig. 186: 4) was patinated but the microwear traces (Pl. 5) looked identical to those (Pl. 6) on the unpatinated blade (Fig. 186: 3). The first-mentioned blade had heavy retouch on both used edges, while the other had a light unpolished retouch on the only used edge. Both types of retouch appeared to be compatible with re-sharpening.

The third blade with steep retouch on the cutting edge (Fig. 186: 5) was covered with broad random micro-striations which were probably post-depositional (Pl. 7); the fact that strong gloss and microscopic polish covered both aspects of the edge suggested that it had been used to cut plants, although no conclusion could be reached as to the plant species.

Hafting

Hafting traces in the form of polishes have been mentioned in various microwear publications. However, experiments using, amongst other devices, a bow-drill (Unger-Hamilton *et al.* n.d.) demonstrated that even with wedge hafting, hafting traces were absent. Nevertheless, hafting can sometimes be inferred from shape and retouch of a tool, as well as from the polish distribution. The considerable size and irregular shape of the tabular scraper (Fig. 186: 1), together with the fact that it had polish on both lateral edges, indicates that this scraper had been hand-held.

The flake-scraper (Fig. 186: 2) had several flakes removed from its ventral proximal end. It is possible that this was done to fit the scraper into a haft, although it may also have been done to facilitate holding the scraper by hand.

The size, shape, backing (in two cases), and truncation (in two cases) of the 'sickle-blades' (Fig. 186: 3 - 5) indicate that they had been hafted, end to end, in composite sickles (see Fig. 184). This is also suggested by the distribution of wear-traces parallel to the used edges. In one case (Fig. 186: 4) both edges had been used, and the blade may have been turned over in the haft, or else may have been taken out of the haft and used by hand.

CONCLUSION

Only five implements were studied and it is, therefore, impossible to come to any far-reaching conclusions about plant husbandry at the site. It appears that scrapers could have been used to scrape fresh reeds, perhaps in order to make projectile shafts (Clark *et al.* 1974) - although use on an unidentified plant or on wood cannot be ruled out - and that at least two of the 'sickle-blades' were used, as part of composite sickles, to harvest cultivated cereals.

NOTE

I would like to thank G. C. Hillman, Department of Human Environment, Institute of Archaeology, London University, for his help.

7. Other Finds

S.W. HELMS

Pottery and lithics apart, the finds from Jawa are not diagnostic for attribution to specific periods; they do, however, fit into a category which is typical of the later Chalcolithic period (i.e. as it is defined in the term 'Ghassul IV' by Mallon *et al.* 1934, or in Hennessy's phases A and B at the same site: 1969; the Beersheba region [Perrot, reference *passim*]; and also in the main occupation at Abu Hamid: Dollfus and Kafafi 1986, *Abu Hamid*) and the EBA (generally of the early part, or EB I) of Palestine, Transjordan, and southern Syria. In some cases the raw material of which these objects were made can be traced farther abroad. Much, however, was made of locally available basalt. Attempts to trace specific source areas for this material, when it was used in non-basaltic regions of Palestine, have been unsuccessful (Amiran and Porat 1984). The catalogue and the comparative study of the assemblage is arranged as follows.

1. Large basalt objects which have been drilled or hammered to make a variety of vessels such as bowls, mortars, and grinding surfaces, pounders, grinding stones, and hammers (Figs 187 - 194). These are subdivided into general vessels (J668-689), a door socket (J690), and various ancillary devices (J691-697). A specific decorated vessel form consists of J686-689.

2. Smaller drilled and polished objects, often made of materials other than basalt which do not occur naturally in the vicinity of Jawa. These objects were, therefore, imported over some distance (Figs 194 - 197). They include 'mace-heads' (J698-702), a variety of stone rings (J703-707), and 'hoes' (J708-712).

3. Miscellaneous stone objects (Figs 197 - 199): an 'arrow straightener' (J712) and unworked objects which were found at the site and used in some unspecified way (J713-720).

4. Various small drilled objects (Figs 199 - 201): carnelian beads, as well as blanks (J721-724); bone (J725-729); and pierced stones and pottery discs which are sometimes called 'spindle whorls' (J730-732).

5. Unbaked clay figurines, mostly of sheep/goat, when they can be identified (Figs 202 - 204), and other creatures (J733-753).

6. Several small fragments of copper alloy (not illustrated) were found, two of them in EB I A contexts in square C2 503.1 and UT1 703.3. These were submitted for analysis (Institute of Archaeology, London University). Results are not yet available.

This is accompanied by comments on manufacturing techniques, in so far as these might be identified.

COMPARATIVE STUDY

Large basalt objects

The entire group is paralleled in a photograph from the early excavations at Tuleilat Ghassul (Mallon *et al*. 1934: Pl. 34). Specific parallels from the same site for J675 and J675 (Fig. 189) have been published by Hennessy (1969: Fig. 12: 4), and 'saddle' querns accompanied by stone rubbers are common there. These are identical to the examples from Jawa (J696/697: cf. Mallon *et al*. 1934: Fig. 22: 'moulin en basalte'). Similar (later) Chalcolithic parallels come from the Huleh Basin: for example, a pounder similar to J694 (Fig. 193) comes from Tell Turmus (Dayan 1969: Fig. 9: 1); a shallow basalt bowl from Rasm Harbush in the Golan/Jawlan region (Epstein 1978a: Fig. 13). Crude stone vessels and pounders similar to J674 - J677 and J693 (Figs 188, 189 and 193, respectively) are known at Chalcolithic Horvat Beter (Dothan 1959b: Fig. 11: 1, 6, 12, 13). Standard 'saddle' querns occur in assemblages from the Golan/Jawlan region (Epstein 1978a: Fig. 5).

Comparable examples from EBA contexts come from Tel Yarmuth (Ben-Tor 1975: Fig. 9: 19 = J668 [Fig. 187]), including the hole in the base, from Arad (Amiran 1978: Pl. 78   J676 [Fig. 189], cf. also Pl. 79 for a quern = J696 [Fig. 194]), and from O.T. Jericho (Dorrell 1983: Fig. 231: 14 = J668/669 [Fig. 187] in handle form). Door sockets (Fig. 192: J690) occur at EB II Arad in precisely the same positions as at Jawa (Figs 22: FB and BC, 25: wall BC; Amiran 1978: Pl. 191: 1884). Comparison may also be made with a typical 'saddle' quern from Abu Hamid (*Abu Hamid*: Fig. 35).

Farther afield, parallels may be sought in the various assemblages at Hama: e.g. a quern-covered pit (?) in Niveaux L1 (Fugmann 1958: Fig. 18, Foyer no. 42), which is also a common internal house feature at Jawa (Figs 13, 22: F3a, 38: AE). Similar querns appear in EBA contexts at Hama (Fugmann 1958: Fig. 30: K10, 7C 148) and continue in use well into the MBA. Shallow bowls (e.g. Fig. 190: J680) find parallels in Hama K5 (1958: Fig. 46: 'S.N.' bowl), and also in later 'horizons' (1958: Fig. 64 3J 148 No. 42/H11 = J668-670 [Fig. 187]). Parallels can also be found in assemblages from the Amuq region of northern Syria, in Amuq F (Braidwood and Braidwood 1960: Fig. 187: 6, 7 = J674, J679 [Figs 188, 189]), and in Amuq G (1960: Fig. 247: 4 = J675, J676 [Fig. 188]; Fig. 251: 3, a quern = J696 and J697 [Fig. 194]). Byblos provides parallels in both 'énéolithique ancien' and 'récent' (Dunand 1973: Fig. 118: 34858 = J671 [Fig. 188], including the omphaloid base; cf. also Pl. CLVB: 32947 = J680, and 23269 = J687 [Figs 190, 191]).

On the basis of these few comparisons, this group of objects can be dated anytime from the Chalcolithic period (in both Syria and Palestine) up to the end of the EBA, and later in the case of the 'saddle' querns. The vessels and ancillary tools are simple, crude, and completely utilitarian; many similar forms are still in use today in the basaltic regions of Syria and Jordan. In some cases they are newly made; in others ancient objects are reused. With the exception of J668, J669, and J673 (Figs 187, 188), none of these vessels can be regarded as anything but utilitarian. J687-690, however, form a separate group.

Pedestal-based bowls

J686-689 (Figs 191, 192) are utilitarian, but they were more carefully made. Three of them are decorated. In general form (hence the inclusion of J686) they can be regarded as stump- or pedestal-based bowls and as such they are loosely related to more enigmatic forms common in, and apparently unique to, the Golan/Jawlan assemblages of the so-called northern Chalcolithic period (Epstein 1975). Epstein has made much of these objects, interpreting them in symbolic and cultic terms (Epstein 1978b, 1982). Mittmann (p.c.) reports finding a related vessel in an EBA (EB II - EB III) context at Tell Zeraqun near Irbid; he also reports finding a similar form at Jawa (p.c.). However, it is doubtful that the examples from Jawa can be interpreted in this way.

The decorated vessels from Jawa belong to a distinctive genre which can be more closely dated and perhaps also localized in southern Syria, Transjordan, and Palestine during the late Chalcolithic/EB I period: i.e. in absolute terms in about the second half of the 4th millennium BC (but see qualifications regarding absolute dates in Chapter 1).

The form itself (flat-based, heavy pedestal foot, flared rounded or bevelled rim, a band of raised decoration below the lip) can be recognized in some utilitarian forms of the Chalcolithic period. A stone vessel from Tuleilat Ghassul shares these features, but for the decoration (Mallon *et al.* 1934: Fig. 23: 7). A high-footed, shallow vessel from the same site is similar to J686 (Fig. 191: cf. *idem* 1934: Fig. 24). Another parallel comes from Abu Hamid (*Abu Hamid*: Fig. 37). Very similar forms are known in the Huleh Basin and the Golan/Jawlan region (e.g. Dayan 1969: Fig. 9: 9; Epstein 1978a: Figs 6, 13; 1988: Fig. 7). These close parallels presumably belong to the 'northern Chalcolithic' period which is usually considered to be contemporary with 'terminal' Ghassul (i.e. Ghassul IV or Ghassul A/B : see above). In the northern regions, these parallels occur with fenestrated basalt vessels, which are probably related to the slightly later fenestrated pottery forms typical of the 'Esdraelon' wares (e.g. Amiran 1969: Pl. 10: 6-8). In terms of the Jawa group, we might suggest that their origin lies in the Chalcolithic period, perhaps in the northern parts of Palestine and the southern regions of Syria (Hawran/Jawlan), and that the special form and its decorative band(s) is a development which occurred in the late Chalcolithic/EB I period, during the second half of the 4th millennium BC. The broader distribution of the basalt vessels, in comparison with that of the 'Esdraelon' forms, might support the notion that pottery imitated stone on this occasion.

A more common, southern Chalcolithic form (including fenestrated vessels) consists of everted, sharp-rimmed bowls (e.g. *Abu Hamid*: Fig. 40), some with characteristic incised decoration, usually in the shape of triangles near the rim (see examples from Horvat Beter, Dothan 1959b: Fig. 11: 18) which are related to forms known as 'bols coniques' (cf. de Contenson 1956: *passim*).

The form of the Jawa vessels can be paralleled in repertoires from many Palestinian/Transjordanian sites, mostly in the time-range of the late Chalcolithic/EB I period. In terms of decoration, however, we can distinguish two related styles: an apparently north-eastern one in which a band of rounded knobs is preferred, and an apparently central-southern one which favours knobs or raised, 'impressed' or incised patterns in single or double bands. Both styles are found in the same archaeological contexts at Tell Um Hammad in the central Jordan Valley: two examples of the 'north-eastern' style, and one of the 'central-southern (Betts [ed.] in press: Reg. nos 39, 15, and TUH4222, respectively). These parallels at Um Hammad occur in stage 2 whose contexts also include the direct pottery and 'sub-epigraphical' parallels with Jawa (Chapters 3 and 4). At Tell el-Far'ah (N) the examples in stone are undecorated (de Vaux and Steve 1949: Figs 6: 21 = J689, 8: 26 = J687/688, both in 'EB I B' contexts; de Vaux 1951: Fig. 11: 16), but occur together with 'Esdraelon' wares, many of whose raised decoration is similar to the 'central-southern style. Similarly, a vessel from Bab edh-Dhra` (Lapp 1968: Fig. 9: St.1 from Tomb A 76) is undecorated, but occurs together with related pottery forms of the 'central-southern' style (see also below). Examples from Tell Fara (S) are also undecorated (Macdonald 1932, all in basalt, together with fenestrated examples and 'churns': i.e. all of the Chalcolithic period?). An undecorated pottery form may be related to this group of stone vessels, rather than the earlier 'bols coniques': the form has been re-drawn by Hennessy (1967) to resemble an Uruk-style bevelled rim bowl (cf. Kenyon 1965: Fig. 12, Tomb K1: 6, and a similar form from Tell el-Far'ah [N], de Vaux and Steve 1949: Fig. 2: 3; see also Millard 1988 and Beale 1978 for references).

Parallels in the 'north-eastern' style (i.e. direct parallels for the Jawa vessels) come from the following sites: Tell Um Hammad (see above); the Jerash Region Survey (Hanbury-Tenison 1986: Fig. 28: 15 - 17; n.d.: Fig. 6: 12, 14, 15); and from Jebel Mutawwaq (= 'Meghanieh' in Glueck 1951: cf. Pl. 163: 8).

The 'central-southern' style occurs at the following places: Tel Yarmuth (Ben-Tor 1975: Fig. 9: 18); at an unknown site (an unprovenanced vessel: Several 1975); at Lachish (Tufnell 1958: 254-5, Pls 26: 7, 56: 13 [pottery]); Tel Gath/`Areyny (Yeivin 1967: 48); and at Bab edh-Dhra` in Tomb A 76 (Lapp 1968: Fig. 9: St.1) where the vessel is plain, but also associated with a similar form (*idem* 1968: Fig. 10: 8; cf. also the photograph in Fig. 13) whose decoration can be classed as 'central-southern'. This has long been known in regard to the area of Bab edh-Dhra`: similar stone (and one in clay) vessels reputedly come from this area (Saller 1964/5: Fig. 26) with single and double bands of raised or incised decoration. One version of this vessel type has a loop handle (*idem* 1964/5: Fig. 27, basalt mug No. 185) which could also have a typological connection with the broad pottery genre of the late Chalcolithic/EB I period known as 'high loop-handled juglets' (see now Helms 1987a; see also Chapter 3: genre F). It can be argued that many forms attributed to this period (mid- to late 4th millennium BC) have a regional distribution in terms of details and their combination, but at the same time they share formal and structural attributes, suggesting that they all stem from a common source, and/or developed regionally (see arguments in Helms 1987a, also in regard of fenestrated forms; 1987a: Fig. 17: 15, cf. also 17: 16, *passim*). Similar examples come from Nizzanim (Gophna 1979: 136) and Rosh Hanniqra (Tadmor and Prausnitz 1959: 8, Fig. 6: 37).

There may be a relationship between the form (including its pottery versions) and vessels from Palestinian EB II and EB III contexts, such as those from phase VIII at 'Ai (Callaway 1972: Fig. 73: 2, *passim*), Arad (e.g. Amiran 1969: Photo 62), and Beth-Shan Levels XI and XII in EB III (Fitzgerald 1935: Pl. IX: 24, 25). One of the cups from Beth-Shan (*idem* 1935: Pl. IX: 24) can be compared with the basalt cup illustrated by Saller (1964/5: Fig. 27) in terms of its 'high loop handle'. It is possible, though pure speculation, to ask whether these EB III forms may have been an Egyptian inspiration, or (perhaps better) an Anatolian one, say from as far away as the Troad (cf. Ritter Kaplan 1981: Fig. 20, and discussion *passim*.)

Parallels for the decorated, flared, and pedestal-based vessels, therefore, place the examples from Jawa well within the general cultural ambit of the 4th millennium BC; they also suggest a 'cultural' connection with the 'north-eastern' regions of Transjordan and we should   probably   include   here   the   essentially   unexplored

Hawran/Jebel Druze region, and perhaps also the Damascene (al-Ghuta) as a potential geo-economic centre of gravity. Connections with regionally variant, but demonstrably related, genres may suggest diffusion and/or contacts as far south as the southern Ghor in Transjordan, and as far as Lachish/Tell ed-Duweir near the Mediterranean coast.

Mace-heads

Mace-heads are the most accomplished among the stone objects (in the technical sense), but like the rest, they are not useful in terms of close dating: and, because of their wide distribution throughout the ancient Near East, they may not easily provide information about their diffusion. However, together with the other objects from Jawa, they are at least not out of place in a 4th millennium BC setting. If anything, their presence shows that despite Jawa's remoteness and its material (though not technological) poverty, these mace-heads appear to be a common phenomenon, whatever their function may have been.

The earliest examples of this form come from Neolithic contexts (Petrie 1920: 22-24, Pls XXV, XXVI; Speiser 1935: Pl. XLa; Tobler 1950: Pl. CLVIIa) in both Egypt and Mesopotamia. Comparable Chalcolithic examples in a southern Levantine/Syrian and Transjordanian setting come from a number of well-known sites. Chief among these is the 'Cave of the Treasure' where a large repertoire of various genres, in a variety of materials, is represented. All of the forms from Jawa (Fig. 194: J698, piriform, Figs 194 - 195: J699 - J702, oval and smaller variations) can be found in this rich assemblage from Palestine. The metal mace-heads from the 'Cave of the Treasure' have been qualitatively and quantitively related to examples from Nahal Se'elim and Beersheba, both Chalcolithic in date (Bar-Adon 1980: Appendix E; Nahal Se'elim, cf. Aharoni 1961: 14, Pl. 8: 6; Beersheba, cf. Perrot 1955: 79, Pl. 15: A; 1957: 1, Pl. I: 3). Comparable examples in haematite (Bar-Adon 1980: Nos 184-189) have also been related to types from the above-mentioned sites, as well as Bene Beraq (Kaplan 1963: 3000, *passim*), Azor (Perrot 1961: Fig. 43: 4), and Megiddo (Loud 1948: Pl. 270: 11). An example in limestone (Bar-Adon 1980: 423) is piriform (= Fig. 194: J698) and may be compared with mace-heads from Tuleilat Ghassul (Mallon *et al.* 1934: 71-2, Pl. 35; cf. also Hennessy 1969: Fig. 13), from Beersheba (Dothan 1959b: Figs 11: 14, 18: 56, Pl. VII: 2; Perrot 1955: 189), Beth-Shan (Fitzgerald 1935: Pl. III: 26, 27, perhaps better dated in EB I rather than the Chalcolithic, Pl. X: 23, 24, in an EB III context [?]), Megiddo (Loud 1948: Pl. 270: 2, *passim*), O.T. Jericho (Garstang 1936: Pls XXX: 19, XXXVI: 25), and from Nahal Besor, Site H (Macdonald 1932: Pls XXVII: 78, 79, 81, 82, XXVIII: 9).

Recent excavations at Abu Hamid in the Jordan Valley, some 20 kilometres north of Tell Um Hammad, have revealed analogous oval and piriform mace-heads (Dollfus and Kafafi n.d.: Pl. 15: 5-8; *Abu Hamid*: Figs 48-50). These examples are slightly earlier in date than stage 2 at Um Hammad, but very close in time and perhaps also representative of demographic and social relationships between the Chalcolithic populations and those of EB I (A) (cf. now Helms in press).

Mace-heads from late Chalcolithic/EB I contexts related to the Jawa examples come from Tel Arad's Strata IV/III (Amiran 1978: Pl. 76: 1-6), Tel Yarmuth (Ben-Tor 1975: Fig. 21: 1, Pl. 12: 7), Bab edh-Dhra`, Tomb A 76 (Lapp 1968: Fig. 9: St.3; cf. also Saller 1964/5: 191, Fig. 25: 3a and references to parallels, including examples in Egyptian alabaster), `Ain Shems (Grant and Wright 1968: Pl. LIV: 63, 64, together with tabular scrapers [see Chapter 5]), O.T. Jericho (Holland 1983: Fig. 365: 1-11, and a full discussion of parallels, including examples from Gezer, Gaza, etc.), and Tell Um Hammad in stage 2 (Betts [ed.] in press: Reg. Nos 12, 54). More in the same environmental zone as Jawa, similar forms have been found at Khirbet Umbachi/Hébariye (Dubertret and Dunand 1954/5: Pl. VII: bis. 1) together with pottery which might belong to the 4th millennium BC ; on the other hand, there is also extensive EB IV occupation (Braemer p.c.). A broken macehead has also been found at a site near Qasr Burqu' (Site 27000) in levels of Late Neolithic/Early Chalcolithic date (Betts p.c.).

The omnipresence of mace-heads in the ancient world is demonstrated by their appearance in Egypt, Anatolia, and Mesopotamia. All of the Jawa forms can be recognized in these repertoires. Chalcolithic and later examples may be compared with examples at Hama throughout 'horizon' K (Fugmann 1958: K10/9, Fig. 30: 5A 886, 7A 736; K6/5, Fig. 46: 7A 548, 7A 675, 4C 443, the last in polished calcite; K3, Fig. 49: 7A 389, in polished calcite; K1, Fig. 54: 6B 21, also in polished calcite). Very similar types come from the Amuq region (Braidwood and Braidwood 1960: Fig. 250: *passim*, but for no. 4) and also from 'énéolithique récent' Byblos (Dunand 1973: Fig. 181).

The evidence, imprecise as it may be, can suggest a floruit in the use of the mace-heads which are similar to those from Jawa throughout the 4th millennium BC in Palestine, Transjordan, and southern Syria. The parallels at Byblos also seem to support this, as perhaps do those parallels from the north (i.e. Amuq), and as does their appearance at both Abu Hamid and at Um Hammad in the Jordan Valley. In the last two cases, they appear in a purely rural setting. Their function, despite an arguably 'royal' symbolism in the famous palette of Narmer (Petrie 1953), may have been purely utilitarian; on the other hand it is possible to suggest a ceremonial function in terms of a leadership symbol within an hierarchical or stratified society (see below).

Rings

Little can be said about the specific form and function of these objects (Fig. 200: J729 - J728): they are common throughout the Near East, ever since stone could be drilled. A few parallels suffice. Comparison within Palestine/Transjordan can be made with 'spindle whorls' from the 'Cave of the Treasure' (Bar-Adon 1980: ill. 57) and Arad's Strata II/III, in EB II contexts (Amiran 1978: Pl. 76: 7, *passim*).

'Hoes'

'Hoes' are irregular, elongated stone objects, roughly perforated, usually towards one end (Figs 196, 197). They occur in all stone assemblages, from the Neolithic period up to the present and served a variety of functions; as loom, net and stick weights, digging implements, and so forth. Their basic form changes little through time and they are, therefore, of no value as chronological indicators.

Miscellaneous

Most, if not all, of these objects (Figs 197-199: J710-718) were 'manuports' or 'objéts trouvées'. J712, a worked basalt piece with a groove is of a form usually referred to as an 'arrow straightener', and appears to be most at home in an early Neolithic setting. Dorrell (1983) has presented a comprehensive study of such objects from O.T. Jericho: he calls them 'grooved stones' (*idem* 1983: Figs 230: 7, 8, 222: 4, Pl. 10a). Most of them come from the PPNA stage at the site (c. 8th millennium BC: see Table 1) and the single example from Jawa could have been transported from one of the earlier sites nearby (see Appendix A).

The rest of the objects in this general class are unworked and consist of locally available volcanic debris. Their form defies functional identification (? toys: see Betts 1989). J717/718 could have been used as weights, or even buttons or toggles.

Carnelian beads

Beads and bead blanks (Fig. 199: J721-724) are associated with manufacturing waste and flint drill bits (see Chapter 5) and were presumably made in workshops at the site (see also 'unbaked clay figurines' below). A concentration of beads, blanks, and drill bits was found in Test Area B [UT 4] (see Chapter 2; Fig. 5). Similar beads are known at many sites: comparison, for example, may be made with pieces from 'énéolithique récent' Byblos (Dunand 1973: Fig. 189),

Arad's Stratum III, in EB II contexts (Amiran 1978: Pl. 68: 4), and O.T.
Jericho (Talbot 1983: Fig. 364: 1-5).

Unbaked clay figurines

But for one example (Fig. 203: J742), which was found in the earth
and stone matrix of dam D1 (see Chapter 2), all figurines were
discovered in area LF2, virtually in the same locus (see Figs 64, 65:
locus 805). It is debatable whether this evidence could be used to
suggest a specialized workshop in this part of the lower settlement.

In terms of style, the figurines form two groups. Most are
recognizable as animals (J733-751). Two (J752/753) are enigmatic:
they could be anthropomorphic (i.e. J752 could have a 'nose': cf.
Epstein 1975, 1978a, 1982, etc.), but their execution and state of
preservation is so poor that speculation is as senseless as trying to
find meaningful stylistic parallels. The animal figurines, on the other
hand, are recognizable and might be divisible into species. All but
J739 seem to be sheep/goat, some of them perhaps fat-tailed sheep
(i.e. J733, J734, J737, etc.). J739 could represent a bovine creature. If
this is really so, we might recall Köhler's breakdown of species in
Jawa's faunal record (1981) in which cattle, though less numerous, are
more significant because of their relative weight (see also Jawa's rock
'art' in Chapter 8).

Close, though perhaps not meaningful, parallels may be cited.
Similar clay figurines representing animals are known from
Chalcolithic Tuleilat Ghassul, some of them perched on the rims of
pottery vessels; others are actually incorporated into the fabric of the
vessels (Mallon *et al.* 1934: Fig. 35; Hennessy 1969: Fig. 11: 4-6, Pl.
XVb). The 'Cave of the Treasure' produced ostensibly Chalcolithic
examples (Bar-Adon 1980: ill. 11, Reg. No. 61-230). Strata IV/III at
Arad, in EB I and EB II contexts, contained similar figurines, both in
style and scale (Amiran 1978: Pl. 117: 1-4). Farther north, at Hama, a
series of comparable pieces comes from various 'horizons': e.g. Hama
L (Fugmann 1958: Fig. 13: 7A 764), Hama K (*idem* 1958: K7, Fig. 37: 4A
920, 4A 916, 4A 918 = J739; K6/5, Fig. 46: 4A 740, 7A 576, 7A 412, 4A
742 = J739; K4, Fig. 49: 4C 69 = J739; and K2/1, Fig. 54: 4A 496, 4A 68).
Similar pieces are known in phase G in the Amuq region (Braidwood
and Braidwood 1960: Fig. 237: 4 = J739).

SUMMARY

Most of the objects discussed here provide a broad date-range, from
the Chalcolithic period, through the EBA and, in some cases, even
later. This is particularly true of the purely utilitarian vessels and
tools. Pedestal-based bowls, however, appear to be more closely
dated: in either the Chalcolithic period, or in the early part of the

EBA; they, therefore, corroborate Jawa's date of main occupation in the 4th millennium BC. They also point to cultural and perhaps also economic links with the north of Palestine/Transjordan and southern Syria (i.e. 'north-eastern style'), paralleling many of the 'connections' already established by the pottery (Chapter 3). On the other hand, the distribution of comparable mace-heads is much wider and cannot be used to localize socio-economic contact zones. Their date-range is also broader than that of the pedestal-based bowls: from the Chalcolithic (even Neolithic) well into the EBA. The currently available evidence might suggest a floruit of use in the 4th millennium BC, but this is uncertain. The balance of 'other objects' has no chronological value, and only slightly more with regard to links beyond the vicinity of Jawa.

CATALOGUE

Ground stone vessels (Fig. 187)

668	TT1 100.1	basalt, shallow bowl with squared handle, hole in flat base perhaps caused by abrasion through use as a mortar or grinding bowl
669	UT1 705.14	basalt, shallow bowl with rounded handle, flattened base, int. worn or polished through manufacture or use
670	UT2 722.5	basalt, shallow bowl with rounded handle, rough flattened base

Ground stone vessels (Fig. 188)

671	TT1 100.1	basalt, small shallow bowl with rounded handle, omphaloid base
672	F4 410.2	basalt, shallow bowl, irregular shape, flattened base
673	F3 408.1	basalt, shallow bowl, ovoid shape, pierced or drilled ledge, polished through manufacture or use
674	++++++++++	basalt, shallow bowl, flattened base

Ground stone vessels (Fig. 189)

675	F2 405.1	basalt, shallow bowl, slightly omphaloid base, irregular shape
676	UT2 +++++	basalt, shallow bowl, rounded base, irregular shape
677	F4 410.2	basalt, shallow bowl, rounded base, one side wider to form handle (?)
678	P2 +++++	basalt, shallow bowl, slightly omphaloid base, one side wider to form handle (?)

679   UT1 705.1   basalt, bowl, pointed or conical base

Ground stone vessels (Fig. 190)

680   F2 405.1   basalt, bowl
681   ++++++++++   basalt, small shallow bowl
682   C2 504.1   basalt, shallow bowl
683   UT2 720.2   basalt, 1/4 fragment of shallow bowl

Ground stone vessels (Fig. 191)

684   UT1 700.1   basalt, square block with shallow
                                 depression, slightly omphaloid base
685   C2 504.1   basalt, shallow container, originally
                                 triangular shape (?)
686   TT1 100.1   basalt, mortar, shallow depression
                                 in high flat base

Ground stone vessels (Fig. 192)

687   F4 410.2   basalt, flared rim bowl on high
                                 flat base, int. polished
688   F2 405.6   basalt, flared rim bowl on high
                                 slightly omphaloid base, band of
                                 raised rounded knobs about waist
689   ++++++++++   basalt, bowl, pointed in-turned rim,
                                 band of raised rounded knobs near lip
690   C2 504.13   basalt, shallow depression in triangular-
                                 shaped form, rounded irregular base,
                                 door socket (?), see features in area F

Ground stone pounders and grinders (Fig. 193)

691   F3 408.1   basalt, pestle or pounder, square 'handle',
                                 rounded shaft worn through use
692   TT1 100.1   basalt, pestle or pounder, bulbous
                                 end worn through use
693   TT1 100.1   basalt, pestle or pounder, one
                                 end worn through use
694   TT1 100.1   basalt, cuboid pounder or rubbing
                                 stone, worn through use
695   C2 504.1   basalt, flat rounded rubbing
                                 stone for use on stone 'saddle'
                                 quern [cf. J696/697], worn through use

Ground stone saddle-querns and mace-heads (Fig. 194)

696   UT1 702.5   basalt, 'saddle' quern, rounded
                                 irregular base, upper surface
                                 worn through use
697   UT1 700.1   basalt, 'saddle' quern, upper

		surface worn through use
698	LF2 820.1	quarzite?, mace-head, piriform shape, unidirectionally drilled through, surface polished
699	LF2 804.14	quarzite?, mace-head, bidirectionally drilled through, piriform shape, surface highly polished

Ground stone mace-heads (Fig. 195)

700	F4c 420.3	quarzite?, mace-head, bidirectionally drilled through (offset), piriform shape, surface polished
701	LT1 903.4	basalt, mace-head, bidirectionally drilled through, oval shape, surface polished
702	UT1 700.1	basalt, mace-head or weight (?), bidirectionally drilled through
703	D2a 1026.8	basalt, weight (?), bidirectionally drilled through

Ground, pierced stones (Fig. 196)

704	F4 +++++	basalt, weight (?), unidirectionally drilled through
705	++++++++++	basalt, weight (?), bidirectionally drilled through
706	++++++++++	basalt, weight (?), bidirectionally drilled through
707	F3 708.2	basalt, weight (?), bidirectionally drilled through
708	UT2 722.9	basalt, weight or 'hoe' (?), bidirectionally drilled through (off axis)

Ground, pierced stones (Fig. 197)

709	LF4 1500.5	chert, weight or 'hoe' (?), unidirectionally drilled through
710	++++++++++	basalt, 'hoe' (?), bidirectionally drilled through
711	++++++++++	basalt, 'hoe' (?), bidirectionally drilled through
712	++++++++++	basalt, 'arrow straightener' (?), grooved top worn through manufacture or use (Neolithic?)
713	C2 500.2	basalt, polished (?)

Basalt pebbles (Fig. 198)

714	F3 408.1	basalt
715	++++++++++	basalt
716	UT1 700.1	basalt
717	LF2 805.9	basalt
718	LF4 1500.13	basalt

Basalt pebbles and pierced stones (Fig. 199)

719	LF4 1501.3	basalt
720	++++++++++	basalt
721	UT1 703.1	carnelian, bead, flat surface polished, bidirectionally drilled through
722	LF2 830.3	carnelian, bead, surface polished, bidirectionally drilled through
723	LF4 1500.2	carnelian, bead blank, roughly shaped
724	LF4 1500.5	carnelian, bead blank, roughly shaped

Pierced stones (Fig. 200)

725	LT1 900.2	bone, rounded and polished on surface, bidirectionally drilled through
726	UT2 720.3	bone, polished and rounded, bidirectionally drilled through (?)
727	++++++++++	bone, polished and rounded, drilled through and smoothed
728	DX +++++	bone, rounded, drilled through and smoothed
729	UT1 702.1	bone, pin, sides rounded and polished, one rounded end bidirectionally drilled through

Drilled objects (Fig. 201)

730	F4c 420.15a	plaster, pinched and pointed, top partly pierced.
731	F2 405.28	pottery sherd, rounded and bidirectionally drilled through
732	C2 504.6	pottery sherd, rounded and bidirectionally drilled through

Animal figurines (Fig. 202)

733	LF2 805.5	unbaked clay, figurine
734	LF2 805.1	unbaked clay, figurine
735	LF2 804.22	unbaked clay, figurine
736	LF2 802.22	unbaked clay, figurine
737	LF2 1000.4	unbaked clay, figurine
738	LF2 1000.3	unbaked clay, figurine
739	LF2 805.10	unbaked clay, figurine

Animal figurines (Fig. 203)

740	LF2 805.12	unbaked clay, figurine
741	LF2 805+++	unbaked clay, figurine
742	D2a 1026.1	unbaked clay, figurine
743	LF2 805+++	unbaked clay, figurine
744	LF2 805.17	unbaked clay, figurine
745	LF2 805.22	unbaked clay, figurine
746	LF2 805.21	unbaked clay, figurine

Figurines (Fig. 204)

747	LF2 805.6	unbaked clay, figurine
748	LF2 805.6	unbaked clay, figurine
749	LF2 805.10	unbaked clay, figurine
750	LF2 805.22	unbaked clay, figurine
751	LF2 805.12	unbaked clay, figurine
752	LF2 805.10	unbaked clay, figurine
753	LF2 805.17	unbaked clay, figurine

8. Rock Carvings and Inscriptions

S.W. HELMS

The Jawa area is rich in inscriptions (mostly in Safaitic and Arabic scripts) and rock carvings. It was the abundance of Safaitic texts which first drew attention to the site - apart from Poidebard's air photograph (1934) - resulting in Harding and Winnett's surveys (Winnett 1951, 1957) and, ultimately, in the current comprehensive recording by the Corpus of the Inscriptions of Jordan Project of Yarmouk University and the Department of Antiquities of Jordan lead by M.C.A. Macdonald (1982, 1983, forthcoming) which has also undertaken the recording of the rock carvings (Searight 1982, 1983). A full inventory will become available in due course. At this time, however, it may be useful to list a representative selection of rock art and a note on some inscriptions from Jawa and its vicinity, in order to see how this material might be related to the occupational record of the site. Some of the rock art has been published before (Hunt 1976; Helms 1981).

ROCK ART

Jawa's rock art may be divided into two broad categories: representations of animals, and representations of human beings, enigmatic objects and other things.

Drawings of animals may be subdivided according to species (when these can be recognized) as follows: cattle, deer (?), sheep/goat, camels, oryx, gazelle, predators (lions or hyaenas?), horses, donkeys, ostriches, dogs, and so forth. A few of these might be dated through their association with texts (mostly Safaitic), between about the 1st century BC and the 4th century AD. A few carvings of camels may be linked with recent Arabic inscriptions. Modern rock art in the *harra* is occasionally pornographic or restricted to the depiction of trucks (= camels: e.g. Chatty 1986). Drawings of cattle, and possibly also deer (?), are undated and, so far as I know, never linked with any texts. These drawings have some close stylistic and technological parallels in the Syrian steppe and northern Arabia.

Cattle

Rock drawings A1 to A6 (Figs 205 - 210) represent cattle and form a stylistically and technically closed group. The carving and drawing techniques involved hammering or pecking the surface of the basalt to produce the outline (e.g. A4), combinations of outlines, and partially infilled portions of the body and head (e.g. A1), or uniformly rendering the whole form of the animals in this way. In all cases only flat surfaces were used: there are no instances of sculptural use of the stone to augment the liveliness or three-dimensionality of the animals (as, for example, in European painting of the Paleolithic period). It may be possible to reconstruct the carving procedure, from the first pecked outline and internal body divisions (i.e. shoulder, belly, hock, etc.), to completely pecked end-product (see also Bowen in Macdonald, forthcoming). On the other hand, the partially infilled types may have been intended as such: to show distinctive markings (see also Köhler 1981).

These drawings are remarkably uniform in both design and style. Draughtsmanship is lively in most cases (but for A3 and A6 perhaps), and normally the artist strove to create group scenes (e.g. Fig. 206: A2). Both draughtsmanship (outline and stance) and composition combine to produce realistic pictures: for example, the herding of cattle in A2 and the group of three on the left side (middle) of A1 showing a bull, cow and perhaps a suckling calf (see also Helms 1981: Pl. 8). All animals are drawn to the same formula by rendering the body and limbs in profile and the head in plan. It is the composition of the head that provides the best, though by no means conclusive, stylistic criterion for comparison with other drawings of cattle in the greater steppic region of Syria/Transjordan and perhaps also Saudi Arabia (see below). A6 is the only example from Jawa which may be slightly different, but this may simply be because of its rather minor role in a different composition (cf. A21 below): its outline is cruder (although the pecking technique is the same), as is its head whose rendering appears to be abbreviated to showing only the horns in plan.

Four relatively close stylistic and compositional parallels can presently be cited. One parallel comes from al-Ghirqa near the Neolithic site of Dhuweila (Fig. 213c; Betts and Helms 1987). Al-Ghirqa itself is an extensive occupation site of the Late Neolithic period (c. 6th millennium BC); the carving, however, is probably later than this: it was cut on a free-standing building stone and is, therefore, not dated in any strictly archaeological sense. The execution (drawing) of the cattle at al-Ghirqa is cruder and the scale much smaller than at Jawa. The heads, however, were composed in precisely the same way: particularly in the largest of the animals (Fig. 213: lower right).

A second, very similar, set of carvings (Fig. 213 a, b) has been found at al-Wusad, where the TAP-line emerges on the eastern edge of the *harra*. The drawing style and patterning of the bodies (i.e. Fig.

213a, top) is almost identical to those at Jawa. One of the recorded drawings from al-Wusad may include other animals (sheep/goat or dog).

The third parallel comes from Qasr Burqu` on the eastern edge of the *harra* (Fig. 214; Betts p.c.). It is drawn in a somewhat different style, scratched rather than pecked. The body is indicated with a series of curved lines; legs are simple scratched lines. However, it is the combination of body in profile and horns in plan which allows us to relate these drawings from the Burqu` area to those at Jawa and al-Ghirqa.

A fourth set of parallels comes from Saudi Arabia, from Jubba and Bi'r Hima (Adams *et al.* 1977: Pl. 12; 'Jubba-style' cf. Zarins *et al.* 1979: Pl. 9; Zarins *et al.* 1981: Pls 34, 36). The pecking technique and the partitioning of the bodies are closely comparable. Heads are also drawn in much the same way at Jubba (e.g. Adams *et al.* 1977: Pl. 12, lower right), in contrast to the heads from Bi`r Hima. At that site we are dealing with a slightly different combination of profile and plan: the heads are drawn in profile, while the horns appear in either plan or perhaps even in 3/4 view (cf. also a typology in Livingstone *et al.* 1985: Pls 125 - 127). Another difference in both sets of these Arabian parallels is that the Arabian cattle are being hunted and not herded, as we suggested for one of the scenes from Jawa (i.e. Fig. 206: A2: even if we interpret the object held by on human figure as a mace [cf. Chapter 6]). The Arabian scenes include 'speared bovids' who appear with human figures armed with spears and bows. The same 'spearing' appears with camels and oryx in these examples and this might suggest that all of the illustrated species were wild. For the camel, this stage could be as late as the 4th, if not early 3rd millennium BC (Clutton Brock 1987; cf. also Adams *et al.* 1977: Pl. 12, lower right, where a camel is cut over a bull and is possibly contemporary with two inscriptions, also cut over the legs of the 'earlier' animal). For the cattle we of course have proof of domesticated species at Jawa itself, in archaeological contexts of the 4th millennium BC (Köhler 1981). Paintings of horned animals (or 'onagers') are known from Neolithic Umm Dabaghiyah in Iraq (Kirkbride 1975: Pl. VIIa). These, however, are drawn entirely in profile.

Examples of cattle in the art of more distant regions might be cited, although they probably have nothing directly to do with Jawa of the 4th or even early 2nd millennia BC. In proto- and early dynastic Egypt the typical form consists of body and head in profile and horns either in plan or frontal view (e.g. Petrie 1953: pls B, F, G, J, K). A similar rendering is used in a stamped (?) relief on the base of a hole-mouth jar from Beth Yerah (Khirbet Kerak) and attributed to EB II/III

(Sussman 1980). The same general style is common in north Syria and Mesopotamia (e.g. Woolley 1929: Pl. VIIIa).

On stylistic and technical grounds we may conclude that the Jawa cattle represent a south Syrian or north Arabian artistic repertoire which, at this point of research, is limited to the steppic zones. No precise date-range can be assigned on this basis, although we can suggest a range prior to the introduction of the Safaitic script to the region (i.e. c. 1st century BC).

Archaeo-zoological data for the greater region are still scarce, but there is enough evidence to substantiate the presence of *bos primigenius* in the Azraq marshes as early as the Natufian period, in the 10th/9th millennium BC (Garrard *et al.* 1987; cf. also Betts and Helms 1987) and also in the Neolithic (7th-6th millennium BC; Garrard *et al.* in press). Jawa itself has produced a significant percentage of *bos taurus* (8.5 per cent of the total bone count: but close to 50 per cent by weight in comparison with other species, notably sheep/goat: Köhler 1981: Fig. E1). One other site in the region, Khirbet Umbachi, has produced a massive concentration of cattle bones (Dubertret and Dunand 1954/55) associated with a 14C date of 2125 +/- 160 BC, i.e. roughly contemporary with the Palestinian EB IV/MB II A period and maybe a little earlier than Jawa's Stage 2 (the 'citadel' complex). At this point then we have four attested date-ranges for the presence of cattle in the *harra* in archaeo-zoological terms: the 10th/9th millennium BC, the 7th-6th millennium BC, the late 4th millennium BC, and the late 3rd/early 2nd millennium BC, the latter two with domesticated species. None may be relevant to dating Jawa's cattle drawings and their stylistic parallels at al-Ghirqa, al-Wusad and Qasr Burqu`, but the evidence does suggest that cattle were domesticated, bred, and reared in the greater region of the Hawran/Jebel Druze by the 4th millennium BC; and also, that they may have been an important part of the economy then and thereafter.

A7 (Fig. 211b) may be related to the group discussed so far. Its production technique is the same, as is its attitude (i.e. running or bounding). However, the long sinuous horns may identify the animal as something other than cattle. Sheep/goat, one with long curving horns, were drawn on the same stone (to the left; Fig. 211a), using more or less the same technique. There are no associated inscriptions.

Turning now briefly to textual and other sources for references to cattle, we can cite a few relevant examples which, however, only prove the presence of domesticated cattle in adjacent areas: i.e. Jebel Druze (Bashan), the Hawran (and the Ghutah/Damascene?) and, farther west, the Jezre'el Valley up to the Mediterranean coast.

Two quotations from ethnographic accounts are of interest, if nothing else. Alois Musil (1928: 415) recorded various beliefs current among the Rwala bedouin regarding black (basalt) boulders in the *harra (harrat al-rajil)*. Three specific areas are mentioned, of which two probably refer directly to Jawa and its immediate environs. These are Gâwa (= Jawa) and as-Subejce (? = qa' [al-] shubayqa: see Fig. 2). The third is Gennâwa (? Jannawah).

(i) "At as-Subejce there are a few large black boulders said to be inhabited by ginn. Close to them yawns the opening of an ancient well from which they water their herds."

(ii) "In the neighbourhood of Gâwa and Gennâwa lie many boulders shaped like cows. A long time ago the ginn kept a herd of cows there, which pastured on grass grown on firm soil as well as on the rimth and raza' thriving only in sand. Allah, however, forbade them to raise cows and transformed the cows into boulders."

The specific mention of boulders shaped like cows at Gâwa (? Jawa itself) could relate to the subject matter of our rock drawings, particularly to A1. (The boulders, specifically the one with drawing A1, are of course not cow-shaped.) Musil (1928) also reports that the Rwala believed that the 'ginn' have 'underground villages' near the 'ridge of Lâha', near Bâjer and also near al-Mwejsen, a story which is very similar to some current bedouin (Ahl al-Jebal) notions of underground villages near Jawa. These are reported to have been used as shelters by the bedouin to avoid French aerial bombardment some years ago. One such place was identified to us by the bedouin: it turned out to be a lava flow cave (called mughara, 'cave') which had been used as an underground water storage system capturing surface runoff via an intricate series of gravity canals of uncertain date (see Helms 1981: Pl. 32). A similar, but much smaller, cave nearer Jawa was perhaps originally used as a shelter during the Natufian period (see Mugharat al-Jawa in Appendix A); it was later incorporated into the water systems of the 4th millennium BC settlement.

One of the earliest relevant texts referring to cattle in our greater region comes from the 6th dynasty of Egypt (c. 2345-2181 BC), a little before our date for the 'citadel' complex at Jawa. I have tried elsewhere (Helms 1989) to associate Jawa with Upper Retenu (to the west: i.e. the Hawran and Jabal al-Druze) during this period, and in that sense Uni's campaign under Phiops I (Pepi I: c. 2332-2283 B.C.) to the 'Antelope's Nose' may be relevant, if the area of his campaign can be localized near Mount Carmel (Sethe 1908-22: pt. II: 101ff.; Pritchard 1955: 228), and the Jezre'el Valley inland from there, including of course Megiddo. A little later, and perhaps closer to the date-range of Jawa's 'citadel' complex, is the story of Sinuhe, providing that we may regard it as containing some ethnographic data about inland Syria, somewhere east of Byblos, possibly in the

Damascene and/or Hawran/Jebel Druze area (Pritchard 1955: 18-22; see also Helms 1989a). In that story mention is made of cattle, in what can be interpreted as a semi-sedentized and 'sheikhly' nomadic setting to the west and north of Jawa, perhaps near Jebel Druze, the Hawran or the Damascene. Two further Egyptian sources are dated in the 12th dynasty (c. 1991-1786 BC), again close to the construction and occupation date of the 'citadel' complex. The tomb of Meir (under Ammenemes II) contains a mention of 'oxen of the Asiatics...' which may have been brought from Palestine (i.e. from the Jezre'el Valley; Posener 1971: 542). The tomb of Thuthotpe at Deir el-Bersha (under Sesostris III) contains references to 'cattle from Retenu' (Posener 1971: 543). Thuthotpe resided at Megiddo where a 'seal' of the 'steward' or 'accountant of cattle' was found as well as a statue of Thuthotpe himself. By the 18th dynasty (c. 1570-1320 BC) the cattle of Retenu had long been famous, and were obviously valued as booty (and/or imports) by the Egyptians. Thutmosis III (c. 1504-1450 BC), for example, is said to have taken 2000 head of cattle after the siege of Megiddo. It may, therefore, be possible that cattle had been a major part of the Syro-Palestinian economy at least from the 2nd half of the 3rd millennium BC onward, according to these sources. Furthermore, we can localize the region of cattle rearing in northern Cisjordan (Jezre'el, Huleh Basin and Tiberias) and see behind that another, perhaps even more extensive, breeding zone in the Hawran and the Damascene, as well as the eastern slopes of Jebel Druze. The last subzone of course contains both Jawa and Khirbet Umbachi.

Later textual sources mention Jebel Hawran (Druze/Bashan) and its environs: e.g. after Shalmaneser besieged Damascus in 841 BC he says, 'I marched as far as the mountains of Hawran [sade MAT Ha-u-ra-ni]' destroying and burning many towns (Epha'al 1982: 76). Specific mention of cattle comes from biblical sources: i.e. the '[contented] cows of Bashan' along with other produce such as the 'oaks of Bashan' (Isa. 2.13; Ezek. 27.6, etc.). Amos (4.1) is of particular interest with regard to our remarks about cattle from southern Syria and the Jezre'el region of Palestine: i.e. 'cows of Bashan who live [or, graze ?] on the hill of Samaria'.

In conclusion, both archaeo-zoological and textual data provide the possible date-ranges for our cattle drawings, if we include the occupation periods at Jawa: i.e. the Natufian period (10th/9th millennium BC); the Neolithic period (7th-6th millennium BC); the second half of the 4th millennium BC; and about 2000 BC, or a little later. None, of course, need be correct. However, in all of these possible time-ranges (especially the later two: i.e. when domesticated species are attested) we can see an important economic aspect which is certainly augmented by the physical presence of cattle during the

4th millennium BC at Jawa. This aspect is that cattle were important in the region; that Jawa, al-Ghirqa, al-Wusad, and Qasr Burqu` represent wider geographical parameters for the exploitation and grazing of cattle than was hitherto suspected, which, in turn, may mean that some nomadic groups of the time (as also in the 2nd millennium BC) included cattle in their multi-resource economy. This leads to the notion of extending an economic system which by historical times also included trade and commerce from Egypt via the coast to the Jezre'el Valley, the Hawran/Bashan/Damascene, out to the edge of the dry steppe. It also may suggest a new insight into the role of tribally organized people (i.e. bedouin: see Helms 1990; Betts in press) with Jawa itself as a permanent settlement in the 4th millennium BC (a *parembole nomadon*, or a 'colonial' extension eastwards from the Hawran/Jebel Druze) and perhaps a station of some kind encompassing the 'badiya' concept at the beginning of the 2nd millennium BC.

Other animals

A8 (Fig. 212) is pecked in the same way as the cattle discussed above. Its form, however, is different and definitely not cattle-like. The drawing is crude, the body (male) virtually unidentifiable, although we are dealing with a large animal (Fig. 212, right) which is being followed or stalked (?) by a smaller beast with a large head and a long, curving tail (lion?). The shape of the horns of the larger animal - long, wavy, with splayed ends - might suggest a stag (deer: cf. also Fig. 217: A9c below). There are no inscriptions anywhere near this scene. An undistinguished shape is visible above the tail of the horned animal: this might be interpreted as a human figure.

Most of the animal scenes (Figs 218 - 221: A9-A17) belong to the 'era' of the Safaitic bedouin (c. 1st century BC to 4th century AD) and later, up to the recent past, either because a few of them are directly associated with inscriptions of the same patina, which in some cases actually describe the scenes (e.g. Fig. 215: A9; Harding 1953), or by comparison with 'dated', stylistically similar examples. The majority of these carvings should be regarded as undated, and probably undatable. (Macdonald [p.c] notes the unreliability of both association and patina.)

A9 (Figs 215 - 217) demonstrates an example of the relationship of the Safaitic texts, the variety of species, and standard compositions, all on one stone (but see cautionary remarks regarding association and patina above). In Figure 217 we may identify oryx (A9b), perhaps deer (A9c), ostrich (A9d, and also Fig. 218: A10), and lion or hyaena (A9a) among the wild species, and horse and camels among the domesticated ones. The hunting scene (Figs 215, 216: A9a) is typical of Safaitic rock art whose inspiration could be contemporary

Hellenistic and Roman art. A similar scene, clearly associated with a Safaitic text was found south of Jawa (Hunt 1976; see also Macdonald 1981). A11 to A15 (Figs 219 - 220) represent isolated drawings of oryx, gazelle, dog (?) lion/hyaena (?) and also a great many sheep/goat. A16 and A17 are typical renderings of camels: one about to sit (Fig. 221: A16); the other hobbled (Fig. 221: A17). Drawing style varies from crude, simple, even abstract to remarkably realistic; production method varies from pecking and hammering (as in the earlier examples), to scratching and cutting.

However, one carving (Fig. 222: A18) apparently pre-dates those discussed above, and can be compared in production technique, form and style to carvings of gazelle and equids from securely stratified and, therefore, 'dated' deposits. These parallels come from Early Neolithic (late 7th millennium BC) contexts at Dhuweila some 50 kilometres southwest of Jawa (Betts 1987, 1988).

The Dhuweila carvings were found in and around a hunting camp sited on a 'kite' wall overlooking the extensive mudflat of qa' Dhuweila. At a number of similar sites in the vicinity more carvings were found on rocks forming part of the structures or lying nearby. The carvings are faint, heavily patinated, and difficult to see except in strong oblique light. Since the discovery of the stratified figures, further survey in the Jawa area has shown that there are similar carvings in several locations along wadi Rajil. Large flat slabs brought in to reconstruct P1 were probably from an Early Neolithic camp as many of them, on close examination, proved to have figures of animals incised on them in the Neolithic style. Similar carvings were also found during epigraphic survey in the Jawa area (Macdonald p.c.).

Typically, the carvings take the form of an outline produced by fine semi-continuous scratched lines. In some cases detail is added by light, even pecking, particularly on the bodies of the animals. Although some anthropomorphic and abstract designs were found at Dhuweila, none have been identified in the Jawa area. The Jawa area carvings, like most of those from other parts of the *harra*, are quadrupeds, shown in profile. Some have short, upright or curving horns and a short tail. The animals are shown singly or in groups, sometimes overcut one on another. The majority face to the right. Most are standing or running, some are looking back over their shoulder and one or two appear to be grazing. The figures are well observed and lifelike, despite the resistant surface of the basalt cobbles on which they are carved.

The hunting camps in the Dhuweila area, are associated with use of the 'kite' systems, animal traps for the mass killing of herd animals. From the faunal remains at Dhuweila, it appears that gazelle was the main prey, together with more limited exploitation of equids. We should, therefore, expect to find signs of Early Neolithic activity somewhere near Jawa (see Appendix A).

Humans, enigmas and other images

Drawings A19 and A20 (Fig. 223; cf. also Fig. 206: A2) are undated, although examples accompanied by Safaitic inscriptions are known (King p.c.). Both of the illustrated examples are stylized and ostentatiously male. The execution is crude and further analysis probably meaningless, although the more formal pose and composition of A19 can be compared with 'prayer-like' attitudes of stylized figures on pottery vessels (e.g., Saller 1964/65: Fig. 18: 5 for an example from the 4th or 3rd millennium BC). We have already noted this attitude in Chapter 7 in reference to Amiran's hypothesis regarding the representation of deities.

A21 and A22 (Figs 224 - 225), however, may be more plausibly related to cultic matters, although speculation in this direction is probably fruitless and inappropriate at this stage. A short analysis suffices.

A22 (and its parallels in A21; Figs 225, 224, respectively) stand alone and I have no knowledge of a close parallel at Jawa which is accompanied by a clearly contemporary inscription (but see below). The pattern consists of a 'T' shape whose horizontal has a series of pendant lines forming a comb-like image. Various real objects might be seen in this: e.g., a parasol, a rake, head-gear of some kind, and so forth. There are, however, some dated cognate examples (cf. A23) and, therefore, we cannot say more at this time.

But, the example in A21 (Fig. 224: d - g) might be taken further. Firstly, it is clear that the Safaitic and Arabic texts are later on the basis of lighter patina; how much later this might be is of course debatable. Secondly, we have a number of undated, but stylistically and technically similar, images which may represent a contemporary set. There are, first of all, three animals (Fig. 224: A21a - c, A6) consisting of a cow (cf. A6; see also 'cattle' above), and horned animals (sheep/goat, oryx, or even equid, [A21c]: cf. Neolithic examples in Kirkbride 1975: Pl. VIIa) followed, or stalked, by a beast with a long pendant tail (lion?, A21b) recalling the composition of A8. Secondly, there is a number of anthropomorphic figures, each surmounted by comb-like designs which are related to A22. They occur in two forms: a more common one consists of the 'comb-like' pattern above and/or attached to a (headless?) human form (Fig. 224: A21e - g) and one example of a more elaborate arrangement (Fig. 224: A21i). The production method, as we have said, is uniform and similar to that of the pecked lines in the cattle drawings. The patina of these figures in A21 is also much darker (therefore older, usually) than that of A22, although this cannot be used as a reliable dating criterion from one stone to the next (see Betts and Helms 1987: 333ff.; Betts 1987).

The meaning of these figures is obscure and perhaps cultic in some way. Similar carvings have been found at Jawf/Sakkaka in association with cattle carvings. These are attributed to the Chalcolithic period, but only on the basis of nearby artefact scatters (Khan *et al.* 1986: pl. 87). The closest compositional (or iconographic) parallel comes from Neolithic Çatal Hüyük where Mellaart has suggested a funerary practice and cult involving the exposure of corpses to vultures (1967: 167 ff.,Fig.47). Somewhat similar designs, also interpreted as vultures, were found at Neolithic Umm Dabaghiya (Kirkbride 1975: Pl. VIIb). Little is known about funerary practices at Jawa. One dolmen has been found just north of the site. It was empty (but see now Yassine 1985 on the use of dolmen in EB I in the Jordan Valley; see also Epstein 1985b on their use in EB IV and MB II A, i.e. c. 2000 BC, both more or less corresponding to the occupation periods at Jawa). Extensive cairn, or cist-grave, fields have been identified south of Jawa (Fig. 3; Helms 1987e). Several cairns were opened. Nothing was found within or about them and, therefore, evidence regarding the possible ritual significance of this particular type of 'enigmatic' rock art at Jawa is negative.

There are several stylistically related examples of these 'enigmatic' figures near Jawa, all of which might perhaps be dated in the post-Safaitic 'era', after about the 4th centuries AD. Two of these (Figs 226, 227: A23, A24) are accompanied by contemporary, and intriguingly similar, inscriptions. A23 shows a comb-like design with vertical lines pendant on a vertical line which ends in a crescent. The combing is shorter than in the other examples described here. A24, on the other hand, has a comb-like or tasselled base and three horizontal cross-line of which the uppermost is the shortest and thinnest. The larger cross-lines have attached wavy lines: one on the left of the upper cross-line; a similar line on the left of the lower one; and a hook-like design on the left. A24 is also accompanied by a set of wasms (bedouin tribal markings).

The meaning of these two images is, likewise, obscure. They are what may be called 'recent bedouin' in origin; they are both superscribed in cognate ways and this is the one feature which connects them absolutely. The inscriptions, however, cannot be read in any one language, or even any one script. Both are similar (shared letter forms) and could perhaps be 'read' as partly Greek (A23: omega?) but more likely in Latin script. That of A24 (with cognate letters in A23) could, for example, be OJAVII.^{DB} (upside-down), and the form of the drawing could then be interpreted as a crashed biplane (wavy lines = parted stays, short cross-line = propeller, etc.), perhaps one that was shot down during the French troubles. Similar hook-like appendages and a thickened base to the vertical line appear in A25 which is also accompanied by wasms (Fig. 228), as well as a stylized but recognizable hobbled camel. The hook-like object in this case is probably the tail of the beast.

Two wasms (Fig. 229: A26), particularly the one on the right, recall the 'prayer-like' attitude of A19 (Fig. 223) above, here clearly without any cultic content. A27 and A28 (Fig. 229) represent obscure designs, some of which occur with Safaitic inscriptions (see Helms 1981: Pl. 14; the inscriptions, however, has nothing to do with the drawings) and may represent sub-architectural features such as corrals or hut circles. A29 (Fig. 229) is a purely geometric design of unknown significance; it was carved on a stone in pool P5 (Fig. 5).

INSCRIPTIONS

As we have noted above, Macdonald (forthcoming, see also 1982, 1983) is compiling a comprehensive catalogue of inscriptions from the Jawa area and, therefore, only a brief discussion is required here. The main objectives are to present collateral evidence for the later artefactual material (pottery) found at the otherwise proto- and early historical site (see Chapter 2: specifically the lower settlement), and perhaps to show the use of the site and area in the later historical periods.

Safaitic texts

Although the dating of these texts is problematical, those from Jawa which list more than names at least show that bedouin often camped near the site, using it as a source of water (i.e. 'watering place', see Winnett 1951, 1957), and perhaps also as a venue for exchange (i.e. horses: see Winnett 1957: SIJ no. 996 'he traded in horse-trappings'; a text not from Jawa), negotiations, and diplomacy with tribe and state. Nabatean and Roman Bosra would be the closest urban centre. A few texts from Jawa may have some political content (Winnett 1973), perhaps demonstrating bedouin awareness of events on and beyond the verdant fringes of their steppic territories. These inscriptions provide one of the rare firm dates for the use of the Safaitic script in southern Syria and Transjordan: i.e. the late 1st century AD (Winnett 1973).

Greek

Several of the Greek inscription at Jawa have a (Judeo-) Christian content (e.g. the word αδο(υ), αδο(υι), αδο(νι) , crosses, etc.) and may be dated from some time after the official adoption of Christianity as the state religion under Constantine in the early 4th century, though more likely in the 5th and 6th centuries AD. The upper date-range could be well into the early Islamic period. The relatively sudden appearance of Greek (Christian) texts at Jawa can plausibly be connected with the general conversions of the bedouin tribes in the area, and the gradual abandonment of the formal *limes arabicus* (from the later 3rd century AD onwards). The latter resulted in bedouin 'colonization' of erstwhile military installations such as the quadriburgium at Deir al-Kahf near Jawa, and eventually also the establishment of monasteries (especially monophysite establishments in the 6th century) in the steppic zones of which some of the ruins at Deir al-Kinn, only 5 kilometres from Jawa, may be an example. It is, therefore, likely that Jawa itself - particularly its many natural caves - was used by pious hermits and both the Greek inscriptions, as well as a number of stone objects found at the site, bear this out. Several stones inscribed with crosses (Fig. 230), worked basalt slabs with socket pins (doors), and Roman/Late Antique sherd scatters have been found near the caves, along the lower fortifications of the site and on or near various cairns in the vicinity (King *et al.* 1983).

Several inscriptions are accompanied by crosses of various kinds, including the monogram χρι(στος) (Fig. 230): a few of them also mention the ?Lord? (e.g. αδο(υ) etc.), but the majority consists of names strung together in long lists and occasionally separated by και Some of these names are obviously semitic (e.g. Σαδος < sa`d, sa`ud, etc.), others Latin or Greek (e.g. Πετρος). Method of carving varies, and there are examples of over-cutting (e.g. Σαδοσαιλαμου over an older, fainter text, perhaps beginning with χα(ιρ.. [a greeting]....[name] ος , or χα(ρι...]....[a name]). Very similar name lists have been found at Deir al-Kinn itself and as far east as Qasr Burqu` (Field 1960; Helms 1990). The inscriptions from Qasr Burqu` are funerary, again with some graecesized semitic names (e.g., Σαγιος Σω(εδου) < 'shaghi' from Suweida in the Hawran?). The name Αβγαρος appears once at Jawa (Macdonald p.c.) and this name also appears in a rare Greek inscription found by Winnett in the Jawa region, near the Syrian frontier (Jathum). It was published by Mowry (1953) and describes a trip into the desert by a lyrist and a barber (Diomedes and Abchoros: the latter a cognate of Αβγαρος ?) with the commander of the footsoldiers (*strategos opleiton*), all of them stationed near a place called the 'city of Abgar', πο(λις) Αβγαρ(ου). Abgaros was deposed by Caracalla in AD 213-4 and the 'city' of A. would be Edessa in northern Syria, rather far from the *harra* of southern Syria, though not impossible in the context of a troop crossing the desert from, say, the quadriburgium at Deir al-Kahf (Speluncae?), via Jawa, Shubeiqa, Nemara, Palmyra, Rusafa, and so forth, to the Euphrates. A date for the inscription before the abandonment of the *limes* would, therefore, perhaps be logical, and if Mowry's reading of polis is correct, perhaps one before AD 213. On the other hand, Schwabe (1954) suggests that πο(λις) should read σιο(υ) Αβγαρ, σιο(υ) standing for sewa'a (Aram.) < swaya (Syr.) = 'tumulus' (Brockelmann 1928) and suwwa (Arab.) = 'pile of stones' and, therefore, the 'tumulus [even tomb?] of Abgar'. This reading may be more likely: it certainly is apposite to the specific area of Jawa where basalt tumuli, some of them quite formal constructions, are very common. There is one example immediately to the north of Jawa. A lamp fragment (Fig. 231) and other Late Antique sherds were found within it (see now Lenzen in King *et al.* 1983). The earliest date for the Greek inscriptions at Jawa may, therefore, be in the 4th century AD; some of them also may have been written as late as the 7th or 8th centuries.

Arabic

There are many Arabic inscriptions about Jawa, ranging in date from the 15th century AD up to the present (Macdonald 1982: 167; see also Baramki 1964 for Arabic inscriptions from Winnett's expedition).

Appendix A

The Jawa Area in Prehistory

A. V. G. BETTS

The Black Desert Survey Project (1981-3) was initiated to examine the prehistory of the *harra*, specifically to gain a better understanding of early land use in the greater Jawa region. One aim of the project was to find out more about indigenous groups using the area in the proto-historic periods; groups who would have interacted with the settled population at Jawa. Fieldwork was carried out around Jawa, along the TAP-line and the Baghdad Highway, and down the eastern edge of the *harra* from Qasr Burqu` southwards. In the Jawa area, the survey team recorded prehistoric sites in selected areas along wadi Rajil, particularly the western bank of the wadi in the section between Jawa and the mudflats at Shubeiqa. South of Jawa, a section of a 'kite' chain was also surveyed. Here work concentrated on planning of the 'kite' enclosures and a search for artefacts in and around them. Sites were located within +/- 50 metres on topographical maps (Jordan 1: 50,000 Series K737). Soundings were made at one site, the Natufian camp of Khallat 'Anaza (Figs 236 - 239; Site No 1407).

SITE INVENTORY

Abbreviations: Epi = general epipaleolithic; Nat = Natufian; Neo = Neolithic; post-Neo = general post-Neolithic; Jawa = artefacts with stratified parallels at the site (4th millennium BC [EB I A], unless otherwise indicated).

Example:
4) 1404/3454IV/799156 Epi?/Jawa: recent corrals near `Ain Jawa
4) = site number on maps (Figs 232, 233)
1401 = site reference number
3454IV = sheet reference in 1: 50,000 maps series K737
799156 = grid reference on map
Epi?/Jawa = approximate dating of artefacts recovered
recent corrals near Jawa = brief description of site

1) 1401: Jawa, general surface collection from the main site at Jawa.
2) 1402: Epi?/Jawa, east side of wadi Rajil opposite the main site, including systematic exploration (without excavations) of caves.
3) 1403: Jawa, west side of wadi Rajil and lower enclosure of the main site (cf. Fig. 5: B3), including systematic exploration (without

excavations) of caves; a large collection of drills, beads, and bead-making waste was found in slope wash about and below the wall of the upper enclosure.

4) 1404/3454IV/799156: Epi?/Jawa, recent corrals near `Ain Jawa.

5) 1405/3454IV/790148: Epi?/Jawa, fields around `Ain Jawa.

6) 1406/3454IV/795193: Epi/Neo/post Neo, cairn and part of a 'kite' wall on the south side of the Jawa-Shubeiqa track.

7) 1407/3454IV/798188: Nat/post Neo, Khallat 'Anaza is a Natufian site on the north side of the Jawa-Shubeiqa track on a small outcrop of jagged basalt slabs overlooking the wadi Rajil gorge.

8) 1408/3454IV/790192: Neo, small knapping site south of the Jawa-Shubeiqa track.

9) 1409/3454IV/791198: Large 'kite' south of the Jawa-Shubeiqa track.

10) 1410/3454IV/810245: Epi?/Neo?/post Neo, cluster of stone structures of mixed date south of the Jawa-Shubeiqa track.

11) 1411/3454IV/804238: Epi/Neo?/post Neo?, waterfalls on wadi Rajil south of the Jawa-Shubeiqa track.

12) 1412/3454IV/807231: Epi/Neo?/post Neo?, badly disturbed 'kite' south of the Jawa-Shubeiqa track and small flint scatter in the vicinity.

13) 1413/3454IV/809237: Epi/post Neo?, stone-built corral south of the Jawa-Shubeiqa track and small flint scatter nearby.

14) 1414/3454IV/800215: Epi?/Neo small qa' south of the Jawa-Shubeiqa track.

15) 1415/3454IV/812227: Post Neo, graves and corrals on the bank of a large pool in wadi Rajil near the Shubeiqa track.

16) 3454IV/832296: Epi?, flint scatter among rocks on the bank of wadi Rajil where it crosses the Shubeiqa track.

17) 1417/3454IV/808269: Disturbed 'kite' south of the Shubeiqa track.

18) 1418/3454IV/808278: 'Kite' south of the Shubeiqa track.

19) 1419/3454IV/819223: 'Kite' on the north side of wadi Rajil.

20) 1420/3454IV/819228: Epi flint scatter on the hill above site 1419.

21) 1421/3454IV/813222: Epi, flint collection from soil thrown up by recent excavations.

22) 1422/3354I/803111: Nat, Mugharet al-Jawa is a Natufian camp on the west side of wadi Rajil, north of the main site of Jawa (cf. Fig. 3: P1).

23) 1423/3354I/746131: 'Kite' south of Jawa; unlike the rest of the 'kites' nearby, it points east.

24) 0701/3354I/755115: 'Kite' south of Jawa.

25) 0702/3354I/750112: 'Kite' south of Jawa.

26) 0703/3354I/748111: 'Kite' south of Jawa.

27) 0704/3354I/746113: 'Kite' south of Jawa.

28) 3454IV/225765: Mughara, lava flow cave used as a cisterns in historic and recent times; a series of canals run for several kilometres across the basalt to lead water into the cave (cf. Helms 1981: Pl. 32);
29) 3354I/109832: 'Kite' on Jebel Haba.
30) 3354I/100784: 'Kite' southwest of Jawa.
31) 3354I/091772: 'Kite' southwest of Jawa.

THE JAWA AREA IN PREHISTORY

Although Jawa is within the *harra*, its position on the lower slopes of Jebel Druze provides a more favourable environment, with cooler temperatures and higher rainfall, than the steppe to the south and east. There are also has deep pools in the bed of the wadi Rajil gorge which hold winter flood water well into the dry season. However, the area is too far out into the steppe to have seen permanent settlement in the periods prior to the 4th millennium BC, and it appears only to have been used on an intermittent basis by hunter/gatherer/herder groups at various times throughout the later prehistoric periods.

The earliest period for which there is evidence is the Geometric Kebaran, with small flint scatters representing campsites used around the 11th to 12th millennium BC. Artefacts diagnostic of this period, specifically backed and truncated bladelets, were found in a few locations along the edge of the wadi Rajil gorge, mostly near to pools in the wadi bed. The only sites of this period found in the Jawa area were open air camps. Despite careful survey, no trace of epipaleolithic occupation was found in the caves near Jawa although several of them are quite suitable for occupation. The only exception to this was at the Natufian site of Mugharet al-Jawa (see below). The larger caves have seen recent use by beduin shepherds. They are also used by hyaena and foxes; presumably there were other predators in the Epipaleolithic as well which may have acted as a deterrent to occupation. However, if the caves were lived in, subsequent layers of debris covering the epipaleolithic occupation levels may have eclipsed all signs of this early use. Most of the caves have a rock lip which prevents soil inside from spilling out down the hillslope, and this may be a factor in obscuring traces of early occupation by limiting erosion of the upper levels. It is possible also that site location (open air *versus* cave/rockshelter) is related to other, more general factors. It has been noted (Bar Yosef 1981) that Geometric Kebaran sites are most commonly open air, while rockshelters come into use more frequently in the Natufian period.

The evidence from the area around Jawa for this period fits with data from elsewhere in the Levant. Small sites of 12th/11th millennium date are found in steppic areas throughout Syria, Jordan and the Sinai/Negev region, generally in locations close to good water supplies. Sites of this period have been found around the oasis at el-Kowm in north-central Syria (Cauvin [M-C] 1981), around Palmyra (Hanihara and Akazawa 1983) and in the wadi systems running into al-Azraq (Garrard *et al.* 1988; Muheisen 1988). Within the *harra*, Geometric Kebaran camp sites are found only around Jawa and to the south near jebel Qurma where wadi Rajil runs into the Azraq lake bed.

Following this period, there seems to have been a hiatus in use of the Jawa area. This is not exceptional. Throughout the Levant in the early Natufian period, around the 10th millennium BC, the steppic areas seem to have been largely abandoned, while occupation concentrated in the rich, well watered regions of the Mediterranean climatic zone. In the later Natufian, the 9th millennium BC, there was again expansion into the steppic zones in what is today the *badiyat al-sham*, and also the Sinai/Negev region. This period was a time of particular activity around Jawa. Survey work identified two long-term camps with structures, heavy grinding equipment, and bedrock processing areas, one on wadi Rajil just upstream from Jawa, near the waterfall, and one downstream, where the gorge opens out into a more open riverbed. These sites are part of a local Natufian 'complex'. Recent survey has located a similar site on wadi Jilad, a drainage system on the lower slopes of Jebel Druze about twenty kilometres south west of Jawa. Survey at this last site, Huwaynit, produced significant quantities of Dabba 'marble', a friable greenish stone from a source west of Azraq. Greenstone of various kinds occurs in small quantities on many Natufian sites in the Levant. Dabba 'marble' fragments, as well as partly worked and complete beads, occur on all three Natufian sites in the southern Jebel Druze, and it appears likely that the material was traded through local exchange networks, along with seashells and other exotic items found at these sites.

In 1983 a small sounding was made at the best preserved Natufian site, Khallat Anaza. Khallat 'Anaza lies on a small outcrop of jagged basalt slabs overlooking a bend in wadi Rajil. A series of plunge pools in the wadi bed below the site hold water well into the dry season. The location affords a clear view over the surrounding area on all sides, particularly eastwards and downstream towards the Shubeiqa mudflats. The jagged basalt ridge against which the site lies has been joined at either end by a low curving wall to form a small terrace enclosing an area of about 2000 square metres. The outcrop has been re-inforced by a section of walling in the centre of the ridge where the bedrock is lower. This is briefly interrupted but then continues on from the western end of the outcrop, running out to the lip of the gorge. A second wall runs off northwards, also up to the gorge. These walls belong to the Epipaleolithic phase of occupation at the site and have been robbed out in places for burial cairns of a later period, probably of the Safaitic bedouin (c. 1st century BC - c. 3rd/4th century AD). There is a thin scatter of chipped stone on and around the terrace. Traces of stone circles and paved areas are visible at the eastern end, and two narrow conical mortars are cut into bedrock in the central part of the natural outcrop.

A collection of surface material was made and a sounding 12 square metres in extent was excavated to bedrock. There was little depth of occupation. Jagged ridges of bedrock were found all through the excavated area, in some places breaking through the surface. The cracks between ridges were filled with ashy occupation deposits, worked flint and bone fragments. Removal of the sandy topsoil revealed a circular stone hut, constructed partly on bedrock and partly on a thin layer of occupation deposit. A box-like feature consisting of up-ended basalt slab was found set into the 'floor' deposit within the hut.

Finds from the site included basalt hammerstones and a mortar, and a number of beads made from various exotic materials. Some of the beads were made from marine shells, probably of Mediterranean origin (D. Rees, p.c.), and others were of Dabba 'marble'. Bones from the site included a range of species (Garrard 1985). Gazelle (*Gazella sp.*), ovi-caprids (*Ovis/Capra sp.*) and equids (*Equus sp.*) were present, as well as hare (*Lepus cf. capensis*) and canid (*Canis cf. aureus*). Although the larger mammals have now become extinct, these are all animals which would have been typical of the region in earlier times.

In the absence of suitable material for C14 dating, the chipped stone industry has proved a useful comparative dating tool. 5067 artefacts were recovered from the sounding, of which 845 were tools, 84 were cores or trimming and preparation elements, 1216 were blanks and the remainder either the by-products of specialized knapping processes such as burin spalls and microburins, unclassifiable fragments or waste pieces.

The raw material used at the site was mostly fine-grained cherts, and occasionally some smooth creamy translucent chalcedony. There is no flint source in the area, but for pebbles in the wadis. All raw material must have been brought in over a distance of at least 30 to 30 kilometres. The tool assemblage from the site suggests that Khallat 'Anaza represents a local variant of the Late Natufian. Diagnostic artefacts include abruptly backed lunates and low proportions of Helwan lunates. There was limited evidence for use of the microburin technique.

The labour investment represented by the walls, huts, heavy grinding equipment, and bedrock mortars all suggest that the site was probably re-used fairly regularly, possibly on a seasonal basis.

The key factor would have been water supply, with the lesser consideration of the availablity of plant foods. It is most probable that Khallat 'Anaza was occupied during winter and spring when water would have been plentiful and fresh grazing would have attracted animals to the area. The only unusual aspects of the site are the enclosure walls. The main terrace wall linking both ends of the bedrock outcrop presumably functioned as a simple perimeter fence, possibly to discourage wild animals from approaching the camp. The walls leading off to the gorge are harder to account for. One possible explanation is that they functioned as a simple form of animal trap, a precursor to the more elaborate 'kite' systems of the Neolithic and later periods. The site lies above the mouth of the wadi Rajil gorge. Just below the settlement the wadi widens out and a tributary stream enters from the northwest. It would be relatively simple for a small group of people to drive animals up the wadi, block off the mouth of the gorge and turn the herd up the scree slope into the area enclosed by the walls. The steep climb up the side of the wadi would tire the animals and they could be readily dispatched by hunters on the hilltop.

The second Natufian camp, Mugharet al-Jawa, is less well preserved. It lies on the west side of wadi Rajil, north of the main site of Jawa. The site presently consists of a heavily disturbed flint scatter around the mouth of, and inside, a lava flow cave. Although the cave has been used as a cistern (cf. Fig. 3: P1) with resulting disruption to the occupational deposits, it is clear that the site was once fairly extensive, probably very similar to Khallat 'Anaza. Like Khallat 'Anaza, it is located on a bedrock outcrop overlooking the wadi Rajil gorge, with clear views over the open country to the south and west. A circular mortar was cut into the bedrock immediately in front of the mouth of the cave and inside a column of stones is preserved, forming a support for the fractured rock of the cave roof. Flint from the site suggests that Mugharet al-Jawa, like Khallat 'Anaza, represents a Late Natufian presence in the semi-arid steppe. Some worked basalt fragments and a mortar were recovered from the spoil thrown up by the clearance of the cistern. A surface collection of artefacts was made in and around the disturbed area but none of the soil was sieved.

The chipped stone assemblage is generally similar to that of Khallat 'Anaza. There are slight differences in proportions of tool types; these include higher numbers of scrapers at Mugharet al-Jawa but fewer borers. Helwan retouch is rare. As at Khallat 'Anaza, most lunates are shaped by abrupt uni- or bipolar backing. The assemblage seems representative of a generalized tool kit, and is similar to assemblages documented from other Late Natufian sites in steppic areas (Byrd 1987; Olzewski 1986).

Khallat 'Anaza and Mugharet al-Jawa were abandoned by the end of the Natufian period and there is no indication that the Jawa area was exploited in the first stages of the following Neolithic period. This might be expected, as few Pre-Pottery Neolithic A (PPNA) sites are known from the eastern steppe. The only substantial site of this period so far recorded is Jilat 7, west of al-Azraq and on the wet/dry steppic interface. Jilat 7 has early Neolithic levels with Khiam points (Baird p.c.). Other small artefact scatters probably dating to this period have been found around the Azraq lake (Garrard and Stanley Price 1975; Betts 1986), but the evidence suggests less intense use of the steppe in the PPNA than in the preceding Late Natufian. However, throughout the steppe there is evidence for a marked rise in activity by the later Pre-Pottery Neolithic B (PPNB), the mid to late 7th millennium BC. Many of the 'kite' systems were in use by this period and PPNB sites are relatively numerous (Helms and Betts 1987; Betts 1988; Garrard *et al.* 1988). The pattern of land use in the Jordanian steppe during the Neolithic periods is one in which early PPNB sites were in better areas near to water and open country. Their occupants were largely dependent on a mixed hunting/gathering/proto-agricultural economy. Sites of the late PPNB were spread further over the steppe, but divided into two types. Those in the better steppe and/or near to reliable water resources continued the pattern of mixed hunting/gathering/proto-agricultural economies, possibly now with the addition of limited sheep/goat pastoralism. However, it is also in this period that the deep *harra* was first exploited on a wide scale. Late PPNB sites in the *harra* reflect a new and very specific adaptation, one which may have had its roots in earlier periods, but which seems to have flourished extensively at this time. This is the focus on exploitation of gazelle through use of sophisticated mass-kill techniques involving complex networks of animal traps, the 'kite' systems. Several PPNB hunting camps have been found along the TAP-line in the area around Dhuweila and hilltop knapping sites are common throughout the *harra*. Broken and partly worked arrowheads are found on these flint working sites, and they were clearly used by hunters resting at a suitable lookout point to watch for the movement of game. Although no PPNB camps have been found in the Jawa area, rock carvings in the 'Dhuweila' style have been found near Mugharet al-Jawa (see Chapter 8), impact fractured PPNB arrowheads have been found around 'kites' south of Jawa, and small scatters of PPNB artefacts occurred throughout the survey area. However, no substantial sites with structures and preserved occupation deposits were located. The same is true of the Late Neolithic, the 6th millennium BC and later. Elsewhere in the *harra* this period is well represented in the form of a variety of sites including short-term herding camps, longer term hunting camps with structures, and 'villages', large agglomerations of stone huts and enclosures, yet, although a number of artefact scatters were recorded in the Jawa area, no substantial Late Neolithic sites were found. There is greater variety in the types and locations of Late Neolithic sites in the steppe than in the Early Neolithic period. There are short term herder/hunter camps preserved as fairly dense scatters of chipped stone artefacts, sometimes associated with structures of some kind, mainly low-walled enclosures. Sites of this type ('burin Neolithic' camps) are usually located along major wadi systems where rainpools and floodplain vegetation provide optimal conditions for herd animals. These camps have a wide distribution over the steppe from the edge of the Jordan Valley across the *harra* and along the wadi systems of the *hamad* down to the Euphrates. In the *harra*, 'burin sites' are found most commonly on the edges of the basalt massif, where the main wadi systems debouch into the open gravel plains. Few are found deeper into the *harra*, where the ground is more rugged. Although sheep and goat are herded in the *harra* today, in the past it may have been considered less favourable than the surrounding *hamad*. It is consistent with this pattern that there is little evidence for Late Neolithic herding camps in the Jawa area, although small scatters of implements along wadi Rajil indicate limited use of the area in this period.

However, the deep *harra* was used in the Late Neolithic period, but for different purposes. The Early Neolithic site of Dhuweila was reoccupied around the mid-sixth millennium BC by a group who practised a more mixed economy than the original occupants, but who still used the site largely as a hunting station. Arrowheads formed a high proportion of the tools recovered from Late Neolithic Dhuweila, and fractured Late Neolithic points have been found around 'kite' enclosures in the area, suggesting that the 'kite' systems were in use in this period also. As part of the reconstruction of Dhuweila in its second phase of occupation, a 'kite' wall was built up to, and incorporated into the structures on the site. It is likely that the few traces of Late Neolithic activity in the Jawa area were left by similar hunting groups, who favoured the *harra* because the terrain is more suited to hunting that the open *hamad*, whether mass kill techniques are employed or not.

The steppe was certainly used in post-Neolithic periods but it is as yet difficult to identify specific sites. Diagnostic artefacts are fewer and with the introduction of sheep/goat herding in the Late Neolithic, sites began to see regular short-term re-use over millennia, so that traces of early occupation may have been quite obliterated. However, 4th/3rd millennium sites have been identified in the *harra* (Betts in press; see also 'Nature of the evidence' above) and for these few, there must have been many more. It is, therefore, likely that the occupants of Jawa in the 4th millennium BC and also in the Middle Bronze Age were in regular contact, probably both hostile and friendly, with nomadic herder/hunters camping in the *harra* during the colder and wetter months of the year. Some may have stayed in the region all year round.

Evidence for these later periods is limited by the lack of pottery, particularly of diagnostic sherds which would allow closer dating of sites. The small amount of pottery recovered from survey sites consists usually of coarse ware body sherds, often with basalt inclusions, pottery which could have been made in the region at any time from the Chalcolithic period to the recent past. However, isolated finds help to fill out the picture a little. One sherd from a campsite near wadi Qattafi was a broken example of a folded ledge handle, giving a broad date for use of the area in the mid to late part of the Early Bronze Age. Similarly, some diagnostic sherds were recovered from the rock-shelter site of Tell al-Hibr, on the eastern edge of the *harra*, close to the Saudi Arabian border. Vessels from al-Hibr have parallels in the Ghassul/Beersheba tradition of the southern Levant. Other sites in the *hamad* east of Qasr Burqu may also fit into a Chalcolithic/Early Bronze Age timespan. Work is still in progress in the region and a clearer picture should emerge in due course.

Research into sites in the *harra* around and beyond Jawa only serves to re-inforce the peculiar nature of Jawa itself. The fourth millennium foundation is an anomaly in a region where seasonal exploitation and mobile populations are normal. The pattern of short-term settlement in the Jawa area reflects the special nature of local environmental conditions. Groups exploiting the dry steppe - Early Neolithic hunters and Late Neolithic hunter/herders - used the area as part of their wider 'territory', while groups exploiting the moist steppe and mediterranean zone - Epipaleolithic hunter/gatherers - regarded the area as viable but marginal. The key to this pattern lies in Jawa's location on the lower slopes of Jebel Druze, just high enough above the rest of the *harra* to have significantly greater rainfall, but not high enough to be too cold in winter. Added to this are the local geological peculiarities which have created the gorge and pools in wadi Rajil up and downstream from Jawa.

NOTES

1. Area survey of the Jawa region was carried out as part of the Black Desert Survey under the auspices of the British Institute at Amman for Archaeology and History. The project was supported by the British Institute at Amman, the British School of Archaeology in Jerusalem, the G. A. Wainwright Fund, the Central Research Fund (London University, the Gordon Childe and Margery Bequest Funds, the Palestine Exploration Fund, the British Museum, the Ashmolean Museum, the City Museum (Birmingham), the Manchester Museum, Liverpool Museum, and the Pitt Rivers Museum. Permission to undertake the survey was kindly granted by Dr Adnan Hadidi, Director of Antiquity, Department of Antiquities of Jordan. The final report of the Jawa region was prepared while the writer was a British Academy Post-Doctoral Fellow in the Department of Archaeology at Edinburgh University.

2. I am grateful to Dr David Rees for identifying the marine shells.

Appendix B

A Note on the Early Pottery

N. VAILLANT

Seuls quelques tessons des genres A, B, C, E, F, et G (voir Chapitre 3) ont été étudiés (les seuls en ma possession).

GENRE A: 9 échantillons analysés

Technique: Tous sont montés à la main. Pour d'eux d'entre eux, la technique 'slab construction' a peut-être utilisée. Ceci est difficile à déterminer car les tessons analysés sont taille trop petite pour une analyse plus complète. La facture est généneralement grossière et le traitement de surface parfois inexistant.

Pâte: La même argile semble être utilisée pour tous les échantillons analysés. C'est une pâte à structure cordée, très friable, dégraissée principalement au silex. Celui-ci se présente sous la forme d'esquille de deux à trois millimètres de long, parfois chauffées avant leur utilisation comme dégraissant. Dans un cas le dégraissant est de taille plus petite et de forme anguleuse.

Cuisson: Elle s'est effectuée en atmosphère oxydante ou réductrice, la céramique est souvent enfumée.

Décor: Il est constitué par de petites impressions pratiquées avec la section de tiges triangulaires carrée ou informe. La pâte est parfois plutôt incisée.

GENRE B: 11 échantillons analysés

Technique: Ces céramiques son toutes montées à la main, probablement au colombin. La facture est généralement bonne, le lissage est effectué soit au doigt soit à l'aide d'un outil comme une brosse.

Pâte: Tous les exemplaires analysés sont fabriqués dans la même pâte. Peu homogéne, elle contient des grains de calcaire d'une grosseur moyenne de 1,5 millimetre. C'est une pâte maigre et friable. Dans un cas, nous avons à faire à une céramique plus fine, montée dans une pâte dégraisseé par de petits fragments anguleux de silex.

Cuisson: Elle est oxydante.

1 exemple (Table 14:18) n'appartient pas à la même famille. Fabriqué dans une pâte plus dense et moins dégraissée que les autres. Ici la cuisson est réductrice.

Table 14. Pottery fabric analysis: provenance of samples

Genre	No.	Provenance	CATNO/Reference
A	1	LF2 810.13	cf. fig. 110ff
	2	LF2 810.22	cf. fig. 110ff
	3	++++++++	29
	4	D2 +++++	32
	5	D2c 1034.4	36
	6	LF2 802.6	58
	7	++++++++	cf. fig. 110ff
	8	D2c 1031.2	34
	9	LF2 810.3	cf. fig.110ff
B	10	++++++++	cg. fig. 110ff
	11	LF2 820.15	194
	12	++++++++	cf. fig. 122ff
	13	UTTA +++	172
	14	++++++++	cf. fig. 122ff
	15	D2a 1026.6	185
	16	X2 000.3	178
	17	++++++++	cf. fig. 122ff
	18	UTTA +++	171
	19	++++++++	168
	20	C2 507.11	307
C	21	LF2 804.7	cf. fig. 130ff
	22	LF2 820.8	278
	23	++++++++	261
	24	D3 1059.6	cf. fig. 130ff
	25	++++++++	cf. fig. 130ff
	26	LF2 805.1	cf. fig. 130ff
E	27	++++++++	cf. fig. 136ff
	28	++++++++	cf. fig. 136ff
	29	++++++++	cf. fig. 136ff
	30	++++++++	cf. 449
	31	X2 000.3	357
F	32	++++++++	441
	33	++++++++	444
	34	D2a 1026.2	402
	35	++++++++	395
	36	C2 507.1	cf. fig. 140ff
G	37	LF2 803.1	cf.fig. 145: 470-483

GENRE C: 6 échantillons analysés

Technique: Pour les jarres de petites dimensions (types A, B, C: cf. Fig. 130:241-273), la technique du tour a été utilisée. Dans les autres cas, le montage est fait au colombin. Ces céramiques sont de bonne facture, le lissage est fin.

Dans deux cas, un engobe fut appliqué sur les deux faces, puis poli uniquement à l'intérieur du récipient.

Pâte: La pâte utilisée est fine, parfois dégraissée avec des grains de calcaire, parfois sans minéraux apparents, mais dans touts les exemples, le potier a employé un dégraissant végétal.

Cuisson: Ces céramiques sont cuites en atmosphère réductrice. Parfois la dernière phase de la cuisson est oxydante.

GENRE E: 5 échantillons analysés

Technique: Tous sont montés à la main. La qualité est bonne, et le lissage externe soigné. Un seul cas de très mauvaise facture.

Pâte: Différentes pâtes on été utilisées (cf. Chapitre 3: étude comparative).
- pâte à dégraissant de silex de toute forme et de toute taille;
- pâte très fine et peu dégraissée, seulement quelques fragments de silex sont visible;
- pâte maigre, vacuolaire, sans dégraissant visible.

Cuisson: Elle a eu lieu dans tous les cas en atmosphère oxydante.

GENRE F: 5 échantillons analysés

Technique: Montage à la main. La qualité est moyenne, le lissage plus ou moins grossier est fait soit à la main, soit avec un outil.

Pâte: Aucune homogénéité entre les différentes céramiques n'a pu être observée. Toutes sont faites dans des pâtes différentes. L'une est fortement dégraissée à la chamotte (ou avec des grains d'argilite), une autre avec des grains roulés de calcaire, une autre possède un dégraissant trop fin pour être observé par les moyens traditionnels.

Cuisson: Elle a eu lieu soit en atmosphère réductrice, soit en atmosphère oxydante.

Deux échantillons analysés sont des anses. Elle sont faites de deux colombins juxtaposés. La facture est assez grossière. L'une est fabriquée dans une pâte à dégraissant fin, difficile à identifier, l'autre dans une pâte dense à dégraissant varié de taille moyenne.

GENRE G: 1 échantillon analysé

Technique: C'est un fragment de coupe faite à la motte. La fabrication est très grossière, sans lissage ni externe, ni interne. Seule la lèvre, amincie est travaillée.

Pâte: La pâte, grossière contient des inclusions calcaires de taille importante: 2 millimètres.

Cuisson: L'intérieur a été enfumé.

NOTE
1. Voir aussi Homès-Fredericq et Franken (eds) 1985: 78.

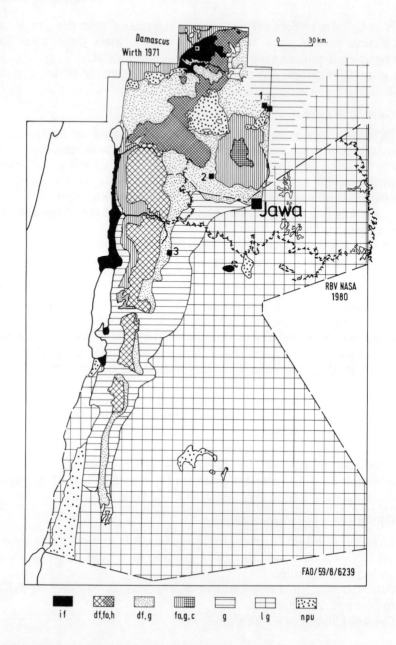

Fig. 1. Landuse Map of southern Syria and Transjordan: if, irrigation farming; df, dry farming; fo, forestry; h, horticulture; g, grazing; lg, limited grazing; npu, no possible use (but for minerals)

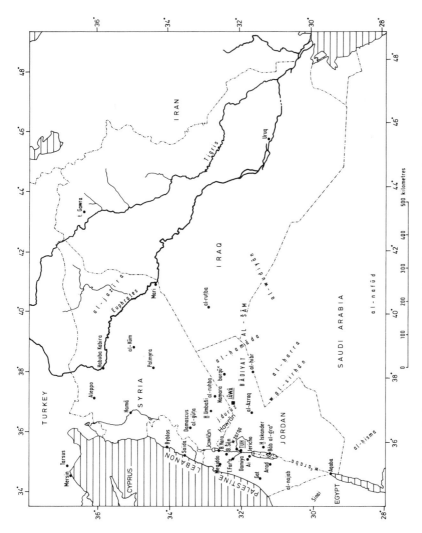

Fig. 2. The Near East: 200 mm isohyet (average year) and relevant sites

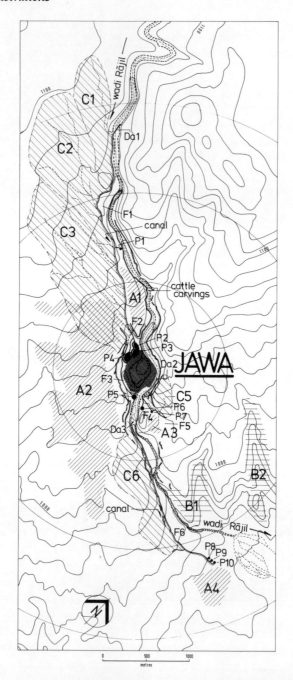

Fig. 3. *The Jawa Area: C, microcatchments (local runoff); A, animal pens (?); B, burial ground (?); Da, deflection dam; P, revetted pools; F, irrigated fields*

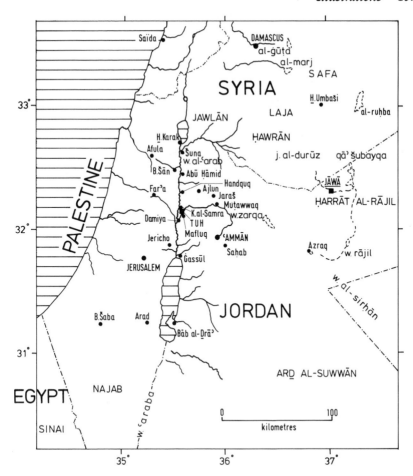

Fig. 4. Jawa and the Jordan Valley: relevant sites

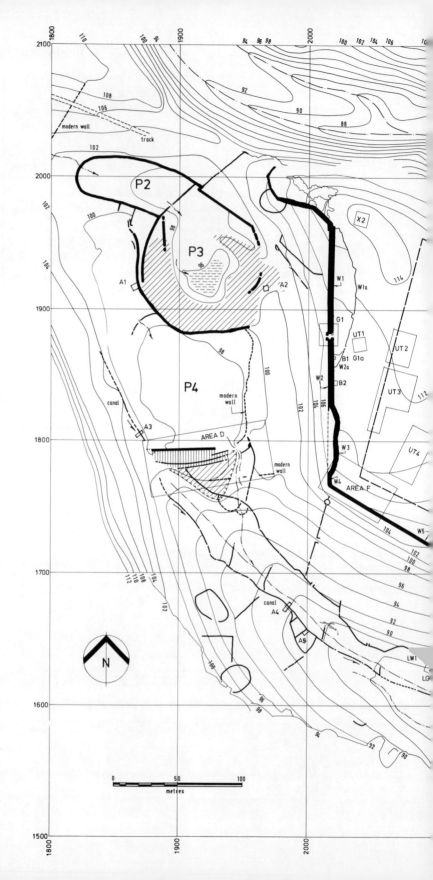

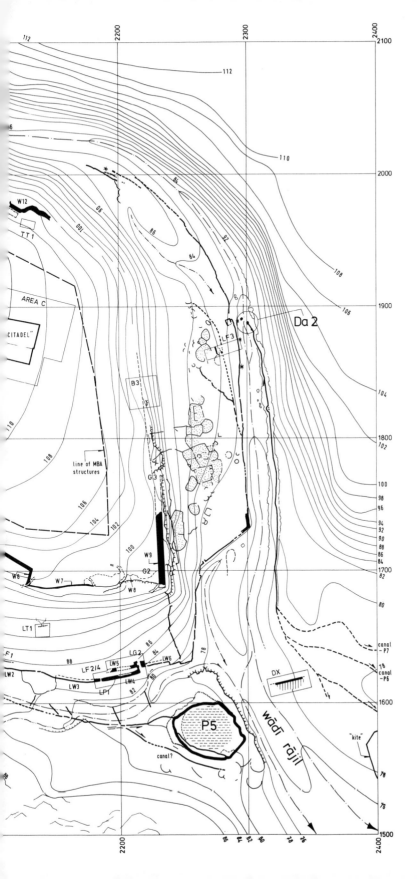

Fig. 5. The site of Jawa

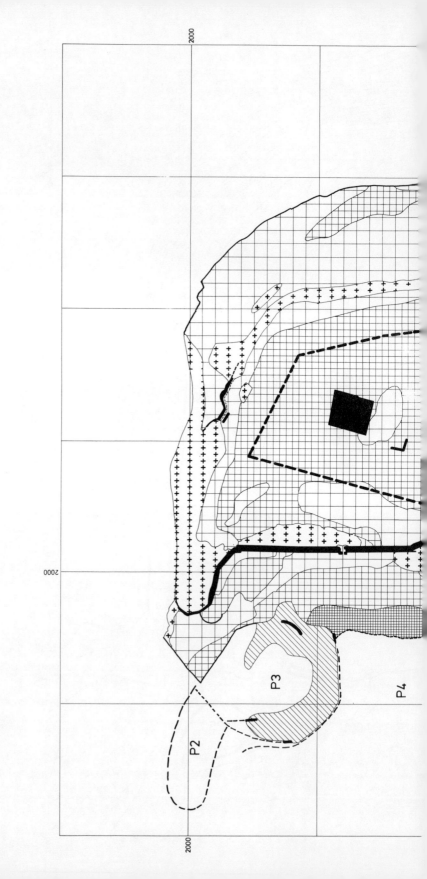

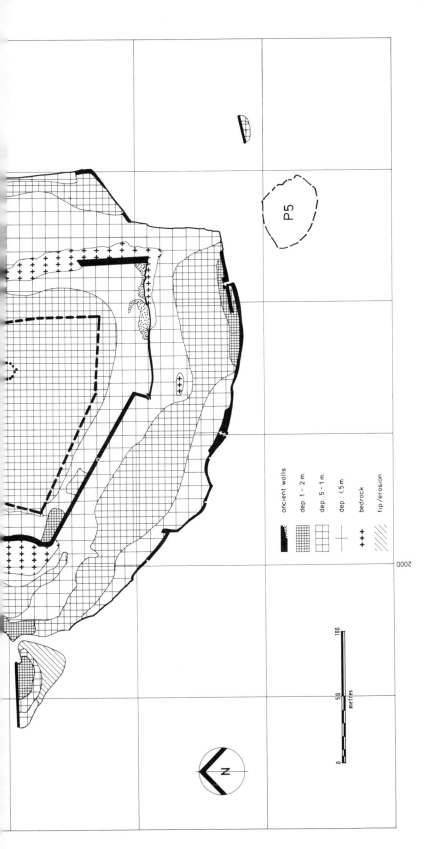

Fig. 6. Depth of archaeological deposition at Jawa

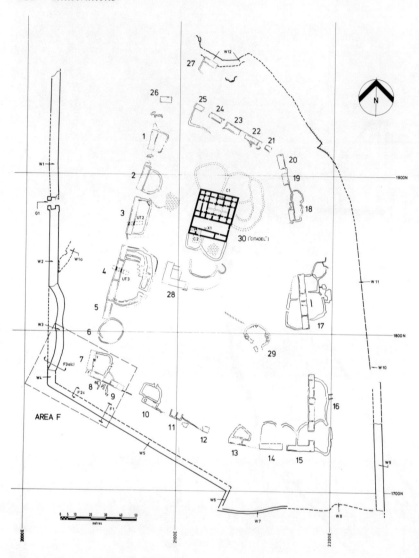

Fig. 7. The Upper Settlement

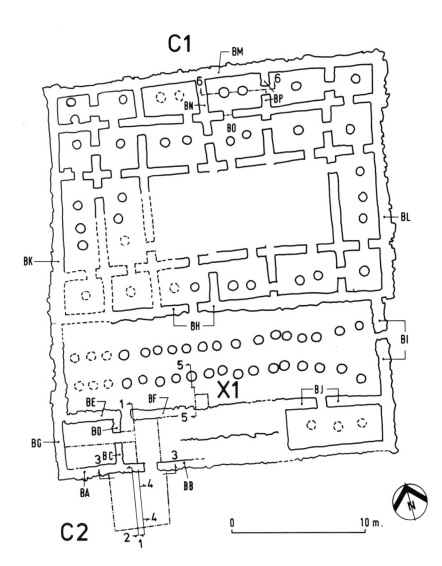

Fig. 8. The 'citadel': excavated areas and key to sections

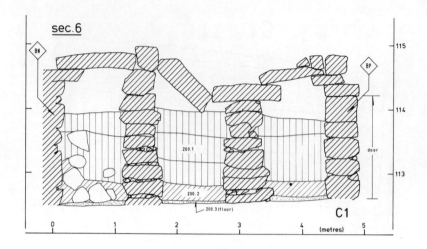

Fig. 9. Square C1: section 6 with piers and corbels

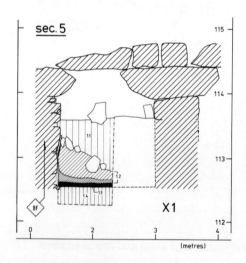

Fig. 10. Square X1: section 5 with pier and corbels

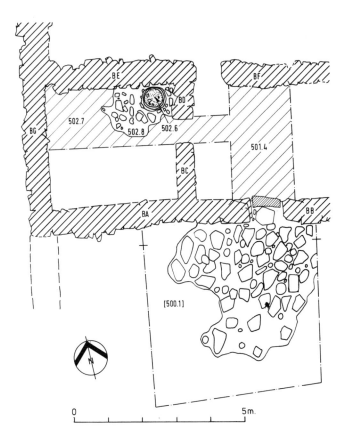

Fig. 11. Square C2: entrance to the 'citadel'

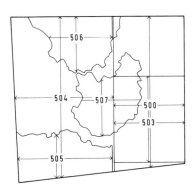

Fig. 12. Square C2: key to loci

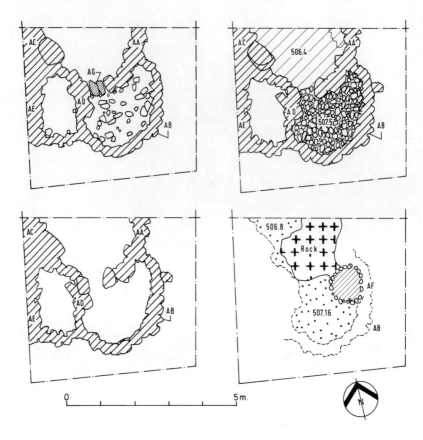

Fig. 13. Square C2: building phases and features

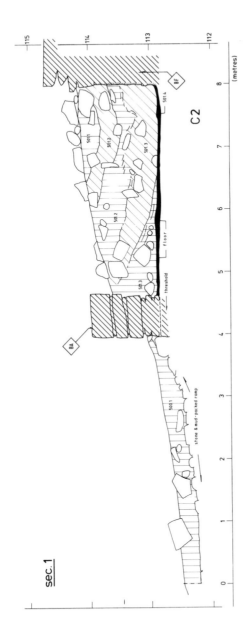

Fig. 14. Square C2: section 1

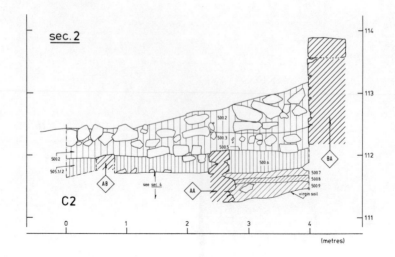

Fig. 15. Square C2: section 2

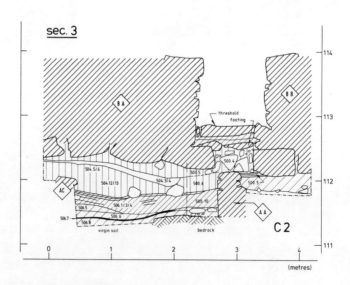

Fig. 16. Square C2: section 3

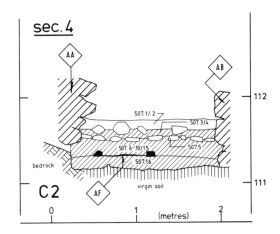

Fig. 17. Square C2: section 4

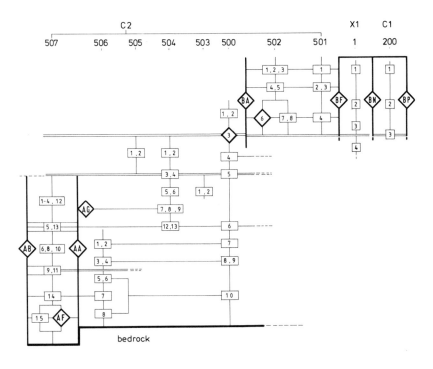

Fig. 18. Area C: stratigraphic matrix

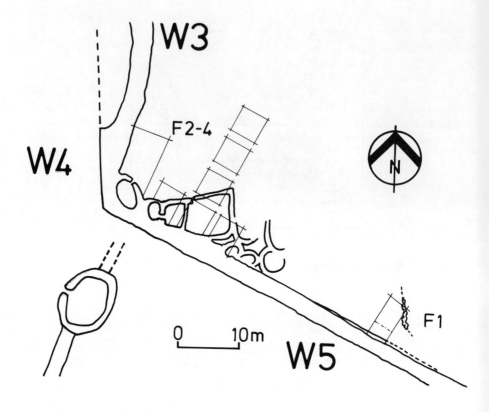

Fig. 19. Area F: plan of squares

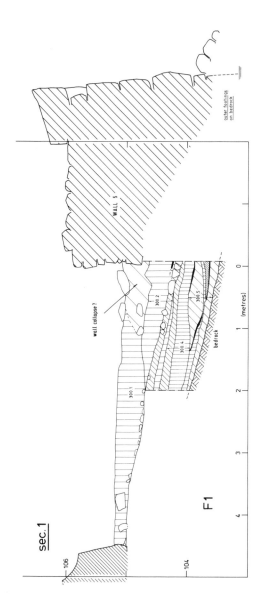

Fig. 20. Square F1: section 1

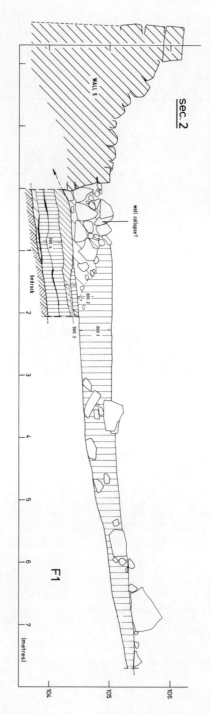

Fig. 21. Square F1: section 2

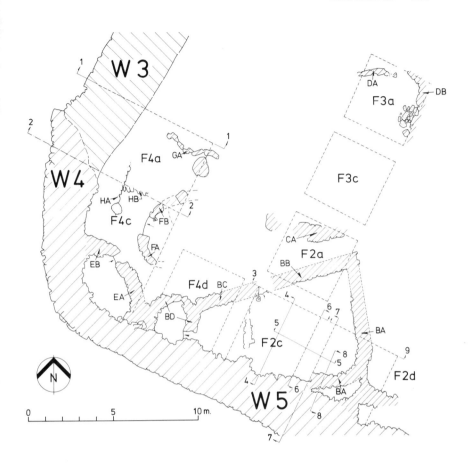

Fig. 22. Area F: squares F2, F3, F4

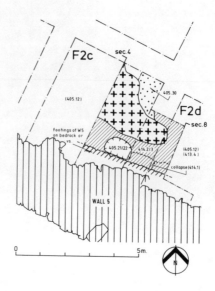

Fig. 23. Square F2c/d: wall W5 and features on bedrock

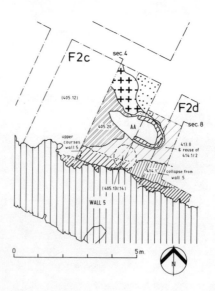

Fig. 24. Square F2c/d: plan of oven and other features

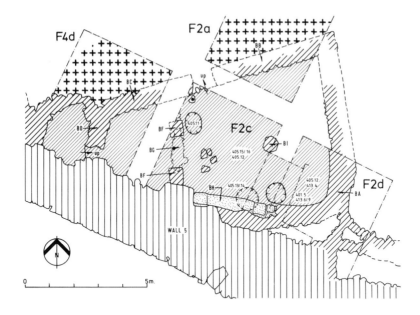

Fig. 25. Squares F2a/c/d and F4d: plan of the latest structures

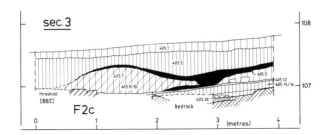

Fig. 26. Square F2c: section 3

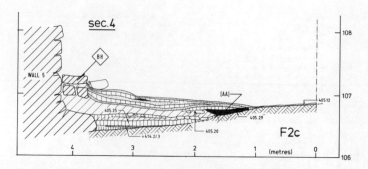

Fig. 27. Square F2c: section 4, fortifications built on bedrock

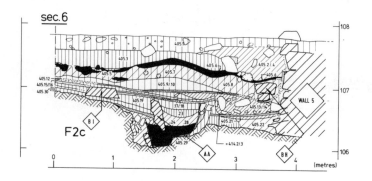

Fig. 28. Square F2c: section 6

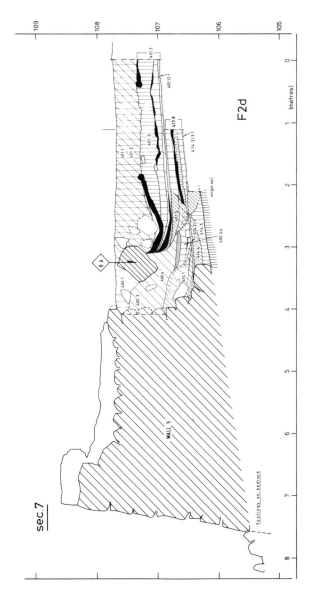

Fig. 29. Square F2d: section 7

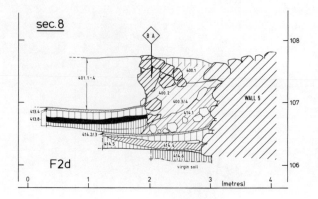

Fig. 30. Square F2d: section 8

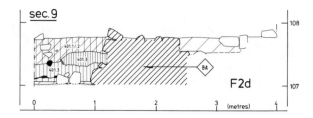

Fig. 31. Square F2d: section 9

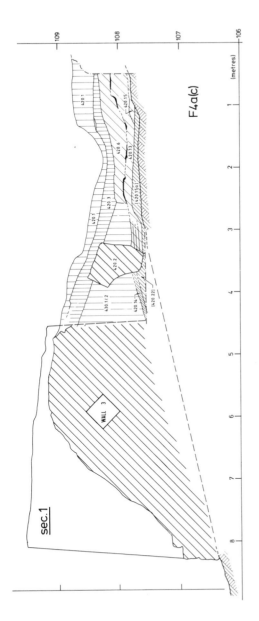

Fig. 32. Square F4a(c): section 1

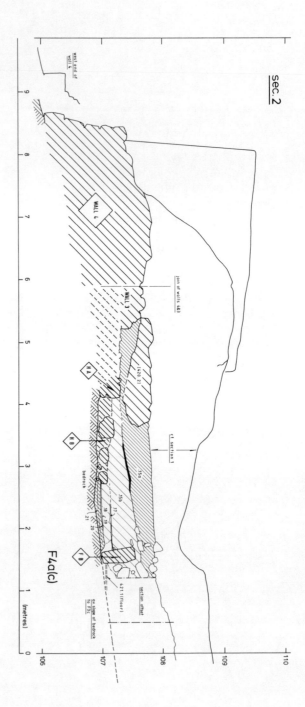

Fig. 33. *Square F4a(c): section 2*

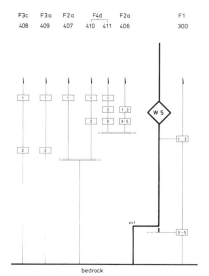
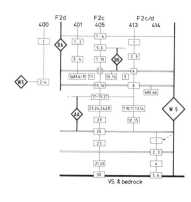

Fig. 34. Squares F1, F2a, F3a/c, F4d: stratigraphic matrix

Fig. 35. Squares F2c/d: stratigraphic matrix

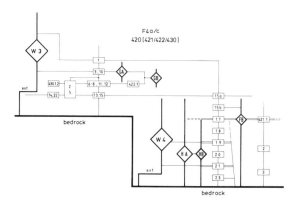

Fig. 36. Square F4a(c): stratigraphic matrix

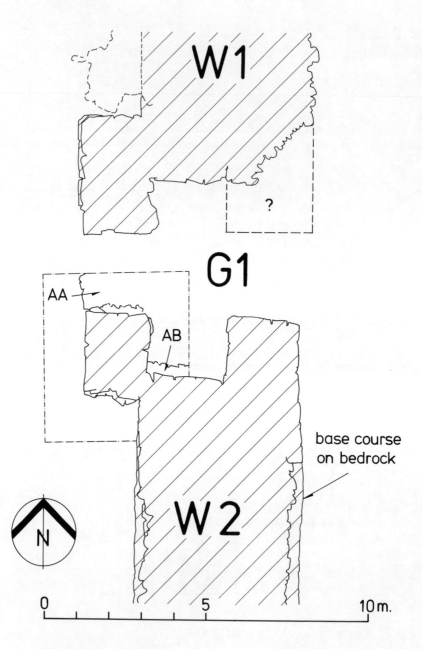

Fig. 37. Gate G1 and sondage

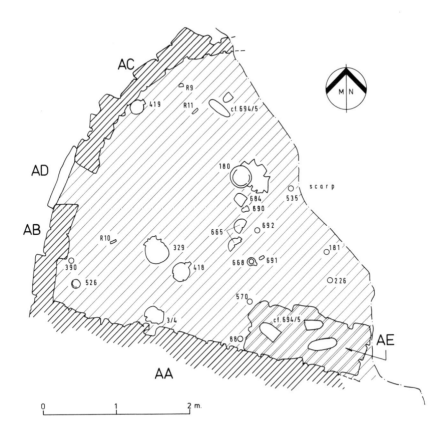

Fig. 38. Square TT1 (1973): rounded structure and finds in situ

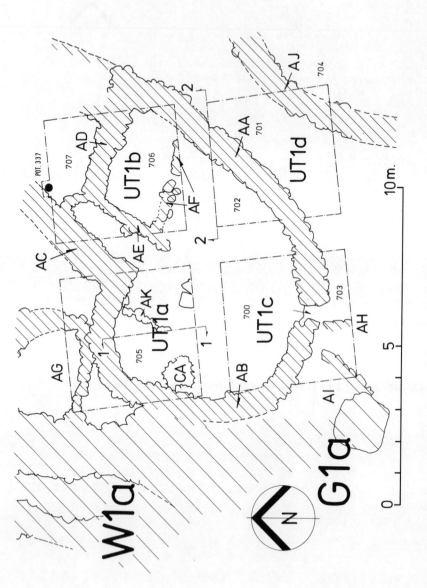

Fig. 39. Square UT1: sub-circular structure

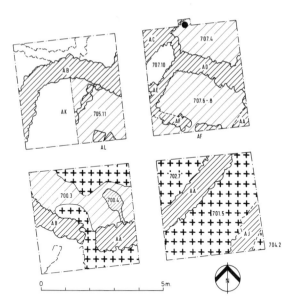

Fig. 40. Square UT1: features on bedrock

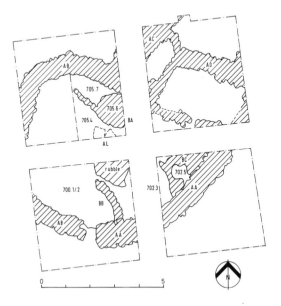

Fig. 41. Square UT1: internal modifications

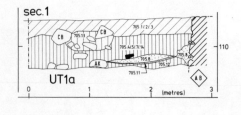

Fig. 42. Square UT1a: the latest features

Fig. 43. Square UT1: section 1

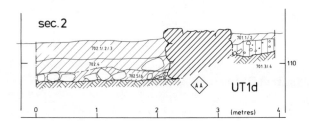

Fig. 44. Square UT1: section 2

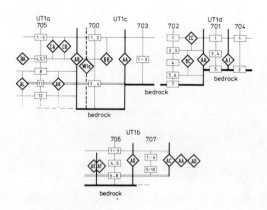

Fig. 45. Square UT1: stratigraphic matrix

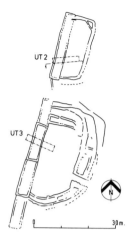

Fig. 46. Squares UT2 and UT3: MBA structures

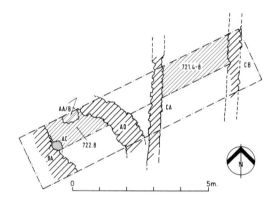

Fig. 47. Square UT2: EB I A and MBA structures

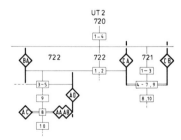

Fig. 48. Square UT2: stratigraphic matrix

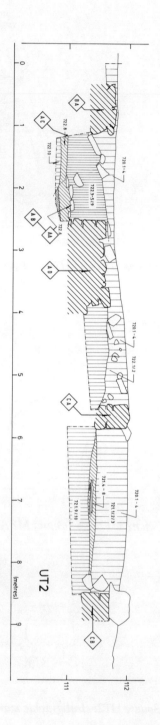

Fig. 49. Square UT2: section 2

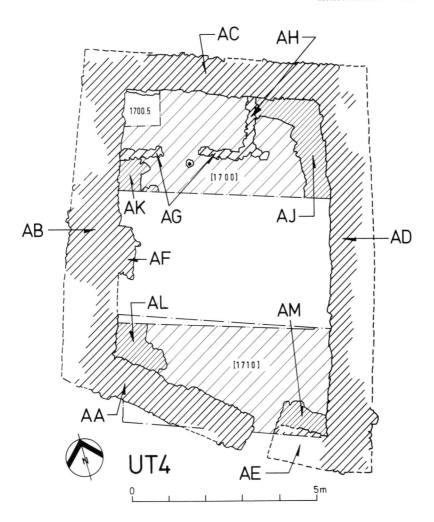

Fig. 50. Square UT4: sub-rectilinear structure

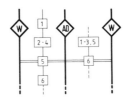

Fig. 51. Square UT4: stratigraphic matrix

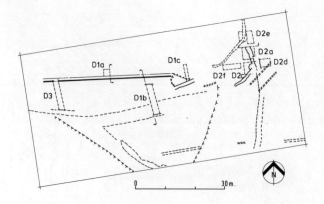

Fig. 52. Area D: general plan of the dams and location of squares

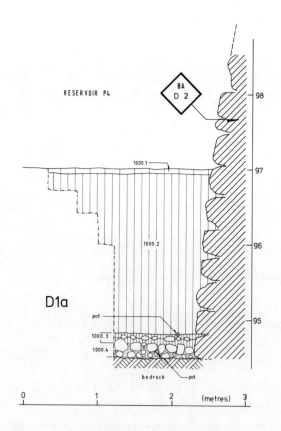

Fig. 53. Square D1a against the waterface of dam D2

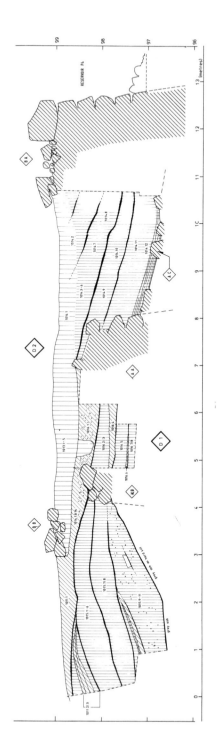

Fig. 54. Area D: section through dams D1 and D2

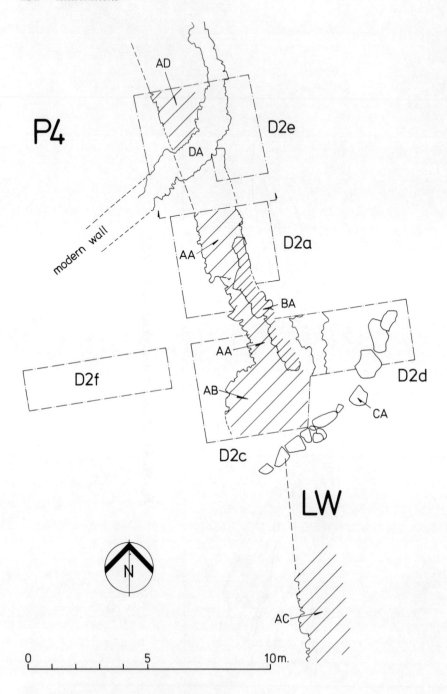

P4

D2e

AD

DA

modern wall

AA

D2a

BA

AA

D2f

AB

D2d

CA

D2c

LW

N

AC

0   5   10 m.

Fig. 55. Squares D2a/c-f: plan of features

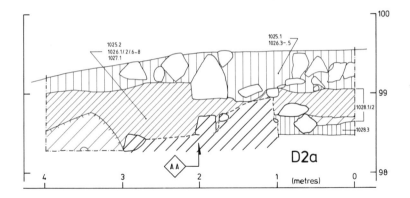

Fig. 56. Square D2a: section

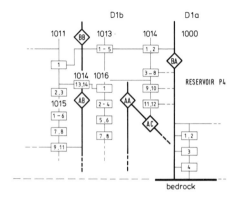

Fig. 57. Square D1a/b: stratigraphic matrix

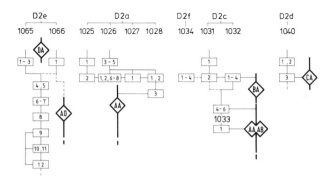

Fig. 58. Squares D2a/c-f: stratigraphic matrix

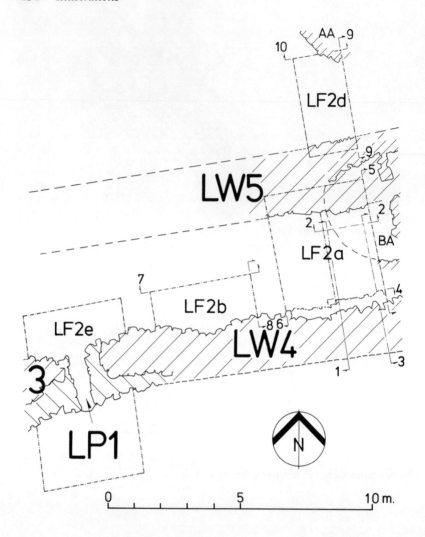

Fig. 59. Square LF2: general plan

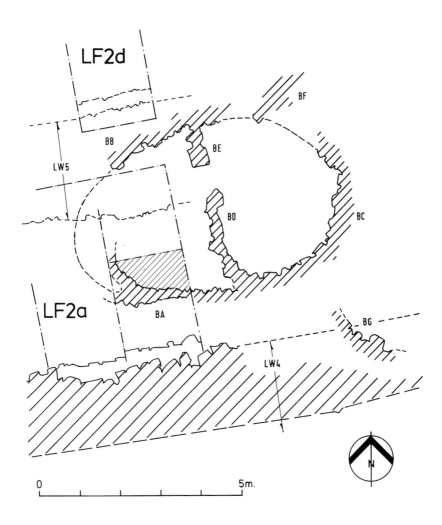

Fig. 60. Squares LF2a/d: latest features

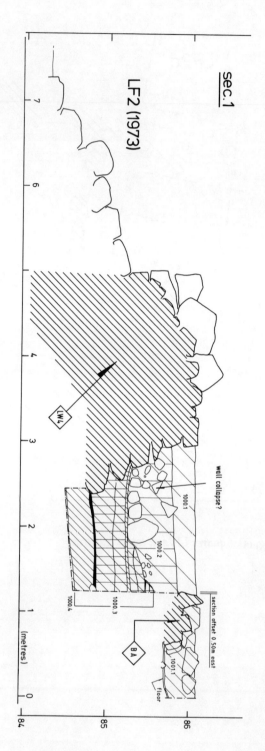

Fig. 61. Square LF2(1973): section 1

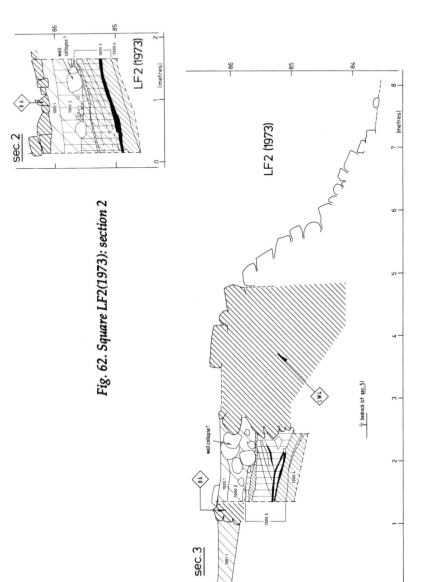

Fig. 62. Square LF2(1973): section 2

Fig. 63. Square LF2(1973): section 3 and the outer lower fortifications

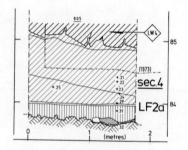

Fig. 64. Square LF2a: section 4

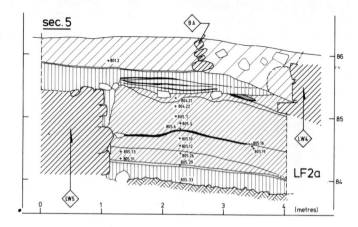

Fig. 65. Square LF2a: section 5

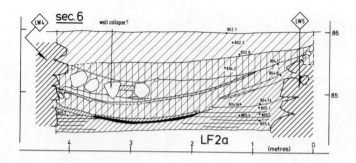

Fig. 66. Square LF2a: section 6

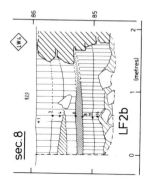

Fig. 68. Square LF2b: section 8

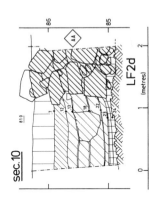

Fig. 70. Square LF2d: section 10

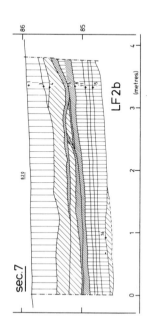

Fig. 67. Square LF2b: section 7

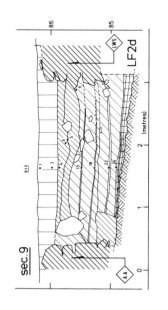

Fig. 69. Square LF2d: section 9

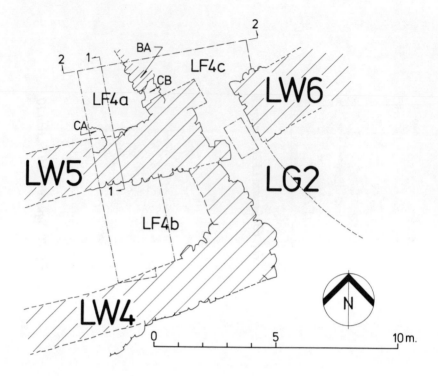

Fig. 71. Square LF4: general plan

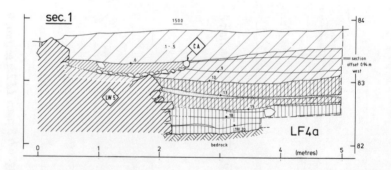

Fig. 72. Square LF4: section 1

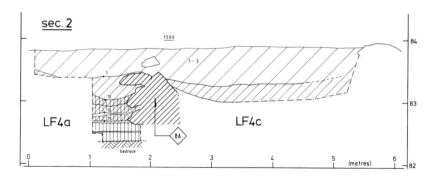

Fig. 73. Square LF4a/c: section 2

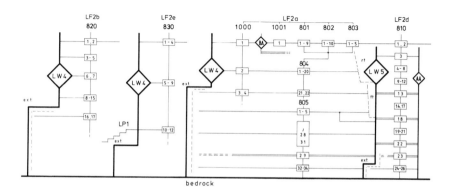

Fig. 74. Square LF2: stratigraphic matrix

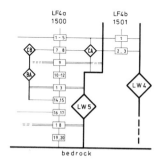

Fig. 75. Square LF4: stratigraphic matrix

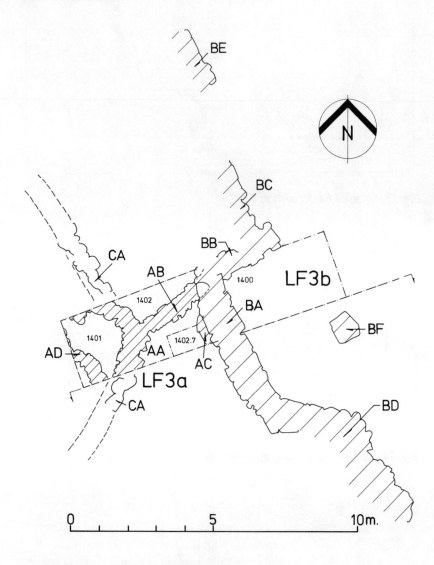

Fig. 76. Square LF3: general plan and key to sections

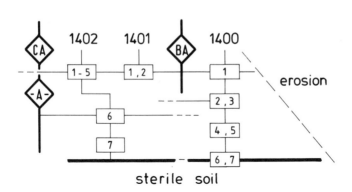

Fig. 77. Square LF3: stratigraphic matrix

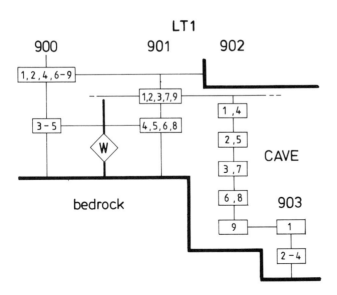

Fig. 78. Square LT1: stratigraphic matrix

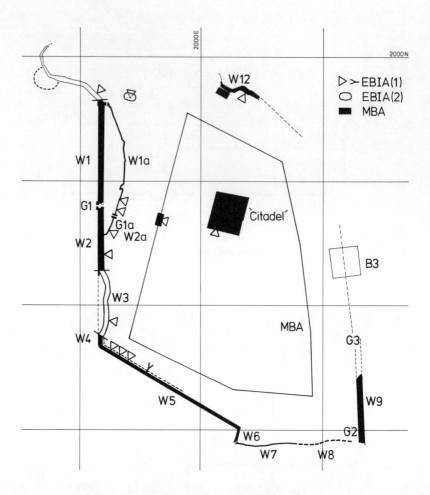

Fig. 79. The upper fortifications

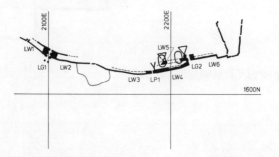

Fig. 80. The lower fortifications (South)

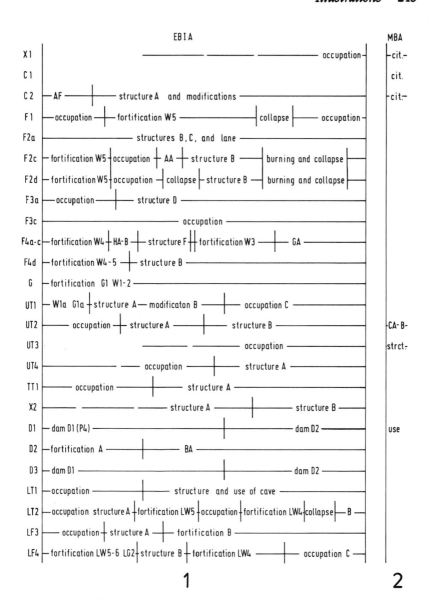

Fig. 81. The stratigraphic matrix of Jawa

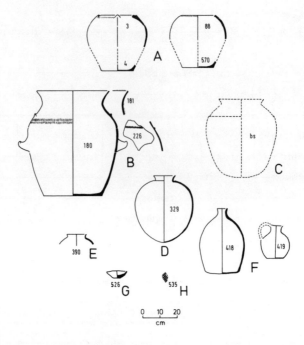

Fig. 82. Pottery vessels from square TT1

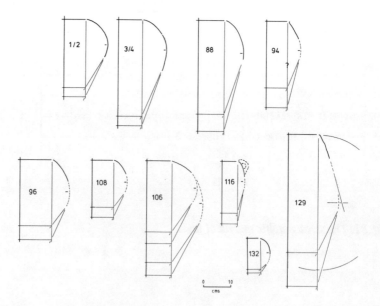

Fig. 83. Genre A: reconstruction of forms

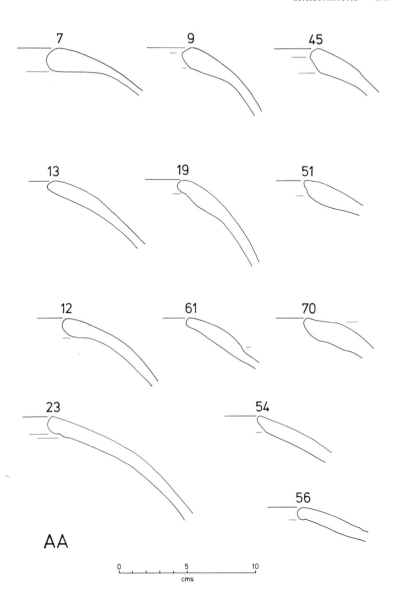

Fig. 84. Genre A: rim profiles (type A)

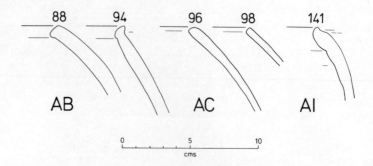

Fig. 85. Genre A: rim profiles (types B/C/I)

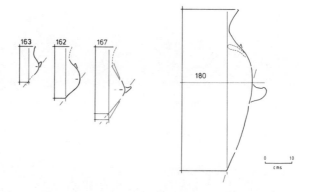

Fig. 86. Genre B: reconstruction of forms

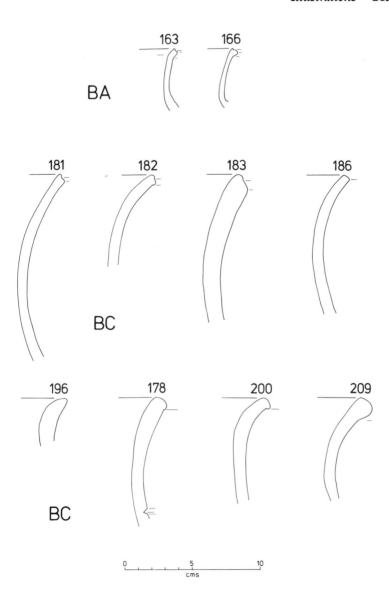

Fig. 87. Genre B: rim profiles (types A/C)

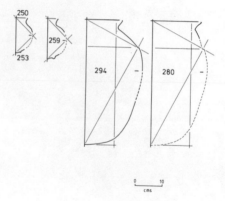

Fig. 88. Genre C: reconstruction of forms

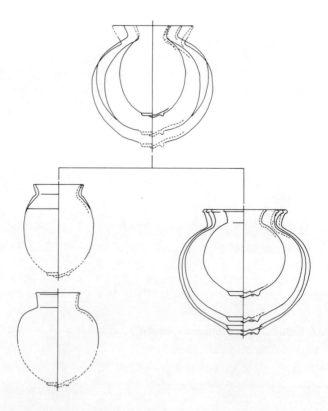

Fig. 89. Genre C: reconstruction of forms

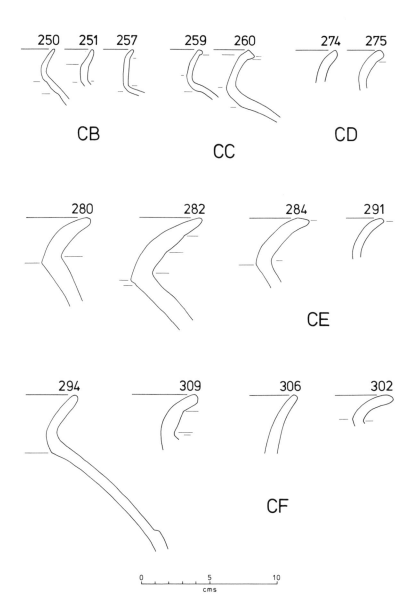

Fig. 90. Genre C: rim profiles (types B/C/D/E/F)

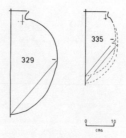

Fig. 91. Genre D: reconstruction of forms

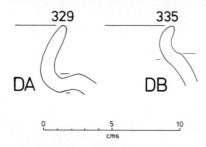

Fig. 92. Genre D: rim profiles (types A/B)

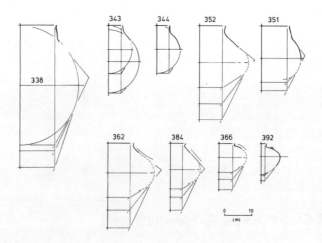

Fig. 93. Genre E: reconstruction of forms (Types A/B/C/E)

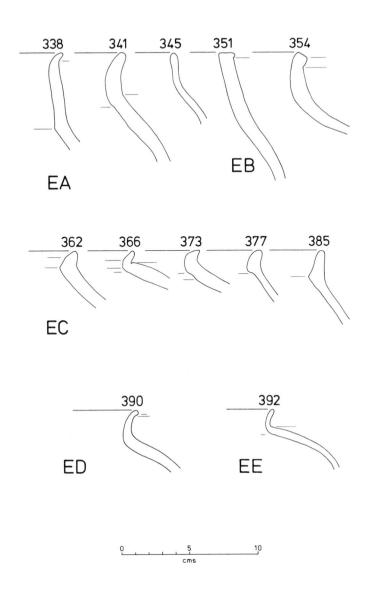

Fig. 94. Genre E: rim profiles (types A/B/C/D/E)

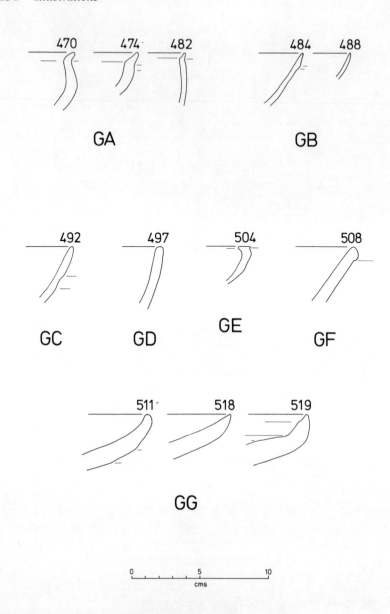

Fig. 95. Genre G: rim profiles (types A/B/C/D/E/F/G)

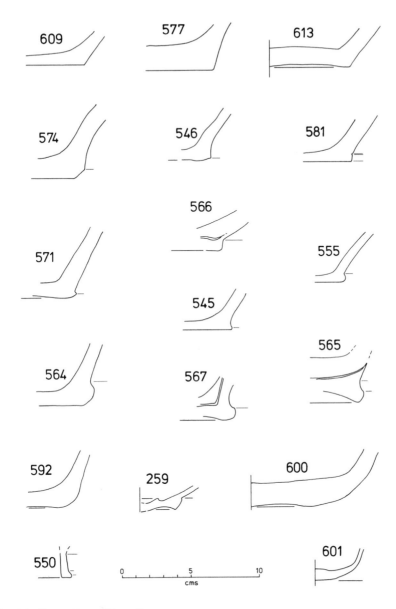

Fig. 96. Genre X: profiles of bases

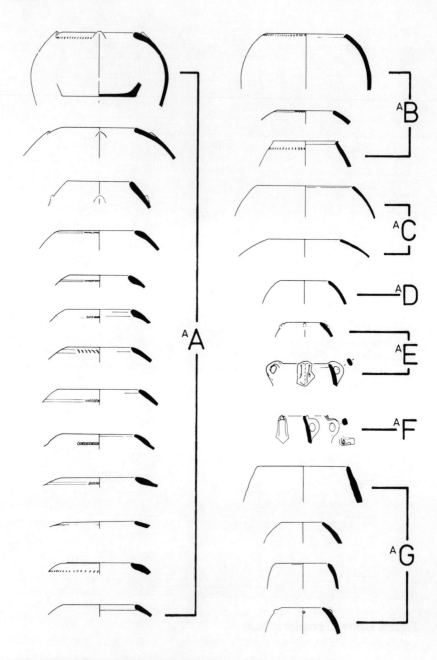

Fig. 97. Summary of Genres and Types: genre A (types A -G)

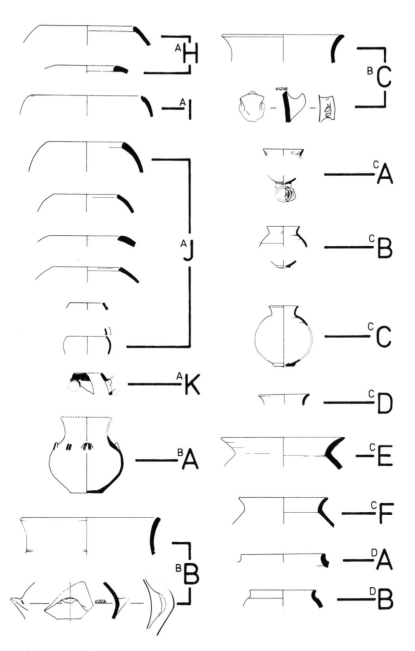

Fig. 98. Summary of Genres and Types: genres A (types H-K), B (types A-C), C (types A-F), D (types A/B)

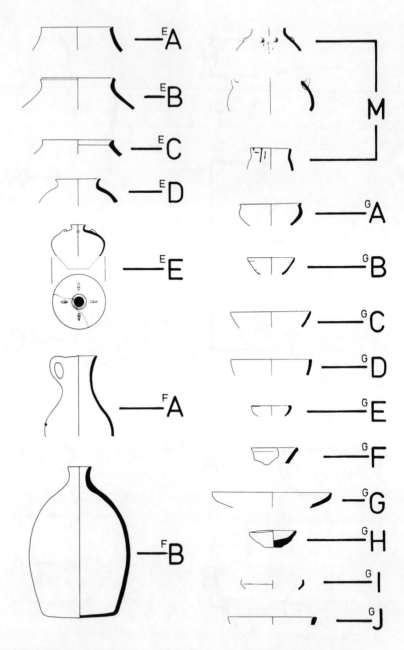

Fig. 99. Summary of Genres and Types: genres E (types A-E), F (types A/B), G (types A-J)

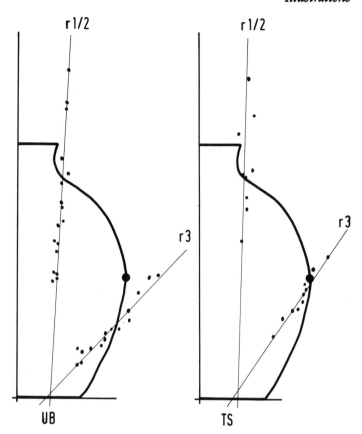

Fig.100. Form and volume: parameters

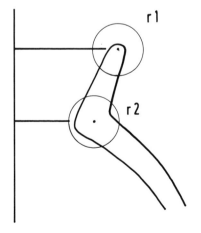

Fig. 101. Rim diameter: parameters

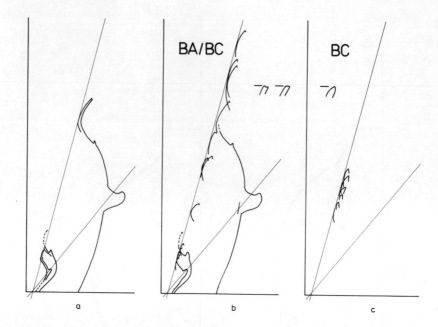

Fig. 102. Volumetric analysis: genre B

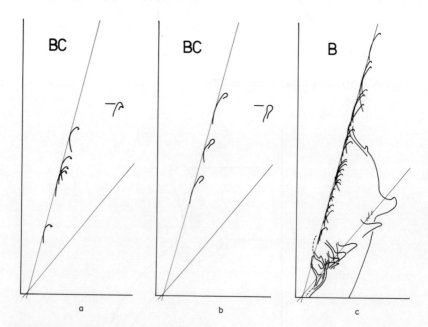

Fig. 103. Volumetric analysis: genre B

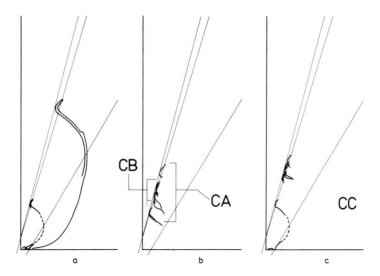

Fig. 104. Volumetric analysis: genre C (types A-C)

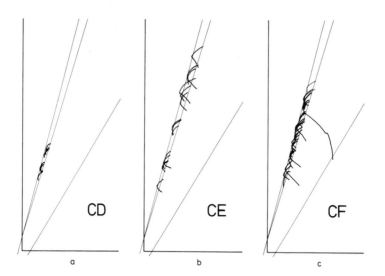

Fig. 105. Volumetric analysis: genre C (types D-F)

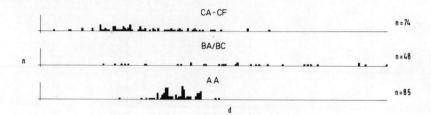

Fig. 106. Comparison of rim dimensions: genres A-C

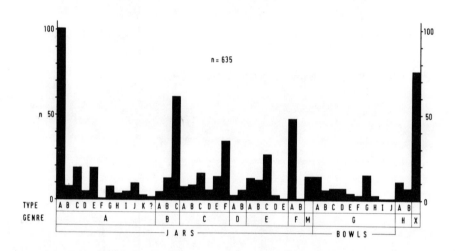

Fig. 107. Frequency of occurrence: genres and types

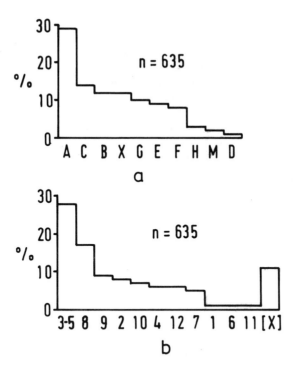

Fig. 108. Frequency of occurrence: (a) genres; (b) fabrics

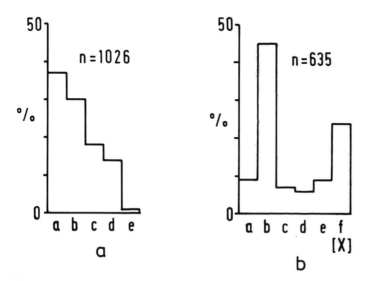

Fig. 109. Frequency of occurrence: genres, (a) test area; (b) excavation

Pottery Catalogue

The illustrated material in the pottery catalogue is arranged in a series of consecutive numbers, followed by the genre and numerical designations used in premilinary reports, the provenance of the material (sq: square designation, loc: locus within square, str: stratum, layer, feature or soil deposition), the genre and type designation (GT), fabric codes (F), and the description. Headings are abbreviated as follows: C (catalogue number), O (old genre/type/variant designation), Provenance, GT, F, and Description.

THE POTTERY OF THE 4TH MILLENNIUM BC

C	O	Provenance	GT	F	Description

Numbers 1-117. Holemouth jars (hmj) (Figs 110-119)

C	O	Provenance	GT F	Description
1	AA1	C2 504.11	AA 08	hmj, 4 pushed up lugs, punctate band at rim
2	AA1	C2 504.11	AA 08	flat base of 1
3	AA2	TT1 100.1	AA 08	hmj, 4 pushed up lugs, punctate band at rim
4	AA2	TT1 100.1	AA 08	flat base of 3
5	AA41	C2 503.2	AA 08	hmj, 4 pushed up lugs, punctate band at rim
6	AA55	UT2 720.4	AA 08	hmj, 4 pushed up lugs, slashed band at rim
7	AA56	F2 406.2	AA 08	hmj, 4 pushed up lugs, slashed band at rim
8	AA39	UT1 702.1	AA 08	hmj, 4 pushed up lugs, punctate band at rim
9	AA40	D2c 1034.4	AA 08	hmj, 4 pushed up lugs, punctate band at rim
10	AA4	LF2 810.5	AA 08	hmj, 4 pushed up lugs, plain
11	AA71	C2 504.15	AA 08	hmj, 4 pushed up lugs, stabbed band at rim
12	AA28	D2c 1032.5	AA 08	hmj, 4 pushed up lugs, punctate band at rim
13	AA38	LF2 804.2	AA 08	hmj, 4 pushed up lugs, punctate band at rim
14	AA53	D2a 1026.7	AA 08	hmj, 4 pushed up lugs, punctate band at rim
15	AA47	LF2 805.7	AA 08	hmj, 4 pushed up lugs, punctate band at rim
16	AA54	LF2 830.10	AA 08	hmj, 4 pushed up lugs, punctate band at rim
17	AA37	C2 507.12	AA 08	hmj, 4 pushed up lugs, punctate band at rim
18	AA64	D2c 1034.3	AA 08	hmj, 4 pushed up lugs, punctate band at rim
19	AA65	F2 413.3	AA 08	hmj, 4 pushed up lugs, stabbed band at rim
20	AA20	D2c 1031.2	AA 08	hmj, 4 pushed up lugs, groove below rim
21	AA22	D2c 1034.4	AA 08	hmj, 4 pushed up lugs, groove below rim
22	AA21	C2 500.8	AA 08	hmj, 4 pushed up lugs, groove below rim
23	AA3	D2c 1034.3	AA 08	hmj, 4 pushed up lugs, plain
24	AA84	++++++++	AA 08	hmj, 4 pushed up lugs, plain
25	AA77	++++++++	AA 08	hmj, punctate band at rim
26	AA82	D2c 1034.4	AA 08	hmj, punctate/slashed band at rim
27	AA45	D2a 1026.6	AA 08	hmj, punctate band at rim
28	AA44	F2 405.9	AA 08	hmj, punctate band at rim
29	AA86	++++++++	AA 08	hmj, punctate band at rim
30	AA46	D2c 1034.3	AA 08	hmj, punctate band at rim
31	AA61	LF2 820.3	AA 08	hmj, slashed band at rim
32	AA68	D2 +++++	AA 08	hmj, punctate band at rim
33	AA63	LF4 1500.6	AA 08	hmj, punctate band at rim

34	AA35	D2c 1031.2	AA 08	hmj, punctate band at rim
35	AA70	D2a 1026.1	AA 08	hmj, punctate/slashed band at rim
36	AA83	D2c 1034.4	AA 08	hmj, punctate band at rim
37	AA73	D2c 1032.2	AA 08	hmj, stabbed band at rim
38	AA69	D2 +++++	AA 08	hmj, punctate/slashed band at rim
39	AA58	D2 +++++	AA 08	hmj, stabbed band at rim
40	AA32	LF3 1400.4	AA 08	hmj, punctate band at rim
41	AA19	D2a 1026.8	AA 08	hmj, groove below rim
42	AA24	LF2 810.5	AA 08	hmj, groove below rim
43	AA25	D2c 1032.2	AA 08	hmj, groove below rim
44	AA76	D2a 1026.2	AA 08	hmj, punctate band at rim
45	AA79	LF2 804.16	AA 08	hmj, stabbed band at rim
46	AA74	D2a 1026.6	AA 08	hmj, stabbed band at rim
47	AA33	++++++++	AA 08	hmj, punctate band at rim
48	AA50	LF2 802.3	AA.08	hmj, punctate band at rim
49	AA43	LF2 507.13	AA 08	hmj, punctate band at rim
50	AA23	LF2 810.5	AA 08	hmj, groove below rim
51	AA30	D2c 1034.4	AA 08	hmj, punctate band at rim
52	AA80	LF4 1500.3	AA 08	hmj, incised/stabbed band at rim
53	AA81	++++++++	AA 08	hmj, punctate band at rim
54	AA51	LF2 804.4	AA 08	hmj, stabbed band at rim
55	AA60	D2a 1026.6	AA 08	hmj, stabbed band at rim
56	AA36	LF2 504.22	AA 08	hmj, punctate band at rim
57	AA66	LF2 802.9	AA 08	hmj, stabbed band at rim
58	AA59	LF2 802.6	AA 08	hmj, stabbed/slashed band at rim
59	AA34	LF2 810.10	AA 08	hmj, punctate band at rim
60	AA48	LF2 805.25	AA 08	hmj, stabbed band at rim
61	AA49	LF2 805.28	AA 08	hmj, stabbed band at rim
62	AA57	LF2 820.3	AA 08	hmj, stabbed band at rim
63	AA52	LF2 804.21	AA 08	hmj, stabbed band at rim
64	AA72	LF2 802.9	AA 08	hmj, stabbed/cut band at rim
65	AA75	LF2 804.9	AA 08	hmj, stabbed band at rim
66	AA42	LF2 804.1	AA 08	hmj, stabbed/punctate band at rim
67	AA62	D2c 1032.5	AA 08	hmj, stabbed band at rim
68	AA26	LF2 804.9	AA 08	hmj, groove below rim
69	AA29	D2c 1031.5	AA 08	hmj, punctate band at rim
70	AA67	LF4 1501.2	AA 08	hmj, stabbed band at rim
71	AA31	D2a 1026.2	AA 08	hmj, punctate band at rim
72	AA78	LF3 1401.2	AA 08	hmj, stabbed/cut band at rim
73	AA10	LF2 810.2	AA 08	hmj, plain
74	AA6	LF2 810.2	AA 08	hmj, plain
75	AA8	LF2 810.5	AA 08	hmj, plain
76	AA7	D2c 1031.2	AA 08	hmj, plain
77	AA5	D2 +++++	AA 08	hmj, plain
78	AA9	LF2 810.10	AA 08	hmj, plain
79	AA11	D2 +++++	AA 08	hmj, plain
80	AA13	LF2 802.6	AA 08	hmj, plain
81	AA14	D2c 1034.4	AA 08	hmj, plain
82	AA12	LF2 836.6	AA 08	hmj, plain
83	AA15	LF2 802.9	AA 08	hmj, plain
84	AA27	LF2 804.2	AA 08	hmj, slurred rim, plain
85	AA17	LF2 802.8	AA 08	hmj, plain
86	AA16	++++++++	AA 08	hmj, plain

87	AA18	F2 414.1	AA 08	hmj, plain

* 14 similar sherds: no catnos

88	AB3	TT1 100.1	AB 08	hmj, punctate band at rim
89	AB4	LF2 820.15	AB 08	hmj, punctate band on rim
90	AB8	++++++++	AB 08	hmj, stabbed band on rim
91	AB5	LF2 805.2[9]	AB 08	hmj, impressed band on rim
92	AB2	LF2 805.6	AB 08	hmj, incised/stabbed band on rim
93	AB6	D2a 1026.2	AB 08	hmj, stabbed band on rim
94	AB1	LF2 805.5	AB 08	hmj/low everted rim jar, stabbed/slashed band below rim
95	AB7	F4 420.3	AB 08	hmj, stabbed band on rim
96	AC2	F4c 420.7[3]	AC 07	hmj, thin body, bevelled/pointed rim, plain
97	AC14	F1 300.4	AC 07	hmj, thin body, bevelled rim, plain
98	AC10	F1 300.5	AC 07	hmj, thin body, bevelled rim, plain
99	AC11	F1 300.5	AC 07	hmj, thin body, bevelled rim, plain, drilled mend-hole
100	AC13	F1 300.4	AC 07	hmj, thin body, bevelled rim, plain
101	AH16	F4c 420.7	AC 07	hmj, thin body, bevelled/rounded rim, plain
102	AH15	F2 414.1	AC 07	hmj, thin body, bevelled/in-folded rim (rolled and bevelled?), plain
103	AC1	F1 300.5	AC 07	hmj, thin body, rounded rim, plain
104	AC4	F1 300.4	AC 07	hmj, thin body, rounded rim, plain
105	AC5	D2a 1028.5	AC 07	hmj, thin body, rounded rim, plain
106	AC6	F4c 420.4	AC 07	hmj, thin body, rounded rim, plain
107	AC7	F1 300.5	AC 07	hmj, thin body, rounded rim, plain
108	AC8	F2 400.3	AC 07	hmj, thin body, rounded rim, plain
109	AC9	F4c 420.7	AC 07	hmj, thin body, rounded/in-turned rim, plain
110	AC12	F4c 420.7	AC 07	hmj, thin body, rounded rim, plain
111	AC3	F1 300.5	AC 07	hmj, thin body, rounded/thickened rim, plain, drilled mend-hole
112	AD14	F2 407.1	AD 07	hmj, rounded rim, plain
113	AD15	UT2 722.1	AD 07	hmj, rounded/pointed rim, plain
114	AD16	D2a 1026.2	AD 07	hmj, pointed/rounded rim, plain
115	AD17	UT1 700.1	AD 07	hmj, rounded rim, plain
116	AD13	LF2 805.6	AE 10	hmj/deep bowl, rounded rim, 1 crude high loop handle at rim, core of handle double
117	AD12	UT2 722.1	AE 10	hmj, pointed/rounded rim, 1 (4?) vertical and pierced lug at rim

Numbers 118-128. Vertical handles (on hmj?) (Fig. 119)

118	AD1	LF2 830.5	AE 10	bs, crude loop handle on shoulder
119	AD2	LF2 804.1	AE 10	bs, crude loop handle near rim
120	AD4	LF4 1500.10	AE 10	bs, crude loop handle
121	AD3	D2a 1028++	AE 10	bs, crude loop handle on shoulder
122	AD5	D1b 1011.2	AE 10	bs, crude loop handle
123	AD6	LF4 1501.2	AE 10	bs, crude loop handle
124	AD7	F1 300.5	AE 10	bs, crude loop handle or lug near shoulder
125	AD8	LF2 810.11	AE 10	bs, crude loop handle
126	AD9	F3c 408.2	AE 10	bs, crude loop handle near shoulder
127	AD10	LF2 805.28	AE 10	bs, crude loop handle or lug
128	AD11	F1 300.4	AE 10	bs, vertical and pierced lug

* 6 sherds, no catnos

Numbers 129-161. Holemouth jars (hmj) (Figs 120-1)

129	AE1	D2c 1031.2	AG 10	hmj, heavy/crude straight rounded rim
130	AE2	LF4 1500.2	AG 10	hmj, heavy/crude slightly bowed rounded/pointed rim
131	AE3	D2c 1032.2	AG 10	hmj, heavy/crude rounded rim
132	AE4	LF2 810.8	AG 10	hmj, heavy/crude pointed and in-turned rim
133	AE5	F4c 420.7	AG 10	hmj, heavy/crude rounded rim
134	AE6	D2c 1032.2	AG 10	hmj, heavy/crude pointed and ext. recessed rim
135	AE7	LF2 807.7	AG 10	hmj, heavy/crude rounded rim
136	000	+++++++++	AG 10	hmj, heavy/crude rounded rim, 1 (4?) raised lump near rim
137	AF1	1028.5	AH 12	hmj, in-rolled rounded/ pointed rim, plain
138	AF2	LF2 802.6	AH 12	hmj, in-rolled rounded rim, plain
139	AF4	LF2 820.15	AH 12	hmj, in-folded (?) rounded/ pointed rim, plain
140	AF3	LF2 804.1	AH 12	hmj, in-folded bevelled/ rounded rim, plain
141	000	+++++++++	AI 12	hmj, pointed and ext. recessed rim
142	AG1	+++++++++	AI 12	hmj, ext. recessed and rounded/squared rim, plain
143	AG4	D2c 1032.4	AI 12	hmj, ext. recessed and pointed/ rounded rim, plain
144	AG2	LF2 1000.3	AI 12	hmj, ext. recessed and rounded rim, plain
145	AG3	LF2 830.9	AI 12	hmj, collared and rounded/ bevelled rim, plain
146	AH1	F2 401.3	AJ 12	hmj, heavy bevelled/rounded rim, plain
147	AH2	D2a 1026.2	AJ 12	hmj, rounded/bevelled rim, plain
148	AH3	LF2 1000.4	AJ 12	hmj, bevelled/rounded rim, plain
149	AH7	LF2 820.6	AC 07	hmj, thin walled (cf. J96-100), bevelled rim
150	AH8	LF2 826.8	AJ 12	hmj, pointed/bevelled and slightly everted rim, plain
151	AH9	LF2 802.4	AJ 12	hmj, rounded/bevelled rim, plain
152	AH4	F4c 420.7	AJ 12	hmj, rolled (?) rounded/bevelled rim, plain
153	AH6	LF2 820.4	AJ 12	hmj, rounded/pointed rim, plain
154	AH5	D2d 1040.2	AJ 12	hmj, rolled rim, rounded and recessed rim, plain
155	AH14	D2a 1026.1	AJ 12	hmj, rounded rim
156	AH13	+++++++	AJ 12	hmj, rounded rim
157	AH10	F4c 420.7	AD 07	hmj, rounded rim (cf. J115)
158	AH17	+++++++	A? 02	hmj, rounded rim, red/brown paint along ext. rim
159	000	+++++++	A? 08	hmj, rounded/pointed rim, 2 bands of slashed decoration near rim (cf. J70 for shape, J180 for dec.)
160	AH11	D2a 1026.6	AC 07	hmj, rounded rim (cf. J103-115)
161	AH12	LF4 1500.11	AC 07	hmj, rounded rim (cf. J103-106), post-firing incised band of chevrons below rim

Numbers 162-212. Flared rim, high-shouldered jars (Figs 122-7)

| 162 | BA4 | C2 503.2 | BA 02 | (rim missing) jar, high neck (everted rim), 4 pushed up lugs with paired stamp impressions on shoulder, similar impression on body, flat base |
| 163 | BA1 | F2 405.8 | BA 02 | jar, high neck, everted grooved rim, 4 pushed up ledge/lug handles at waist, paired stamp impressions on shoulder, base missing (flat) |

164	BA5	D1b 1014.7	BA 02	jar, everted grooved rim
165	BA3	UT1 704.1	BA 02	jar, everted grooved rim
166	BA2	F2 820.8	BA 02	jar, everted grooved rim
167	BB2	D2c 1032.5	BB 03	bs, up-turned ledge handle and finger impressions
168	BB1	++++++++	BB 03	bs, up-turned ledge handle or crude lug
169	000	UTTA +++	BB 03	bs, up-turned and rounded ledge handle
170	000	UTTA +++	BB 03	bs, up-turned and rounded ledge handle
171	000	UTTA +++	BB 03	bs, up-turned and rounded ledge handle, punctate band along sharp edge and on body of jar
172	000	UTTA +++	BB 03	bs, fragment of up-turned and rounded/pointed ledge handle, slashed band along sharp edge
173	000	++++++++	BB 03	bs, rounded ledge handle, brown slip
174	000	UTTA +++	BB 03	bs, up-turned and rounded ledge handle, stamp impression centre upper side
175	BB3	D2c 1031.2	BB 03	bs, up-turned and rounded ledge handle
176	BB4	F4c 720.18a	BB 03	bs, up-turned and rounded ledge handle, double stamp impression centre upper side
177	BB5	LF2 830.12	BB 03	bs, up-turned and rounded ledge handle
178	000	X2 000.3	BB 03	bs, everted rounded and out-rolled/folded rim, deep groove at junction of neck and body
179	000	X2 000.3	BB 03	bs, everted rounded/bevelled and out-rolled/ folded rim, groove at junction of neck and body
180	BC1	TT1 100.1	BC 03	jar, flaring neck, everted grooved rim (cf. also J162-166), high shoulder, flat base, (4) up-turned lugs on shoulder, (2) heavy up-turned lump handles at waist, double band of slashed decoration on shoulder, drilled mend-holes
181	BC2	TT1 100.1	BC 03	jar, everted grooved rim
182	BC7	UT2 722.1	BC 03	jar, everted grooved and down-turned rim
183	BC4	F2 405.11	BC 03	jar, everted rilled/grooved rim, drilled mend-hole
184	BC3	UT1 702.4	BC 03	jar, everted bevelled rim
185	BC9	D2a 1026.6	BC 03	jar, everted bevelled rim
186	BC8	F2 406.5	BC 03	jar, everted bevelled rim
187	000	++++++++	BC 03	jar, everted bevelled/grooved rim
188	BC29	++++++++	BC 03	jar, everted bevelled/rounded rim
189	BC15	UT2 722.4	BD 03	jar, everted bevelled/rounded rim, vertical band of stabbed decoration from rim
190	BC30	LF2 804.12	BD 03	jar, everted bevelled/rounded rim
191	BC17	C2 507.12	BD 03	jar, everted bevelled rim
192	BC31	LF2 810.2	BE 03	jar, everted bevelled and rounded rim
193	BC5	LF2 804.4	BC 03	jar, everted rounded rim
194	BC25	LF2 820.15	BC 03	jar, everted rounded/pointed rim
195	BC16	LF2 1001.1	BC 03	jar, everted rounded rim
196	BC24	D2a 1026.6	BC 03	jar, everted pointed/rounded rim
197	BC18	D2c 1034.4	BC 03	jar, everted pointed/rounded rim
198	BC19	LF2 836.6	BC 03	jar, everted rounded rim
199	BC20	++++++++	BC 03	jar, everted rounded rim

200	BC6	F2 405.5	BC 03	jar, everted rounded out-rolled rim
201	BC12	D2c 1031.2	BC 03	jar, everted rounded/bevelled out-rolled rim
202	BC10	D2a 1026.8	BC 03	jar, everted pointed/rounded slightly int. recessed out-rolled rim
203	BC11	D2c 1034.3	BC 03	jar, pointed/bevelled slightly int. recessed out-rolled/down pointed rim
204	BC27	D2c 1034.4	BC 03	jar, everted rounded/pointed rim
205	BC13	D2c 1034.3	BC 03	jar, everted bevelled pointed rim
206	BC14	D2a 1026.6	BC 03	jar, everted pointed/rounded slightly down-turned rim
207	000	++++++++	BC 03	jar, round rolled rim, drilled mend-holes
208	BC22	++++++++	BC 03	jar, everted rounded bulbous rim
209	BC23	D2c 1031.2	BC 03	jar, everted rounded bulbous rim
210	BC21	D2 1034.2	BC 03	jar, everted (int. bevelled) rounded bulbous rim
211	BC26	LF2 820.2	BC 03	jar, everted rounded rim
212	BC28	++++++++	BC 03	jar, everted rounded rim

Numbers 213-225. Flared rim, high shouldered jar handles (Fig. 128)

213	BD1	LF2 810.4	BC 03	bs, up-turned squared/rounded lump handle
214	BD2	D2 +++++	BC 03	bs, up-turned rounded flaring lump handle
215	BD3	LF2 810.4	BC 03	bs, up-turned pointed flaring lump handle
216	BD4	LF2 810.5	BC 03	bs, up-turned pointed flaring lump handle, thumb impressions upper side
217	BD5	D2a 1026.8	BC 03	bs, up-turned pointed flaring lump handle
218	BD6	F2 401.3	BC 03	bs, up-turned rounded flaring lump handle
219	BD7	LF2 820.8	BC 03	bs, up-turned flaring lump handle
220	BD8	LF2 805.2	BC 03	bs, flaring lump handle
221	000	UT +++++	BC 03	bs, rounded lump handle, slashed decoration under
222	BD9	++++++++	BC 03	bs, flaring pointed lump handle
223	000	++++++++	BC 03	bs, up-turned rounded flaring lump handle
224	000	++++++++	BC 03	bs, fragment, flaring lump handle, impressed band at end
225	BD0	C2 507.13	BC 03	bs, up-turned rounded lump handle

Numbers 226-240. Flared rim, high-shouldered jar decoration (Fig. 129)

226	BE1	TT1 100.1	BC 03	bs, impressed circles on raised band at shoulder
227	BE2	F2 405.8	BC 03	bs, impressed circles on raised band, drilled mend-hole
228	BE3	D2a 1026.1	BC 03	bs, impressed circles on raised band
229	BE4	D2c 1032.2	BC 03	bs, impressed/cut circles
230	BE5	UT4 1700.4	BC 03	bs, impressed circles on raised band
231	BE6	LF2 810.8	BC 03	bs, impressed circles on raised band
232	BE7	UT1 705.3	BC 03	bs, impressed circles on raised band
233	BE8	D2 +++++	BC 03	bs, impressed circles on raised band
234	BE9	D3 1058.2	BC 03	bs, impressed/stabbed circles on raised band
235	000	++++++++	BC 03	bs, impressed ovoids on raised band
236	000	++++++++	BC 03	bs, impressed/stabbed circles on raised band
237	FA12	LF3 1400.4	BC 03	bs, incised patterns on raised horiz. and vert. bands
238	FD1	D2a 1026.8	BC 03	bs, vestigial lug, grooved line beneath

| 239 | FD2 | C2 506.2 | BC 03 | bs, vestigial lug or raised undecorated band |
| 240 | FD3 | LF3 1400.4 | BC 03 | bs, vestigial lug |

Numbers 241-273. Everted rim jars with high shoulders (J249 - pattern burnished) (Fig. 130)

241	CA1	LF2 820.15	CA 01	bs, jar, everted rim, wheel-made, whitish slip ext.
242	CA5	D2a 1028.3	CA 01	bs, jar, everted rim from sharp inverse carination, wheel-made, whitish slip ext.
243	CA2	LF2 802.8	CA 01	jar, pointed rim, wheel-made, whitish slip ext.
244	CA4	D2 +++++	CA 01	jar base, wheel-made, whitish slip ext.
245	CA3	LF4 1500.8	CA 01	jar shoulder, wheel-made, whitish slip ext.
246	CA6	LF2 802.4	CA 01	jar base, ring base and protruding body, wheel-made, whitish slip ext.
247	UT	++++++++	CA 01	jar neck, wheel-made, whitish slip ext., mend-hole
248	LF2	++++++++	CA 01	jar base, ring base and protruding body, wheel-made, whitish slip ext.
249	CB2	++++++++	CB 04	jar, everted pointed rim
250	CB1	++++++++	CB 04	jar, everted pointed rim joined to neck at slight int. scar, tucked carination at shoulder
251	CB4	LF3 1400.4	CB 04	jar, everted rounded/pointed int. recessed rim
252	CB5	LF2 802.6	CB 04	jar, everted pointed slightly int. recessed rim
253	000	++++++++	CB 04	jar base, ring base and protruding body
254	CB6	LF2 820.10	CB 04	jar, everted rounded rim
255	CB3	++++++++	CB 04	jar, everted rounded slighly int. recessed rim
256	CB8	F1 300.4	CB 04	jar, everted rounded int. bevelled/recessed rim
257	CB7	LF2 1000.3	CB 04	jar, everted int. bevelled rounded rim, high rounded shoulder, near vertical neck
258	CC1	LF2 802.8	CC 04	jar, everted rounded rolled rim
259	CC14	LF2 820.6	CC 04	jar, everted rounded rolled rim, bulbous body, ring base with down protruding body
260	CC2	LF2 +++++	CC 04	jar, everted pointed and bevelled slightly int. recessed down-turned rim
261	000	++++++++	CC 04	jar, everted pointed bevelled rim
262	CC3	F2 405.1	CC 04	jar, everted rounded rim
263	CC4	++++++++	CC 04	jar, everted rounded rim
264	CC15	LF2 802.1	CC 04	jar, ring base with down protruding body
265	CC6	LF2 820.8	CC 04	jar, everted rounded rim
266	CC7	D1b 1014.7	CC 04	jar, everted pointed bevelled rim
267	CC5	LF2 1000.2	CC 04	jar, everted pointed bevelled rim
268	CC9	LF2 802.8	CC 04	jar, everted rounded bevelled rim
269	CC10	F4c 420.15	CC 04	jar, everted rounded and pointed rim
270	CC8	++++++++	CC 04	jar, everted rounded and pointed rim
271	CC12	D2a 1026.3	CC 04	jar, everted rounded and bevelled rim
272	CC11	F2 400.2	CC 04	jar, everted rounded and pointed rim
273	CC13	D2a 1026.6	CC 04	jar, everted rounded and pointed rim

Numbers 274-328. Everted rim jars with high shoulders (red pattern burnished) (Figs 131-4)

| 274 | CD1 | LF2 +++++ | CD 09 | jar, everted rounded rim |
| 275 | CD2 | LF2 804.9 | CD 09 | jar, rounded slightly rolled rim |

276	CD3	LF2 804.9	CD 09	jar, everted rounded/pointed rim
277	CD4	LF2 802.6	CD 09	jar, everted rounded rim
278	CD5	LF2 820.8	CD 09	jar, everted rounded rim
279	CD6	LF2 804.10	CD 09	jar, everted rounded rim
280	CE1	LF2 804.4	CE 09	jar, everted pointed/rounded rim, sharp inv. carination at neck/shoulder junction
281	CE2	F2 401.1	CE 09	jar, everted pointed/rounded rim, sharp int. carination
282	CE3	F2 413.3	CE 09	jar, everted pointed rim, shallow scallops ext. neck, sharp int. carination
283	CE4	LF2 820.2	CE 09	jar, everted pointed rim
284	CE5	++++++++	CE 09	jar, everted pointed (bevelled) rim, sharp int. carination
285	CE6	++++++++	CE 09	jar, everted pointed/rounded rim, sharp int. carination
286	CE8	++++++++	CE 09	jar, rounded/pointed rim
287	CE7	LF2 804.4	CE 09	jar, everted rounded/pointed rim
288	CE9	LF2 802.4	CE 09	jar, everted rounded/pointed rim
289	CE10	C2 506.5	CE 09	jar, everted rounded/pointed rim
290	CE11	LF2 820.4	CE 09	jar, everted rounded/pointed rim, sharp int. carination
291	CE12	LF2 802.4	CE 09	jar, everted rounded/pointed rim
292	CE13	LF2 805.28	CE 09	jar, everted rounded/pointed rim, sharp int. carination
293	CE14	LF2 804.20	CE 09	jar, everted pointed rim, sharp int. carination
294	CF1	C2 506.4	CF 09	jar, everted rounded rim, sharp int. carination, indented high shoulder, horizontal pattern burnish on rim, radial/vert. on shoulder, horiz. on body
295	CF2	F2 405.11	CF 09	jar base, round
296	CF3	LF4 1500.3	CF 09	jar, everted rounded rim, sharp int. carination
297	CF4	LF2 804.4	CF 09	jar, everted rounded rim
298	CF5	D2c 1034.4	CF 09	jar, everted rounded slightly down-pointed rim
299	CF6	LF4 1500.6	CF 09	jar, everted rounded rim
300	CF7	LF2 805.24	CF 09	jar, everted rounded rim
301	CF8	LF2 820.5	CF 09	jar, everted rounded rim, sharp int. carination
302	CF29	LF2 504.5	CF 09	jar, sharply everted rounded rim
303	CF28	D2c 1034.3	CF 09	jar, everted bevelled rim
304	CF11	LF2 802.4	CF 09	jar, everted rounded slightly rolled rim, ext. scallop, sharp int. carination
305	CF10	LF2 805.10	CF 09	jar, everted rounded rim
306	CF27	LF2 802.9	CF 09	jar, high everted rounded rim
307	CF26	C2 507.11	CF 09	jar, everted pointed/rounded rim
308	CF9	LF2 805.28	CF 09	jar, everted rounded rim, sharp int. carination
309	CF12	C2 506.5	CF 09	jar, everted rounded int. bevelled rim, slight scalloped ext.
310	CF13	LF2 805.12	CF 09	jar, everted rounded rim
311	CF15	LF2 1000.2	CF 09	jar, everted rounded slightly rolled rim
312	CF14	LF2 820.6	CF 09	jar, everted rounded rim
313	CF16	LF2 1000.2	CF 09	jar, everted rounded rim, slighty int. recessed
314	CF17	LF2 820.6	CF 09	jar, everted rounded rim
315	CF22	F2 405.16	CF 09	jar, everted rounded down-turned rim

316	CF20	LF4 1500.6	CF 09	jar, everted rounded rim, sharp int. carination
317	CF18	LF2 820.11	CF 09	jar, everted rounded rim
318	CF19	UT4 1700.4	CF 09	jar, everted rounded rim
319	CF31	LF2 804.9	CF 09	bs, jar, everted rim
320	000	+++++++++	CF 09	jar, everted rounded rim
321	000	X2 000.2	CF 09	jar, everted rounded rim, slight scallops ext.
322	CF21	F2 405.16	CF 09	jar, everted rouned rim, sharp int. carination
323	CF30	F2 405.20	CF 09	jar, narrow high neck, everted rounded rim
324	CF23	LF2 810.10	CF 09	jar, rounded rim
325	CF24	F2 405.16	CF 09	jar, everted rounded/squared rim, slight bulge in neck
326	CF25	D2c 1032.5	CF 09	jar, everted rounded slightly int. recessed rim
327	CF32	LF2 810.14	CF 09	bs, jar shoulder, indented
328	CF33	LF2 810.14	CF 09	bs, jar shoulder, indented

Numbers 329-337. Low everted rim jars, high indented shoulders and round bases (Fig. 135)

329	DA1	TT1 100.1	DA 11	jar, rounded rim, indented shoulder, rounded base
330	000	+++++++++	DB 11	jar, rounded and bevelled rim, sharp int. carination
331	DB3	LF2 810.6	DB 11	jar, rounded bevelled rim, indented shoulder, int. carination
332	DB5	D2a 1026.1	DB 11	jar, rounded rim
333	EC23	D2a 1026.1	DB 11	jar, rounded rim, indented shoulder (?)
334	DB1	+++++++++	DB 11	jar, rim broken, indented shoulder, int. carination
335	DB2	D2a 1026.2	DB 11	jar, rounded rim, indented shoulder
336	DB4	D2a 1026.6	DA 11	jar, rounded rim
337	DA2	UT1 707.1	DA.11	jar, rim broken, indented shoulder, rounded base

Numbers 338-361. Bag-shaped jars (Figs 136-7)

338	000	+++++++++	EA 03	jar, everted pointed rim, in-sloping neck, sharp int. carination
339	EA3	UT1 705.8	EA 03	jar, everted pointed rim, in-sloping neck
340	EA4	LF2 830.11	EA 10	jar, everted rounded and grooved rim
341	000	+++++++++	EA 10	jar, everted rounded rim, scar at neck/shoulder
342	000	+++++++++	EA 10	jar, everted rounded rim from in-sloping neck, (4?) up-turned rounded lugs below rim (cf. J1-24, J162, J180, J449)
343	EA6	+++++++++	EA 10	jar, vertical pointed rim, slight scar at neck/shoulder
344	EA1	D2a 1025.2	EA 03	jar, vertical rounded rim
345	EA2	LF2 802.1	EA 03	jar, vertical slightly bowed rounded rim
346	EC24	LF2 830.12	EA 03	jar, vertical rounded rim
347	EA5	UT1 700.1	EA 10	jar, bulging rounded/bevelled rim
348	EA7	LF2 805.6	EA 10	jar, everted/vertical bevelled rim
349	EA8	F2 405.1	EA 10	jar, rounded rim

350	000	D2 1034.4	EA 10	jar, rounded slightly bowed rim
351	EF2	LF2 830.12	EB 02	jar, bevelled rim with ext. ridge, 1 doubled high loop handle from shoulder to rim, in-sloping neck
352	000	+++++++	EB 02	jar, everted bevelled rim, thickened join at in-sloping neck
353	EB1	C2 507.13	EB 02	jar, bevelled/rounded rim, int. carination
354	EB2	D2a 1026.1	EB 02	jar, bevelled/squared rim
355	EB3	D2a 1026.1	EB 02	jar, rilled/grooved rim, int. carination
356	000	++++++++	EB 02	jar, bevelled/rounded rim
357	000	X2 000.3	EB 02	jar, bevelled/rounded rim
358	EB4	UT1 702.4	EB 02	jar, bevelled/rounded rim
359	EB5	LF2 830.4	EB 02	jar, bevelled/rounded rim
360	EB6	D2c 1034.3	EB 02	jar, bevelled rim
361	EB7	LF3 1400.4	EB 02	jar, heavy bevelled rim

Numbers 362-392. Bag-shaped jars with low everted rims (Figs 138-9)

362	EC1	D2a 1026.6	EC 02	jar, bevelled/rounded rim, sharp int. carination, concave shoulder
363	EC3	D2a 1028.5	EC 02	jar, bevelled/rounded rim, flat shoulder
364	EC10	F2 405.1	EC 02	jar, bevelled/rounded rim, sharp. int./ext. carination
365	EC13	LF2 802.4	EC 02	jar, rounded rim, int. carination, scalloped shoulder
366	EC7	++++++++	EC 02	jar, bevelled and slightly int. recessed rim, harply indented convex shoulder, sharp int. carination
367	EC15	++++++++	EC 02	jar, rounded int. recessed rim, convex/scalloped shoulder, sharp int. carination
368	EC7	++++++++	EC 02	jar, rounded rim, flat shoulder, int. carination
369	EC14	++++++++	EC 02	jar, rounded bevelled and int. recessed rim, concave shoulder, int. carination
370	EC16	++++++++	EC 02	jar, near vertical pointed/rounded rim, convex shoulder, int. carination
371	000	++++++++	EC 02	jar, rounded/pointed rim, concave shoulder
372	000	++++++++	EC 02	jar, rounded slightly int. recessed rim, flat/concave shoulder
373	EC12	LF2 830.12	EC 02	jar, bevelled/pointed rim, concave shoulder, int. concave carination
374	EC19	D2c 1032.4	EC 02	jar, vertical pointed rim, concave shoulder
375	EC18	D2c 1034.1	EC 02	jar, rounded rim, in. carination, convex shoulder
376	EC25	++++++++	EC 02	jar, rounded int. recessed rim (shape MBA?; fb EB I)
377	EC22	D2a 1028.5	EC 02	jar, rounded almond-shaped rim, concave shoulder, int. sharp carination
378	EC2	LF2 830.5	EC 02	jar, rounded bevelled rim, int. carination, flat shoulder
379	EC4	LF2 830.12	EC 02	jar, rounded rim, flat shoulder
380	EC5	LF2 830.4	EC 02	jar, rounded/pointed rim, flat/concave shoulder

381	EC6	++++++++	EC 02	jar, rounded and bevelled rim, int. carinations, flat shoulder
382	EC8	LF2 820.1	EC 02	jar, rounded and int. recessed rim, int. carination, convex/flat shoulder
383	EC9	LF2 802.4	EC 02	jar, rounded rim
384	EC11	F2 405.8	EC 02	jar, rounded rim, ext. carination, flat shoulder
385	000	++++++++	EC 02	jar, near vertical rounded int. recessed rim, flat/convex shoulder
386	EC21	LF2 810.2	EC 02	jar, rounded rim
387	000	++++++++	EC 02	jar, pointed rim
388	EC20	D2c 1034.2	EC 02	jar, pointed rim, concave shoulder
389	000	++++++++	ED 02	jar, pointed bevelled rim, sharp int. carination
390	EE2	TT1 100.1	ED 02	jar, rounded everted rim
391	EE1	D2c 1034.4	ED 02	jar, everted rounded rim
392	ED1	UT1 702.1	EE 02	jar, narrow necked, everted rounded rim, high convex shoulder, 4 vertical pierced lugs on shoulder, base missing

Numbers 393-417. Narrow-necked jars (Fig. 140)

393	FA1	LF2 802.8	FA 3/5	jar, everted pointed rim, 1 loop handle at rim,impressed lug at shoulder
394	FA2	C2 506.1	FA 3/5	jar, everted rounded rim
395	000	++++++++	FA 3/5	jar, rim missing, incised linear pattern on shoulder
396	FA25	C2 405.8	FA 3/5	bs, impressed/incised lug
397	FA4	LF2 801.8	FA 3/5	bs, imprssed lug
398	FA5	D2a 1026.2	FA 3/5	bs, impressed lug
399	FA3	D2c 1034.1	FA 3/5	bs, impressed lug
400	FA7	D2a 1026.1	FA 3/5	bs, incised lug
401	FA8	D2a 1026.8	FA 3/5	bs, impressed lug
402	FA9	D2a 1026.2	FA 3/5	bs, incised lug
403	FA15	F2 405.8	FA 3/5	bs, incised lug
404	FA6	D2 +++++	FA 3/5	bs, impressed lug
405	FA11	D2c 1032.2	FA 3/5	bs, impressed lug/band (cf. also J226-237)
406	FA13	LF4 1400.2	FA 3/5	bs, impressed lug
407	FA15	F2 405.8	FA 3/5	bs, incised lug
408	FA20	+++++++	FA 3/5	bs, incised/impressed lug
409	000	D2a 1026.2	FA 3/5	bs, impressed lug
410	FA16	D2a 1026.6	FA 3/5	bs, incised lug
411	FA17	D2 +++++	FA 3/5	bs, incised bands either side of ridge
412	FA18	++++++++	FA 3/5	bs, impressed band (cf. J226-237)
413	FA19	D2a 1026.1	FA 3/5	bs, incised band/lug
414	FA21	LF2 820.1	FA 3/5	bs, impressed band
415	FA22	LF3 1401.2	FA 3/5	bs, incised lug
416	FA23	D2a 1026.6	FA 3/5	bs, incised lug
417	FA24	D2c 1031.2	FA 3/5	bs, incised lug

Numbers 418-428. Jars and body sherds (Fig. 141)

| 418 | FB1 | TT1 100.1 | FB 10 | jar, narrow necked, everted rounded rim, convex base |
| 419 | FC1 | TT1 100.1 | FA 3/5 | jar, everted rounded rim, (broken) high loop handle from shoulder, red slip, flat base |

420	FC2	UT1 700.4	FA 3/5	(jar), loop handle
421	EF1	D2c 1034.4	FA 3/5	(jar), loop handle, impressed ovoids on top
422	FF1	D2a 1026.8	HB 12	bs, incised lines
423	FF2	UT2 722.4	HB 12	bs, impressed/stabbed band
424	FF3	D2a 1026.1	HB 12	bs, punctate band
425	FF4	LF2 810.5	HB 12	bs, stabbed band
426	J13	LF4 1500.2	HB 12	bs, raised band of circles
427	J1	D2e 1065.8	HB 12	bs, incised pattern (see chapter 4)
428	J9	UT1 707.1	HB 12	bs, raised circular lug (cf. J136, J450)

Numbers 429–448. Handles (Figs 142–143)

429	FE1	D2a 1026.1	FA 3/5	strap handle
430	FE2	D2a 1026.1	FA 3/5	doubled strap handle
431	FE12	D1b 1011.1	FA 3/5	loop handle
432	FE6	LF2 820.3	FA 3/5	doubled loop handle
433	FE7	C2 503.2	FA 3/5	loop handle
434	FE3	C2 503.2	FA 3/5	strap handle
435	FE8	D2c 1034.3	FA 3/5	loop handle
436	FE5	LF4 1500.5	FA 3/5	loop handle
437	FE9	D2a 1026.2	FA 3/5	loop handle
438	FE11	D2c 1032.5	FA 3/5	loop handle
439	FE10	C2 503.2	FA 3/5	loop handle
440	FE13	LF2 820.3	FA 3/5	loop handle, incised/stabbed decoration
441	000	++++++++	FA 3/5	doubled loop handle, stabbed design
442	FE15	LF2 1000.2	FA 3/5	loop/strap handle
443	FE14	F2 401.3	FA 3/5	loop handle
444	000	++++++++	FA 3/5	doubled loop handle, red painted pattern ext.
445	FE4	++++++++	FA 3/5	loop handle
446	HA7	LF2 820.6	FA 3/5	bs, start of loop handle, red painted vertical stripes
447	000	++++++++	AF 03	bowl, loop handle at rim with applied decoration
448	HA8	UT1 707.3	FA 3/5	loop handle, red painted net pattern ext.

Numbers 449–469. Miscellaneous jars (Figs 143–4)

449	000	++++++++	EB 02	jar, rim missing, in-turned neck, 1 (4?) pushed up rounded stabbed lug at waist (shape: cf. J351–388)
450	000	++++++++	M 12	jar, rim missing, everted neck/rim, brownish slip and vertical lines of pattern burnish on shoulder below two rounded lugs
451	000	++++++++	FA 3/5	jar, rim missing, high loop handle
452	HB3	++++++++	AK 12	spout
453	HB1	LF2 1000.2	AK 12	spouted bowl/hmj, rounded in-turned rim, reddish painted band along ext. rim
454	HB2	D2 1034.2	AK 12	spout
455	HA5	LF2 802.1	M 3/5	jar, everted rounded rim (cf. J344?), red painted vert. and horiz. lines ext.
456	HA4	LF2 810.14	M 3/5	jar, vertical/everted rounded rim (cf. J435?), painted red horiz. and vert. stripes
457	J8	UT1 707.3	G? 12	deep bowl, rounded/pointed rim
458	000	++++++++	M 05	jar/bowl, everted rounded/pointed rim, 1 vert. pierced lug at rim, red painted diagonal stripe

459	J2	LF2 804.10	M 05	jar, everted pointed rim (cf. J393-4)
460	J6	UT1 705.10	M 12	jar, rounded everted rim
461	HA6	D2a 1026.6	AJ 03	bowl, inturned rounded/pointed/ bevelled rim, red paint along top of rim
462	HA3	LF2 830.8	M 12	jar/flat bowl (?), rounded rilled/grooved rim, red painted horiz. and diagonal stripes
463	J5	C2 504.10	M 12	jar, everted rounded/pointed rim
464	J3	LF2 805.1	M 12	jar, everted rounded rim, whitish slip int./ext.
465	HA1	C2 506.2	M 05	jar, everted pointed/rounded rim, red painted diagonal stripes from rim
466	HA2	LF2 810.14	M 3/5	jar, everted pointed/rounded rim, traces red paint
467	J4	C2 504.10	M 12	jar, everted rounded bulbous (rolled?) rim
468	J7	LF3 1400.1	M 12	jar, everted rounded rim, slight scallop ext. neck
469	J1	LF2 804.10	M 12	jar neck/shoulder, rim missing, band of incised decoration

Numbers 470-489. Small bowls (Fig. 145)

470	GA1	D2c 1032.2	GA 3/5	bowl, everted pointed rim, slight int. carination
471	000	++++++++	GA 3/5	bowl, everted pointed rim
472	000	++++++++	GA 3/5	bowl, everted pointed rim
473	GA2	LF2 810.8	GA 3/5	bowl, everted rounded/bevelled rim, slight ext. carination
474	GA3	D2a 1026.6	GA 3/5	bowl, everted pointed slightly int. recessed rim, int. carination
475	GA4	LF4 1500.6	GA 3/5	bowl, everted pointed rim, int. carination
476	GA10	LF2 804.1	GA 3/5	bowl, everted pointed rim, slight int. carination
477	GA5	C2 500.8	GA 3/5	bowl, everted pointed bevelled and slightly int. recessed rim, int. carination
478	GA9	C2 506.7	GA 3/5	bowl, int. recessed pointed rim
479	GA6	LF4 1500.5	GA 3/5	bowl, everted int. recessed pointed rim, int. carination
480	GA7	LF2 804.4	GA 3/5	bowl, everted int. recessed pointed rim
481	GA8	LF2 820.1	GA 3/5	bowl, everted bevelled pointed rim
482	GA11	LF2 804.1	GA 3/5	bowl, everted int. recessed pointed rim
483	000	++++++++	GA 3/5	bowl, everted int. recessed pointed rim, int. carination
484	GB1	LF2 1000.3	GB 04	bowl, pointed slightly thickened rim, slight multiple carination ext. body
485	GB2	LF2 1000.2	GB 04	bowl, slightly in-turned pointed rim
486	GB3	LF2 820.13	GB 04	bowl, pointed rim
487	GB4	++++++++	GB 04	bowl, slightly in-turned pointed rim
488	GB5	LF2 1001.1	GB 04	bowl, pointed rim
489	GB6	LF2 1000.1	GB 04	bowl, pointed rim
490	GC1	++++++++	GC 07	bowl, rounded rim

Numbers 490-530. Bowls (Figs 146-8)

491	GC2	LF2 804.2	GC 07	bowl, rounded almond-shaped rim
492	GC3	++++++++	GC 07	bowl rounded rim, slight indentation ext. body
493	GC4	LF2 820.15	GC 07	bowl, rounded rim

494	GC5	LF2 800++	GC 07	bowl, rounded rim
495	GC6	LF2 804.2	GC 07	bowl, rounded rim
496	GC7	++++++++	GC 07	bowl, rounded rim, flat body below rim
497	GD1	D2a 1028.5	GD 06	bowl, rounded rim
498	GD2	F4c 420.7	GD 06	bowl, rounded rim
499	GD3	C2 507.6	GD 06	bowl, rounded rim
500	000	++++++++	GD 06	bowl, rounded rim
501	GD5	C2 506.3	GD 06	bowl, rounded rim
502	GF2	LF2 820.11	GD 06	bowl, rounded rim
503	GD4	F4c 420.7	GD 06	bowl, rounded rim
504	GE1	LF2 820.8	GE 04	bowl, horiz. bevelled in-turned rim with ext. groove
505	GE2	LF2 820.11	GE 04	bowl, horiz. bevelled in-turned rim with ext. groove
506	GF1	LF2 820.8	GE 04	bowl, horiz. bevelled rim
507	GF3	LF2 505.28	GE 04	bowl, bevelled rim with ext. groove
508	GG1	C2 504.2	GF 12	bowl, rounded rolled rim
509	GG2	F2 406.1	GF 12	bowl, bevelled rounded/rolled rim
510	GG3	++++++++	GF 12	bowl, bevelled rim
511	000	++++++++	GG 10	shallow bowl, slightly in-turned rounded rim
512	GJ1	++++++++	GG 10	shallow bowl, rounded rim
513	GJ2	LF2 820.6	GG 10	shallow bowl, rounded rim
514	GJ3	LF3 1400.4	GG 10	shallow bowl, bevelled rim
515	GJ4	D2a 1026.8	GG 12	shallow bowl, pointed rim, slight ext. carination
516	GJ5	LF2 820.13	GG 10	shallow bowl, pointed rim, slight double ext. carination
517	GJ6	LF2 836.6	GG 10	shallow bowl, pointed rim
518	GJ7	LF2 836.6	GG 10	shallow bowl, pointed rim
519	GH1	D2c 1034.4	GG 10	shallow bowl/platter, pointed rim, int. carination
520	GH2	LF2 810.2	GG 10	shallow bowl/platter, rounded rim, int. double carination
521	GH3	LF2 810.14	GG 10	shallow bowl/platter, rounded rim with ext. groove
522	GK1	UT2 722.4	GG 10	bowl, rounded rim
523	GK2	LF2 820.10	GG 10	bowl, rounded rim
524	GK3	D2 ++++++	GG 10	bowl, rounded rim
525	GK4	D2c 1034.4	GG 10	bowl, pointed everted rim, external ridge
526	GL1	TT1 100.1	GH 3/5	lamp (burning on lip), rounded rim, flat base
527	GL2	LF2 1000.3	GH 3/5	lamp (burning on spout), rounded rim, 1 shallow spout
528	GL3	LF2 810.14	GH 3/5	lamp (?), rounded rim
529	J11	LF2 804.2	GI 12	bowl (?), sharp ext. carination
530	J10	C2 504.22	GJ 12	bowl, bevelled/rounded rim

Numbers 531-550. Painted vessels (Fig. 149)

531	HA15	LF2 810.2	HA 3/5	bs, jar neck (?), red painted net pattern and stripes int./ext.
532	000	F2c 405.15	HA 3/5	bs, red painted chevrons in vert. register(s)
533	HA9	LF2 820.5		plan: (= J544)
534	HA16	C2 507.13	HA 3/5	bs, red painted chevrons and net pattern

535	HA22	TT1 100.1	HA 3/5	bs, red painted net pattern
536	HA18	D2a 1026.8	HA 3/5	bs, red painted chevrons and vert. (?) stripes
537	HA21	LF2 830.3	HA 3/5	bs, red painted stripes and cross-lines
538	HA26	++++++++	HA 3/5	bs, red painted lines
539	HA17	D2a 1026.8	HA 3/5	bs, red painted chevrons and lines
540	HA19	C2 507.13	HA 3/5	bs, red painted chevrons
541	HA20	LF2 805.1	HA 3/5	bs, red painted diagonal stripe
542	HA11	++++++++		plan: (= J547)
543	HA23	LF2 820.11	HA 3/5	bs, red painted splash
544	HA9	LF2 820.5	X 3/5	flat base with slight ridge, red painted vert. and horiz. stripes (cf. J533 plan)
545	HA10	LF2 805.6	X 3/5	flat out-curving base, red painted chevrons/triangles in horiz. register(s)
546	000	++++++++	X 3/5	flat stump base, red painted broad vert. stripes and circles between
547	HA11	++++++++	X 3/5	flat stump base, red painted wavy lines (cf. J542, plan)
548	HA12	LF2 830.9	X 3/5	flat stump base. red painted broad vert. stripes
549	HA13	LF2 820.4	X 3/5	flat stump base, red painted lines
550	HA14	F4c 420.15a	X 12	pedestal base, red painted stripe about junction of body and base, flared foot, light slip ext.

Numbers 551-619. Bases (Figs 150-153)

551	X13	D2a 1026.7	X	flat rounded disc base
552	X31	LF2 1000.2	X	flat rounded disc base
553	X33	LF2 805.12	X	flat rounded disc base
554	X35	LF2 803.1	X	flat rounded disc base
555	X34	LF2 803.1	X	flat rounded disc base
556	X42	D2a 1026.1	X	flat rounded disc base
557	X43	LF2 810.10	X	flat rounded disc base
558	X28	LF2 804.13	X	flat rounded/bevelled disc base
559	X44	D2c 1031.2	X	flat rounded disc base
560	X11	LF2 805.28	X	flat low pedestal base, thumb impressed pattern
561	X17	LF2 805.12	X	flat low pedestal base
562	X14	LF2 810.2	X	flat low pedestal base
563	X18	+++++++++	X	flat low pedestal base
564	X24	D2a 1026.8	X	flat low pedestal base, thumb impressed pattern
565	X36	LF2 820.15	X	hollow low pedestal base, composite construction, thumb-impressed band
566	X37	D2a 1026.2	X	flat low pedestal base, composite construction
567	X38	LF2 810.10	X	hollow low pedestal base, composite construction
568	X12	D2a 1026+	X	flat bevelled base
569	X61	C2 507.12	X	flat rounded base
570	X15	TT1 100.1	X	flat base, rounded
571	X55	D2 +++++	X	flat base, ridge
572	X16	D2c 1034.4	X	flat base
573	X21	+++++++++	X	flat base, disc
574	X19	C2 507.2	X	flat base, bevelled
575	X20	F2 400.2	X	flat base, bevelled, thumb-impressed

576	X22	F2 413.2	X	flat base, rounded
577	X7	F2 405.8	X	flat base, rounded
578	X32	LF2 810.14	X	flat base
579	X25	LF2 804.16	X	flat base, rounded/bevelled
580	X26	LF2 1000.1	X	flat base, rounded
581	X40	LF2 810.10	X	flat base, bevelled/grooved
582	X39	F2 405.15	X	flat base
583	X41	LF2 810.10	X	flat base, bevelled
584	X27	++++++++	X	flat base, bevelled
585	X30	C2 503.2	X	flat base, bevelled
586	X46	F4c 420.7	X	flat base, rounded, mend-hole
587	X2	D2c 1034.2	X	flat base
588	X45	C2 506.5	X	flat base, rounded
589	X47	C2 506.3	X	flat base, rounded
590	X65	C2 504.12	X	flat base, rounded
591	X50	LF2 804.7	X	flat base, rounded
592	X62	C2 504.12	X	flat base, rounded
593	X67	UT1 702.1	X	flat base, rounded
594	X23	D2c 1031.2	X	flat base, rounded
595	X29	D2c 1031.2	X	flat base, rounded
596	X5	LF2 810.5	X	flat base
597	X49	++++++++	X	flat base
598	X52	D2c 1031.1	X	flat base, rounded
599	X66	D2a 1026+	X	flat base, rounded
600	X64	C2 507.3	X	rounded hollow base
601	J12	D2c 1034.2	X	rounded base
602	X68	++++++++	X	rounded base
603	X6	D2c 1034.1	X	flat base
604	X1	D2a 1026.1	X	flat base, impressed decoration
605	X4	++++++++	X	flat base
606	X53	LF2 804.5	X	flat base, slight ridge
607	X51	D2c 1034.2	X	flat base
608	X10	UT2 720.4	X	flat base
609	X9	F2 401.3	X	flat base
610	X48	F2 405.3	X	hollow base
611	X3	++++++++	X	hollow base
612	X60	LF2 820.2	X	hollow base
613	X58	F2 401.3	X	hollow base
614	X8	D2c 1031.2	X	hollow base
615	X57	LF2 810.5	X	hollow base
616	X54	C2 506.5	X	hollow base
617	X56	++++++++	X	hollow base
618	X63	D2c 1031.2	X	hollow base
619	X59	C2 503.2	X	hollow base

For 620, 621, both incised body sherds, see Chapter 4.

MIDDLE BRONZE AGE POTTERY

C	Provenance	Description
622	UT ++++	bowl, inturned bevelled/rounded rim,(2) rounded horizontal ledge handles at rim with incised band on edge, slashed band on top
623	C2 501.4	bowl, inturned rounded rim, (2) rounded horizontal ledge handles at rim with incised band on edge
624	C2 501.4	bowl, inturned rounded rim, (2) rounded horizontal ledge handles at rim with incised band on edge
625	C2 502.7	bowl, inturned bevelled rim, (2) trapezoidal horizontal ledge handles at rim with incised band on edge
626	C2 502.5	bowl, inturned bevelled rim, (2) rounded horizontal ledge handles at rim with incised band on top
627	C2 502.8	base (bowl/hmj), flat
628	X1 1.2	bowl, inturned rounded rim, (2) rounded horizontal ledge handles at rim with incised/slashed band on top
629	C1 200.2	deep bowl, inturned almond-shaped collared rim, external groove below lip, internal carination
630	UT ++++	bowl, bevelled/rounded rim, external groove below lip
631	C2 502.5	bowl, rounded rim, flat base
632	C2 502.1	krater, everted bevelled and squared rim or flange
633	UT ++++	bowl, almond-shaped rolled rim with external groove below lip
634	UT ++++	deep bowl (?), out-rolled down-pointing rim
635	C2 502.5	bowl,evertedroundedrimsharp ext./int. carination at waist
636	C2 504.2	bowl, rounded internally recessed rim (carinated at waist)
637	UT ++++	bowl, rounded internally recessed rim, internal grooves (carination at waist ?)
638	C2 502.7	bowl, pointed internally recessed rim
639	X1 1.2	bowl, everted rounded rim, slight raised band (ridge) at neck/shoulder junction, rounded body, horizontal bands of of reserved slip
640	C2 500.1	bowl, rounded everted rim, raised band on neck
641	C2 500.1	heavy storage jar, flared neck with bevelled pointed triangular rim
642	C2 ++++	storage jar, flared neck with pointed/ rounded and externally recessed triangular rim, shallow raised band about neck, groove cut about neck/shoulder junction
643	UT ++++	storage jar, flared neck, rounded triangular rim with slight external recess at lip
644	C2 502.7	jar, pointed triangular rim
645	UT ++++	jar, rounded externally recessed rim

646	C2 ++++	jar, near vertical neck, rounded rilled elongated rim
647	X1 1.2	jar, flared (?) neck, rounded rilled rim
648	UT 720.1	jar, vertical neck, internally bevelled and recessed rim with external rilling
649	C1 100.1	jar, inturned neck, rounded rim with small rounded flange (or rilling) at lip
650	UT2 720.3	jar, everted rounded/pointed rim, large loop handle from rim to shoulder (?)
651	UT ++++	jar, rounded thickened everted rim
652	UT ++++	jar, vertical neck, rolled rounded rim with external groove
653	UT ++++	jar, vertical neck, rounded rolled rim with external groove, internal ledge
654	C2 502.1	bs., rounded body (waist ?) with small loop handle
655	C2 502.6	bs., storage jar (cf. J643), raised band at neck/shoulderjunction (cf. J639, J640, J657), combed wavy band in combed horizontal register on shoulder
656	X1 1.2	bs., shoulder/neck of jar, horizontal combed band
657	C2 500.1	bs., shoulder/neck junction of jar, raised band
658	C2 506.1	bs., parallel horizontal combed bands
659	UT2 720.3	bs., horizontal combed band
660	C2 504.2	bs., horizontal combed band(s)
661	D1a 1000.3	bs., horizontal combed bands
662	UT2 720.3	bs., sharp carination at waist (?)
663	UT ++++	flat base
664	C2 502.6	base of juglet, dark burnished exterior
665	C2 504.2	ring base
666	C2 501.4	ring base
667	C2 ++++	base of juglet, dark burnished exterior

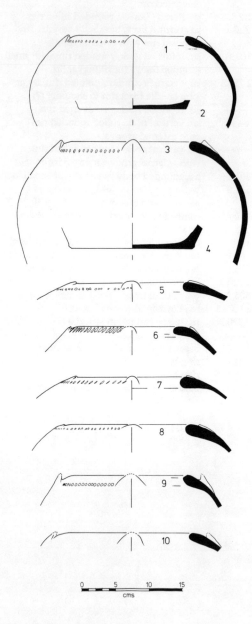

Fig. 110. Pottery catalogue: genre A (1 - 10)

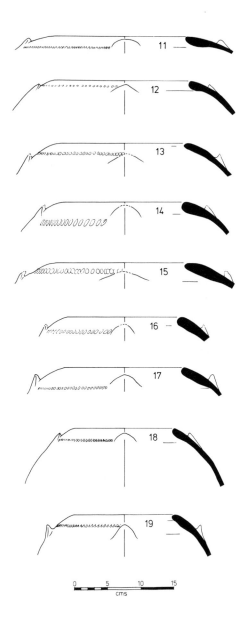

Fig. 111. Pottery catalogue: genre A (11 - 19)

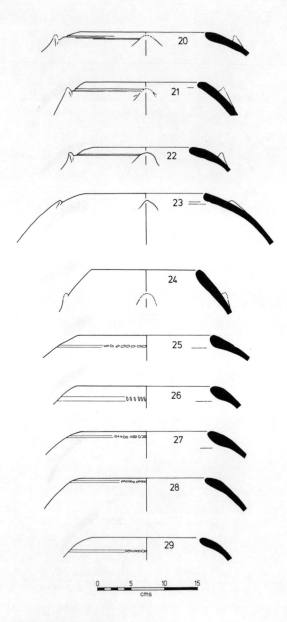

Fig. 112. Pottery catalogue: genre A (20 - 29)

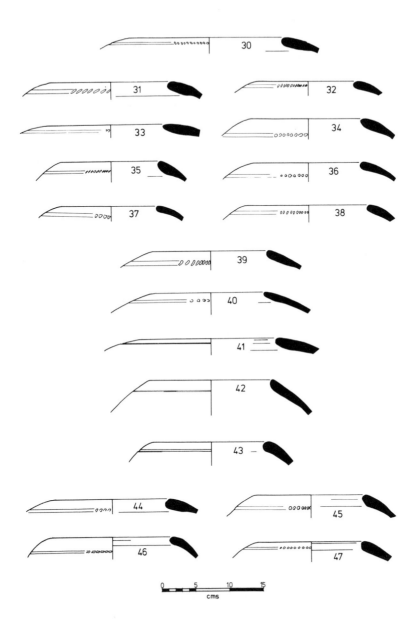

Fig. 113. Pottery catalogue: genre A (30 - 47)

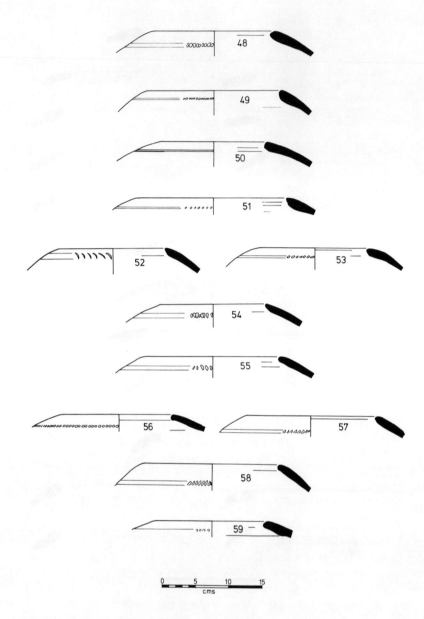

Fig. 114. Pottery catalogue: genre A (48 - 59)

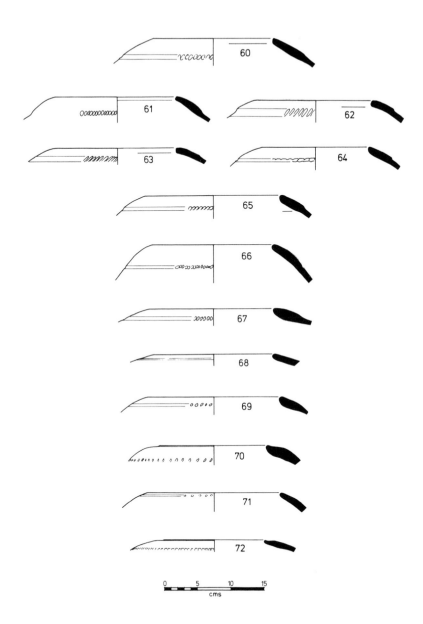

Fig. 115. Pottery catalogue: genre A (60 - 72)

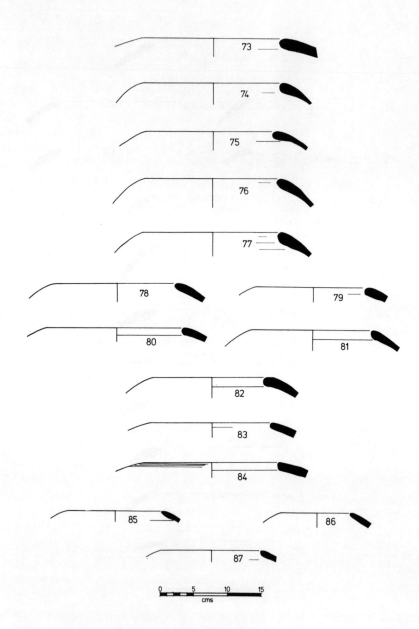

Fig. 116. Pottery catalogue: genre A (73 - 87)

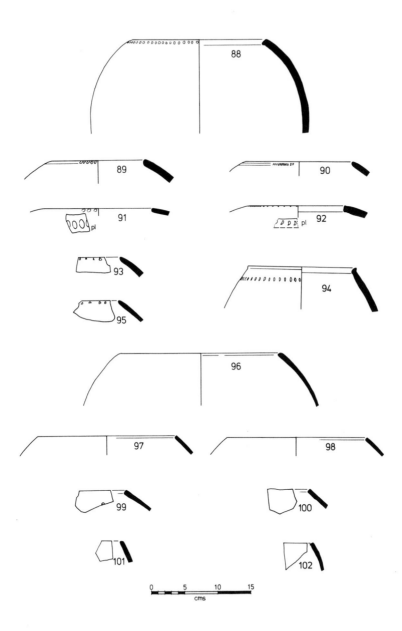

Fig. 117. Pottery catalogue: genre A (88 - 102)

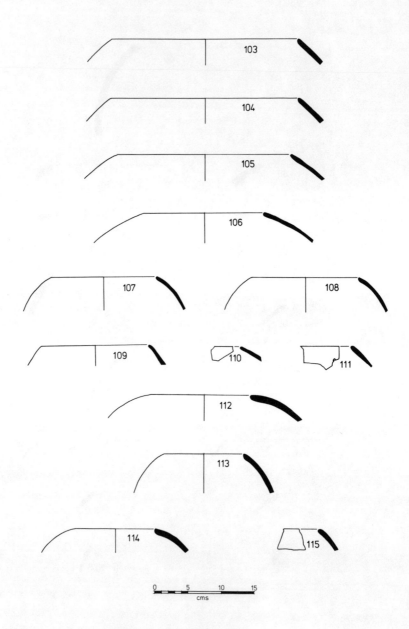

Fig. 118. Pottery catalogue: genre A (103 - 115)

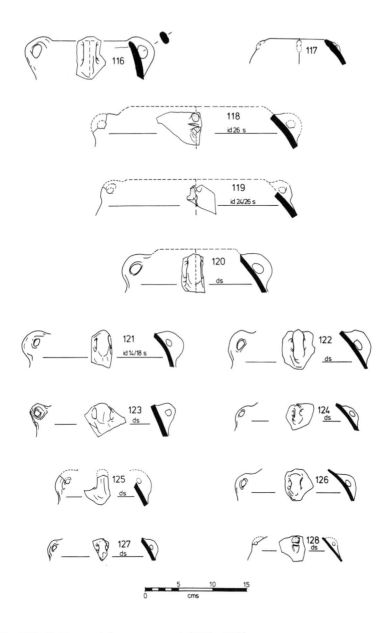

Fig. 119. Pottery catalogue: genre A (116 - 128)

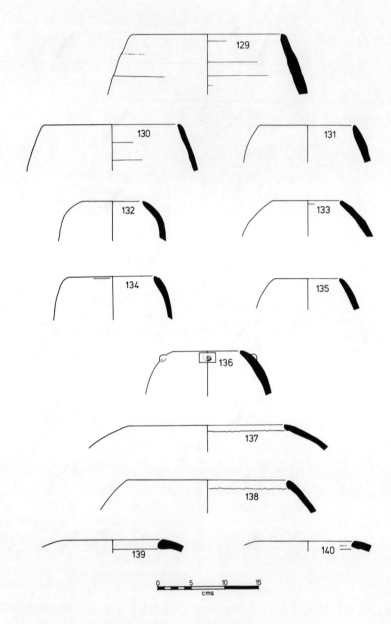

Fig. 120. Pottery catalogue: genre A (129 - 140)

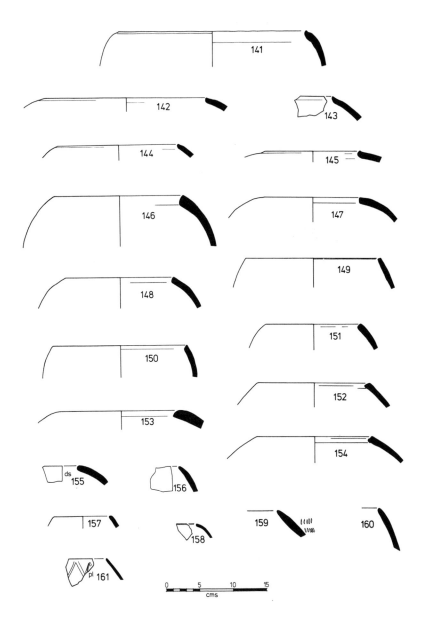

Fig. 121. Pottery catalogue: genre A (141 - 161)

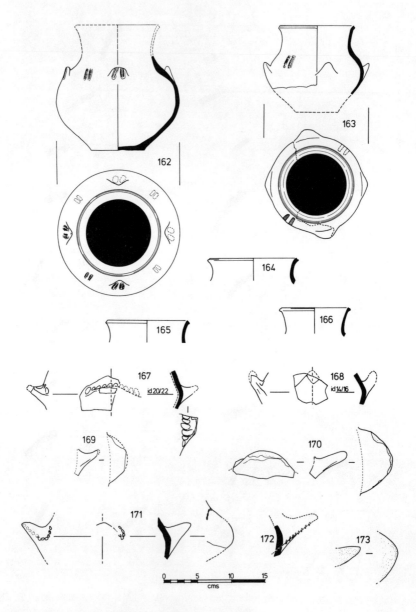

Fig. 122. Pottery catalogue: genre B (162 - 173)

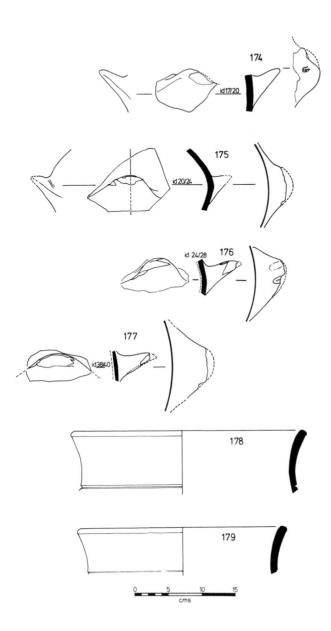

Fig. 123. Pottery catalogue: genre B (174 - 179)

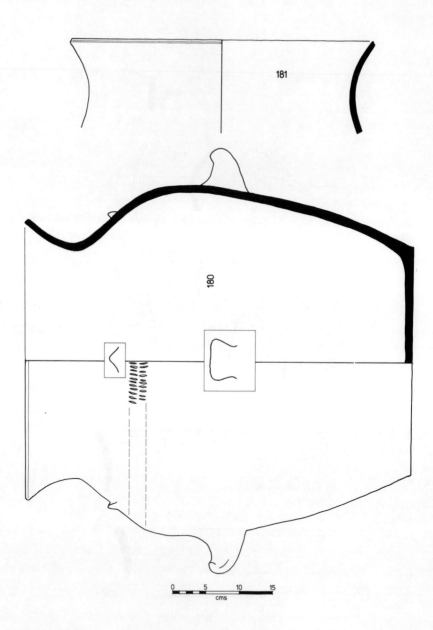

Fig. 124. Pottery catalogue: genre B (180 - 181)

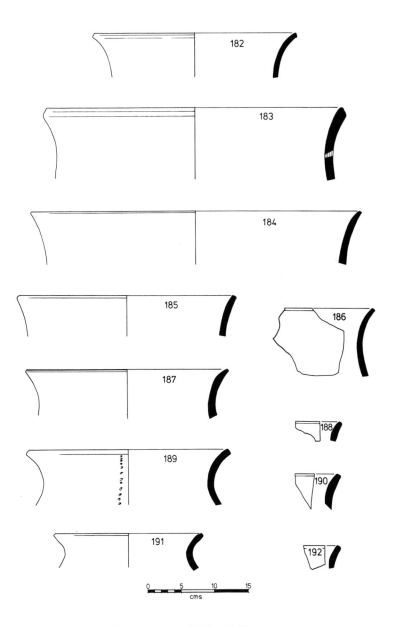

Fig. 125. Pottery catalogue: genre B (182 - 192)

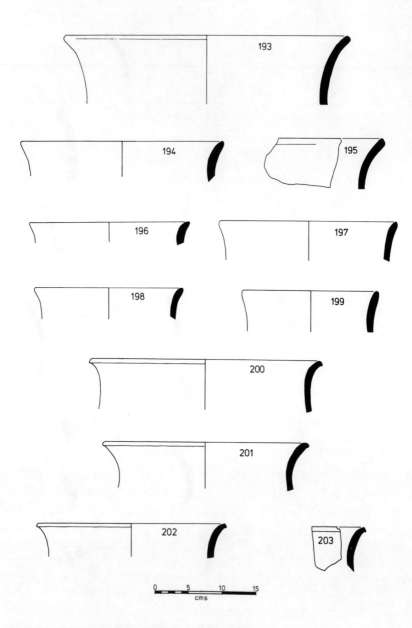

Fig. 126. Pottery catalogue: genre B (193 - 203)

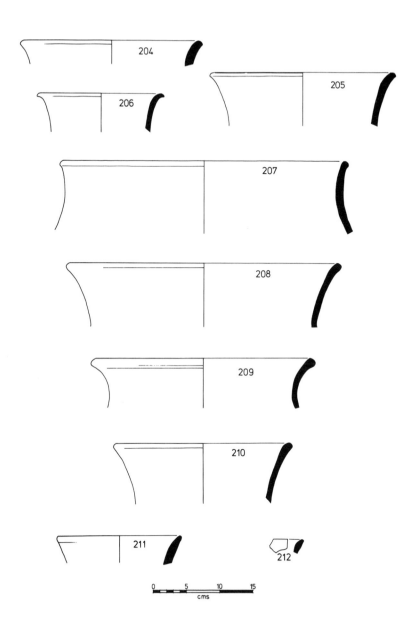

Fig. 127. Pottery catalogue: genre B (204 - 212)

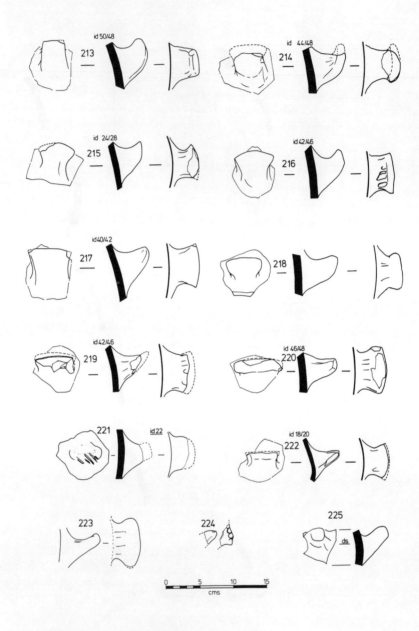

Fig. 128. Pottery catalogue: genre B (213 - 225)

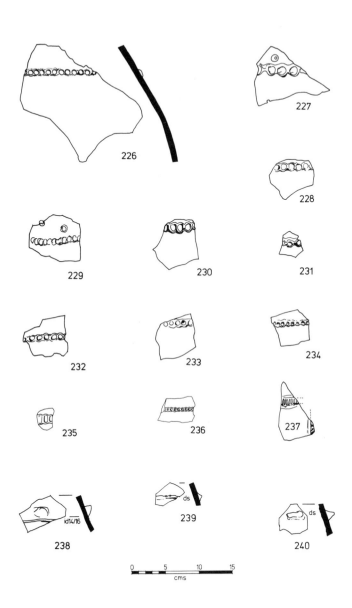

Fig. 129. Pottery catalogue: genre B (226 - 240)

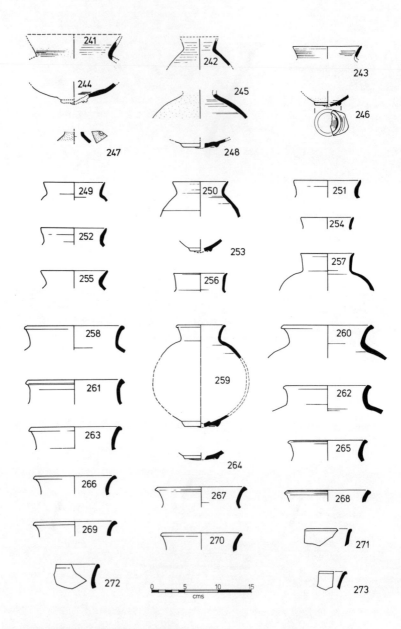

Fig. 130. Pottery catalogue: genre C (241 - 273)

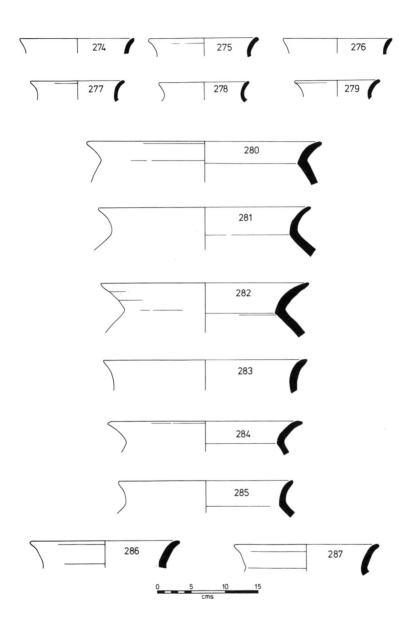

Fig. 131. Pottery catalogue: genre C (274 - 287)

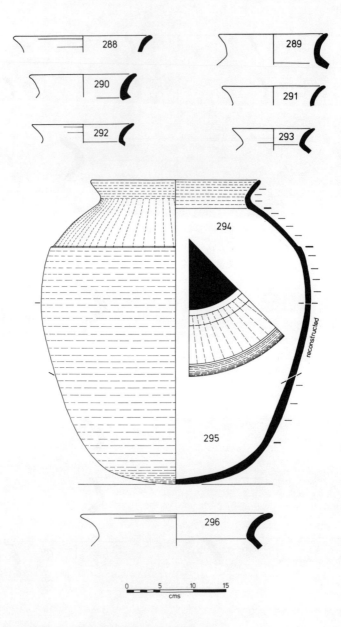

Fig. 132. Pottery catalogue: genre C (288 - 296)

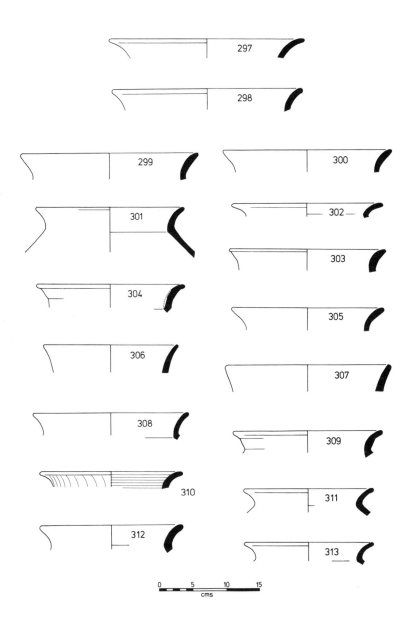

Fig. 133. Pottery catalogue: genre C (297 - 313)

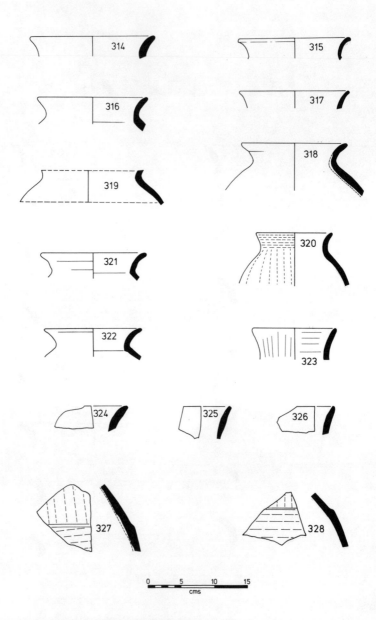

Fig. 134. Pottery catalogue: genre C (314 - 328)

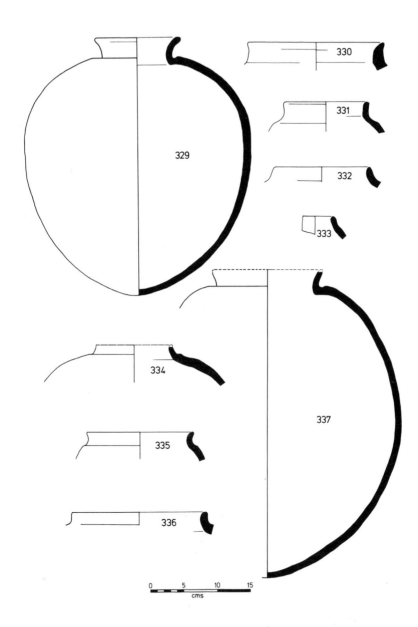

Fig. 135. Pottery catalogue: genre D (329 - 337)

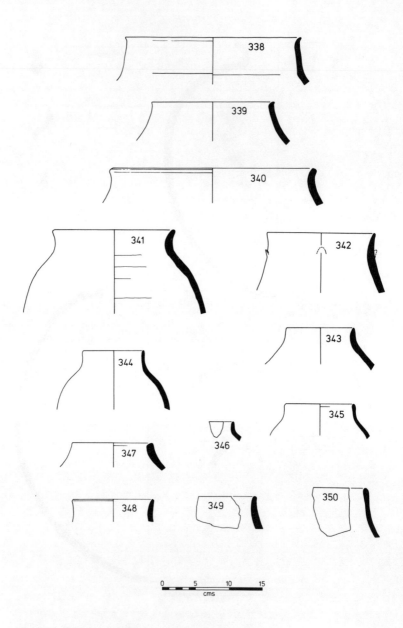

Fig. 136. Pottery catalogue: genre E (338 - 350)

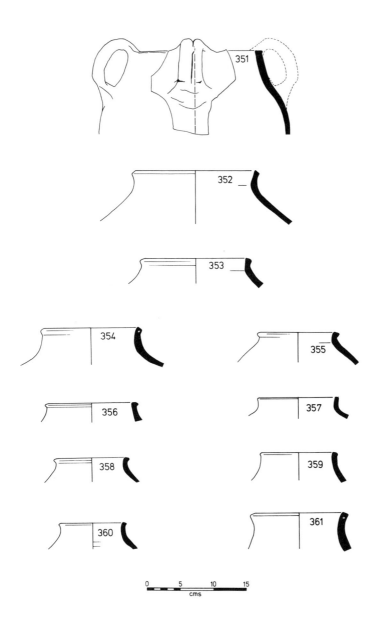

Fig. 137. Pottery catalogue: genre E (351 - 361)

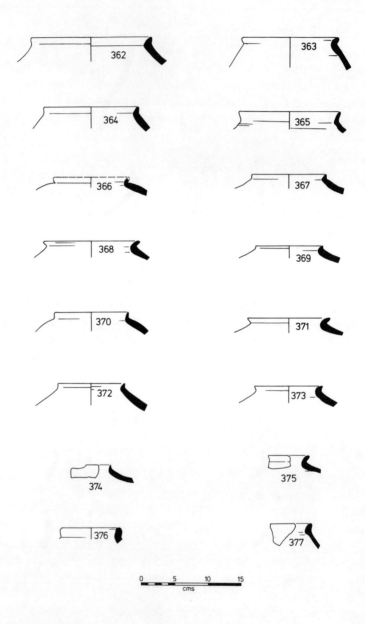

Fig. 138. Pottery catalogue: genre E (362 - 377)

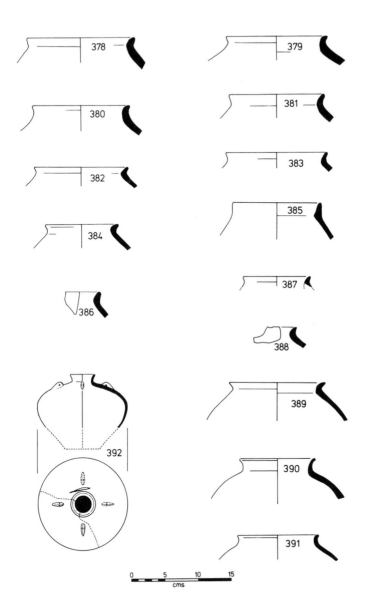

Fig. 139. Pottery catalogue: genre E (378 - 392)

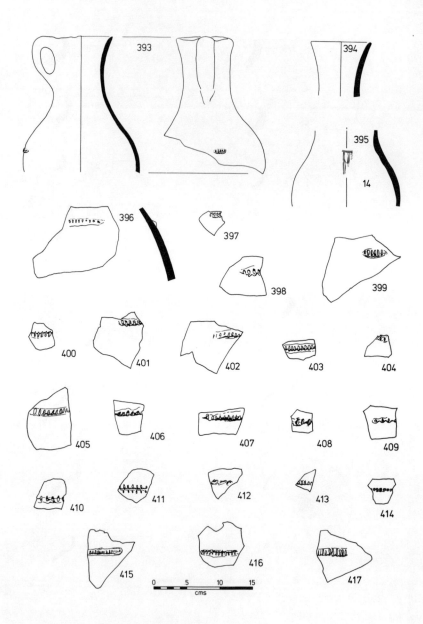

Fig. 140. Pottery catalogue: genre F (393 - 417)

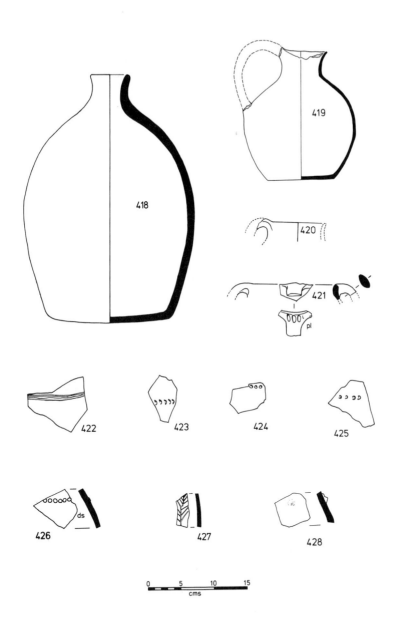

Fig. 141. Pottery catalogue: genre F/H (418 - 428)

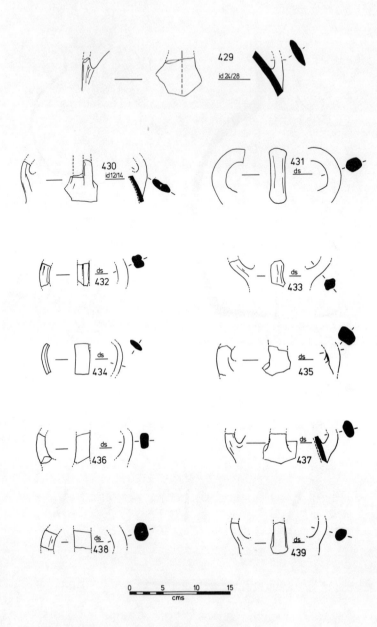

Fig. 142. Pottery catalogue: genre F (429 - 439)

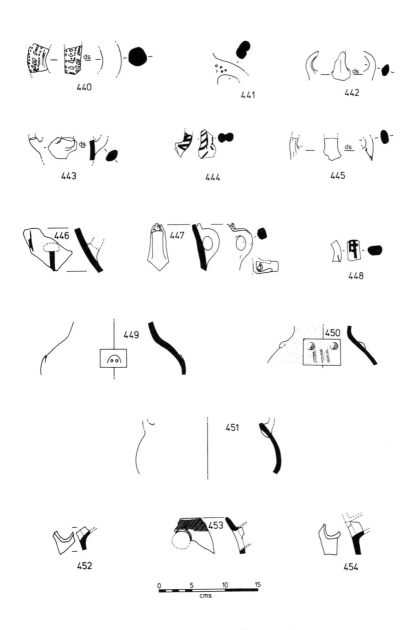

Fig. 143. Pottery catalogue: genre F/E/M/A (440 - 454)

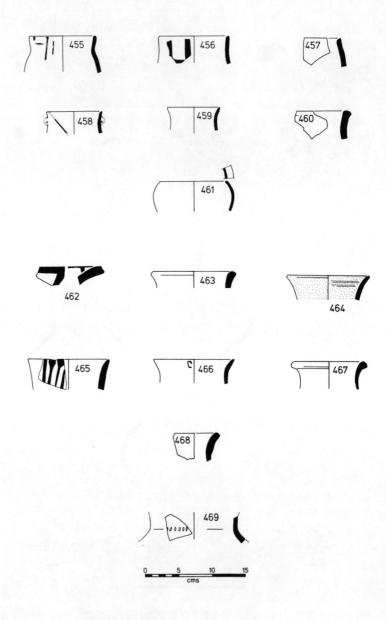

Fig. 144. Pottery catalogue: genre M/G (455 - 469)

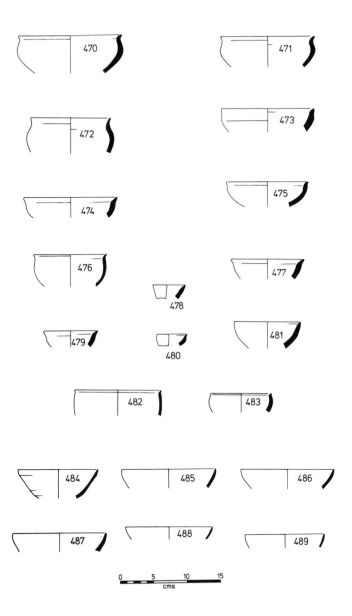

Fig. 145. Pottery catalogue: genre G (470 - 489)

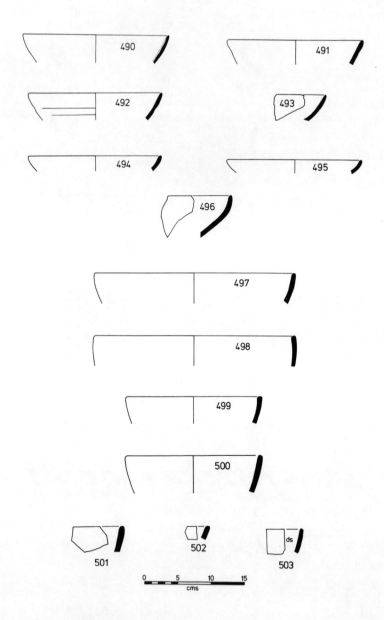

Fig. 146. Pottery catalogue: genre G (490 - 503)

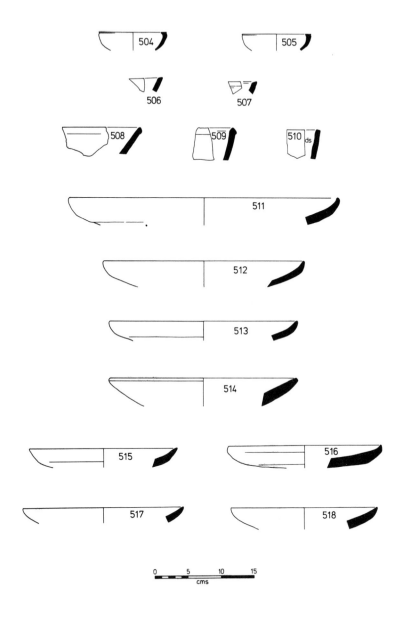

Fig. 147. Pottery catalogue: genre G (504 - 518)

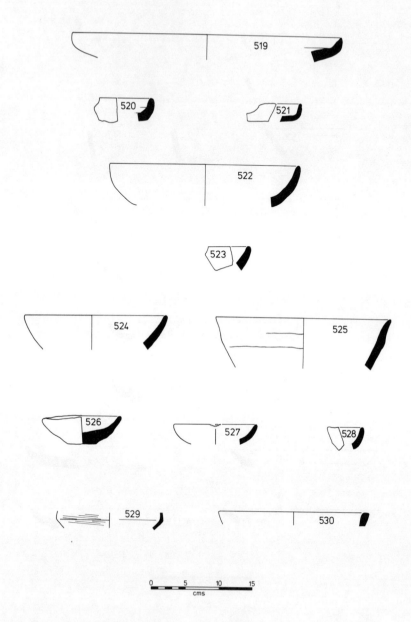

Fig. 148. Pottery catalogue: genre G (519 - 530)

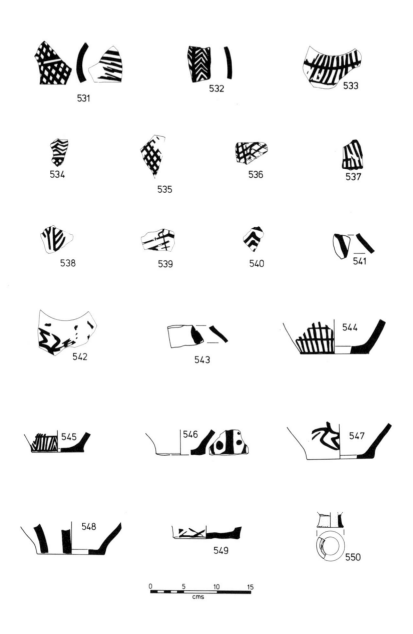

Fig. 149. Pottery catalogue: genre H/X (531 - 550)

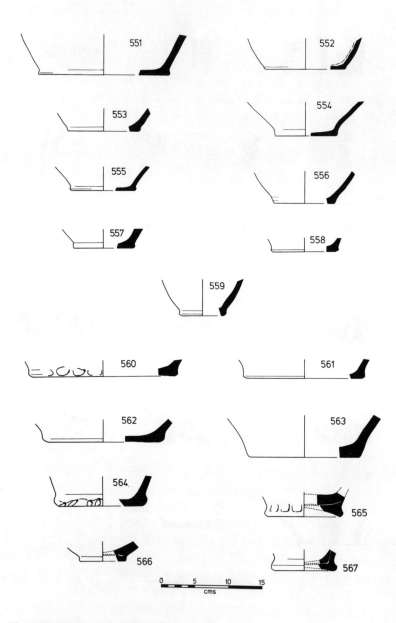

Fig. 150. Pottery catalogue: genre X (551 - 567)

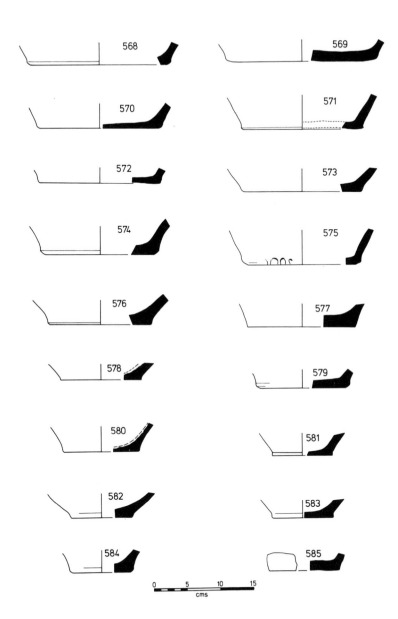

Fig. 151. Pottery catalogue: genre X (568 - 585)

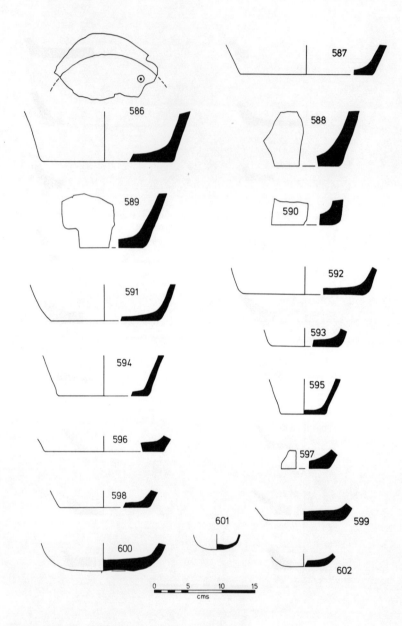

Fig. 152. Pottery catalogue: genre X (586 - 602)

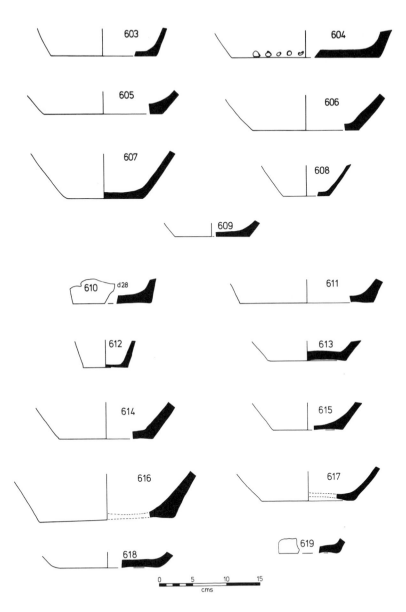

Fig. 153. Pottery catalogue: genre X (603 - 619)

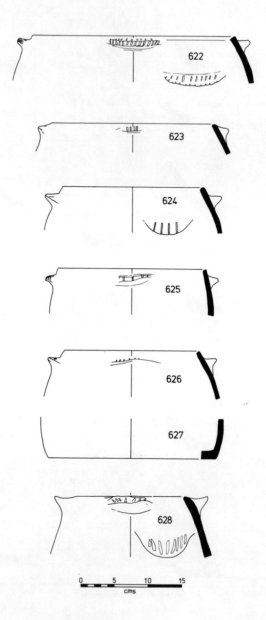

Fig. 154. Pottery catalogue: MBA (622 - 628)

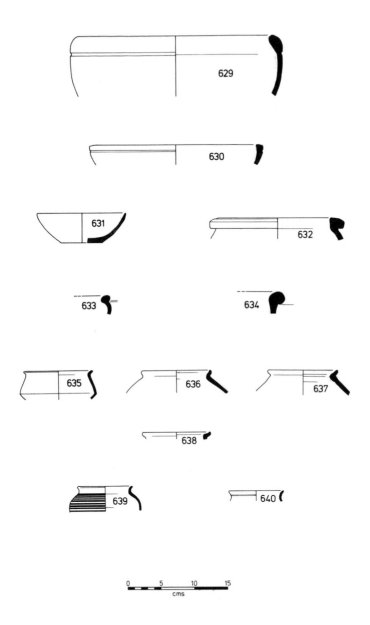

Fig. 155: Pottery catalogue: MBA (629 - 640)

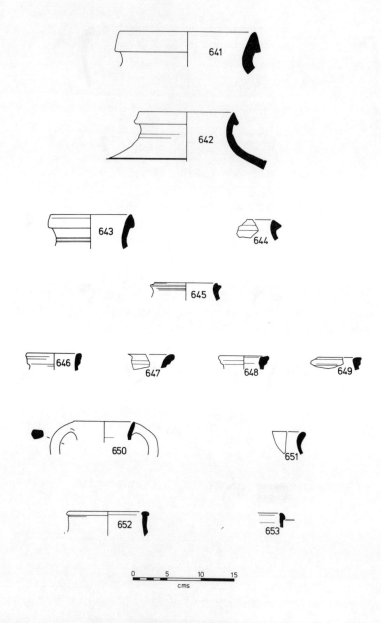

Fig. 156. Pottery catalogue: MBA (641 - 653)

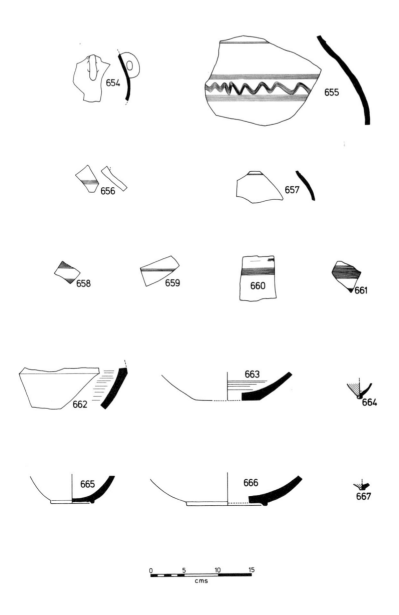

Fig. 157. Pottery catalogue: MBA (654 - 667)

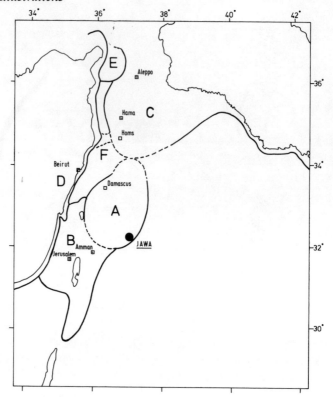

Fig. 158. Distribution of pottery parallels (repertoires and genres)

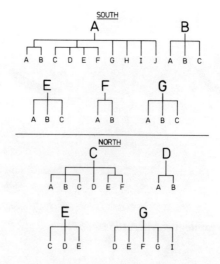

Fig. 159. Seriation: 4th millennium BC pottery repertoires

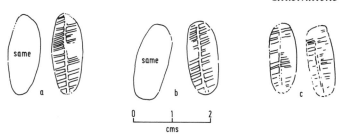

Fig. 160. Stamp seal impression: J162

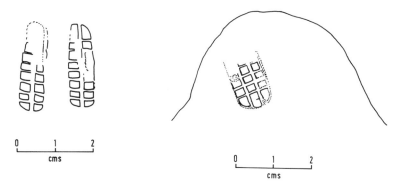

Fig. 161. Stamp seal impression: J163

Fig. 162. Stamp seal impression: J174

Fig. 163. Stamp seal impression: J176

Fig. 164. Impressions: J449

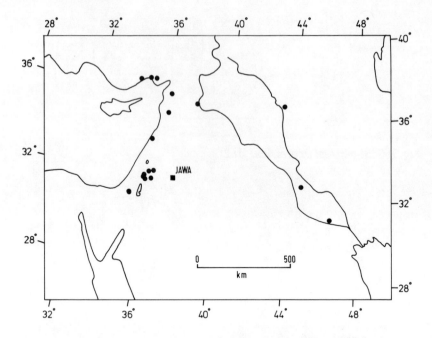

Fig. 165. Location of parallels for stamp seal impressions and seals

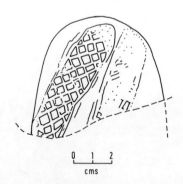

Fig. 166. Stamp seal impressions: Tell Um Hammad

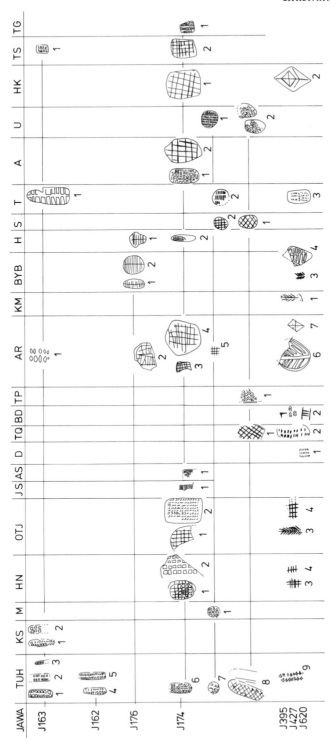

Fig. 167. Survey of seal impressions

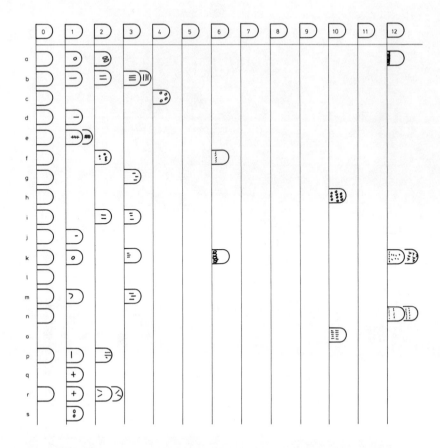

Fig. 168. Blank impressions on handles: a, Jawa; b, Tell Um Hammad (Sharqiyah); c, Tell Mafluq; d, Katarat al-Samra'; e, Tell Handaquq; f, Jericho (O.T.); g, Katar Yuba; h, Dhiyaba; i, Ras Abu Lofeh; j, Fakhat; k, Jerash Survey; l, Azor; m, Megiddo; n, Tell al-Fara'ah (North); o, Beth Yerah; p, Affulah; q, Kinneret; r, Beth Shan; s, Ghrubba

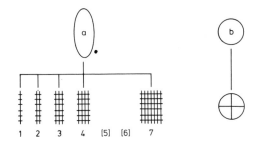

Fig. 169. Stamp seal impressions: numerical ranking?

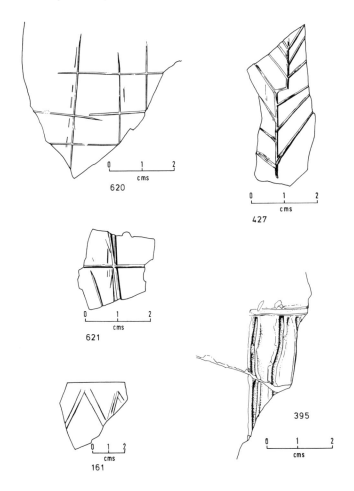

Fig. 170. Incised sherds

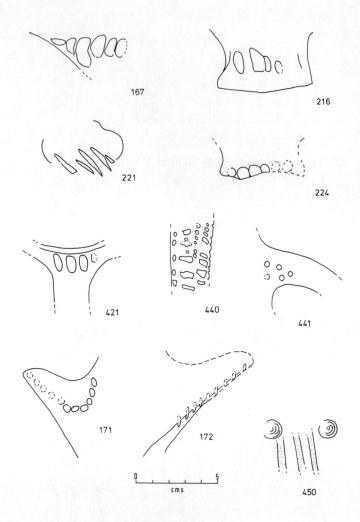

Fig. 171. Impressed and decorated handles

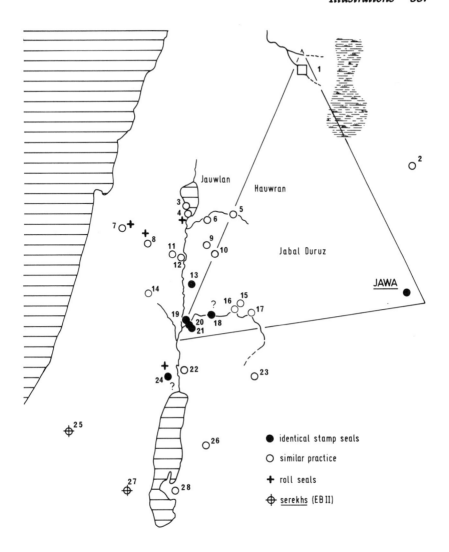

Fig. 172. Distribution of handle types and stamped impressions

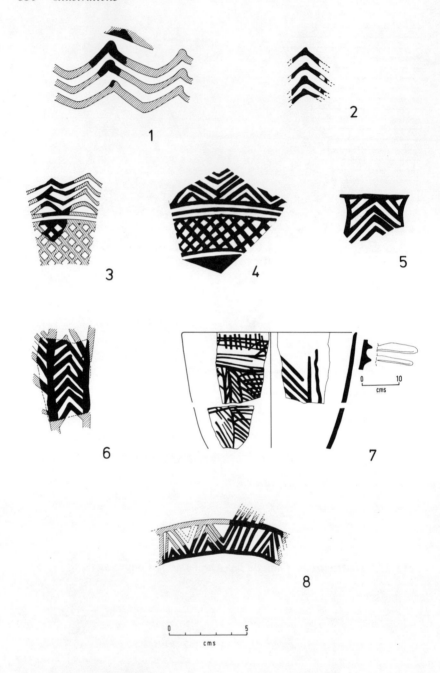

Fig. 173. Painted Designs

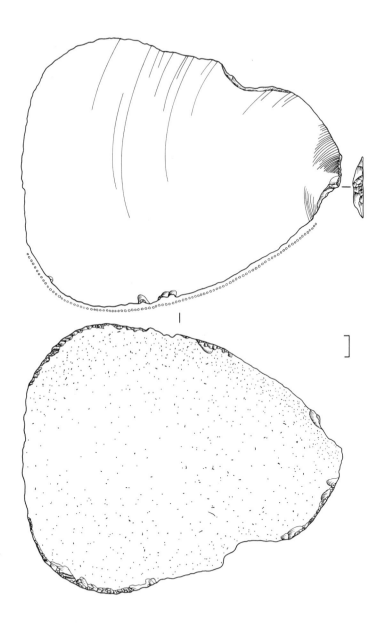

Fig. 174. Chipped stone: scraper (a)

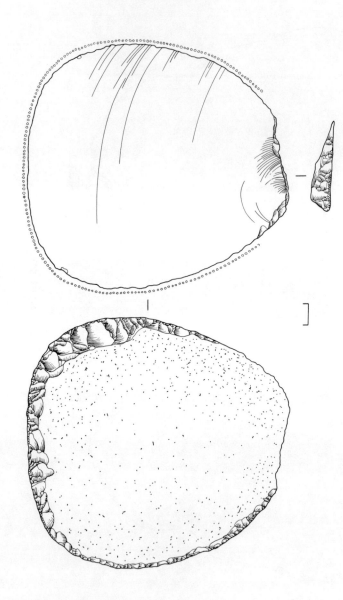

Fig. 175. Chipped stone: scraper (a)

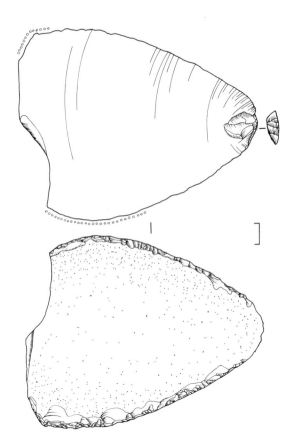

Fig. 176. *Chipped stone: scraper (a)*

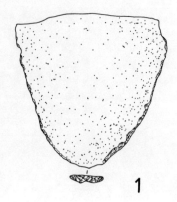

1

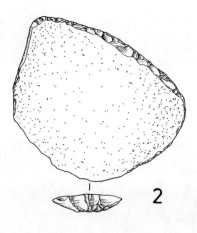

2

Fig. 177. Chipped stone: scrapers (a)

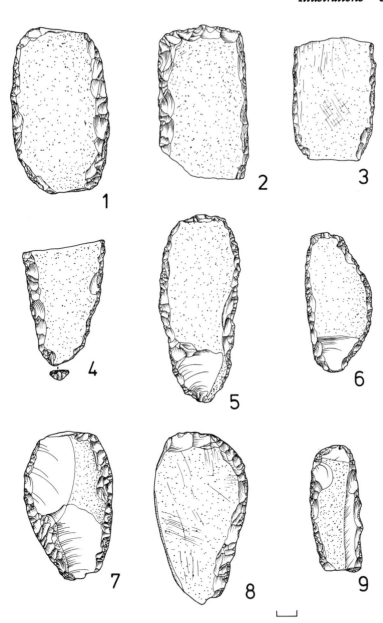

Fig. 178. Chipped stone: scrapers (b)

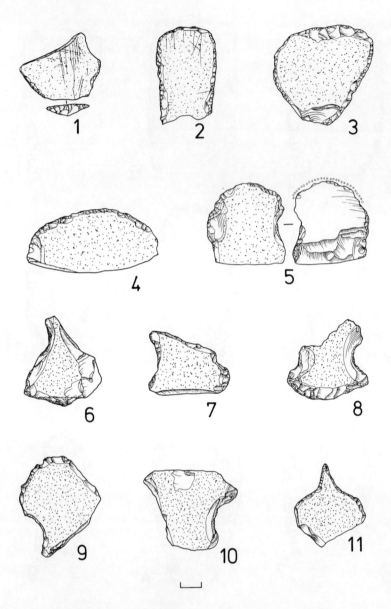

Fig. 179. Chipped stone: 1-5. scrapers (b), 6-10. (c), 11. point (a)

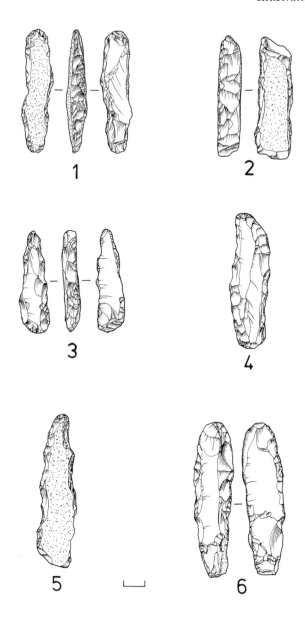

Fig. 180. Chipped stone: points (b)

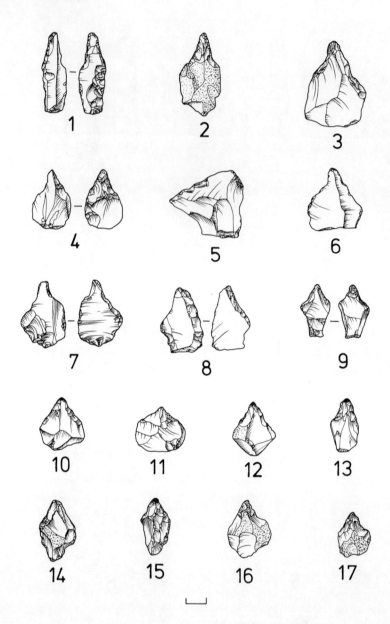

Fig. 181. Chipped stone: 1-8. points (b), 9-17. (c)

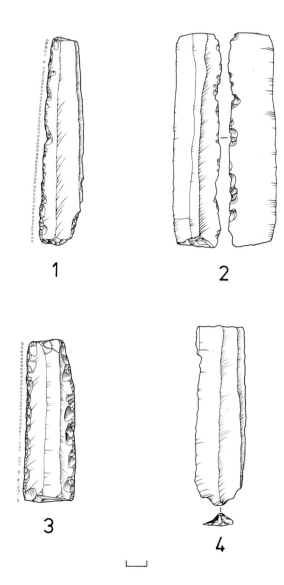

1

2

3

4

Fig. 182. Chipped stone: knives (a)

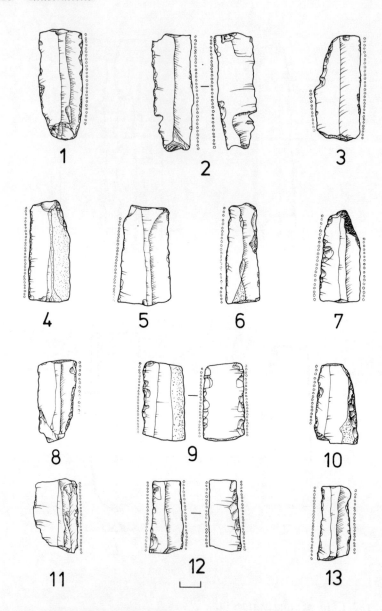

Fig. 183. Chipped stone: knives (b)

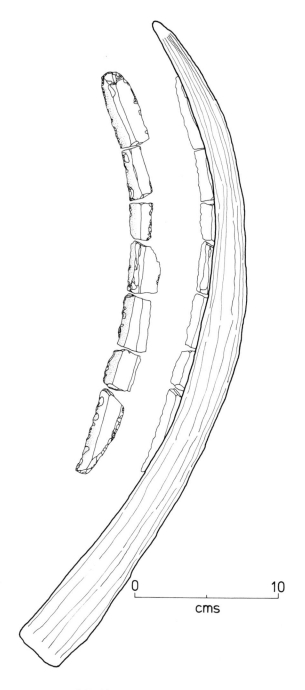

Fig. 184. Reconstructed Sickle

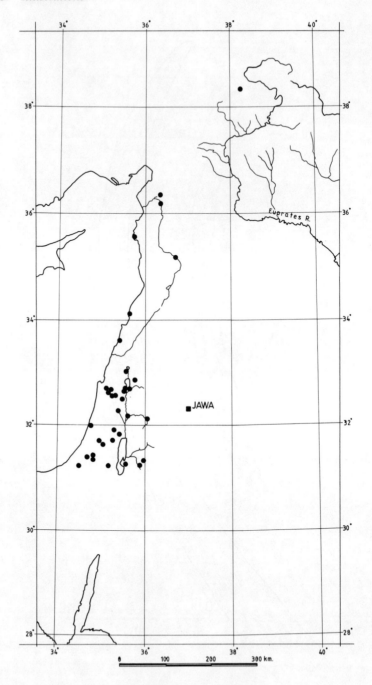

Fig. 185. Distribution of parallels for chipped stone

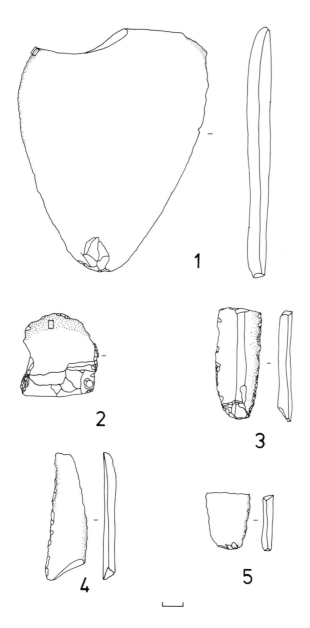

Fig. 186. Wear Analysis

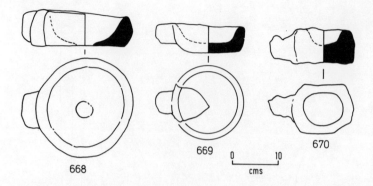

Fig. 187. Ground stone vessels

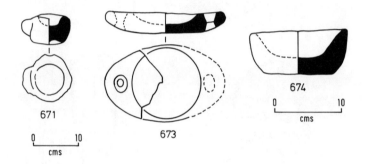

Fig. 188. Ground stone vessels

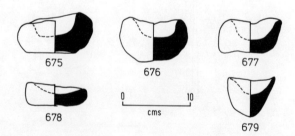

Fig. 189. Ground stone vessels

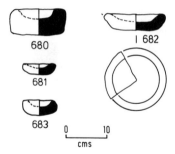

Fig. 190. Ground stone vessels

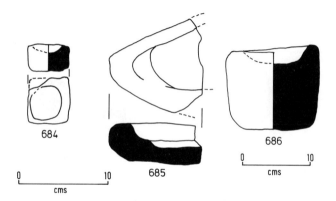

Fig. 191. Ground stone vessels

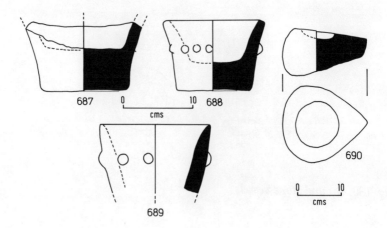

Fig. 192. Ground stone vessels

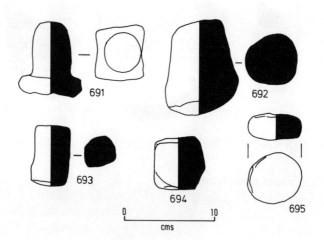

Fig. 193. Ground stone pounders and grinders

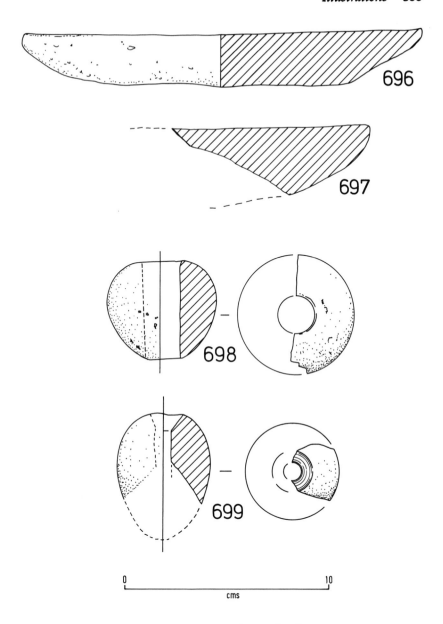

Fig. 194. Ground stone saddle querns and mace-heads

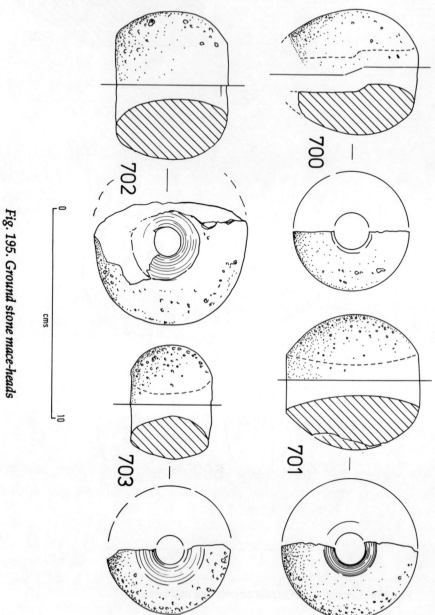

Fig. 195. Ground stone mace-heads

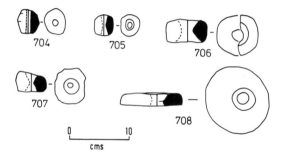

Fig. 196. Ground stone objects: pierced stones

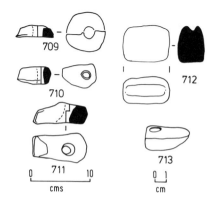

Fig. 197. Ground stone objects: pierced stones

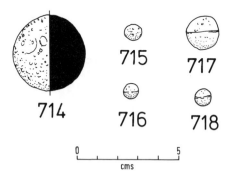

Fig. 198. Basalt pebbles

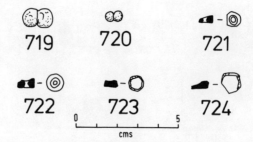

Fig. 199. Basalt pebbles and pierced stones

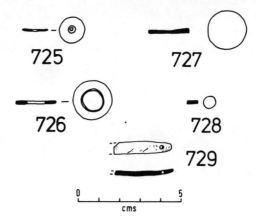

Fig. 200. Pierced stones

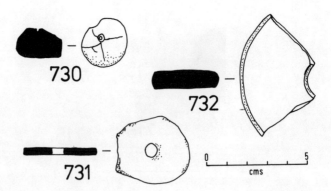

Fig. 201. Drilled objects

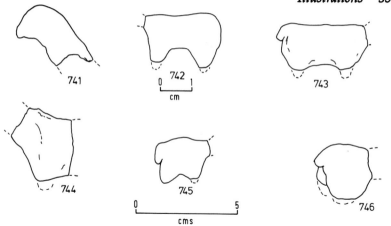

Fig. 202. Animal figurines

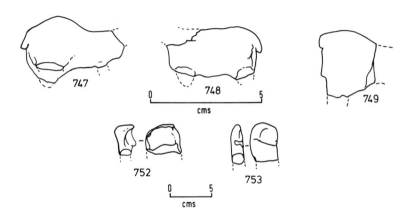

Fig. 203. Animal figurines

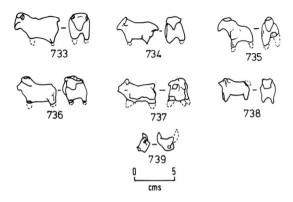

Fig. 204. Figurines

Fig. 205. Rock carvings: cattle (A1)

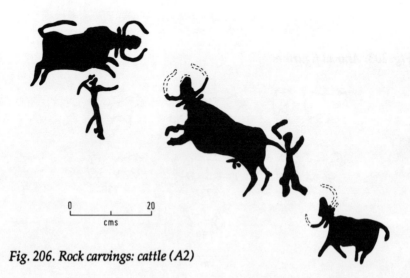

Fig. 206. Rock carvings: cattle (A2)

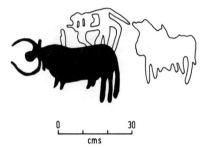

Fig. 207. Rock carvings: cattle (A3)

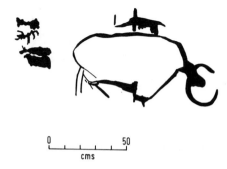

Fig. 208. Rock carvings: cattle (A4)

Fig. 209. Rock carvings: cattle (A5)

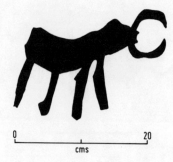

Fig. 210. Rock carvings: cattle (A6)

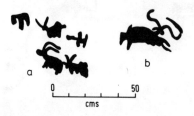

Fig. 211. Rock carvings: horned beasts (A7)

Fig. 212. Rock carvings: horned beasts (A8)

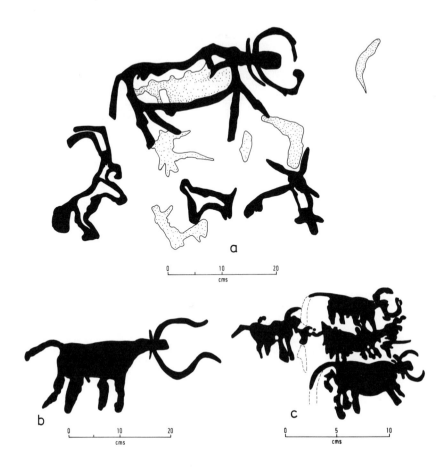

Fig. 213. Rock carvings: cattle from a, al-Wusad; b, al-Wusad; c, al-Ghirqa

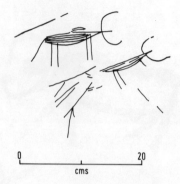

Fig. 214. Rock carvings: cattle from near Qasr Burqu`

Fig. 215. Rock carvings: Safaitic text (A9) and hunting scene

Fig. 216. Rock carvings: hunting scene (A9a)

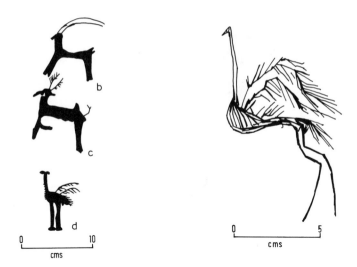

Fig. 217. Rock carvings: ibex (A9b), deer ? (A9c), ostrich (A9d)

Fig. 218. Rock carvings: ostrich (A10)

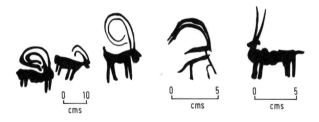

Fig. 219. Rock carvings: various animals (A11 and A12)

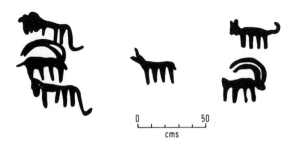

Fig. 220. Rock carvings: various horned animals (A13, A14, A15)

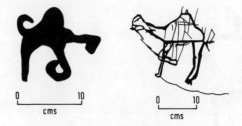

Fig. 221. Rock carvings: camels (A16, A17)

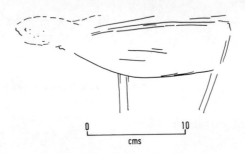

Fig. 222. Rock carvings: animal (A18)

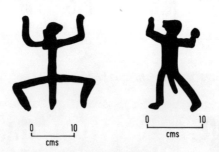

Fig. 223. Rock carvings: human figures (A19, A20)

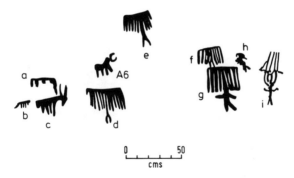

Fig. 224. Rock carvings: animals [A6: cf. Fig. 210], enigmatic figures and
designs (A21)

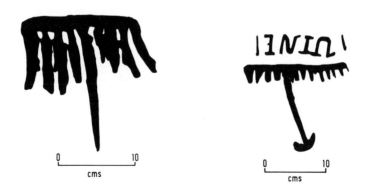

Fig. 225. Rock carvings: enimatic design (A22)

Fig. 226. Rock carvings: enigmatic designs (A23)

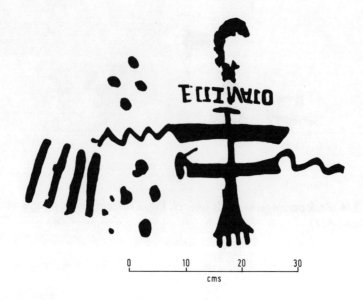

Fig. 227. Rock carvings: enimatic designs (24)

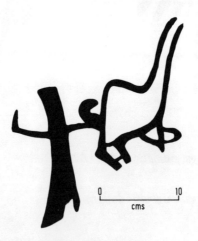

Fig. 228. Rock carvings: man and camel (A25)

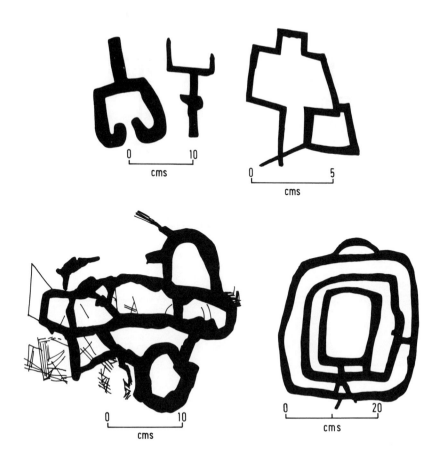

Fig. 229. Rock carvings: wasms (A26), various designs (A27, A28, A29)

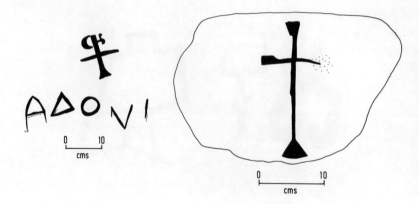

Fig. 230. *Rock carvings: cross and inscription (E1) and a cross*

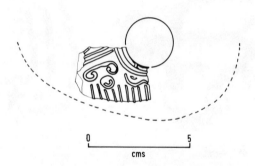

Fig. 231. *Lamp fragment from tumulus north of Jawa*

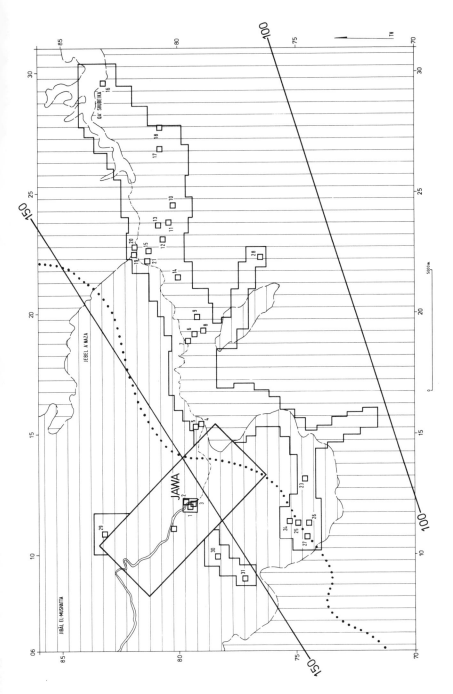

Fig. 232. The Jawa Survey Area: location of sites

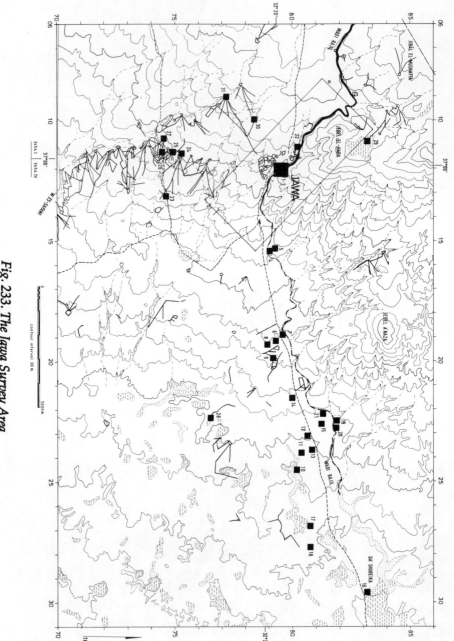

Fig. 233. The Jawa Survey Area

Fig. 234. Desert "Kites" near Jawa (cf. Figs 232/3)

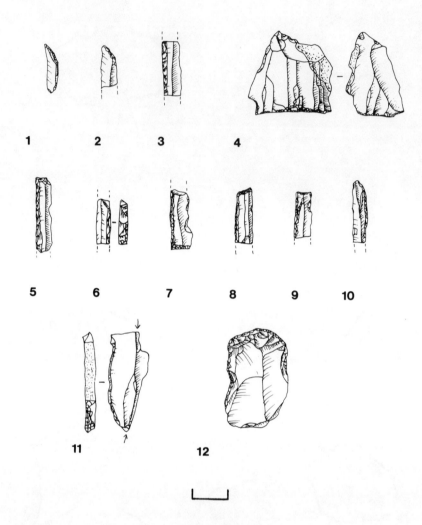

Fig. 235. Chipped stone (misc. epipaleolithic sites)

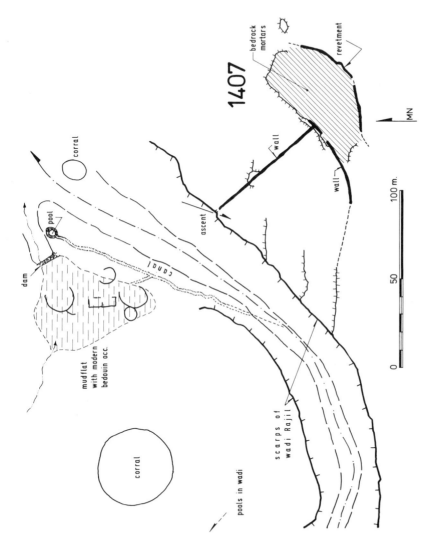

Fig. 236. Khallat `Anaza: plan of visible remains

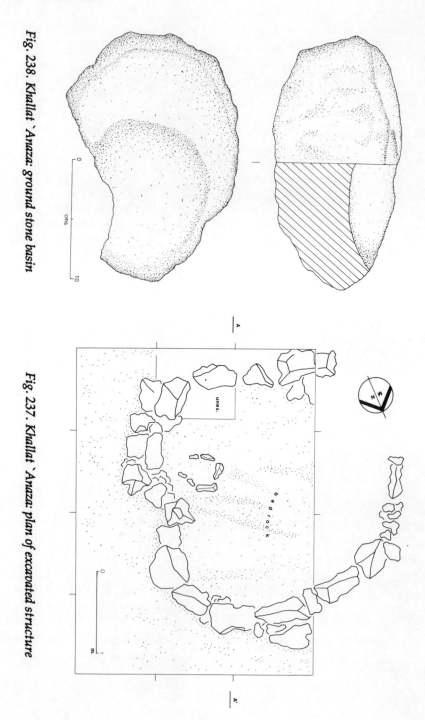

Fig. 238. *Khallat `Anaza: ground stone basin*

Fig. 237. *Khallat `Anaza: plan of excavated structure*

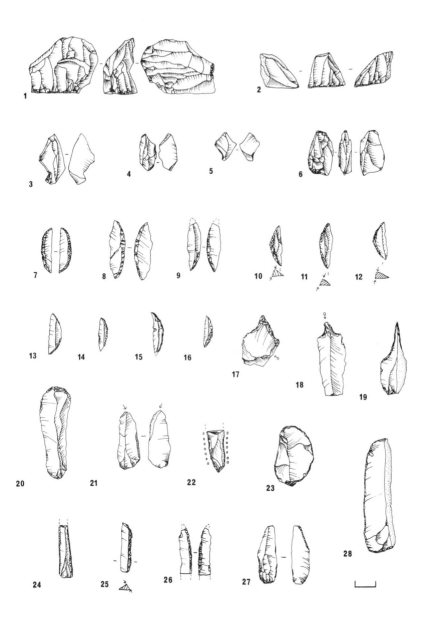

Fig. 239. Khallat `Anaza: chipped stone

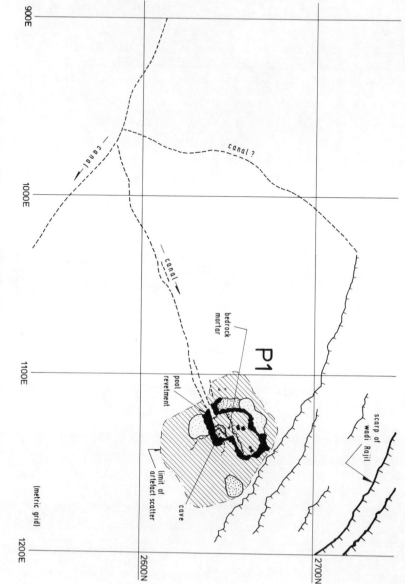

Fig. 240. Mugharet al-Jawa: plan of visible remains

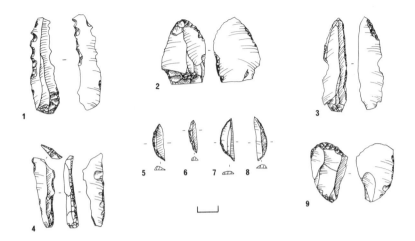

Fig. 241. Mugharet al-Jawa: chipped stone

Pl. 1. Polish and striations on experimental blade used to harvest domestic emmer (M 100x)

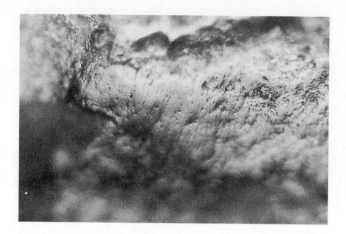

Pl. 2. Polish and striations on tabular scraper from Jawa (M 200x)

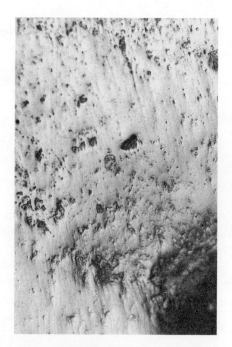

Pl. 3. Polish and striations on flake scraper from Jawa (M 100x)

Pl. 4. Polish on experimental reed scraper (M 200x)

Pl. 5. "Sickle blade" from Jawa (M 100x)

Pl. 6. "Sickle blade" from Jawa (M 100x)

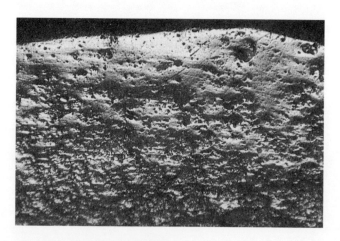

Pl. 7. "Sickle blade" from Jawa (M 50x)

Bibliography

ABBREVIATIONS

AAA Liverpool Annals of Archaeology and Anthropology
AAAS Annales Archéologiques Arabes Syriennes
AASOR Annual of the American Schools of Oriental Research
ADAJ Annual of the Department of Antiquities of Jordan
AJA American Journal of Archaeology
ANET Ancient Near Eastern Texts (see Pritchard 1955)
ATLAL The Journal of Saudi Arabian Archaeology
ATU Ancient Texts from Uruk (see Falkenstein 1936)
BAR British Archaeological Reports
BASOR Bulletin of the American Schools of Oriental Research
BiArR Biblical Archaeological Review
CNRS Centre National de la Recherche Scientifique
DAFI Délégation Archéologique Française en Iran
IEJ Israel Exploration Journal
IFAPO Institut Français d'Archéologie du Proche-Orient
JAOS Journal of the American Oriental Society
JESHO Journal of Economic and Social History of the Orient
JNES Journal of Near Eastern Studies
JPOS Journal of the Palestine Oriental Society
PEFQS Palestine Exploration Fund Quarterly Series
PEQ Palestine Exploration Quarterly
QDAP Quarterly of the Department of Antiquities in Palestine
RB Revue Biblique
ZDPV Zeitschrift des Deutschen Palästina Vereins

Abu al-Soof, B. (1968). 'Tell es-Sawwan Excavations (Fourth Season)', *Sumer*, 24, 3-16.
Abu Hamid: Village du 4e millénaire de la vallé du Jourdain. (1988), (Centre Culturel Français et Département des Antiquités de Jourdaine) Amman.
Adams, W. Y. (1968). 'Invasion, Diffusion, Evolution?', *Antiquity*, 42, 194-215.
Adams, R., Parr, P. J., Ibrahim, M. and Mughannum, A. S. (1977). 'Saudi Arabian Archaeological Reconnaissance -1976. Preliminary Report on the First Phase of the Comprehensive Archaeological Survey Program', *ATLAL*, 1, 21-40.
Aharoni, Y. (1961). 'The Expedition to the Judean Desert 1960: Expedition B', *IEJ*, 11, 11-24.
Albright, W. F. (1933). 'The Excavation of Tell Beit Mirsim Vol. IA. The Bronze Age Pottery of the Fourth Campaign', *AASOR*, 13, 55-127.
Albright, W. F. (1938). *The Excavation of Tell Beit Mirsim. Vol. II. The Bronze Age*, New Haven: American Schools of Oriental Research (AASOR 17).
Albright, W. F., Kelso, J.L. and Palin Thorley, J.(1944). 'Early-Bronze Pottery from Bâb ed-Dra` in Moab', *BASOR*, 95, 3-13.
Amiran, R. (1961). 'Tombs of the Middle Bronze Age I at Ma`ayan Barukh', *'Atiqot*, 3, 84-92.
Amiran, R. (1968). 'Chronological Problems of the Early Bronze Age', *AJA*, 72, 316-318.
Amiran, R. (1969). *Ancient Pottery of the Holy Land from its Beginnings in the Neolithic Period to the End of the Iron Age*, Jerusalem: Massada Press.
Amiran, R. (1970). 'The Beginnings of Urbanization in Canaan', in Saunders (ed.) (1970), 83-100.
Amiran, R. (1972a). 'A cult Stele from Arad', *IEJ*, 22, 86-8.
Amiran, R. (1972b). 'Reflections on the Identification of the Deity at the EB II and EB III Temples at Ai', *BASOR*, 208, 9-13.

Amiran, R. (1978). *Early Arad I: the Chalcolithic settlement and Early Bronze city*, Jerusalem: Israel Exploration Society.

Amiran, R. (1981). 'Some Observations on Chalcolithic and Early Bronze Age Sanctuaries and Religion', in Biran (ed.) (1981), 47-53.

Amiran, R. (1986). 'The Fall of the Early Bronze Age II City of Arad', *IEJ*, 36, 74-6.

Amiran, R. and Porat, N. (1984). 'The Basalt Vessels of the Chalcolithic Period and Early Bronze Age I', *Tel Aviv*, 11, 3-19.

Anati, E. (1963). *Palestine before the Hebrews: a history, from the earliest arrival of man to the conquest of Canaan*, London: Cape.

Anati, E. (1971). 'Excavations at Hazorea, in the Plain of Esdraelon, Israel', *Origini*, 5, 59-148.

Ariel, D. T., Sharon, I., Gunneweg, J. and Perlman, I. (1985). 'A Group of Stamped Hellenistic Storage-Jar Handles from Dor', *IEJ*, 35, 135-52.

Bar-Adon, P. (1980). *The Cave of the Treasure*, Jerusalem: The Israel Exploration Society.

Baramki, D, (1964). 'Arabic inscriptions in the Syrian Desert', *al-Abhâth*, 17, 317-46 (Arabic).

Bar Yosef, O. (1981). 'The Epi-Paleolithic Complexes in the Southern Levant', in Cauvin and Sanlaville (eds) (1981), 389-408.

Bates, D. G. (1971). 'The Role of the State in Peasant-Nomad Mutualism', *Anthropological Quarterly*, 44, 109-31.

Beale, T. W. (1978). 'Bevelled Rim Bowls and their implications for changes and economic organization in the later fourth millennium BC', *JNES*, 37, 289-313.

Beaulieu, R. (1944). 'La Première Civilisation du Djebel Druze', *Syria*, 24, 237-250.

Beck, P. (1984). 'The Seals and Stamps of Early Arad', *Tel Aviv*, 11, 97-114.

Beck, P. (1985). 'The Middle Bronze Age II A Pottery from Aphek 1972-1984: First Summary', *Tel Aviv*, 12, 181-203.

Beit-Arieh, I. (1984). 'New Evidence on the Relations between Canaan and Egypt during the Proto-Dynastic Period', *IEJ*, 34, 20-23.

Beit-Arieh, I. (1986). 'Two Cultures in Southern Sinai in the Third Millennium B.C.', *BASOR*, 263, 27-54.

Bender, F. (1968). *Geologie von Jordanien* (English edn. 1974), Berlin: Beitr. 3, Regionalen Geol. d. Erde, Bd 7.

Ben-Tor, A. (1966). 'Excavations at Horvat Usa', *'Atiqot*, 3 (Hebrew Series, English Summary), 1-3.

Ben-Tor, A. (1973). 'Excavations at Two Burial Caves at Azor', *Qadmoniot*, 6, 48.

Ben-Tor, A. (1975). 'Two burial caves of the Proto-Urban period at Azor, 1971', *Qedem*, 1, 1-53.

Ben-Tor, A. (1978). *Cylinder Seals of Third-millennium Palestine*, Cambridge, Mass.: American Schools of Oriental Research.

Betts, A. V. G. (1984). 'Black Desert Survey, Jordan: Second Preliminary Report', *Levant*, 16, 25-34.

Betts, A.V.G. (1985). 'Black Desert Survey, Jordan: Third Preliminary Report', *Levant*, 17, 29-52.

Betts, A. V. G. (1986). *The Prehistory of the Black Desert, Transjordan: an analysis*, unpubl. Ph.D. thesis, University of London.

Betts, A. V. G. (1987). 'The hunter's perspective: 7th millennium BC rock carvings from eastern Jordan', *World Archaeology*, 19, 214-25.

Betts, A. V. G. (1988). '1986 Excavations at Dhuweila, Eastern Jordan: A Preliminary Report', *Levant*, 20, 7-21.

Betts, A. V. G. (1989). 'Ancient ar-Risha: Stone Implements', in Helms (1990), 159-168.

Betts, A.V.G. (in press). Tell el-Hibr: a rockshelter occupation of the 4th millennium BC in the Jordanian badiya', *BASOR*.

Betts, A.V.G. (ed.) (in press). *Excavations at Tell Um Hammad 1982-1984. The Early Assemblages (EB I-II)*, Edinburgh: Edinburgh University Press.

Betts, A. V. G. and Helms S. W. (1987). 'A Preliminary Survey of Late Neolithic Settlements at el-Ghirqa, Eastern Jordan', *Proceedings of the Prehistoric Society*, 53, 327-336.

Betts, A., Helms, S., Lancaster, W., Jones, E., Lupton, A., Martin, L. and Matsaert, F. (1990).'The Burqu`/Ruweishid Project: preliminary report of the 1988 field season', *Levant*, 22, 1-20.

Betts, A., Helms, S, and W. and F. Lancaster (1991). 'The Burqu`/Ruweishid Project: preliminary report on the 1989 field season', *Levant*, 23, 7-28.

Binford, L. R. (ed.) 1977. *For Theory Building in Archaeology*, New York: Academic.

Bingen, J, Cambier, G. and Nachtergael, G. (eds) (1975). *Le monde grec: Hommage a Claire Preaux*, Brussels: University of Brussels.

Bikai, P. M. (1978). *The pottery of Tyre*, Warminster: Aris and Phillips.

Biran, A. (ed.). (1981). *Temples and high places in biblical times: proceedings of the colloquium in honor of the centennial of Hebrew Union College - Jewish Institute of Religion, Jerusalem 14-16 March 1977*, Jerusalem: Nelson Glueck School of Biblical Archaeology of Hebrew Union College - Jewish Institute of Religion.

Bocco, R. (n.d.). Paper presented at Yarmouk University: Pastoralist Workshop (April 1987).

Bowersock, G. W. (1975). 'The Greek-Nabataean Bilingual Inscription at Ruwwafa, Saudi Arabia', in Bingen *et al.* (eds) (1975), 513-22.

Braemer, F. (1984). 'Prospections archéologiques dans le Hawran (Syrie)', *Syria*, 61, 219-50.

Braemer, F. (1988). 'Prospections archéologiques dans le Hawran. II. Les réseaux de l'eau', *Syria*, 65, 99-137.

Braidwood, R. J. and Braidwood, L. S. (1960). *Excavations in the Plain of Antioch. I*, Chicago: University of Chicago Oriental Institute Publications 61.

Braidwood, R.J. and Willey, G. (eds) (1960). *Courses Towards Urban Life*, Chicago: Chicago University, Oriental Institute Studies in Ancient Oriental Civilisations, No. 31.

Brandes, M. A. (1980). 'Modelage et imprimerie aux débuts de l'écriture en Mesopotamie', *Akkadica*, 18, 1-30.

Braun, E. (1984). 'Yiftah'el', Notes and News, *IEJ*, 34, 191-4.

Braun, E. (1985). *En Shadud. Salvage Excavations at a Farming Community in the Jezreel Valley, Israel*, Oxford: BAR Int. Ser. 249.

Braun, E. (1987). 'Book Reviews' (Review of Hanbury-Tenison 1986), *Mitekufat Haeven: Journal of the Israel Prehistoric Society*, 20, 186-90.

Brockelmann, C. (1928). *Lexicon syriacum* (2nd edn), Alis Saxonum: Niemeyer.

Burleigh, R. (1983). 'Radiocarbon Dates', in Kenyon and Holland (1983), 760-5.

Byrd, B. F. (1987). Beidha and the Natufian: *Variability in Levantine Settlement and Subsistence*. unpubl. PhD thesis, University of Arizona.

Callaway, J. A. (1964). *Pottery from the Tombs at 'Ai (et-Tell)*, London: Quaritch.

Callaway, J. A. (1972). *The Early Bronze Age Sanctuary at Ai (et-Tell)*, London: Quaritch.

Callaway, J. A. (1978). 'New Perspectives on Early Bronze III in Canaan', in Moorey and Parr (eds) (1978), 46-58.

Callaway, J. A. (1980). *The Early Bronze Age Citadel and Lower City at Ai (et-Tell)*, Cambridge Mass.: American Schools of Oriental Research.

Camps-Fabrer, H. and Courtin, J. (1982). *Essaie d'approche technologique des faucilles préhistoriques dans le bassin Méditerranéen*. Traveaux du Laboratoire d'Anthropologie, de Préhistoire et d'Ethnologie des Pays de la Méditerranée Occidentale, Etude 8 (Université de Provence).

Caneva, I. (1973). 'Note sull'industria litica de Arslantepe', in A. Palmieri (1973), 55-228.

Cauvin, J. and Sanlaville, P. (eds). (1981). *Préhistoire du Levant*. Paris: CNRS.
Cauvin, J. and Aurenche, O. (eds). (1985). *Cahiers de l'Euphrate 4*. Paris: Publication de l'URA 17.
Cauvin, J. and Stordeur, D. (1985). 'Une occupation d'époque Uruk en Palmyréne: le niveaux supérieur d'el Kowm 2 - Caracol', in Cauvin and Aurenche (eds) (1985), 191-205.
Cauvin, M.-C. (1973). 'Problèmes d'Emmanchement des Faucilles du Prôche-Orient: les Documents de Tell Assouad (Djezireh, Syrie)', *Paléorient*, 1, 101-6.
Cauvin, M.-C. (1981). L'Epipaleolithique de Syrie d'après les premières recherches dans la cuvette d'el Kowm (1978-1979)' in Cauvin and Sanlaville (eds) (1981), 375-388.
Cauvin, M. -C. (ed.) (1983). *Traces d'Utilisation sur les Outils Néolithiques du Prôche Orient*, Lyon: Traveaux de la Maison de l'Orient, Tôme 5.
Chatty, D. (1986). *From Camel to Truck: The Beduin in the Modern World*, New York: Vantage Press.
Childe, V. G. (1950). 'The Urban Revolution', *Town Planning Review*, 21, 3-17.
Clarke, D, Phillips, J. L. and Staley, P. S. (1974). 'Interpretation of Prehistoric Technology from Ancient Egyptian and other Sources. Part I: Ancient Egyptian Bows and Arrows and their relevance for African Prehistory', *Paléorient*, 2, 323-88.
Clutton Brock, J. (1987). *A Natural History of Domesticated Animals*, Cambridge: Cambridge University Press
Collon, D. (1987). *First Impressions. Cylinder Seals in the Ancient Near East*, London: British Museum Publications.
Commenge-Pellerin, C. (1987). *La poterie d'Abou Matar et de l'Ouadi Zoumeli (Beershéva) au IVe millénaire avant l'ère chrétienne*, (Les Cahiers du Centre Recherche Français de Jérusalem, vol. 3), Paris: Association Paléorient.
Contenson, H. de (1956). 'La céramique chalcolithique de Beersheba, étude typologique', *IEJ*, 6, 163-79, 226-38.
Contenson, H. de (1960). 'Three soundings in the Jordan Valley', *ADAJ*, 4-5, 12-66.
Crowfoot Payne, J. (1960). 'Appendix I: Flint Implements from Tell al-Judaidah', in Braidwood and Braidwood (1960), 525-39.
Crowfoot Payne, J. (1983). 'Appendix C: The Flint Industries of Jericho', in Kenyon and Holland (1983), 622-759.
Curwen, E. C. (1930).'Prehistoric flint sickles', *Antiquity*, 4, 179-86.
Curwen, E. C. (1937). 'Notes and News: Tribulum flint from Sussex', *Antiquity*, 11, 93-94.
Dayan, Y. (1969). 'Tell Turmus in the Huleh Valley', *IEJ*, 19, 65-78.
Delougaz, P. (1952). *Pottery from the Diyala Region*, Chicago: Chicago University, Oriental Institute Publications, Vol. 63.
Dever, W. G. (1970). 'Vestigial features in MB I: an illustration of some principles of ceramic typology', *BASOR*, 200, 19-30.
Dever, W. G. (1974). 'The Middle Bronze Age Occupation and pottery of 'Araq en-Na'saneh (Cave II)', in Lapp and Lapp (eds) (1974), 41, 33-48.
Dever, W. G. (1980). 'New Vistas on the EB IV ('MB I') Horizon in Syria-Palestine', *BASOR*, 237, 35-64.
Diamond, G. (1979). 'The nature of so-called polished surfaces on stone artifacts', in Hayden (ed.) (1979) 159-66.
Dollfus, G. and Encrevé, P. (1982). 'Marques sur poteries dans la Susiane de Ve millénaire. Réflexions et comparaisons'. *Paléorient*, 8, 107-15.
Dollfus, G. and Kafafi, Z. (1986). 'Abu Hamid, Jordanie. Premiers résultats', *Paléorient*, 12, 91-100.
Dollfus, G. and Kafafi, Z. (n.d.). 'Abu Hamid. Mission jordano-française', IFAPO.
Dornemann, R. H. (1979). 'Tell Hadidi: A Millennium of Bronze Age City Occupation', *AASOR*, 44, 113-51.

Dornemann, R. H. (1984). 'The Syrian Euphrates Valley as a Bronze Age Cultural Unit, See[n] from the Point of View of Mari and Tell Hadidi', in Symposium International Histoire de Deir Ez-Zor et ses Antiquités, (*AAAS*, numero spéciale, 2-6 Oct. 1983), 63-87.

Dorrell, P. G. (1983). 'Stone Vessels, Tools , and Objects', in Kenyon and Holland (1983), 485-75.

Dossin, G. (1956). 'Les Bédouins dans les textes de Mari', in Gabrielli (ed.) (1956), 35-51.

Dothan, M. (1957). 'Excavations at Meser: 1956. Preliminary Report on the First Season', *IEJ*, 7, 217-28.

Dothan, M. (1959a). 'Excavations at Meser: 1957. Preliminary Report on the Second Season', *IEJ*, 9, 13-29.

Dothan, M. (1959b). 'Excavations at Horvat Beter (Beersheba)', '*Atiqot*, 2, 1-42.

Dothan, M. (1971). 'The Late Chalcolithic Period in Palestine - Chronology and Foreign Contacts', *Eretz Israel*, 10, 126-31 (Hebrew), xii-xiii (English Summary).

Dubertret, C. and Dunand, M. (1954/5). 'Les Gisements Ossifers de Khirbet el Umbachi et de Hébariye (Safa)', *AAAS*, 4-5, 59-76.

Duckworth, R. (1976). 'Appendix C: Notes of the Flint Implements from Jawa', in Helms (1976b), 31-5.

Dunand, M. (1937). *Fouilles de Byblos. I. 1926-1932*, Paris: Geuthner.

Dunand. M. (1973). *Fouilles de Byblos. V*, Paris: Adrien Maisonneuve.

Dyson-Hudson, R. (1980). 'Towards a General Theory of Pastoralism and Social Stratification', *Nomadic Peoples*, 7, 1-7.

Egami, N. (1983). 'The Archaeological Researches in Idlib prefecture', *AAAS*, 33, 75-82.

Ehrich, R. W. (ed.) (1965). *Chronologies in Old World Archaeology*, Chicago: University of Chicago Press.

Eisenstadt, S. N. (1977). 'Sociological theory and an analysis of the dynamics of civilization and of revolutions', *Daedalus*, 106, 59-78.

Eitan, A. (1969). 'Excavations at the Foot of Tel Ras ha`ayin', '*Atiqot*, 5, 49-68.

Elliott, C. (1977). 'The Religious Beliefs of the Ghassulians c. 4000-3000 B.C.', *PEQ*, 3-25.

Eph'al, I. (1982). *The Ancient Arabs. Nomads on the Borders of the Fertile Crescent 9th-5th Centuries B.C.*, Jerusalem: Magnes Press.

Epstein, C. (1975). 'Basalt Pillar Figures from the Golan', *IEJ*, 25, 193-201.

Epstein, C. (1978a). 'A New Aspect of Chalcolithic Culture'. *BASOR* 229: 27-45.

Epstein, C. (1978b). 'Aspects of Symbolism in Chalcolithic Palestine', in Moorey and Parr (eds.) (1978), 23-35.

Epstein, C. (1982). 'Cult Symbols in Chalcolithic Palestine', *Bulletino del Centro di Studi Preistorici* 19, 63-82.

Epstein, C. (1985a). 'Laden Animal Figurines from the Chalcolithic Period in Palestine', *BASOR*, 258, 53-62.

Epstein, C. (1985b). 'Dolmens excavated in the Golan', '*Atiqot*, 17, 20-58.

Esse, D. L. (1984). 'Archaeological Mirage: reflections on Early Bronze IC in Palestine', *JNES*, 43, 317-30.

Falkenstein, A. (1936). *Archäische Texte aus Uruk*, Berlin: Bearb. und hrsq. v. A. Falkenstein (Ausgr. d. Deut. Forschungsgemeinsch. in Uruk Warka, 2).

Fabietti, U. (n.d.). Paper presented at Yarmouk University: Pastoralist Workshop (April 1987).

Field, H. (1960). *North Arabian Desert Archaeological Survey 1925-1950*. (Peabody Museum Papers 45/2). Cambridge Mass.: Peabody Museum.

Fitzgerald, G. M. (1935). 'The Earliest Pottery of Beth Shan', *The Museum Journal*, 24, 5-22.

Fleming, D. (1976). 'Appendix B: Vertical Photography at Jawa', in Helms (1976b), 30-1.

Friberg, J. (1984). 'Numbers and Measures in the Earliest Written Records', *Scientific American*, February: 78-86.

Fried, M. (1967). *The Evolution of Political Society, an Essay in Political Anthropology*, New York: Random House.

Fritz, V. (1986). 'Kinneret. Vorbericht über die Ausgrabungen auf dem Tell el-`Oreme am See Genazaret in den Jahren 1982-1985', *ZDPV* 102: 1-39.

Fugmann, E. (1958). *Hama: Fouilles et recherches 1931-1938: II1. L'architecture des périodes préhellénistiques*. Copenhagen: Nationalmuseet.

Gabrielli, F. (ed.) 1956. *L'antica società beduina*. (Studi Semitici 2) Rome: Università di Roma (Centro de Studi Semitici).

Gardiner, A. (Sir) (1969). *Egyptian Grammar. 3rd edn*. London: Oxford University Press.

Garrard, A. (1985). 'Faunal Remains', Appendix I in Betts (1985), 48-52.

Garrard, A. and Stanley Price, N. (1975). 'A Survey of Prehistoric Sites in the Arzqq Basin, Eastern Jordan', *Paléorient*, 3, 109-123.

Garrard, A., Betts, A., Byrd, B. and Hunt, C. (1987). 'Prehistoric Environment and Settlement in the Azraq Basin: an interim report on the 1985 excavation season', *Levant*, 19, 5-25.

Garrard, A. Betts, A., Byrd, B. Colledge, S. and Hunt, C. (1988). 'Summary of Palaeoenvironmental and Prehistoric Investigations in the Azraq Basin', in Garrard and Gebel (eds) (1988), 311-337.

Garrard, A. and Gebel, H.G. (eds) (1988). *The Prehistory of Jordan: the state of research in 1986*, Oxford: BAR Int.Ser. 396 i, ii.

Garstang, J. (1932). 'Jericho, City and Necropolis', *AAA*, 19, 3-22.

Garstang, J. (1935). 'Jericho, City and Necropolis, Fifth Report', *AAA*, 22, 143-84.

Garstang, J. (1936). 'Jericho, City and Necropolis: Reports for the Sixth and Concluding Season, 1936', *AAA*, 23, 67-100.

Garstang, J. (1937). Exploration in Cilicia, *AAA*, 24, 53-68.

Garstang, J. (1953). *Prehistoric Mersin: Yümük Tepe in Southern Turkey*, Oxford: Clarendon Press.

Gerstenblith, P. (1983). *The Levant at the Beginning of the Middle Bronze Age*, Philadelphia: AASOR Dissertation Series no. 5.

Gitin, S. (1975). 'Middle Bronze I "Domestic" Pottery at Jebel Qa`aqir. A ceramic inventory of cave G23'. *Eretz Israel*, 12: 46-62.

Glueck, N. (1951). 'Explorations in Eastern Palestine, IV. Parts 1 and 2, *AASOR*, 25-28.

Goldman, H. (1956). *Excavations at Gözlü Kule, Tarsus. Vol.II, From the Neolithic through the Bronze Age*, Princeton: Princeton University Press.

Gophna, R. (1979). 'Two Early Bronze Age Basalt Bowls from the Vicinity of Nizzanim', *Tel Aviv*, 6, 136-7.

Gophna, R. (1984). 'The Settlement Landscape of Palestine in the Early Bronze Age II - III' and the Middle Bronze Age II', *IEJ*, 34, 24-31.

Gophna, R. (1990). 'The Early Bronze Age I Settlement at `En Besor Oasis', *IEJ*, 40, 1-11.

Gophna, R. and Sadeh, S. (1988-9). 'Excavations at Tel Tsaf: an early chalcolithic site in the Jordan Valley', *Tel Aviv*, 15-16, 3-36.

Grant, E. and Wright, G. E. (1938). *Ain Shems Excavations. Part IV (Pottery)(Plates)*, Biblical and Kindred Studies, No.7, Haverford College, Haverford.

Gregory, S. and Kennedy, D. (1985). *Sir Aurel Stein's Limes Report*, Oxford: BAR Int. Ser. 272, i, ii.

Gustavson-Gaube, C. (1985). 'Tell esh-Shuna North 1984: a Preliminary Report', *ADAJ*, 29, 43-87.

Gustavson-Gaube, C. (1986) 'Tell esh-Shuna North, 1985: A Preliminary Report', *ADAJ*, 30, 69-113.

Haas, J. (1982). *The Evolution of the Prehistoric State*, New York: Columbia University Press.

Hadidi, A. (ed.) (1982). *Studies in the History and Archaeology of Jordan I*, Amman: Department of Antiquities.

Hadidi, A. (ed.) (1987). *Studies in the History and Archaeology of Jordan III*, Amman, London and New York: Department of Antiquities and Routledge and Kegan Paul.

Hanbury-Tenison, J. W. (1986). *The Late Chalcolithic to Early Bronze I Transition in Palestine and Transjordan*, Oxford: BAR Int. Ser. 311.

Hanbury-Tenison, J. W. (1987). 'Jarash Region Survey, 1984', *ADAJ*, 31, 129-57.

Hanbury-Tenison, J. W. (1989). 'Desert Urbanism in the Fourth Millennium?', *PEQ*, 55-63.

Hanbury-Tenison, J. W. (n.d.) 'Jebel Mutawwaq 1986'.

Hanihara, K. and Akazawa, T. (eds) (1983). *Paleolithic Site of Douara Cave and Paleogeography of Palmyra Basin in Syria III*, Tokyo: Tokyo Museum.

Harding, G. L. (1953). 'The Cairn of Hani', *ADAJ*, 2, 8-56.

Hassan, F. (1981). *Demographic Archaeology*, New York: Academic.

Hayden, B. (ed.) (1979). *Lithic Use-Wear Analysis*, New York: Academic.

Hayes, J. W. (1972). *Late Roman Pottery*, London: The British School at Rome.

Heinrich, E. (1936). *Kleinfunde aus den Archäischen Tempelschichten in Uruk*, Leipzig: Harrassowitz.

Helms, S. W. (1973). 'Jawa - an Early Bronze Age Fortress?', *Levant*, 5, 127-8.

Helms, S. W. (1975). 'Jawa 1973: a preliminary report', *Levant*, 7, 20-38.

Helms, S.W. (1976a). *Urban Fortifications of Palestine During the Third Millennium BC*, unpubl. Ph.D. thesis, University of London.

Helms, S. W. (1976b). 'Jawa Excavations 1974 - a preliminary report', *Levant*, 8, 1-35.

Helms, S. W. (1977). 'Jawa, Excavations 1975: Third Preliminary Report', *Levant*, 9, 21-35.

Helms, S. W. (1981). *Jawa: lost city of the black desert*, London and New York: Methuen and Cornell University.

Helms, S. W. (1983). 'The EB IV (EB-MB) Cemetery at Tiwal esh-Sharqi in the Jordan Valley, 1983', *ADAJ*, 28, 55-85.

Helms, S. W. (1984a). 'Excavations at Tell Umm Hammad esh-Sharqiya in the Jordan Valley, 1982', *Levant*, 16, 35-54.

Helms, S. W. (1984b). 'The Land behind Damascus: urbanism during the 4th millennium in Syria/Palestine', in Khalidi (ed.) (1984), 15-31.

Helms, S. W. (1986). 'Excavations at Tell Um Hammad, 1984', *Levant*, 18, 25-50.

Helms, S. W. (1987a). 'Jawa, Tell Um Hammad and the EB I/late Chalcolithic landscape', *Levant*, 19, 49-81.

Helms, S. W. (1987b). 'A Question of Economic Control during the Proto-Historical Era of Palestine/Transjordan', in Hadidi (ed.) (1987), 41-51.

Helms, S. W. (1987c). 'A Note on some 4th Millennium Stamp Seal Impressions from Jordan', *Akkadica*, 52, 29-31.

Helms, S. W. (1987d). 'A Note on EB IV "Symbols" from Palestine/Transjordan', *Akkadica*, 52, 32-4.

Helms, S. W. (1987e). 'Jawa, site chalcolithique', *Dossiers Histoire et Archéologie*, 118, 92.

Helms, S. W. (1989a). 'Jawa at the beginning of the Middle Bronze Age', *Levant*, 21, 141-68.

Helms, Svend [W.] (1989b). 'An EB IV Pottery Repertoire at Amman, Jordan', *BASOR*, 273, 17-36.

Helms, Svend [W]. (1990). *Early Islamic Architecture of the Desert. A bedouin station in eastern Jordan*, Edinburgh: Edinburgh University Press.

Helms, Svend [W.] (in press). 'The "Zerqa Triangle": a preliminary appraisal of protohistorical settlement patterns and demographic episodes', (IVth Conference on the History and Archaeology of Jordan, Lyon 1989 = *Studies in the History and Archaeology of Jordan IV*).

Helms, S. W. (in progress). *Excavations at Jawa 1972 - 1986: Architecture, Water and Irrigation Systems*.

Helms, S. [W.] and Betts, A. [V. G.] (1987). 'The Desert "Kites" of the Badiyat al-Sham and North Arabia', *Paléorient*, 13/1, 41-67.

Helms, Svend [S. W.] and McCreery, David (1988). 'Rescue Excavations at Umm el-Bighal: The Pottery', *ADAJ*, 32, 319-47.

Hennessy, J. B. (1967). *The Foreign Relations of Palestine during the Early Bronze Age*, London: Quaritch.

Hennessy, J. B. (1969). 'Preliminary Report on a First Season of Excavations at Teleilat Ghassul', *Levant*, 1, 1-24.

Hestrin, R. and Tadmor, M. (1963). 'A Hoard of Tools and Weapons from Kfar Monash', *IEJ*, 13, 265-88.

Holland, T. A. (1980). 'Incised pottery from Tell Sweyhat, Syria and its Foreign Relations', in Margueron (ed.) (1980).

Holland, T. A. (1983). 'Appendix M: Stone Mace-heads', in Kenyon and Holland (1983), 804-13.

Homès-Fredericq, D. (1963). 'Cachets protohistoriques Mésopotamiens et Susiens', *Iranica Antiqua* 3: 85-101.

Homès-Fredericq, D. (1970). *Les cachets Mésopotamiens protohistoriques*, (Documenta et monumenta orientis antiqui ... volumen quattrodecem), Leiden: Brill.

Homès-Fredericq, D. and Franken, H. J. (1985). *Argile, source de vie: sept millenaires de céramique en Jordanie*, Brussels and Tongeren: Musées Royaux d'Art et d'Histoire and Provinicaal Gallo-Romeins Museum.

Hours, F. (1979). 'L'industrie lithique de Saida-Dakerman', *Berytus*, 27, 57-76.

Hunt, L-A. (1976). 'Appendix A: Rock Carvings', in Helms (1976b), 24-9.

Hütteroth, W-D. and Abulfattah, K. (1977). *Historical Geography of Palestine, Transjordan and Southern Syria in the late 16th Century*, Erlangen.

Ibrahim, M, Sauer, J. and Yassine, K. (1976). 'The East Jordan Valley Survey, 1975', *BASOR*, 222, 41-66.

Jidejian, N. (1968). *Byblos through the Ages*, Beirut: Dahr el-Machreq.

Kamp, K. A. and Yoffee, N. (1980). 'Ethnicity in Ancient Western Asia During the Early Second Millennium B.C.: Archaeological Assessments and Ethnoarchaeological Prospectives', *BASOR*, 237, 85-104.

Kampschulte, I. and Orthmann, W. (1984). *Gräber des 3. Jahrtausends v. Chr. im syrischen Euphrattal: Ausgrabungen bei Tawi 1975 & 1978*, Bonn: Habelt.

Kantor, H. J. (1965). 'The Relative Chronology of Egypt with that of other parts of the Near East', in Ehrich (1965), 1-27.

Kaplan, J. (1958). 'Excavations at Teluliot Batashi in the Vale of Sorek', *Eretz Israel* 5: 9-14 (Hebrew), 83-84 (English Summary).

Kaplan, J. (1963). 'Excavations at Benei Beraq 1951', *IEJ*, 13, 300-12.

Kaplan, J. (1969). `Ein el-Jarba. Chalcolithic Remains in the Plain of Esdraelon', *BASOR*, 194, 2-39.

Keeley, L. H. (1980). *Experimental Determination of Stone Tool Uses: a Microwear Analysis*, Chicago: University of Chicago.

Kempinski, A. (1978). *The Rise of Urban Culture: The Urbanization of Palestine in the Early Bronze Age, 3000-2150 B.C.*, Jerusalem.

Kempinski, A. (1983). 'Early Bronze Age Urbanization of Palestine: Some Topics in a Debate', *IEJ*, 33, 235-41.

Kempinski, A. (1986). Review of Helms 1981, *IEJ*, 6, 280-1.

Kempinski, A. and Gilead, I. (1988). 'Tel `Erani, 1987', *IEJ*, 38, 88-90.

Kenyon, K.M. (1952a). *Beginning In Archaeology*, London: Phoenix House.

Kenyon, K. M. (1952b). 'Excavations at Jericho, 1952', *PEQ*, 62-82.

Kenyon, K. M. (1960). *Excavations at Jericho. I*, London: British School of Archaeology in Jerusalem.

Kenyon, K. M. (1965). *Excavations at Jericho. II*, London: British School of Archaeology in Jerusalem.

Kenyon, K. M. (1974). Review of de Miroschedji 1971, *Biblica*, 55, 88-90.

Kenyon, K. M.(1979). *Archaeology in the Holy Land, 4th edn*, London: Benn.

Kenyon, K. M. (1981). *Excavations at Jericho. III*, London: British School of Archaeology in Jerusalem.

Kenyon, K. M. and Holland, T. A. (1982). *Excavations at Jericho. IV*, London: British School of Archaeology in Jerusalem.

Kenyon, K. M. and Holland, T. A. (1983). *Excavations at Jericho. V*, London: British School of Archaeology in Jerusalem.

Khalidi, T. (ed.) (1984). *Land Tenure and Social Transformation in the Middle East*, Beirut: American University of Beirut.

King, G., Lenzen, C.J. and Rollefson, G.O. (1983). Survey of Byzantine and Islamic Sites in Jordan. Second Preliminary Report 1981', *ADAJ*, 28, 385-436.

Kirkbride, D. (1975). 'Umm Dabaghiya 1974. A Fourth Preliminary Report', *Iraq*, 37, 3-10.

Kochavi, M. (1969). 'Excavations at Tel Esdar', *'Atiqot*, 5, 14-48.

Kochavi, M., Beck, P. and Gophna, R. (1979). 'Aphek-Antipatris, Tel Poleg, Tel Zeror and Tel Burga: Four Fortified Sites of the Middle Bronze Age II A in the Sharon Plain', *ZDPV*, 95, 121-65.

Köhler, I. (1981). 'Appendix E: Animal Remains', in Helms (1981), 249-52.

Koeppel, R. (1940). *Teleilat Ghassul II: compte rendu des fouilles de l'Institut Biblique Pontifical 1932-36*, Rome: Institut Biblique Pontifical.

Kohl, P. L. (ed.) (1981). *The Bronze Age Civilisation of Central Asia: recent Soviet discoveries*, New York: Sharpe.

Korobkova, G. F. (1981). 'Ancient reaping tools and their productivity in the light of experimental tracewaer analysis', in Kohl (ed.) (1981), 325-349.

Kühne, H. (1976). *Die Keramik von Tell Chuera und ihre Beziehungen zu Funden aus Syrien-Palästina, der Türkei and dem Iraq*, Berlin: Mann.

Kuschke, A., Mittmann, S., Müller, V. and Azoury I. (1976). *Archäologischer Survey in der nördlichen Biqa`, Herbst 1972*, Wiesbaden: Reichert.

Labat, R. (1948). *Manuel d'épigraphie akkadienne (signes, syllabaire, idéogrammes)*, Paris: Imprimérie Nationale.

Laere, R. van (1980). 'Techniques hydrauliques en Mésompotamie ancienne', *Orientalia Lovaniensia Periodica*, 11, 11-53.

Lancaster, W. (1981). *The Rwala Bedouin today*, Cambridge: Cambridge University Press.

Lancaster, W. and Lancaster, F. (1990). 'Modern ar-Risha: a permanent address', in Helms (1990), 67-70.

Lapp, P. W. (1966). *The Dhahr Mirzbaneh Tombs: Three Intermediate Bronze Age Cemeteries in Jordan*, (Publications of the Jerusalem School 4), New Haven: American Schools of Oriental Research.

Lapp, P. W. (1968). 'Bab edh-Dhra' Tomb A 76 and Early Bronze I in Palestine', *BASOR*, 189, 12-41.

Lapp, P. W. (1970). 'Palestine in the Early Bronze Age', in Saunders (ed.) (1970), 101-131.

Lapp, P. W. and Lapp, N. L. (eds) (1974). *Discoveries in the wadi ed-Daliyeh*, Cambridge, Mass.: American Schools of Oriental Research (AASOR 41).

Le Brun, A. (1978). 'Le niveaux 17B de l'acropole de Suse (campagne de 1972)', *Cahiers de la DAFI*, 9, 57-156.

Lee, J. R. (1973). *Chalcolithic Ghassul: new aspects and master typology*, unpubl. Ph.D. thesis, Hebrew University.

Leonard, A. (1983). 'The Proto Urban/Early Bronze I Utilization of the Kataret es-Samra Plateau', *BASOR*, 251, 37-60.

Leonard, A. (1989). 'A Chalcolithic 'Fine Ware' from Khirbet es-Samra in the Jordan Valley', *BASOR*, 276, 3-14.

Leonard, A. (n.d.). *Preliminary Plates from the 1953 Sounding in the Jordan Valley conducted by James Mellaart.*

Levi-Sala, I. (1986). 'Use-wear and post-depositional surface modification: a word of caution', *Journal of Archaeological Science*, 13, 229-44.

Levy, T. E. (1986). 'The Chalcolithic Period', *Biblical Archaeologist*, 49, 82-108.

Levy, T. E. (ed.) (1987). *Shiqmim I*, Oxford: BAR Int. Ser. 356.

Levy, T. E. and Menahem, N. (1987). 'The Pottery from the Shiqmim village: typological and spatial considerations', in Levy (ed.)(1987), 313-31 (611-52).

Livingstone, A., Khan, M., Zahrani, A., Sallok, M. and Shaman, S. (1985). 'Epigraphical Survey. 1404-1984', *ATLAL*, 9, 128-44.

Loud, G. (1948). *Megiddo II: Vol. II. Plates*, (University of Chicago Oriental Institute Publications LXII), Chicago: Chicago University Press.

Mabry, J. (n.d.) 'Investigations at Tell el-Handaquq, Jordan (1987-88)'. *(ADAJ).*

Macdonald, E. (1932). *Beth Pelet II, Prehistoric Fara*, London: British School of Archaeology in Egypt.

Macdonald, M. C. A. (1981). 'Appendix G: Notes on some Safaitic inscriptions', in Helms (1981), 257-63.

Macdonald, M. C. A. (1982). 'The Inscriptions and Rock-Drawings of the Jawa area: A Preliminary Report on the first season of field-work of the Corpus of Inscriptions of Jordan Project', *ADAJ*, 26, 159-72.

Macdonald, M. C. A. (1983). 'Inscriptions and Rock-Art of the Jawa Area, 1982: A Preliminary Report, *ADAJ*, 27, 571-6.

Macdonald, M. C. A. (forthcoming). *Jawa Inscriptions*, Irbid: Yarmouk University Institute of Archaeology and Anthropology (Monograph Series).

Mallon, A., Koeppel, R, and Neuville, R. (1934). *Teleilat Ghassul I, (Comptes rendus des fouilles l'institut biblique pontifical, 1929-1932)*, Rome: Scripta Pontifici Instituti Biblici.

Mallowan, M. E. L. (1936). 'The Excavations at Tall Chagar Bazar, and an Archaeological Survey of the Habur Region 1934-5', *Iraq*, 3, 1-86.

Mallowan, M. E. L. and Cruikshank, R. J. (1935). 'Excavations at Tall Arpachiyah, 1933'. *Iraq*, 2, 1-178.

Maqdissi, M. al-. (1984). 'Compte rendu des traveaux archéologiques dans la Ledja en 1984', *Berytus*, 32, 7-17.

Margueron, J. Cl. (ed.) (1980). *Le Moyen Euphrate. Zone de contacts et d'échanges*, (Actes du Colloque de Strasbourg, 10-12 mars 1977), Leiden: Brill.

Marquet-Krause, J.(1949). *Les fouilles de 'Ay (et-Tell). 1933-1935: La résurection d'une grande cité biblique*, (Institut Francais d'Archaeologie de Beyrouth. Bibliotèque archéologique et historique 45), Paris: Geuthner.

Marx, E. (1978). 'The Ecology and Politics of Nomadic Pastoralists in the Middle East', in Weissleder (ed.) (1978), 41-74.

Marx, E. (1980) 'Wage Labour and Tribal economy of the Bedouin in South Sinai', in Salzman (ed.) (1980), 111-23.

Marx, E. (1984). 'Economic Change among Pastoral Noamds in the Middle East', in Marx and Shmueli (eds) (1984), 1-6.

Marx, E. and Shmueli, A. (eds) (1984). *The Changing Beduin*, New Brunswick.

Mathias, V. and Parr, P. J. (1989). 'The Early Phases at Tell Nebi Mend: A Preliminary Account', *Levant*, 21, 13-32.

Matthiae, P. (1980). *Ebla: An Empire Rediscovered*. London: Hodder and Stoughton.

McConaughy, M. (1979). *Formal and Functional Analysis of Chipped Stone Tools from Bab edh-Dhra'*, unpubl. Ph.D. thesis, Ann Arbor.

McNicoll, A., Smith, R. H. and Hennessy, J. B. (1982). *Pella in Jordan 1*, Canberra: Australian National Gallery.

Mellaart, J. (1956). 'The Neolithic Site of Ghrubba', *ADAJ*, 3, 24-30.

Mellaart, J. (1962). 'Preliminary Report of the Archaeological Survey in the Yarmuk and Jordan Valley', *ADAJ*, 6-7, 126-32.

Mellaart, J. (1966). *The Chalcolithic and Early Bronze Ages in the Near East and Anatolia*, Beirut: Khayats.

Mellaart, J. (1967). *Çatal Hüyük: a neolithic town in Anatolia*, London: Thames and Hudson.

Mellaart, J. (1975). *The Neolithic of the Near East*, London: Thames and Hudson.

Mellaart, J. (1979). 'Egyptian and Near Eastern Chronology - A Dilemma?', *Antiquity*, 53, 6-18.

Mesnil du Buisson, R. du (1935). *La Site archéologique de Mishrife-Qatna*, Paris: Boccard.

Millard, A. R. (1988). 'The bevelled-rim bowls: their purpose and significance', *Iraq*, 50, 49-57.

Miroschedji, P. R. de (1971). *L'Epoque Pré urbaine en Palestine*. Paris: Cahiers de la Revue Biblique 13, Paris: Gabalda.

Mittmann, S. (1970). *Beiträge zur Siedlung und Territorialgeschichte der Nördlichen Ostjordanlandes*, Wiesbaden: DPV.

Moorey, P. R. S. (1988). Review of Collon 1987, *Antiquaries Journal*, 68, 141-2.

Moorey, P. R. S. (ed.) (1984). [Buchanan, B.]. *Catalogue of Ancient Near Eastern Seals in the Ashmolean Museum. Volume II. The Prehistoric Stamp Seals*, Oxford: Ashmolean Museum.

Moorey, P. R. S. and Parr, P. J. (eds) (1978). *Archaeology in the Levant: essays for Kathleen Kenyon*, Warminster: Aris and Phillips.

Moormann, F. (1959). *Report to the Government of Jordan on the Soils of East Jordan* (Report Np. 1132, FAO/59/86239), Rome.

Mowry, L. (1953). 'A Greek inscription at Jathum in Transjordan', *BASOR*, 132, 34-41.

Muheisen, M.J. (1988). 'The Epipaleolithic phases of Kharaneh IV', in Garrard and Gebel (eds) (1988), 353-367.

Museum (1982). *Land des Baal*, Museum für Vor- und Frühgeschichte, Berlin.

Musil, A. (1928). *The manners and customs of the Rwala Bedouins*, (Oriental Explorations and Studies. Number 6), New York: American Geographical Society.

Na'aman, N. (1986). 'Hezekiah's Fortified Cities and the LMLK stamps', *BASOR*, 261, 5-21.

Nelson, C. (ed.) (1973). *The Desert and the Sown*, Berkley: University of California.

Nissen, H. J. (1985). 'The Emergence of Writing in the Ancient Near East', *Interdisciplinary Science Reviews*, 10, 349-61.

North, R. (1961). *Ghassul 1960 Excavation Report*, (Analectica Biblica 14), Rome: Pontifical Biblical Institute.

Olszewski, D. (1986). *The North Syrian Late Epipaleolithic*, Oxford: BAR Int. Ser. 309.

Ory, J. (1938). 'Excavations at Ras el-'Ain', *QDAP*, 6, 99-120.

Osten, H. H. von der (1956). *Svenska Syrienexpeditionen I: Die Grabungen von Tell es-Salihiyeh*, Lund.

Otte, M. (1976). 'Données nouvelles sur le Néolithique d'Apamée (sondage A4)', *AAAS*, 26, 101-18.

Palmieri, A. (1973). 'Scavi nell'area sud-occidentale di Arslantepe', *Origini*, 7, 55-228.

Palmieri, A. (1981). 'Excavations at Arslantepe (Malatya)', *Anatolian Studies*, 31, 101-19.

Palumbo, G. (1987). '"Egalitarian" or "Stratified" Society? Some Notes on Mortuary Practices and Social Structure at Jericho in EB IV', *BASOR*, 267, 43-59.

Parr, P. J. (1956). 'A Cave at Arqub el-Dhahr', *ADAJ*, 3, 61-73.

Parr, P. J. (1960). 'Excavations at Khirbet Iskander', *ADAJ*, 4-5, 128-33.

Parr, P. (1983). The Tell Nebi Mend Project', *AAAS*, 33, 99-117.

Peebles, C. S. and Kus, S. M. (1977). 'Some Archaeological Correlates of Ranked Societies', *American Antiquity*, 42, 421-48.

Perrot, J. (1955). 'The Excavations at Tell Abu Matar, near Beersheba', *IEJ*, 5, 17-40, 73-84, 167-189.

Perrot, J. (1957). 'Les Fouilles d' Abou Matar près de Beersheba', *Syria*, 34, 1-38.

Perrot, J. (1961). 'Une tombe à ossuaires à Azor', *'Atiqot*, 3, 1-83.

Perrot, J. (1962). 'Palestine-Syria-Cilicia', in R. Braidwood and G. Willey (eds) (1962), 147-64.

Perrot, J., Zori, N. and Reich, Y. (1967). 'Neve Ur, un nouvel aspect du Ghassoulien', *IEJ*, 17, 201-32.

Petrie, W. M. F. (1920). *Prehistoric Egypt*, London: Quaritch.

Petrie, W. M. F. (1953). *Ceremonial Slate Palettes*, London: British School of Egyptian Archaeology, Quaritch. (BSEA vol. 66 [A]).

Poidebard, A. (1934). *La Trace de Rome dans le désert de Syrie*, Paris: Geuthner.

Posener, G. (1971). 'Syria and Palestine c. 2160-1780 B.C.', *Cambridge Ancient History*, I2A, 532-58.

Potts, D. (1981). 'The Potters Marks of Tepe Yahya', *Paléorient*, 7, 107-22.

Prag, K. (1971). *A Study of the Intermediate Early Bronze - Middle Bronze Age in Transjordan, Syria and Lebanon*, unpubl. D.Phil. dissertation, Oxford.

Prag, K. (1974). 'The Intermediate Early Bronze - Middle Bronze Age: an Interpretation of the evidence from Transjordan, Syria and Lebanon', *Levant*, 6, 69-116.

Prag, K. (1986). 'The Intermediate Early Bronze - Middle Bronze Age Sequences at Jericho and Tell Iktanu Reviewed', *BASOR*, 264, 61-72.

Pritchard, J. B. (1955). *Ancient Near Eastern texts relating to the Old Testament*, (2nd edn.) Princeton: Princeton University Press.

Pritchard, J. B. (1958). *The Excavation at Herodian Jericho, 1951*, New Haven: American Schools of Oriental Research (AASOR 32-3).

Rast, W. E. (1980). 'Palestine in the 3rd millennium. Evidence for Interconnections', *Scripta Mediterranea*, 1, 5-20.

Rast, W. E. and Schaub, R. T. (1980). 'Preliminary Report of the 1979 Expedition to the Dead Sea Plain, Jordan', *BASOR*, 240, 21-61.

Rast, W. E. and Schaub, R. T. (eds) (1981). 'The Southeastern Dead Sea Plain Expeditions: an Interim Report of the 1977 Session', *AASOR*, 46.

Redman, C. L. (ed.) (1978). *Social Archeology: Beyond Subsistence and Dating*, New York: Academic.

Richard, S. (1980). 'Towards a Concensus of Opinion on the End of the Early Bronze Age in Palestine-Transjordan', *BASOR*, 237, 5-34.

Richard, S. (1987). 'The Early Bronze Age. The Rise and Collapse of Urbanism', *Biblical Archaeologist*, 50, 22-43.

Ritter Kaplan, H. (1981). 'Anatolian Elements in the EB III Culture of Palestine', *ZDPV*, 97, 18-35.

Rosen, S. A. (1982). 'Flint Sickle-blades of the Late Protohistoric and Early Historic Periods in Israel', *Tel Aviv*, 9, 139-45.

Rosen, S. A. (1983a). *Lithics in the Bronze and Iron Ages in Israel*, unpubl. Ph.D. thesis, University of Chicago.

Rosen, S. A. (1983b). 'The Canaanean Blade and the Early Bronze Age', *IEJ*, 33, 15-29.

Rosen, S. A. (1983c). 'Tabular Scraper Trade: a model of material cultural dispersion', *BASOR*, 249, 79-86.

Ross, J. F. (1980). 'The Early Bronze Age in Palestine', in K. Newmyer (ed.) Historical Essays in Honor of Kenneth R. Rossman, 147-70.

Rowe, A. (1936). *A Catalogue of Egyptian Scarabs, Scaraboids, Seals and Amulets in the Palestine Archaeological Museums*, Cairo: Institut Français d'Archéologie Orientale.

Rowton, M. (1974). 'Enclosed Nomadism', *JESHO*, 17, 1-30.

Rowton, M. (1976). 'Dimorphic Structure and Topology', *Oriens Antiquus*, 15, 17-31.

Saghieh, M. (1983). *Byblos in the Third Millennium B.C.: A Reconstruction of the Stratigraphy and a Study of the Cultural Connections*, Warminster: Aris and Phillips.

Saidah, R. (1979). 'Fouilles de Sidon-Dakerman: l'agglomeration chalcolithique', *Berytus*, 27, 29-56.

Saller, (1964/5). 'Bab edh-Dhra", *Liber Annuus*, 15, 137-219.

Salzman, P.C. (ed)(1978). 'Ideology and Change in Middle Eastern Tribal Societies', *Man*, 13, 618-37.

Salzman, P.C. (1980). *When Nomads Settle*, New York: Bergin.

Sanders, W. and Webster, D. (1978). 'Unilinealism, Mutualism and the Evolution of Complex Societies', in Redman (ed.) (1978), 249-302.

Sartre, M. (1982). *Trois études sur l'Arabia romaine et byzantine*, Brussels: Collection Latomus, Volume 178.

Saunders, J.A. (ed.) (1970). *Near Eastern Archaeology in the Twentieth Century, (Essays in Honor of Nelson Glueck)*, New York: Doubleday.

Schaeffer, F. A. (1962). *Ugaritica IV*, Paris: Geuthner.

Schaub, R. T. (1981). 'Patterns of Burial at Bab edh-Dhra' and Ceramic Sequences in the Tomb Groups at Bab edh-Dhra', in Rast and Schaub (eds) (1981), 44-68, 69-118.

Schaub, R. T. (1982). 'The origins of the Early Bronze Age walled town culture of Jordan', in Hadidi (ed.) (1982), 67-75.

Schaub, R. T. (1987). 'Ceramic Vessels as Evidence for Trade Communications during the Early Bronze Age in Jordan', in Hadidi (ed.) (1987), 247-50.

Schaub, R. T. and Rast, W. E. (1984). 'Preliminary Report of the 1981 Expedition to the Dead Sea Plain, Jordan', *BASOR*, 254, 35-60.

Schmandt-Besserat, D. (1977). 'An archaic recording system and the origin of writing', *Syro-Mesopotamian Studies*, 1/2, 1-32.

Schmandt-Besserat, D. (1978). 'The earliest precursor of writing', *Scientific American*, (June) 238, 6, 50-9.

Schwabe, M. (1954). 'Note of the Jathum Inscription', *BASOR*, 135, 38.

Searight, A. (1982). 'The Rock-Art Survey of the Jawa Area, 1981', in Macdonald (1982), 168-70.

Searight, A. (1983). 'The Rock-Art Survey 1982', in Macdonald (1983), 575-6.

Seeden, H. (1986). 'Bronze Age Village Occupation at Busra. AUB Excavations on the northwest Tell 1983-84', *Berytus*, 34, 11-81.

Service, E. R. (1962). *Primitive Social Organization*, New York: Random House.

Service, E. R. (1975). *The Origins of the State and Civilization*, New York: Norton.

Sethe, K. (1908-22). *Die altägyptischen Pyramidentexte*, (Volumes I-IV), Leipzig: Hinrichs

Several, M. W. (1975). 'Archaeological Notes II: An Early Bronze Basalt Bowl in the Skirball Museum', *Levant*, 7, 139-41.

Speiser, E. A. (1933). *The Pottery of Tell Billa*, Pennsylvania Museum Journal 23, No. 3, 249-283.

Speiser, E. A. (1935). *Excavations at Tepe Gawra I*, (American Schools of Oriental Research), Philadelphia: University of Pennsylvania Press

Spurrell, F. C. (1982). 'Notes on early sickles', *Archaeological Journal*, 49, 53-68.

Stekelis, M. (1935). *Les monuments mégalithiques de Palestine*, Paris: Masson.

Stordeur, D. (ed.) n.d. *Manches et Emmanchements Préhistoriques*, CNRS, St. André de Creuzière.

Strommenger, E. (1977). 'Ausgrabungen der Deutschen Orient-Gesellschaft in Habuba Kabira', *AASOR*, 44, 63-78.

Strommenger, E. (1980). *Habuba Kabira. Eine Stadt vor 5000 Jahren*, Mainz: Von Zabern.

Sürenhagen, D. (1978). *Keramikproduktion in Habuba Kabira-Süd*, Berlin: Bruno Hessling.

Sukenik, E. (1936). 'Late Chalcolithic Pottery from Affuleh', *PEFQS*, 68, 150-4.

Sukenik, E. L. (1948). 'Archaeological Investigations at Affula', *JPOS*, 21, 1-9.

Sussman, V. (1980). 'A Relief of a Bull from the Early Bronze Age', *BASOR*, 238, 75-7.
Swidler, W. (1973). 'Adaptive Processes Regulating Nomad-Sedentary Interaction in the Middle East', in Nelson (ed.) (1973), 23-41.
Tadmor, M. (1978). 'A Cult Cave of the Middle Bronze Age I near Qedesh', *IEJ*, 28, 1-30.
Tadmor, M. and Prausnitz, M. (1959). 'Excavations at Rosh Hanniqra', '*Atiqot*, 2, 72-88.
Tainter, J. A. (1977). 'Modeling Change in Prehistoric Social Systems', in Binford (ed.) (1977), 327-51.
Talbot, G. C. (1983). 'Appendix K: Beads and Pendants from the Tombs', in Kenyon and Holland (1983), 788-801.
Tobler, A. J. (1950). *Excavations at Tepe Gawra II*, Philadelphia: University of Pennsylvania Press.
Tubb, J. N. and Wright, M.W. (1985). 'Excavations in the Early Bronze Age Cemetery of Tiwal esh-Sharqi. A Preliminary Report', *ADAJ*, 29, 115-30.
Tubb, J.N. (1990). *Excavations at the Early Bronze Age Cemetery of Tiwal esh-Sharqi*, London: British Museum.
Tufnell, O. (1958) *Lachish IV. The Bronze Age*, London: Oxford University Press.
Unger-Hamilton, R. (1983). 'An investigation into the variables affecting the development and the appearance of plant polish on flint blades', in Cauvin, M.-C. (ed.) (1983), 243-50.
Unger-Hamilton, R. (1984). *Method in Microwear Analysis: Sickles and Other Tools from Arjoune, Syria*, unpubl. Ph.D. thesis, London University.
Unger-Hamilton, R. (1985). 'Microscopic striations on flint sickle-blades as an indication of plant cultivation: preliminary results', *World Archaeology*, 17, 121-6.
Unger-Hamilton, R. n.d. [a] 'Experimental microwear analysis: some current controversies'. (*L'Anthropologie*).
Unger-Hamilton, R. n.d. [b] 'Early harvesting of plant resources in Palestine: a new approach using microscopic studies of sickle-blades'.
Unger-Hamilton, R, Grace, R., Miller, R. and Bergman, C. A. n.d. 'Experimental replication, use and microwear analysis of spindle-tipped borers from Abu Salabikh, Iraq', in Stordeur [ed.] n.d.
Vaux, R. de (1951). 'La troisième campagne de fouilles à Tell el-Far'ah, près Naplouse - la nécropole', *RB*, 58, 566-93.
Vaux, R. de (1952). 'La quatrième campagne de fouilles à Tell el-Fara'ah, près Naplouse', *RB*, 62, 541-89.
Vaux, R. de (1955). 'Les Fouilles de Tell el-Far'ah, près Naplouse, cinquième campagne', *RB*, 62, 541-89.
Vaux, R. de (1957). 'Les fouilles de Tell el-Far'ah, près Naplouse, sixième campagne', *RB*, 64, 552-88.
Vaux, R. de (1970a). 'Palestine during the Neolithic and Chalcolithic Periods', *The Cambridge Ancient History*, I, 1, 499-538.
Vaux, R. de (1970b). 'On the right and wrong uses of archaeology', in Saunders (ed.) (1970), 64-80.
Vaux, R. de (1971). 'Palestine in the Early Bronze Age'. *The Cambridge Ancient History*, I, 2A, 208-37.
Vaux, R. de and Steve, A. M. (1947). 'La première campagne de fouilles à Tell el Fara'ah, près Naplouse', *RB*, 54, 394-433.
Vaux, R. de and Steve, A. M. (1949). 'La deuxième campagne de fouilless à Tell el-Far'ah, près Naplouse: la nécropole', *RB*, 56, 102-38.
Vayson de Pradennes, A. (1919). 'Faucille préhistorique de Solferino (étude comparative)', *L'Anthropologie*, 29, 393-422.
Weinstein, J. M. (1984). 'The Significance of Tell Areini for Egyptian-Palestinian Relations at the Beginning of the the Bronze Age', *BASOR*, 256, 61-9.
Weissleder, W. (ed.) (1978). *The Nomadic Alternative*, The Hague: Mouton.

Willcox, G. H. (1981). 'Appendix D: Plant Remains', in Helms (1981), 247-8.

Winnett, F. V. (1951). 'An Epigraphical Expedition to North-Eastern Transjordan', *BASOR*, 122, 49-52.

Winnett, F. V. (1957). *Safaitic Inscriptions from Jordan*, (Near and Middle East Series No. 2), Toronto: University of Toronto Press.

Winnett, F. V. (1973). 'The Revolt of Damasi: Safaitic and Nabatean Evidence', *BASOR*, 211, 54-7.

Wirth, E. (1971). *Syrien: eine geographische Landeskunde*, Darmstadt: Wissenschaftliche Buchgesellschaft.

Wittvogel, K. (1964). *Le despotisme oriental. Etude comparative du pouvoir total*, Paris.

Woolley, C. L. (1929). *Ur of the Chaldees. A Record of Seven Years of Excavations*, London: Ernest Benn.

Wright, G. E. (1937). *The Pottery of Palestine from the Earliest Times to the End of the Early Bronze Age*, (American Schools of Oriental Research), New Haven: Publications of the Jerusalem School.

Wright, G. E. (1958). 'The Problem of the Transition between the Chalcolithic and Bronze Ages', *Eretz Israel*, 5, 37-45.

Wright, G. E. (1961). 'The Archaeology of Palestine', in Wright (ed.) (1961), 73-112.

Wright, G. E. (1971). 'The Archaeology of Palestine from the Neolithic through the Middle Bronze Age', *JAOS*, 91, 282-93

Wright, G. E. (ed.) (1961). *The Bible and the Ancient Near East*, London: Kegan Paul.

Wright, H. T. and Johnson, G. A. (1975). 'Population, exchange, and early state formation in southwestern Iran', *American Anthropologist*, 77, 267-89.

Yadin, Y., Aharoni, Y., Amiran, R., Dothan, T., Dunayevsky, I., and Perrot, J. (1958). *Hazor I. An account of the first season of excavations, 1955*, Jerusalem: Magnes Press.

Yassine, K. (1985). 'The Dolmens: Construction and Dating Reconsidered', *BASOR*, 259, 63-9.

Yassine, K. (ed.) (1988). *Archaeology of Jordan: Essays and Reports*, Amman: University of Jordan.

Yassine, K., Ibrahim, M. and Sauer, J. (1988). 'The East Jordan Valley Survey, 1976', in Yassine (ed.) (1988), 187-207.

Yeivin, S. (1961). *First Preliminary Report on the Excavations at Tell "Gat" (Tell Sheykh 'Ahmad el-Areyney, Seasons 1956-1958)*, Jerusalem: Dept. of Antiquities.

Yeivin, M. S. (1967). 'A New Chalcolithic Culture at Tel `Erany and its Implications for Early Egyptian-Canaanite Relations', Jerusalem: *Fourth World Congress of Jewish Studies-Papers*, 45-8.

Yoffee, N. (1979). 'The decline and rise of Mesopotamian civilization: an ethno-archaeological prespective on the evolution of social complexity', *American Antiquity*, 44, 5-35.

Zarins, J., Ibrahim, M., Potts, D. and Edens, C. (1979). 'Saudi Arabian Archaeological Reconnaissance 1978', *ATLAL*, 3, 9-42.

Zarins, J., Murad, Abd al-J. and al-Yish, K. S. (1981). 'The Comprehensive Archaeological Survey Program: a. The Second Preliminary Report on the Southwestern Province', *ATLAL*, 5, 9-42.

Zeuner, F. E. (1956). 'The Radiocarbon Age of Jericho', *Antiquity*, 30, 195-7.